Black Post-Blackness

Black Post-Blackness

The Black Arts Movement and
Twenty-First-Century Aesthetics

MARGO NATALIE CRAWFORD

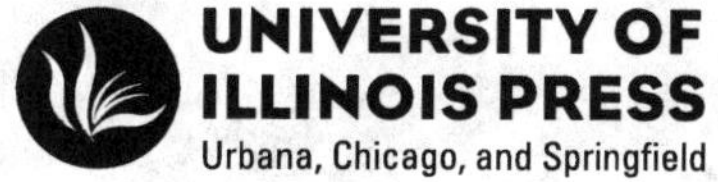

UNIVERSITY OF
ILLINOIS PRESS
Urbana, Chicago, and Springfield

Library of Congress Control Number: 2017931625
ISBN 978-0-252-04100-6 (hardcover)
ISBN 978-0-252-08249-8 (paperback)
ISBN 978-0-252-09955-7 (e-book)

for the homespun who trespass

Contents

Acknowledgments

This book aims to deepen our understanding of the 1960s and early 1970s Black Arts Movement as well as early twenty-first-century African American literature and visual culture. My desire to bring "black" and "post-black" together was sparked by the vibrant work emerging in studies of the 1960s and 1970s Black Arts Movement and twenty-first-century black art. I have benefited immensely from scholars revisiting the Black Arts Movement as well as scholars who are paving the way for a twenty-first-century new wave of black aesthetic theory. My bringing together of the Black Arts Movement and the twenty-first century breaks out of the typical approach to these movements and uncovers "black post-blackness"—a new way of thinking about radical black aesthetics as a constant push to what is unimaginable and a constant holding on to the radicalness of black life in an antiblack world.

The entire jam session of the Black Arts Movement was *a love supreme*. In the poem "Numbers, Letters," Amiri Baraka writes, "There is no guilt in love." Love can be revolutionary. This book was a jam session since its very beginning, and I was fortunate to jam with so many kindred spirits. The vibrating edge of the ensemble included Amiri Baraka, Haki Madhubuti, Eleanor Traylor, Sonia Sanchez, Cheryl Clarke, Kalamu ya Salaam, Nelson Stevens, Quo Vadis Gex-Breaux, and Jerry Ward, who led me to the deep water. I was blessed to wade in the water with their precious counsel.

Key conferences and collaborations shaped the flow of this book. Many panels pushed me to think about how the framing of the Black Arts Movement has shaped nascent attempts to frame and theorize twenty-first-century black literature and visual art. I thank Aldon Lynn Nielsen, Evie Shockley, Christina

Sharpe, Meta DuEwa Jones, Carter Mathes, Erica Edwards, GerShun Avilez, James Smethurst, Fred Moten, Shana Redmond, Keith Leonard, Dana Williams, Howard Rambsy, Soyica Colbert, Robert Patterson, La Marr Jurelle Bruce, Kai Green, Stéphane Robolin, Tsitsi Jaji, Rebecca Wanzo, and Rizvana Bradley for all of the "BangClash" we have created in our jam sessions.

Being a part of Houston Baker and Merinda Simmons's edited volume *The Trouble with Post-Blackness* was tremendously useful. The earlier conference, "The Trouble with Post-Blackness," at Rochester University was a phenomenal gathering of scholars with diverse approaches to twenty-first-century black studies. The *Callaloo* conferences have also provided an ideal audience. *Callaloo*'s bringing together of literature and visual art has greatly nurtured my own breaking of the boundaries between literary and visual studies. I thank Charles Rowell for his visionary leadership.

In the visual art zone, the Porter Colloquium, sponsored by Howard University's art history department, has been an intellectual home. The artists I met after delivering one of the 2016 Porter Colloquium keynotes have greatly enhanced this book's approach to black abstraction. I thank Ben Jones, Kevin Cole, Adrienne Gaither, and Ernest Shaw for sharing their work during the book's final stages. During the early stage of the book, Rebecca Zorach asked me to be one of the writers for the 2013 AfriCOBRA exhibit at the DuSable Museum of African American History. These direct connections with art historians gave me the wings to do this "word and image" work.

I thank the following kindred spirits for being non-guiding lights in this crucial "disorder" (as Robert Reid-Pharr describes it) that we might call global black studies: Greg Thomas, Sylvia Wynter, Fred Moten, Souleymane Bachir Diagne, Hortense Spillers, Cheryl Wall, Houston Baker, Mark Anthony Neal, Aldon Lynn Nielsen, James Smethurst, Kokahvah Zauditu-Selassie, Farah Jasmine Griffin, Jennifer De Vere Brody, Robert Reid Pharr, Imani Perry, Sharon Holland, Kevin Quashie, Herman Beavers, Salamishah Tillet, Bill Maxwell, Erica Edwards, Evie Shockley, Brent Edwards, E. Patrick Johnson, Jeremy Glick, L. H. Stallings, and Dr. James Turner.

At Cornell University, Dagmawi Woubshet and Lyrae Van Clief-Stefanon have been friends, air, food, water, and pure love. So many dimensions of this book have been nurtured by the Cornell jam session with Dagmawi Woubshet, Lyrae Van Clief-Stefanon, Riché Richardson, C. Riley Snorton, Carole Boyce Davies, Gerard Aching, Naminata Diabate, Mary Pat Brady, Noliwe Rooks, Satya Mohanty, Helena Viramontes, and Ken McClane. While teaching and mentoring Donelle Renita Boose, Robert Jiles, Danielle Fuentes Morgan, Elena Guzman, Elizabeth Alexander, Marquis Bey, Anisha Warner,

Esmeralda Arrizon-Palomera, Nasrin Olla, and Maya Durham, I discovered new dimensions of this book.

Dawn Durante has been an exquisite editor whose support throughout the publication process has been invaluable. I thank Matt Mitchell for being such an ideal copyeditor. Jennifer Comeau directed the production of the book with precious care and commitment. The two external reviewers gave precious insight about the paradigm shifts this book could set in motion. For me, the book was spoken into existence through these reviews. I thank Christopher Harter and the staff at the Amistad Research Center at Tulane University. I also thank Third World Press and the Moorland-Spingarn Research Center.

I thank Koritha Mitchell for being my amazing accountability partner during the year this book was completed. I thank Yomaira Figueroa for finding *Half-Past Nation Time* and for being the beautiful spirit she is. I thank Jennifer De Vere Brody for our vacations during hard times. I finished the Harlem Renaissance chapter while enjoying the Harlem Renaissance pad that Nicole Fleetwood offered. I thank Kalamu ya Salaam for all of the interviews and BLKARTSOUTH connections he provided and for the second line we stumbled upon. I thank Quo Vadis Gex-Breaux for her precious poetry and for opening up a whole new perspective on black feminism during the Black Arts Movement. I thank Kokahvah Zauditu-Selassie for bringing *hum* to New Orleans as I finished the book, and I thank my dear sister Syeeda Naima, my brother-in-law Kwasi, and my amazing niece Zoe for bringing their joy to New Orleans during that final writing stage. I thank George Hutchinson for the "post-emergency surgery" *life* of "blessings, hope, and bells."

The Black Arts Movement was a turned corner and a cornerstone of my father's (Bob Crawford's) life work (1939–2015). His phenomenal photographic archive first led me to see the nuances and textures of this complicated cultural movement. Amiri Baraka signed my father's copy of *Black Art* (1966) in the following manner: "For Bob Crawford → The Seeing Eye + Margo, Asante for being so Black." I cherish that "seeing eye." This book is dedicated to him and others who remain grounded enough (*homespun*) to see the movements within movements.

Homespun love sustains me. I thank my mother, Margo Barnetta Crawford, for remaining my model for revolutionary thinking, grace, and true insight. I thank all my homespun friends and siblings for their unconditional homespun love. Like Stevie Wonder sings, "You can rest your mind assure / That I'll be loving you always."

Introduction

What is the edge of this event? [. . .] What is the
beautiful? What will blackness be?
—Fred Moten, *In the Break*

Baraka was able to reterritorialize the shock of the new.
—Aldon Lynn Nielsen, *Black Chant*

This book unveils the surprising connections between the 1960s and early
1970s Black Arts Movement (BAM) and early twenty-first-century black aesthetics. In *Black Is Beautiful: A Philosophy of Black Aesthetics*, Paul C. Taylor
offers a lucid definition of "black aesthetics": "the practice of using art, criticism, or analysis to explore the role that expressive objects and practices play
in creating and maintaining black life-worlds."[1] In a 1967 issue of *Soulbook*,
a California-based BAM journal, an advertisement used the word "rhythm"
to crystallize the meaning of "black aesthetics": "Rhythm is the *vibratory
shock*, the force which, through our sense, grips us at the root of our being.
It is expressed through corporeal and sensual means; through lines, surfaces,
colours, and volumes in architecture, sculpture, or painting; through accents
in poetry and music, through movements in dance. But doing this, rhythm
turns all these concrete things towards the light of the spirit" (italics mine).[2]
The "vibratory shock" of the Black Arts Movement and twenty-first-century
black aesthetics can only be appreciated when we break out of a linear sense
of black aesthetics and imagine it as a space in which, as Martha Buskirk
explains, there is a "possibility of skipping backward or forward in the succes-
sion of rooms or chapters [that] yield a different message, that message being
the simultaneous availability of all periods and styles."[3] Skepticism about any
fixed notion of "black art" plays a profound role in the 1970s "second wave"
of the BAM and early twenty-first-century mobilizations of "post-black" art.
As the BAM became the first cultural movement determined to make art that

is specifically and unapologetically black, the artists' search for the specificity of black art led to a wide horizon of shaping and unshaping blackness that I call "black post-blackness." This book's comparison of the BAM and the early twenty-first century shows how black art (in its most innovative forms) is always a remaking of "black" and "post-black" within the layered circle of black post-blackness.[4]

The words "black post-blackness" are another way of thinking about the "changing same," as Amiri Baraka named black aesthetics during the BAM.[5] It matters that the changing same was first theorized (and the very words introduced) during the BAM. The architects of the movement discovered the Black Power of the changing same. They seized the power of framing blackness as the art of moving forward and remaining grounded.[6] In Kalamu Ya Salaam's essay "*BlkArtSouth*—New Orleans" in a 1972 issue of *Black World*, the notion of "post" appears in the following fashion: "Art, as we know it, is a post-experience (or should be) suggestion. I mean, we must first experience (in one way or another) that which we attempt to translate into an art form."[7] Black post-blackness is the circular inseparability of the lived experience of blackness and the translation of that lived experience into the world-opening possibilities of art. In his introduction to Larry Neal's poetry volume *Black Boogaloo* (1969), Amiri Baraka proclaims that the BAM is "post-literary" as he makes blackness itself stretch out like the words "It's nation time eye ime" in his signature BAM poem "It's Nation Time."[8] Black post-blackness is this state of suspension we see and hear when Baraka stretches out the word "time" into "time eye ime." In this state of suspension, black consciousness-raising and black experimentation are inseparable; being and becoming cannot be separated.

In *Splay Anthem* (2002), Nathaniel Mackey provides a new grammar for understanding the circularity of black aesthetic traditions. His theory of seriality captures the circular tension of black post-blackness: "A desperate accent or inflection runs through seriality's recourse to repetition, an apprehension of limits we find ourselves up against again and again, limits we'd get beyond if we could. [. . .] Recursiveness can mark a sense of deprivation fostered by failed advance, a sense of alarm and insufficiency pacing a dark, even desperate measure, but this dark accent or inflection issues from a large appetite or even a utopic appetite."[9] This tension between pacing back and forth with a sense of stasis (a "failed advance") and pacing back and forth as one feels propelled by a "large appetite" is the difference between moving linearly and moving in a "tidalectic" manner. This idea of "tidalectics" emerges in a 1995 dialogue between Mackey and Kamau Brathwaite. As Brathwaite explains his theory of "tidalectics," he captures the nonlinear, back-and-forth, black radical tradition of continuity *and* rupture that propels my theory of black post-blackness. Mackey explains, "It's not a linear movement, except in the sense of thesis-antithesis-synthesis. That is an overall idea. But since I started that, it has been superseded with the idea of tidalectics, which is dialectics with my difference. In other words, instead of the notion of one-two-three, Hegelian, I am now interested in the movement of the water backwards and forwards as a kind of cyclic, I suppose, motion, rather than linear."[10] Frantz Fanon, in *Black Skin, White Masks*, famously critiqued his comrade Jean-Paul Sartre's use of the Marxist dialectic when he asserted that there is a next step after black consciousness-raising (that *négritude* is a "minor term" in a larger dialectic). Fanon (like Brathwaite with his theory of tidalectics) insists that the most radical black aesthetic movements are always anticipating the next step "beyond blackness" and actually shaping whatever blackness is around the impulse to imagine the unimaginable. When the BAM mobilized the word "black" in the most radical manner, it was a way of naming the unknown dimensions of freedom and self-determination. In the most radical BAM usages, the word "black" always gestures to a profound overturning of the identity category "Negro" and a desire to reenchant black humanity as much more than an identity category. "Black" signaled excess, the power of the *unthought* (that which José Munoz, in *Cruising Utopia*, describes as the "not yet here").

This book opens up a space in which the *not yet here* of the 1960s and early 1970s Black Arts Movement converges with the *not yet here* of early twenty-first-century African American literature and visual art. We now have foundational studies of the BAM, such as James Smethurst's groundbreaking *The Black Arts Movement: Literary Nationalism in the 1960s and 1970s* (2005), Amy Ongiri's *Spectacular Blackness* (2009), Daniel Widener's *Black Arts West: Culture and Struggle in Postwar Los Angeles* (2010), Howard Rambsy's *The Black Arts Enterprise and the Production of African American Poetry* (2013), and Carter Mathes's *Imagine the Sound: Experimental African American Literature after Civil Rights* (2015),[11] that signal the vibrant new wave of further interpretation of the movement. *Black Post-Blackness* argues that the full innovativeness of the BAM only emerges when we recognize the movement's full anticipation of the "beyond black art" waves of twenty-first-century black aesthetics. The BAM has much more in common with twenty-first-century African American literature and visual art than we often realize. The push to the mixed media, abstraction, satire, and sheer experimentation in twenty-first-century African American literature and visual art is sometimes framed as a push away from the narrowness of the category "black art," but it is often a push *back* to the mixed media, abstraction, satire, and experimentation in the BAM.

Amiri Baraka's introduction to his short-story collection *Tales of the Out & the Gone* (2007) begins with the following words: "What should be obvious in these tales, are the years, the time passing and eclipsed."[12] In the second paragraph, Baraka adds an image of the layers of residue that shape the cultural mood of this "passing of time": "What is left of what has left." Baraka's puzzling play with what changes and what remains, in this introduction to this collection of short stories written from 1974 to 2007, is one way to understand the pulse of this book—the cultural mood of black post-blackness. This feeling does not emerge after the 1960s and 1970s BAM and its mobilization of "black" as a unifying political and aesthetic concept. Black post-blackness is a way to understand the continuity between the BAM and the twenty-first-century African American literature and culture that seems to be "post-black" (or not invested in "black representational space," Darby English's term in *How to See a Work of Art in Total Darkness*).[13] Black post-blackness was the cultural mood of the BAM's simultaneous investment in blackness *and* a type of freedom that broke the boundaries of blackness.

By the 1970s, as the BAM entered its second wave, black post-blackness is staged, repeatedly, in essays and poems that dramatize the difference between the movement's 1960s hailing of blackness and the early 1970s need to pause and add new dimensions to this movement that remained in motion. The push for a post-blackness that is actually "blacker" than the 1960s enactments of blackness is the focus of the editors' introduction to the "edge of the 1970s," spring 1969 issue of *Black Dialogue*. The editors end the introduction with these words: "The few years between 1965 and 1969 brought many changes to Black America and BLACK DIALOGUE tried to keep up with those changes, but not always with success. We've stubbornly refused to be whipped by the forces that attempt to co-opt and strangle all things black. [. . .] Our determination is still Black. Our printer is still Black. We are still distributed and sold (where possible) Black. [. . .] In the year 1969, we hope you'll meet with us quarterly and have a BLACK(ER) DIALOGUE with us so that we can be around in 1970 when things are sure to get even blacker."[14] The early 1970s marked the beginning of the end of the BAM and the beginning of all of the reverberations the movement produced. These were the vital years when people in the movement looked back at the 1960s and knew that a crucial, although limited, black cultural revolution did indeed take place. In "The Seventies: A Poem for Blacks of the Sixties," Tom

Dent of BLKARTSOUTH depicts this 1970s looking back at the 1960s black cultural revolution: "if you thought we had finally begun to turn the corner in this / century, suppose you thought that . . . / [. . .] check us out on the merrygoround / spinning round & round & around."[15] The mood of the early 1970s BAM ranged from this cynicism to the anticipation of a "blacker" next step (in the editorial statement in *Black Dialogue*). When the mood of the "spinning round & round & around" was not only cynicism and despair but the anticipation of something "blacker," the early 1970s BAM became a pensive, "what will blackness be?" form of black post-blackness.

In 1971, in her *Black World* essay "Uh Nat'chal Thang—The WHOLE TRUTH—US," Carolyn Rodgers, one of the most significant BAM poets, framed the early 1970s mood of black post-blackness in the following manner:

> Let us all grow Black WHOLE human beings and know our REAL selves, together. Let us touch, feel, each every Black other.
>
> To some extent, we know who we are. Angry, oppressed, frustrated, anxious, Black slaves. 1971 style.[16]

This unromanticized search for a way of talking about a black wholeness (that emerges as a productive frustration with what Rodgers, in this same essay, describes as a 1960s style of "shouted, screamed, and writhed" blackness) is the full spirit of black post-blackness.

The title of Charles Johnson's 1972 collection of satirical editorial cartoons—*Half-Past Nation Time*—evokes the midpoint mystery of the "what's next?" early 1970s mood of black post-blackness. Johnson begins with a discussion of "lateness":

> The hour is late. [. . .] It is dusk and the fierce, Mau Mau cries of "Nation Time, Nation Time" ring from the lightless ghettos. [. . .] *Half-Past Nation Time* is about the time bomb ticking of evolution's clock; it is about black folks in search of new forms and symbols. [. . .] It is about the surge of black nationalism that has reshaped America in its eleventh hour, the charcoal élan vital that injected new blood into the tired veins of Western culture. It is also about the clots in that new blood which coagulated and grew sluggish as it degenerated from Black Power to Green Power; from "au natural" hairstyles to assembly line Afro wigs; from the promise of the Black Panther party to fashionable, expensive bandelero dresses more chic than anything from Christian Dior's studio; from men of faith like Malcolm X to dime store revolutionaries with a mouthful of Mao and a pocketful of ripped-off poverty program funds. It's about the revolution in black America.[17]

This late-style 1970s BAM energy was looking back at the promise and limits of the first wave of the movement. The "new blood" and the "clots in that new blood" of the early 1970s "half-past nation time," suspended state of black post-blackness was described by Edward Spriggs, as he announced the 1973 Studio Museum exhibit of Afri-COBRA, in the following manner: "The black artist of the '70s will move beyond the protest art of the '60s and renew the celebration and pageantry of our collective ethos. [. . .] It is an age for moving beyond mere rage—it's Nation Time and black artists are searching. Black artists are immigrating into self, family, and nationhood—and celebrating the process."[18] Spriggs recognizes that the second wave of the BAM made the search for nation into a search for self. When Derek Conrad Murray argues, in *Queering Post-Black Art: Artists Transforming African-American Identity after Civil Rights*, that the BAM was the stage of "black romantic art" that comes before the post-black quest for individuality, he identifies the frames that I trouble in this book.[19] Black post-blackness is the often illegible mood of both the 1970s second wave of the BAM and the early twenty-first century that makes the black collective romance inseparable from frustration with a black collective sensibility. The romance and frustration build on each other as black artists somehow continue to hold on to an aesthetic flow that keeps moving and changing.

Toward a Theory of Black Post-Blackness

The black post-blackness of the BAM was most nuanced when it understood movement itself as the ethos of black style; the black post-blackness of the twenty-first century is most nuanced when it troubles blackness without worrying about the loss of blackness. "Change" is the last word in the dizzying array of vertical and horizontal layers in Larry Neal's consummate BAM manifesto "Some Reflections on the Black Aesthetic" (1972).[20] The note-taking aesthetic in Neal's manifesto is visualized in a 1967 photograph by Gordon Parks (fig. 1) of Stokely Carmichael (whose 1966 call for "Black Power" made him, like Malcolm X, a core part of the BAM worldview). This photograph of Carmichael holding onto chalk and looking at his audience as the conversation changes in a classroom where he is giving a lecture on Black Power visualizes what is at stake in this book.[21] Carmichael has written many words—such as "Afrika," "ideology," "Nkrumah," "inward," and "just" on the board—but Parks captures his right hand suspended in motion, making marks that look like a series of strokes that could be a tally (a counting of something) that is being discussed. Carmichael looks intently at his audience as if he is waiting for someone to finish what they are saying before he continues to write. I situate this book in this photograph's suspended motion that captures the state of suspense of any pedagogy for the oppressed. What will the next lesson be? What will the next word be? What is not yet legible? The photograph conveys both the stillness and the motion of the Black Power era and its artistic kindred spirit, the BAM. The intent stare of Carmichael accentuates what we cannot know about this classroom lecture and what we may have misunderstood about the BAM. What happened in this classroom as the lecture or dialogue was led by the person who first set the words "Black Power" in motion as the civil rights movement gave birth to the Black Power movement? How can we lean into the photograph's dramatizing of a liminal state of anticipation that makes Carmichael's black consciousness-raising too open-ended to be the point of closure that a "post-black" generation would push against as they propel themselves into motion?

In 2008, the *New Yorker*'s cover image of Michelle and Barack Obama (fig. 2) put the spotlight on how easy it is to parody the Black Power movement as "new" types of blackness are imagined. In Obama-era parodies of Black Power, militancy is rendered as the ridiculous urge to stay "black and angry" in a world that is moving so quickly past all the effects of America's "original sin" of slavery that a black man can actually be elected president

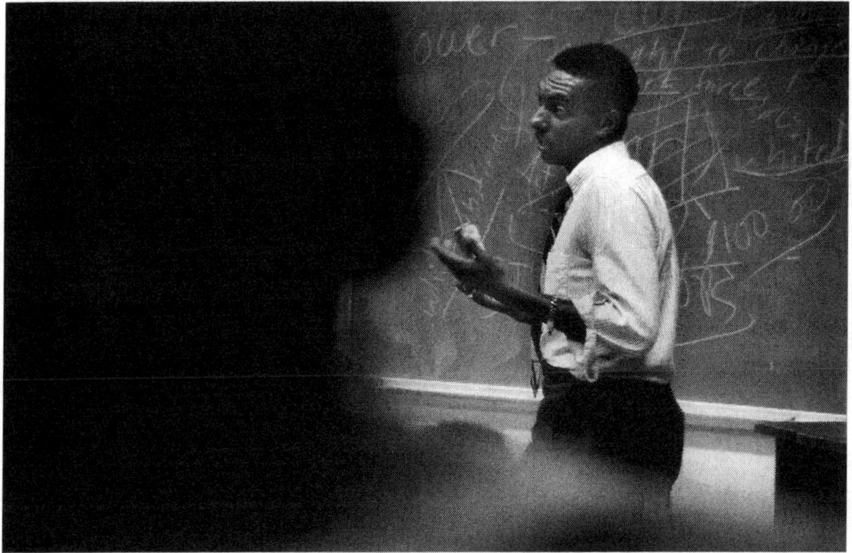

Figure 1. Stokely Carmichael, Los Angeles, 1967. Photograph by Gordon Parks. Courtesy of and copyright the Gordon Parks Foundation.

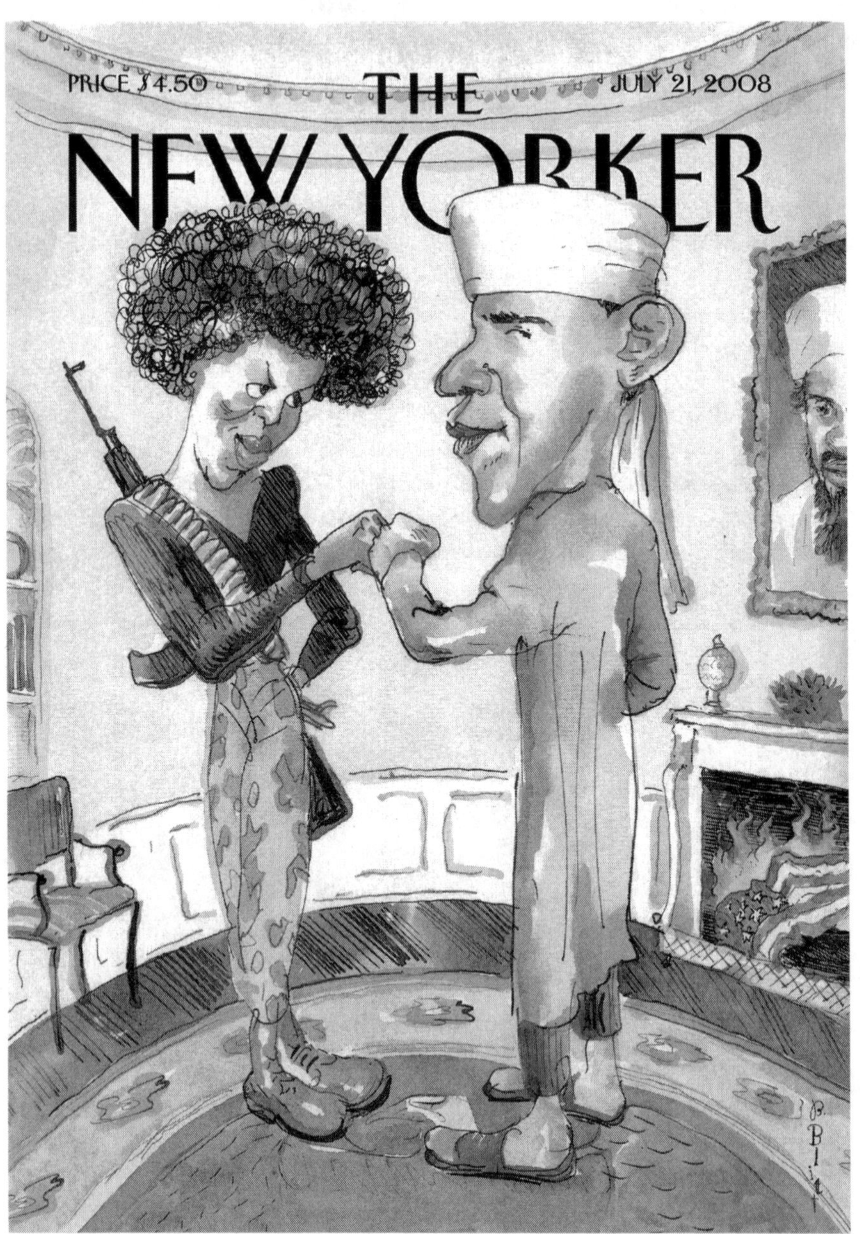

Figure 2. Barry Blitt, "The Politics of Fear." Cover image, *New Yorker*, July 21, 2008.

of the United States. This cover image of the *New Yorker* circulated during Obama's first presidential campaign. The parody suggested that some of the critical responses to Barack Obama's "fist bump" with Michelle Obama (before he took the stage to accept the 2008 Democratic presidential nomination) were latent fears of intimacy between African Americans turning into anti-American sentiments. The image makes it seem ridiculous that some people unconsciously see the Afro and the rifle when they see a black presidential candidate and a potential black first lady bumping fists, but it also ridicules the Black Power movement in the process of ridiculing antiblack racism. Iconic images of black militant resistance are flattened, in this cover image, and the iconic Black Power gesture, the elevated fist, hovers in its absence. The image suggests that the Black Power movement must be stripped of any substance if African Americans want to be embraced as full citizens. The crushing of Black Power becomes the "price of the ticket," the cost of the admission into the seeming post-racial future.

This notion of admission into a "beyond blackness" space is directly engaged in Danzy Senna's short story "Admission" in her volume *You Are Free* (2011). Senna imagines an African American upper middle-class woman playwright, Cassie, who is initially seduced by the possibility of her two-year-old child being able to attend the most elite preschool in Los Angeles and then gradually repulsed by the assumption that no one would want to refuse this "admission," once she receives the acceptance letter and the school representative repeatedly calls her and then comes to her house because she cannot believe that she and her husband are not accepting the admission. The full experience of visiting and being interviewed by the school makes Cassie remember her own experiences in elementary school and the classmate, Tasha, who was ostracized and ridiculed by the other students because she wore a wig (her mother had burned her scalp). Cassie keeps remembering Tasha's burned scalp as she works through her conflicted feelings about wanting her "honey-colored" child to be in the safe white world of privilege. Cassie's husband, whom she accuses of "making everything political," is never seduced by the prospect of their son being admitted into this ridiculously expensive preschool.[22] In this short story, he represents the voice of "I don't want to be admitted" that approaches the betrayal of race and class privilege that is embodied in BAM literature. In her novel *Caucasia* (1998), Senna directly responds to the Black Arts Movement when she imagines a biracial child adding a question mark to the words "Black Is Beautiful" during the alternative pledge of allegiance in Nkrumah, a black consciousness-raising school.

Senna's twenty-first-century critique of African American desire to be admitted into white privilege is inseparable from her desire to understand the fundamental impulse to be seduced by the possibility of a post-trauma state of existence. Like Senna's short stories, Elizabeth Alexander's 2009 poem "Praise Song for the Day," written for Barack Obama's inauguration, opens up space for the remembering of black struggle and a letting go of the fixation on black struggle. The tension between Alexander's inauguration poem and Amiri Baraka's "Somebody Blew Up America" (2001), a response to the 9/11 terrorist attacks, reveals the tension, in twenty-first-century black aesthetics, between the opening up of space and the continued sense of the struggle to breathe. Alexander's words, "Say it plain: that many have died for this day," take on a new dimension when compared to the final explosion in "Somebody Blew Up America": "Who and Who and WHO who who Whoooo and Whooooooooooooooo-oooooo!" Her post-rage praise song takes for granted that we know who has died for this day. When these poems (and the performance of them) are compared, Alexander's words, "say it plain: that many have died for this day," and Baraka's repeated "who who who" open us the complexity in each poem. Baraka's "who who who" reminds us that Alexander is not "making it plain"; she is not naming those who have died or providing any direct naming that would "blacken" this praise song. In a similar sense, Alexander's "say it plain" reminds us that Baraka, throughout "Somebody Blew Up America," keeps asking "who?" but never provides the "plain" answer, as the word "who" at the end of the poem becomes more of a sound than a word. The move to abstraction in both poems, even while holding on to a concrete (even when subtle, in the case of "Praise Song for the Day") invocation of the history of struggle, is the impulse of black post-blackness that is explored in this book.

Where, in the BAM, do we see concrete signs of this black post-blackness? Consider the depiction of being "Black, / Blacker, / and Blackless sometimes" in the poem "What Color Is Lonely?" by Carolyn Rodgers, one of the poets in the core, inner circle of the movement and a cofounder of Third World Press, one of the black publishing companies created during the movement. Rodgers ends the poem with the black feminist query, "Tell me sister, / What color is lonely?" As an insider (not a outsider to the movement), Rodgers writes:

> and I know that I am Black
> 　　　Blacker
> 　　　　　and Blackless sometimes[23]

The layers in this poem are registered visually, as Rodgers breaks the lines so that readers move downward from "Black" to "Blackless." The knowing that the speaker announces—"I know that I am Black"—cannot be separated from her awareness that the BAM is insisting on a collective process of becoming "Blacker." But the full force of black post-blackness emerges when Rodgers adds the deepest level of this line breakage—the fact that, in the midst of this collective assumption of blackness, there are also feelings of "Blackless[ness]."

Why "Black Post-Blackness"?

The word "post-black" has circulated, in the first years of the twenty-first century, as a way of understanding contemporary black aesthetics. African American curators and visual artists spearheaded "post-black" discourse. It is significant that this unnaming begins in the field of African American visual culture. Through the dialogue between curators and visual artists, this anti-name is produced as if, from its very beginning, the term is a way of visualizing an opening-up of space. In the catalog for the 2001 Studio Museum *Freestyle* exhibit, Thelma Golden explains that, as soon as the visual artist Glenn Ligon said "post-black," she "knew exactly" what he meant.[24] Not having to explain the unname allows Ligon and Golden to set up the exhibit as an interior space in which blackness is taken for granted to such an extent that it does not need to be a master sign. The first uses of the term "post-black" appeared as Golden and Ligon joked about their "inside" awareness of what the term might mean.

I first started thinking about the relation between the neologism "post-black" and "post–Black Arts Movement" when I read Golden's introduction to the catalog of the 2001 *Freestyle* exhibit at the Studio Museum. In this framing of the exhibit as "post-black," she pauses at one point to note that the term may be shorthand for "post–Black Arts."[25] The notion that this elision is sometimes shorthand (and not an attempt to erase the significance of the Black Arts Movement) competes with many other circulations of the term that do not cling to the words "black arts" or the "black aesthetic."

In the United States, the words "black aesthetic" first began to circulate widely as a way of thinking and seeing during the mid-1960s. The movement was often *the black aesthetic movement,* as people engaged in a constant theorizing about the function and power of aesthetics. In the pages of the most central archive of the movement, Hoyt Fuller's *Black World* (first named *Negro*

Digest), there is a steady attempt to flesh out the meaning of the words "black aesthetic." The BAM's steady need to define the black aesthetic differs from the twenty-first-century circling around "post-black" and its performance of the unnaming.

There is no way of knowing the originary utterance of "post-black," but Thelma Golden's 2001 explanation of the affect tied to the term lingers. The affect is comparable to a nod—taking something for granted and therefore not needing to remain defined by that term. It could be also likened to a wink. The affect of the wink is exemplified in the following performative dialogue between the curator Lowery Sims and the performance artist and curator William Pope.L: "Lowery Sims: Are you still black? William Pope.L: Obviously. Of course not."[26] The wink here becomes "black post-blackness" in the space between "obviously" and "of course not." In the definitive space (marked by the period), the wink makes it "obvious" that people can feel both black and post-black.

During the BAM, outer space, abstraction, and the eccentricity that Larry Neal simply referred to as the "weird" were steadily invoked, but they were not imagined as being post-black. In the poem "Don't Say Goodbye to the Porkpie Hat," as in many other poems in the long final layer of *Hoodoo Hollerin' Bebop Ghosts* (1974), Neal captures the full style of this black weirdness: "Shape to shape, horn to horn / the Porkpie Hat resurrected himself / night to night, from note to note / skimming the horizons, flashing bluegreenyellow lights / and blowing black stars / and *weird* looneymoon changes, chords coiled about him / and he was flying" (italics mine).[27] As we remember the normativity of much of the gender discourse and the racial-authenticity impulses of the BAM, we must also remember the "weird"—what A. B. Spellman describes as the "Negritudinous surreal dream."[28] The BAM pivoted on a dialectic between collective mirrors and collective collages, which were a layering that gave blackness depth. This depth was a spatial and temporal strategy of resistance that insisted on blackness as the past, present, and future. Black aesthetics' time of entanglement (echoing Achille Mbembe's words) is what many post-black performances erase. Many post-black advocates fail to understand black abstraction, black improvisation, and even *black* post-blackness. The irony of the post-black critiques of essentialized blackness is that the emerging post-black "marketing" obscures the transnational motion that was created when "black" was mobilized as a unifying concept full of layers and different temporalities. Post-blackness is often stuck in a misunderstanding of black aesthetic movement.

Black Arts / Post–Black Arts

Some of the texts and visual images that might be tagged "post-black" deserve less marketable names such as "post–Black Arts" and "black post-black." Consider, for example, Percival Everett's novel *Erasure* (2001) as an extension of the BAM critique of the publishing industry. *Erasure* is a harsh critique of the marketing of African American literature as the literature of "pafology." Everett's protagonist wants to publish a type of literature that will not cater to this marketable "pafology," and he also does not want to be a writer of racial uplift and black respectability. This dual desire is a vital part of the BAM sensibility. The short play *Malcolm: '71, or Publishing Blackness: Based upon a Real Experience* (1971), by Ed Bullins, is the type of BAM parody that, when read alongside *Erasure*, exposes the changing same of African American frustration with the publishing industry's marketing of a certain version of blackness and the BAM anticipation of the post-movement *play* that would ridicule the serious playfulness and productive experimentation that the movement itself represented. Bullins shapes the tension of this short play around a white woman editor's inability to understand why naming her dog after Malcolm X is deeply offensive to the African American writer she calls to ask for a submission to the "Black Culture" project she is editing. The writer hears the dog barking and hears her call him "Malcolm"; after receiving confirmation that he has heard her correctly, he simply hangs up the phone. He cannot bear to explain to her the irony of her reduction of Malcolm X to a domesticated pet, given her supposed expertise on the subject of blackness and her current position as a white editor of black texts.

This play captures the movement's awareness of not only the power of self-naming but also the power of a dominant culture industry to distort the names mobilized during decolonizing movements. One of the best ways to fight this distortion is to refuse to accept the dominant culture industry's marketing of the "new" and to refuse to accept that twenty-first-century African American cultural productions are necessarily removed from the earlier movements of black self-determination. When frames cut frames (Black Arts / Post–Black Arts), we see prisms of what lingers (the splitting of the "black light" that is often depicted in the BAM). Harryette Mullen's poem "Denigration" (2002) is a classic prism of Black Arts / post–Black Arts.[29]

Mullen cuts the word "nigger" into sounds (as she thinks about all of the other words that contain some of these cut up sounds). The full prose poem is worth citing:

Did we surprise our teachers who had niggling doubts about the picayune brains of small black children who reminded them of clean pickaninnies on a box of laundry soap? How muddy is the Mississippi compared to the third-longest river of the darkest continent? In the land of the Ibo, the Hausa, and the Yoruba, what is the price per barrel of nigrescence? Though slaves, who were wealth, survived on niggardly provisions, should inheritors of wealth fault the poor enigma for lacking a dictionary? Does the mayor demand a recount of every bullet or does city hall simply neglect the black alderman's district? If I disagree with your beliefs, do you chalk it up to my negligible powers of discrimination, supposing I'm just trifling and not worth considering? Does my niggling concern with trivial matters negate my ability to negotiate in good faith? Though Maroons, who were unruly Africans, not loose horses or lazy sailors, were called renegades in Spanish, will I turn any blacker if I renege on this deal?

The closing line, "will I turn any blacker if I renege on this deal?" captures the embeddedness of the "nig" sound in words that have no etymological relation to "nigger." As Mullen plays with the sound of words such as "denigration," "niggling," "nigrescence," "neglect," and "renege," she makes her readers hear a sonic racial terror that is so terrifying, the poem suggests, precisely because it is embedded in the everyday affect of those who have never been called a nigger. Like Mullen, Black Arts poets were (as Baraka explains in his introduction to Larry Neal's *Black Boogaloo*) "dealing in sound." Baraka uses the phrase "post-literary" to describe this sound work: "Post 'literary' because we are men who write. [...] Literary sound like something else . . . sound like it ain't sound. And sound is what we deal in . . . in the real world . . . sound for sounding."[30] Many of the current "post-black" assessments of BAM poetry do not understand the post-literary. These critiques often focus on the supposed lack of "literary" worth and ignore the innovations with sound. The power of the Mullen/BAM "frame-cutting-frame" is the power of rehearing the 1960s Black Power "reneging on the deal" of assimilation. Mullen's poem "Denigration" sonically performs an African American neverending process of counternaming. Each word that almost sounds like "nigger" grates against the word "blacker" in the final line. Mullen seems to tell us that there is no ethical way, in the face of transnational structural antiblack racism, to revel in a state of post-denigration (subjects of antiblack racism cannot get "any blacker"). Her poem can be read, slantwise, as yet another troubling of the post-black brand.

The BAM led some writers to a nascent interest in "more than black" as opposed to "post-black." The "more than" impulse has a temporal dimension that differs from the linearity of the post-black brand. Carolyn Rodgers helps us grasp the productive play with time as "nation time" was performed. In her poem "All the Clocks," she presents the image of clocks that are "off" or "have stopped in the Black ghetto" and the idea that people "don't know what TIME it is."[31] She paints this picture of stopped clocks (due to the lack of resources in the "ghetto" neighborhoods), but the stopped time also signals the speaker's sense that the rhetoric of nation time has not reached the everyday people on the street. We can imagine that James Brown's "Say It Loud, I'm Black and I'm Proud" might have resonated more, in some of the streets of "stopped time," than Baraka's elongated powerful chant of "It's nation time eye ime." Brown's lyrics "I'm black and I'm . . ." are rarely heard with the emphasis on "and," because the rhyme of "loud" and "proud" makes us hear the opposite of what Kevin Quashie calls the "sovereignty of quiet."[32] The move from "I'm Black" to "and I'm" has the "more than black" texture that, clearly, in the song is inseparable from the full assertion of blackness.

Rodgers dramatizes the everyday experience of the "stopped time" that would make people who live in the ghetto unable to answer the resonant Black Power question, "What time is it?" The only answer may not be "nation time"; it may be simply "time to fix the clocks in the neighborhood," but it is hard to imagine that the answer should ever be "It's post-black time." These words sound like a shutdown of earlier flows. The temporal flow of black aesthetics remains the trope of "flow, layering, and rupture" that Tricia Rose uses in her analysis of hip-hop.[33] "Post-black" stages the rupture while neglecting the flow and layering that produce the power of the ongoing rupture in the dialectic of the three energies.

At the beginning of *Interrogating Post-Feminism: Gender and the Politics of Popular Culture* (2007), the editors write, "Postfeminism broadly encompasses a set of assumptions, widely disseminated with popular media forms, having to do with the 'pastness' of feminism, whether that supposed pastness is merely noted, mourned, or celebrated."[34] The tone of celebration in Touré's *Who's Afraid of Post-Blackness* (2011) is the most troubling feature of the post-black brand. The BAM celebrated such a different sense of past, present, and future in its focus on both *being* black and *becoming* black. Fred Moten's question, in *In the Break*, remains: "What will blackness be?"[35] And we might hear the liminality and the self-fulfilling circle (the hailing will become the *matter*; black begets black). As the power of black enchantment continues, Claire Colebrook's focus on *becomings* that attach to other *becomings* may be one way to understand the black post-blackness. Colebrook writes, "Here, becoming does not realize and actualize itself, does not flourish into presence, but bears a capacity to annihilate itself, to refuse its ownness."[36] But the vital point is that the refusal of the ownness and the lack of a "flourishing into presence" were only achieved, in the BAM consciousness-raising, through the *collective becoming*, the collective movement. The "flourishing into presence" was a collective performance. The post-black brand, in contrast, relies on a fetishism of individuality and the dead end of exceptionalism.

Amiri Baraka, in "Heathen Technology at the End of the Twentieth Century," in *Tales of the Out and the Gone*, refuses to accept this "dead end." In this science-fiction story, Baraka imagines an apocalypse that includes the "dis/imaging" of people, a type of mind control that makes people disappear by stealing and collecting their image making.[37] The first-person narrator is a witness linked to other survivors who resist the mind control by listening "eight times a day" to John Coltrane's jazz recordings and looking "eight times a day" at Aaron Douglas's images.[38] This counter-hypnotism harkens back to BAM images of black collective resistance to dominant image making. The story's call for continued belief in collective resistance emerges most clearly when the narrator asks his apocalypse-era listeners to "remember" and then realizes that "remembering" is no longer possible in the era of the "brain switch," but nonetheless continues to remember the power of "bound metaphor."[39] This bound metaphor is described in the following manner: "If the metaphors of a heavy group were rendered collective and focused on whatever, energy and power could be produced."[40] This language captures Baraka's recognition that the power of the BAM's mobilization of blackness as a unifying concept was the power of people realizing that blackness is a productive collective metaphor.

Baraka's poem "SOS" was painted on the BAM mural *The Wall of Respect* (Chicago, 1967). The words in the painted poem gradually disintegrate until the final lines cannot be read without squinting and performing a "close looking." Glenn Ligon's twenty-first-century text paintings of passages from African American literature demand a similar "close looking." As Darby English teaches us, Ligon's text paintings show "the transformation brought about when the word graduates to picturehood."[41] The BAM painting of the poem "SOS" sheds light on James Stewart's theory, in the BAM anthology *Black Fire*, of the movement's critique of art that becomes a monument, an object that aims to last forever. The ephemeral nature of the *Wall of Respect*, the precariousness of art on an abandoned building, signals that the frustrated reading performed in the mural painting of "SOS" is a frustration with the need to fix and make the happening into an eternal monument. The notion of frustrated reading explains the new type of reading practice that is needed, a way of reading the frustrating black post-blackness that connects the BAM and the twenty-first century. The past-tense emphasis in twenty-first-century post-narratives, such as Kenneth W. Warren's *What Was African American Literature?* (2012) and Charles Johnson's "The End of the Black American Narrative" (2008),[42] assumes that the goal of black identity politics is the creation of an eternal model, the creation of a black "object." The BAM's critique of the text as object and monument was tied to a type of identity politics that combined strategic abstraction and strategic Afrofuturism. The *jazz* of blackness, when considered as the larger ethos of the great experimentation during the BAM, is the force that unsettles the movement's steady, complex impulse to frame blackness.

In *What Was African American Literature?* Warren thinks about "our age" as retrospective in contrast to the pre–Jim Crow era of African American literature (what African American literature used to be). He claims that African American writers and critics used to think about what will come, hailing the opening up of the literary tradition, and he implies that now that what was being hailed has happened, there is no conceptual integrity to the category "African American literature."[43] Now that the Jim Crow walls have broken down, the writers are not writing within the enclosure nor breaking down an enclosure (the dual actions that defined African American literature). Warren explains that he considered the title "What was Negro Literature?" before choosing the title "What was African American Literature?" The original title would have connected with the rhetoric of the BAM that insisted on the transformation of "Negro" into "Black." In contrast to the BAM emphasis on the rebirth signaled by Black (not "Negro") consciousness and on establishing new criteria for understanding the specificity of African American art, Warren hails the end of any ability to refer to the specificity, signifying difference, or ongoing tradition of African American literature.[44] The post–Jim Crow moment that Warren sees as the end of African American literature is hailed, during the BAM, as the *beginning* of a literary tradition that can be specifically "Black."

Black Post-Blackness shows how blackness remains that elusive "flash of the spirit" that moves through the Black Arts Movement to twenty-first-century black aesthetics. As I uncover the role of self-criticism, humor, exhaustion, and cynicism in the 1970s, second wave of the BAM and the early years of the twenty-first century, I shape each chapter around the following tensions and inquiries that are at the core of both movements: anticipation, abstraction, counter-literacy (mixed media), the global-local, satire, public interiority, and the substance of style.

1

The Aesthetics of Anticipation

Anticipation: The early sounding of one or more tones of
a succeeding chord to form a temporary dissonance
—Merriam-Webster Online Dictionary

Harlem is vicious
modernism. BangClash.
—Amiri Baraka, "Return of the Native"

As the Black Arts Movement was approaching its final wave in the 1970s, Dudley Randall (the founder of Broadside Press and one of the most influential Black Arts writers) wrote the most insightful comparison of the BAM and the 1920s and 1930s Harlem Renaissance. In "The Black Aesthetic in the Thirties, Forties, and Fifties" (1970), Randall argues that the "closest thing [during the Harlem Renaissance] to a black aesthetic was Langston Hughes's declaration in 'The Negro Artist and the Racial Mountain' (1926)."[1] Randall quotes the final words in Hughes's powerful manifesto and then offers the following analysis:

> This sounds much like the Black Aesthetic credo, but there are significant points of difference. For instance, Hughes uses the word Negro. Some Negro ideologues have forbidden Negroes to call Negroes Negroes. Hughes stresses individualism ("express our individual dark-skinned selves"). In the Black Aesthetic, individualism is frowned upon. Feedback from black people, or the mandates of self-appointed literary commissars, is supposed to guide the poet. But Hughes says, "If colored people are pleased we are glad. If they are not, their displeasure doesn't matter either." (Another expression of individualism.) Hughes says, "We know we are beautiful. And ugly too." In the Black Aesthetic, Negroes are always beautiful.[2]

Randall is only drawn to these "significant points of difference" because the confluence between Hughes's discourse and Black Aesthetic discourse (in other parts of this iconic Harlem Renaissance manifesto) seems so remarkable. As he analyzes the opening words in "The Negro Artist and the Racial Mountain," he asserts, "This is as close to the Black Aesthetic cry of 'I'm black, and beautiful!' as it is possible to come."[3]

Certain Harlem Renaissance texts that can almost pass as Black Arts texts pivot on the conceptual edge of the Harlem Renaissance, an edge of this cultural movement that was not fully formed and that approached the aesthetic theory and practice of the BAM. These liminal texts remind us that cultural movements do not always *settle*; the integrationist aesthetic and the white-patron influence of the Harlem Renaissance did not cancel out the writers' attempts to carve out a space of black self-determination. Harlem Renaissance writers anticipated the BAM, and some of those anticipatory visions greatly shaped the more militant tones of the Harlem Renaissance.

When we read some Harlem Renaissance texts, we almost forget the difference between the tone of the "New Negro" (one of the Harlem Renaissance's monikers) and the tone of the BAM insistence on being "Black," not "Negro." The emphasis on "racial pride" resounds in Alain Locke's opening essay in *The New Negro* (1925), but this pride often seems tame compared to the black pride of the BAM. But the Harlem Renaissance texts that gesture toward another movement of black self-determination allow us to understand why Kalamu ya Salaam argues that the movement should be instead known as the "Garvey era."[4] Locke's "The New Negro" offers a clear way of processing the limits and usefulness of the term "Garvey era" as a means of understanding the Harlem Renaissance. The "counter-hate" and "defiant superiority feeling" that, Locke warns, could emerge is one way that 1920s Garveyism and 1960s black nationalism are described by critics. Locke's conciliatory tone is remarkably different from black-nationalist refusals to apologize for black radicalness and rage. Locke writes, "Only the steadying and sobering effect of a truly characteristic gentleness of spirit prevents the rapid rise of a definite cynicism and and a defiant superiority feeling."[5] As Locke announces the arrival of this cultural movement, he explains both the "race pride" and the assimilationist sensibility of the New Negro. Locke argues that the New Negro is a "forced radical," but the BAM understood black radicalism as the most genuine, *natural* response to white supremacy and viewed assimilation as a dead end.[6]

When the art of these movements is compared, radicalism's liminality surfaces. We see, for example, the process of a mobilization of black consciousness, the texture of an ad hoc territory of black aesthetics. In the 1960s, black aesthetics remained not yet settled, as improvisation and experimentation continued. But the BAM did name and consciously seek to define "the Black

Aesthetic" in a manner that the Harlem Renaissance did not. As a starting point in the uncovering of the radicalism of the Harlem Renaissance that anticipates the BAM (and can only be fully recognized when we see the liminality that shaped both movements), we can begin with the poem "Colors" (1927) by Countee Cullen, which plays with the red, black, and green colors of Garvey's United Negro Improvement Association. Cullen begins with the word "(Red)" in parentheses and moves to "(Black)" at the beginning of the second stanza, but he ends with "(The Unknown Color)," placed at the beginning of the closing stanza.[7] The final move to the unknown matters; as he rewrites the expected "red, black, and green" triad, Cullen makes "red, black, and the unknown" convey a sense of the need to wait to see what that final color will be. The questioning of aesthetics throughout the poem is tied to the appearance of the unexpected and the unknown. The first stanza introduces a scene of sad subjection and powerful resistance. A woman, described as "ugly, black, and fat," is told, while shopping, that a red hat suits her, but "behind her back" the compliments become laughs. The onlookers laugh "to see it glow against the black."[8] The woman walks out of the store with pride. Has she been set in motion by the deceptive compliments of the storekeepers, or is her prideful strut fueled by her own sense of her beauty in the red hat? In this stanza, Cullen makes the opening word "(Red)" connect to the violence of the storekeepers' deception and laughter, but the red also signals the visual shock and surprise of the red hat against dark skin. Cullen, by virtue of foregrounding the pan-African colors (the *colors* of black liberation), makes this red hat also conjure up the redness of blood (the blood of kinship and the blood of those wounded by the transnational white supremacy that Garvey was fighting). When contrasted with the final stanza and its opening words, "(The Unknown Color)," this first stanza is clearly what Cullen sees as the "known" colors—the script of dominant white aesthetics clashing with a black woman's impulse to see herself as beautiful. The final stanza is the surprise. After the depiction of the white gaze and then lynching, in the second and third stanzas, we arrive at a lighter sequence that remains quite heavy: "I've often heard my mother say, / When great winds blew across the day, / And, cuddled close and out of sight, / The young pigs squealed with sudden fright / Like something speared or javelined, / 'Poor little pigs, they see the wind.'"[9] This Harlem Renaissance poem "sees the wind" as it gestures, in the opening stanza, toward the need for black aesthetic warfare and a "black is beautiful" sensibility. The BAM was blowing in the wind as Cullen wrote this poem.

The Harlem Renaissance / Black Power Edge

The anticipatory wind of black radicalism swept up Marita Bonner. Her play *The Purple Flower* (1926) is an uncanny anticipation of the rhetoric and radicalness of the BAM. As Jennifer Wilks explains in *Race, Gender, and Comparative Black Modernism: Suzanne Lacascade, Marita Bonner, Suzanne Cesaire, Dorothy West,* Bonner "portend[s] the 'black revolutionary drama' of the 1960s and 1970s."[10] Cullen's poem "Colors" performs the beginning of a *black can be beautiful* awareness that approaches the BAM's full performance of aesthetic warfare (the rage against the white aesthetic), but *The Purple Flower* is an overt performance of warfare against white power. When we read this play as an anticipation of the BAM, we gain a heightened understanding of the power of anticipation in the black radical tradition. Bonner, in the 1920s, envisioned the emergence of a black freedom struggle shaped around a deep analysis of the spatial dimensions of power. Before the Black Power movement happened, Bonner could see it on the horizon. Radical cultural movements are imagined first, before they can happen. Some of the liminal, anticipatory texts of the Harlem Renaissance have a militancy that has been overshadowed by the wave of scholarship focusing on interracial intimacies (beginning with George Hutchinson's groundbreaking *The Harlem Renaissance in Black and White*). In *Modernism and the Harlem Renaissance,* Houston Baker gave us the foundation for a deeper understanding of the role of black self-determination and black nationalism in the Harlem Renaissance. Bonner's *The Purple Flower* is a deeply black-nationalist play that teaches us, as Wahneema Lubiano has argued, that black nationalism is sometimes simply black common sense, a deep awareness, for example, that when oppression has penned you in you must claim your own space in order to breathe.[11]

In *The Purple Flower,* Bonner's engagement with the spatial dimensions of power (the image of a valley with "white devils" living on a hill) leads her not only to a profound anticipation of the Hurricane Katrina crisis (New Orleans as a "bowl," with disempowered black people living inside it) but also to a profound anticipation of the Black Arts and Black Power movement theorizing about the need to create a "nation within a nation" as colonized space is transformed into black space. Bonner's play is both theater and criticism. In the opening notes, which have the tone of an essay, Bonner explains that "[t]he Skin-of-Civilization must be very thin. A thought can drop you through it."[12] These characters who can fall through the cracks and become almost post-human (or prehuman) shapes are a part of "Us," who are set apart, in their valley, from the "white devils" who live on hills. The set has a horizontal division of the stage into an upper and lower level. The most innovative part of this play is the description of how the actors on the upper level sometimes fall through the boards and become "twisted" and "curled" mounds. This strange image of the fall that makes the black people lose their "civilized" state and become the mounds is a stunning representation of what happens when a mind is decolonized, when just a clear thought of liberation can take you into not only a different state of consciousness but even a different state of embodiment. The mound may appear to suggest inanimateness, but it may also signal a collectivity. The process of decolonizing the mind that was at core of the BAM was a movement of young people who were shattering their former sense of self and discovering a collective black identity that was inchoate, amorphous, and nonetheless galvanizing.

The white devils in *The Purple Flower* are described as being "artful little things"; there is something delicate about these devils that "have soft wide eyes such as you would expect to find in an angel."[13] In contrast to the standard depiction of whiteness, in BAM texts, as purely negative images of violence and oppression, Bonner suggests that white supremacy is still inchoate. Bonner ends the play with the note of listening and the question, "Is it time?" The final stage directions are: "All the Us listen. All the valley listens. Nowhere listens. All the white devils listen. Somewhere listens. Let the curtain close leaving all the Us, the White Devils, Nowhere, Somewhere, listening, listening. Is it time?)."[14] Bonner, in 1926, anticipates the rhetoric of "white devils" that began circulating two years after the publication of the play, when W. D. Fard first laid the foundation for the Nation of Islam. But the final question, "Is it time?" anticipates the question and answer "What time is it? Nation time!" that echoes throughout the Black Power movement. Bonner teaches us that before powerful slogans such as "nation time" emerge, there are powerful questions that have not yet been fixed, questions that are still looking for full elaboration. The play leads us to a core question: What does black rage sound like? Do we only hear it in the last spoken words in the play ("You have taken blood: there can be no other way. You will have to give blood! Blood!"), or can we hear it in the final stage directions that present the tense listening process? Black rage, in this play, is both the unabashed call for bleeding of the white devil and the quiet at the end, after the curtain closes and the "listening" refuses to stop.

Jean Toomer's Evanescent Black Aesthetic

The art of the Harlem Renaissance has more black rage than we sometimes see; it anticipates the black rage of the BAM. The liminal Harlem Renaissance/Black Arts texts remind us that rage takes many forms and that the black rage of the BAM was inseparable from black love (an intense collective love affair with a newly embraced identity that was called "black"). The black rage/black love dynamic is performed in Jean Toomer's *Cane*, the text that is most often canonized as the literary masterpiece of the Harlem Renaissance. *Cane* ends with the rage of Kabnis directed at the mute "old man" who won't say anything "new an up t date."[15] The immobility of the old man and his ties to slavery make him represent a type of authentic blackness that Kabnis cannot bear to accept. But Toomer's anticipation of a love affair with blackness is dramatized in earlier sections of *Cane*. In "Esther," Toomer anticipates the "black is beautiful" sensibility of the BAM and also anticipates the reasons why this falling in love with blackness may be painful and impossible for some to sustain. Toomer foresees that black women, for example, might quickly lose their affection for blackness if the black consciousness-raising movements are fueled by the performance of black male chauvinism.

Analysis of Toomer's depiction of falling in love with "magnetic blackness" in "Esther," coupled with analysis of the final section, "Kabnis," opens up the nuances of Toomer's anticipation of the southern BAM. Tom Dent, one of the founders of the performance collective BLKARTSOUTH, explains the emergence of the name of the collective in the following manner: "In other words what I'm driving for now is a sort of Black Arts South, localized, centralized in New O . . . which will among other things produce material for the touring company and bring to the whole fucking black arts concept a southern orientation, a source of material coming from the South."[16] In *Cane*, Toomer also tries to find that southern orientation of black aesthetics, but Toomer is more similar to his frustrated character Kabnis, who despairs that he will never be the "face of the South" (as opposed to Lewis, who "merges with his source [the South]."[17] During the BAM, *Cane* was embraced as one of the models of consummate black aesthetics even as the movement framed the Harlem Renaissance as an interracial party or spectacle of assimilation in which the self-determination of the Negro was constantly jeopardized. BAM writers critiqued the role of white patrons in the Harlem Renaissance and an alleged desire, on the part of the African American writers, to assimilate into a dominant (white) aesthetic. Amiri Baraka, in "The Myth of a 'Negro

Literature'" (1966), for example, argues that the majority of Harlem Renaissance literature remained mediocre art due to the imitation of white "high art." But Baraka cites Toomer as one of the few black writers who produced substantial literature.[18]

We need to rethink what the BAM saw in *Cane*. It may be that the texture of the southern black aesthetic was the appeal; the black northerner's longing to know the South and his remarkable closeness to that which seems so far away was similar to the BAM longing to know Africa as they sought to purge themselves of whiteness. After the publication of *Cane*, Toomer did not want to be defined as a black writer, whereas the urgency and passion of the BAM created desire to produce "black art." Reading "Esther" and other parts of *Cane* through the lens of the BAM sheds light on the ways in which the Harlem Renaissance's anticipation of the BAM sometimes led to the rejection of the sensibility that would become Black Arts. Toomer captures "black is beautiful" as it fades; just as he explains that the impetus of *Cane* was the "folk spirit that was walking in to die on the modern desert," his glimpse of "black is beautiful" is an intoxicating, powerful reflection of that which he could not hold onto. Alice Walker, in *In Search of Our Mothers' Gardens* (1983), advises that those of us who are invested in the ongoing tradition of black aesthetics keep *Cane* and let Toomer go.[19]

In *Cane*, Toomer anticipates a discovery of an alternative aesthetic that sees black southernness (black rootedness) as beautiful and also anticipates that this love affair with a black South would be too heavy and disorienting for some to hold onto without rushing back to the comfort of a world that is, in the words of Louis Armstrong, less "black and blue." When BAM devotees saw something they loved in *Cane*, they may have been loving the intensity of someone falling deeply in love with a black folk spirit; they may, unconsciously, have been connecting Toomer's complicated love affair with the black South to their own complicated love affairs with the *regions* of blackness they were discovering.

"Esther" revolves around a young, light-skinned black girl who "decides that she loves" King Barlo, a man whom she views as "magnetically" black. His blackness makes her feel an awakening; her class status and light skin color connect her to an aesthetic of whiteness that makes her feel dead, and Barlo's magnetic blackness is a wake-up call. The intentionality of Esther's love (her *decision* to love) signals that this new way of seeing (loving magnetic blackness) is a swerve, a new worldview. Like the BAM mobilization of black love that overcomes the internalization of antiblack racism, when Esther falls in love with Barlo she is overcoming a dominant aesthetic structure that has demonized blackness. Toomer anticipates the ethos of the BAM when black respectability is no longer the only way that black people admire blackness. Barlo's blackness is admired because it is riotous and free. He is a preacher, but he is preaching Black Power, not conciliatory Christianity. His sermon includes the following direct focus on Black Power: "An Lord Jesus whispered strange good words deep down, O way down deep, deep in my ears. An He said, 'Tell em till you feel your throat on fire.' I saw a vision. I saw a man arise, and he was big an black an powerful—."[20] Esther falls into a state of trance once Barlo "became the starting point of the only living patterns that her mind was to know."[21] These words capture the deep connection between the depiction of her decision to fall in love with Barlo and the BAM mission of loving blackness as a means of decolonizing the mind. This same passage also suggests that she has an entirely new worldview, comparable to what happens when the mind is purged of the antiblack racism instilled by white power.

At the end of the story, Toomer portrays Esther's state of trance (this new type of pro-black conditioning) in a negative light. King Barlo, she discovers, is a drunk, crude man who lacks the serious commitment to Black Power performed in his street sermons. As Toomer depicts Esther's disenchantment, he portrays the color black in a very different manner from the magnetic blackness that first seduces her. Black now becomes a frightening state of *blackout* that profoundly disorients and almost kills Esther (taking her back to the deadness of her "white" existence before magnetic blackness woke her up). Toomer critiques the need to project authentic blackness onto bodies. He also seems to critique any conditioning process that makes a person become zombie-like, even if the conditioning is tied to black resistance and consciousness raising. Esther, Toomer suggests, would need (if we lean on Ntozake Shange's language in *For Colored Girls Who Have Considered Suicide / When the Rainbow Is Enuf*) to find the King Barlo *in herself*; in order to be truly liberated, she would need to become the "starting point" of her own "living patterns."[22] This tension produces Amiri Baraka's melancholy in *In Our Terribleness,* when he warns readers that he cannot lead them in the decolonizing state of counter-hypnotism (the dominant hypnotism being white power)—they must close their own eyes and create their own alternative visions of liberation. The ties between Toomer's depiction of Esther's dilemma and the BAM imaging of this deconditioning process are striking. As Esther escapes from home and searches the streets for Barlo, she shuts her eyes and then decides that the act of closing her eyes simply reminds her that she has not found Barlo yet (she has not been liberated yet). This image of the liberating black interior that is so hard to locate is remarkably similar to Baraka's tender call, in *In Our Terribleness*, for a closing of the eyes that will allow the black subjects being hailed to "see [their] own face."[23]

The difference between Toomer's vision and Baraka's vision is the move, in "Esther," to the negative image of the drunken, "hideous" Barlo. Toomer does not let the decision to fall in love with blackness remain a viable option. He kills it at the end of "Esther," and this is how he sets the stage for the rage of Kabnis against the sight of Father John, at the end of *Cane*. Kabnis's great frustration with Father John makes Toomer's anticipation of 1960s black consciousness-raising even more nuanced. Young black people in the era of the Black Power movement could not always understand that their notions of older black people's apparent passiveness and acceptance of oppression were often faulty. In contrast to Esther's impulse to decide to love the figure who seems magnetically black, Kabnis is not attracted to Father John, whose blackness seems too old and immobile to him. Kabnis's insistence that Father John say something that is "new and up to date" sets up a generational gap between the young black northerner who has come to the South to teach in a black school and the much older black man whose knowledge Kabnis cannot recognize. Kabnis views Lewis as as a "better version" of himself. Lewis is the figure who most approaches a Black Power militancy and commitment to the black freedom struggle. He won't leave the Georgia town until be finishes his investigation of the lynchings. He feels a tie to Father John and shows him the love that Kabnis cannot feel. Lewis is also not a distant collector of information about the South but rather someone who "merges with his source."

Throughout *Cane*, Toomer includes moments when black love of blackness surfaces as a particular way of living and thinking about the world. Paul, in "Box Seat," claims this black love when he rages against Muriel's fear of the dwarf who is offering her a rose. Muriel, the epitome of racial uplift and assimilation, sees "blackness" when she is offered this rose, as the entire theater audience watches her: "Muriel, tight in her revulsion, sees black, and daintily reaches for the offering."[24] Her self-consciousness, haughtiness, and sense of humiliation is tied to her inability to accept the display of affection from the dwarf. Muriel, through the lens of the black solidarity of the Black Power movement, is a self-hating, colonized mind. Toomer's description of the dwarf highlights his novel's uncanny anticipation of a black aesthetic that would translate that which a dominant (white) aesthetic views as the black grotesque into a profound type of unadulterated, grounded, rooted, undiluted type of black beauty. Toomer writes, "Muriel flinches back. The dwarf steps forward, diffident; threatening. Hate pops from his eyes and crackles like a brittle heat about the box. The thick hide of his face is drawn in tortured wrinkles. Above his eyes, the bulging, tight-skinned brow. Dan looks at it. It grows calm and massive. It grows profound. It is a thing of wisdom and tenderness, of suffering and beauty."[25] Dan's alternative vision anticipates so many aspects of the Black Power worldview: the reclamation of the black phallus ("It grows calm and massive"); the conflation of black mind and the black body ("It is a thing of wisdom"); the reclamation of the black gaze, the power of black people looking at each other and creating counter-hegemonic visions ("Dan looks at it"); and the transformation of human/beast racialized binaries into the power of *animated* blackness (the smoothing out and energizing of the "thick hide of his face" and the "tortured wrinkles").

Toomer sees the power of a collective move to "black is beautiful." He imagines the force of Haki Madhubuti's call "Don't Cry, Scream," as he depicts Dan yelling "JESUS WAS ONCE A LEPER!" Toomer captures the aesthetic warfare between Muriel's fear that the color of her dress might clash with the color of the theater seats and Dan's thoughts of guerrilla warfare when he realizes that someone passing by might think he is a burglar ("Break in. Get an ax and smash in. Smash in their faces. I'll show em. [. . .] Baboon from the zoo."[26] But Toomer's beautiful images of "face flowing in her eyes" and "her skin [. . .] like dusk on the eastern horizon" are what we remember when we think of this Harlem Renaissance classic. The black rage and the anticipation of a black-is-beautiful movement fade away just as the "folk spirit was walking in to die on the modern desert." Toomer does not allow this black militancy to settle down and gain roots. Like Esther and Kabnis, he needs air; he is not prepared to linger too long in this black aesthetic underground.

Langston Hughes's Sonic Edge

In contrast to Jean Toomer, Langston Hughes willingly lingers in this underground; he anticipates the BAM and calls it into being. *Ask Your Mama* (1961) was published literally on the edge of the 1960s, calling and calling (as Baraka's iconic poem "SOS" insists) for black people "to come on / in." The indelible mark of the BAM on *Ask Your Mama* is rooted in the refrain "AND THEY ASKED ME [. . .] / IF MY BLACKNESS, WOULD IT RUB OFF? / I SAID, ASK YOUR MAMA."[27] The poem presents the decision to embrace blackness as a bold refusal to be erased in a global system of racialized capitalist oppression. Hughes wrote the poem in direct response to the riot at the 1960 Newport Jazz Festival (when young white people had difficulty getting into the festival). As Scott Saul explains, in *Freedom Is, Freedon Ain't: Jazz and the Making of the Sixties*, Hughes was in a precarious position at the festival. He was the emcee for what became "the mop-up act for the festival after it was summarily canceled by the city council in the wake of the Saturday night riot."[28] For the "mop-up" event, Hughes wrote the lyrics to "Goodbye Newport Blues" (which was performed by Muddy Waters and Otis Spann). The lyrics include the words: "What's gonna happen to my music? / What's gonna happen to my song?"[29] Hughes started writing *Ask Your Mama* at a hotel in Newport. *Ask Your Mama* is an extension of this question, "What's gonna happen to my music?" The answer (given the diverse range of music the poem brings together) seems to be: black music mixes with everything as the categories ("blues" and "world music") become inseparable. But this anticipation ("What's gonna happen to my music?") leads Hughes to something much more complex than a "we are the world" sensibility. Universal sounds make him hear the notes that are not *specifically* black, but *still* black. His anticipation of the poetics of the BAM lies in this sounding out of the layers that create deep political, aesthetic, and *pleasurable* investments in blackness.

The pleasure of being black was a core part of the cultural revolution staged during the BAM. Reading Black Arts texts, we often fail to see the power of the pleasure factor. The humor cannot be separated, at times, from the rage. And in the post–Black Power landscape, as the price of the ticket for many admissions into nuanced, open (post-black?) identities becomes the tacit agreement that the black consciousness-raising of the 1960s was silly, violent, and ineffective, people create a parody of the Black Power and Black Arts movements. The use of humor in the movement itself is lost as people laugh at the movement. Hughes, in *Ask Your Mama*, seems to anticipate that the power of *black rage* humor would be reduced to twitches and not recognized as winks. *Ask Your Mama* is a sustained wink. Each time Hughes uses the refrain "AND THEY ASKED ME [. . .] / IF MY BLACKNESS, WOULD IT RUB OFF?" the words "ASK YOUR MAMA" have the gestural effect of a wink that asks other kindred spirits to remember that we should not continue to explain who we are (that too many of the inquiries themselves have been deeply offensive). Too many of the framing questions have made blackness into a problem that must be "rubbed off."

Ask Your Mama's critique of these oppressive framing questions explodes in the eighth mood, titled "Is it True?" Hughes writes: "FROM THE SHADOWS OF THE QUARTER / SHOUTS ARE WHISPERS CARRYING / TO THE FARTHEREST CORNERS SOMETIMES / OF THE NOW KNOWN

WORLD / UNDECIPHERED AND UNLETTERED / UNCODIFIED UN-PARSED / IN TONGUES UNANALYZED UNECHOED / UNTAKEN DOWN ON TAPE— / NOT EVEN FOLKWAYS CAPTURED / BY MOE ASCH OR ALAN LOMAX / NOT YET ON SAFARI."[30] Like Hughes, Zora Neale Hurston critiques any collection of the "black folk" that translates a process of creating sound into an object that contains the sounds. In the introduction to *Mules and Men* (1935), Hurston writes, "Folk-lore is not as easy to collect as it *sounds*" (italics added).[31] These words brilliantly express the need for a collection process that allows the sound to continue to *sound* (that does not convert the living, dynamic sound into a frozen object of study). Hurston's and Hughes's worry about the safari approach to the collection of the "black folk" is the worry that shapes the BAM's direct attack on white appropriation and commodification of black culture.

James T. Stewart's manifesto "The Development of the Black Revolutionary Artist" (1968) is a signature example of the BAM critique of white commodification of black culture. Stewart argues:

> The work ["temples made of mud that vanish in the rainy seasons," rice-paper drawings made with ink and spit, and the "newssheets circulated in our bars today"] is fragile, destructible; in other words, there is a total disregard for the perpetuation of the product, the picture, the statue, and the temple. Is this ignorance? According to Western culture evaluations, we are led to believe so. The white researcher, the white scholar, would have us believe that he "rescues" these "valuable" pieces. He "saves" them from their creators, those "ignorant" colored peoples who would merely destroy them. Those people who do not know their value. What an audacious presumption![32]

Hughes's critique is equally strong. He was thinking about the sounds that are captured in the "safari" led by the white collectors of folk music and world music. His reference to Moe Asch and Alan Lomax shows that he was not only thinking critically about those who intentionally collect the culture of others in a "safari" that hurts those who are being observed and hunted, but also about the seemingly benevolent souls who may have never really thought about their power as collectors of those who cannot collect their own material.[33] Hughes was anticipating the BAM call for black collection of blackness.

When Hughes writes "TONGUES UNANALYZED," he sets up what the BAM would later insist upon as the type of black self-determination that refuses to be an object of study within a white-dominated discourse. The liner notes in *Ask Your Mama* and the use of an overwhelming number of allusions throughout the poem are not only a riff on *The Waste Land*; they are also a refusal to explain. The dedication of the liner notes—"For the Poetically Unhep"—displays a disdain for readers who may be on the "safari" trip that worries Hughes. Only the "unhep" would need a key to the text; only the "unhep" would not remember the earlier words in the eighth mood, "UNCODIFIED UNPARSED / IN TONGUES UNANALYZED." The subtitle of the text—"12 Moods for Jazz"—underscores Hughes's hopes that moods will not be analyzed; moods should be experienced, not decoded. He does not want this book to be comparable to a Folkways recording of the music that must be preserved: "NOT EVEN FOLKWAYS CAPTURED / BY MOE ASCH OR ALAN LOMAX / NOT YET ON SAFARI." Hughes hopes that *Ask Your Mama*'s experimental, loose form will be understood as an open text that does not aim to "capture." As he experiments with unboundness, he adds musical directions to the lines of poetry. In a marginal column, the lines are given sound waves such as "Gospel music with a very heavy beat as if marching forward against great odds, climbing a high hill—to again fade into the dry swish of maracas in cha-cha time."[34] The poetry and music flow together and produce a composite mood that is emergent and unsettled.

If Hughes had dedicated the liner notes to the ideal reader of this uncapturable text, his language would approach "To the Unborn Beast," the dedication in Carlene Hatcher Polite's Black Arts–era novel *The Flagellants*.[35] Polite, like Hughes, inveighs against the impulse to "capture." Early in the novel, she sets up the difference between "gestures" and "clutch." She links gesture to dance and the process of falling in love, but she uses the image of clutching to signal the problems of possession. In this explosive novel, Polite presents a traumatic love story that forces readers to acknowledge how entangled love and rage can be. The lovers (Jimson and Ideal) use the word "dog" as a way of insulting each other, but the dedication to the unborn beast hails a new type of black human being, someone who finds a way to be fierce (unafraid to express black rage) without hurting other black people as this rage is expressed and, in fact, even learning through the expression of this black rage to love other wounded black people.

In the eleventh mood of *Ask Your Mama*, Hughes directly calls for the expression of black rage: "IN THE NEGROES OF THE QUARTERS / PRESSURE OF THE BLOOD IS SLIGHTLY HIGHER / IN THE QUARTER OF THE NEGROES / WHERE BLACK SHADOWS MOVE LIKE SHADOWS / CUT FROM SHADOWS CUT FROM SHADE / IN THE QUARTER OF THE NEGROES / SUDDENLY CATCHING FIRE / FROM THE WING TIP OF A MATCH TIP / ON THE BREATH OF ORNETTE COLEMAN."[36] These words dramatize the full anticipation of the BAM. The title of the central Black Arts anthology, *Black Fire,* is on the tip of Hughes's tongue. The free jazz of Ornette Coleman spoke to many of the poets of the BAM as they searched for the word-and-sound interplay that Hughes created in *Ask Your Mama.* Hughes titles this eleventh mood "Jazztet Muted." As he dreams, in *Ask Your Mama,* about black resistance "suddenly catching fire," he throws a flame on the more "muted" resistance in *Fire!!* (1926), the Harlem Renaissance publication that he produced with Wallace Thurman (the editor), Zora Neale Hurston, Aaron Douglas, and others. Hughes's poetic foreword to *Fire!!* begins with the following words: "*FIRE . . . flaming, burning, searing, and penetrating far beneath the superficial items of the flesh to boil the sluggish blood.*"[37] Even during the Harlem Renaissance, as he remained under the influence of white patronship, Hughes could see that a different type of movement of black aesthetic warfare would happen, that what he calls "black shadows" (in *Ask Your Mama*) would become "Black Light" (the BAM term for the new epistemology of light and darkness that the artists were creating).

Theorizing Anticipation

The productive force of anticipation is its difference from waiting. Anticipation is much more active than waiting. Anticipation, like invisibility (as in Ralph Ellison's *Invisible Man*), gives one a "different sense of time"; it makes one's present deeply tied to the future. After setting up the twelve moods in *Ask Your Mama,* Hughes makes the mood of anticipation linger. We hear the raw power of this mood in the final words in the foreword to *Fire!!*: "Fy-ah, / Fy-ah, Lawd, / Fy-ah gonna burn ma soul!"[38] Anticipating fire makes one sweat before the actual heat. During the Black Power and Black Arts movements, the "actual heat" was the revolution that people in the movement believed was "right around the corner." The BAM was as tied to the anticipation of fire as the more militant moods of the Harlem Renaissance. During the BAM, the anticipation often masqueraded as postanticipation; the black cultural revolution (black cultural nationalism) was an experimentation with new self-images and ways of walking through the *actual new world* that was anticipated. The Black Arts cultural workers were not waiting for the world to change; they were anticipating change, believing that change could happen, and creating art that would, in the words of Ed Bullins, create a "sense of reality confronted" and "consciousness assaulted."[39] Given this mood of anticipation, Sun Ra's Afrofuturism found an unsettled home on the jazz mobile of the Black Arts Repertory Theatre. Sun Ra was drawn to the BAM's future-oriented engagement with the present, and his resonant query—"Suppose we came not *from* Africa but *to* Africa"—reflects what "Africa" symbolized in the BAM.[40] The idealization of "Africa" was rooted in Afrofuturism—an anticipation of a new understanding of heritage as not where one is *from* but *to* where one must travel (what pulls one forward and makes one believe, in spite of global antiblack oppression, in a *black future*).

The question "What is Africa to me?" in Countee Cullen's iconic Harlem Renaissance poem "Heritage" (1925) anticipates the Afrofuturism of the BAM. The Harlem Renaissance posed many questions that the BAM strove to answer. Cullen's final move in this poem—the speaker's confession that sometimes he wants to imagine that God is not white—is reshaped, in BAM literature, into the explicit discourse of black liberation theology. *Journey to Africa* and *Black World* (the titles of the texts of Hoyt Fuller, one of the deans of the BAM) show the inseparability of the new black worldview that Cullen was anticipating and Sun Ra's sense that "Africa" is where black diasporic subjects can arrive (not begin). The title of Fuller's travel narrative—*Journey to Africa*—echoes as much as *Black World*, the name of the journal Fuller edited as he became one of the prime architects of the BAM.[41] We must remember that Cullen (whom we might too quickly understand as a poet who did not want to be known as a "black poet") anticipated that the answers to the question "What is Africa to me?" will pivot on the powerful impulse of black colonized people to somehow see themselves with their own eyes: "Lord, I fashion dark gods, too, / Daring even to give to You / Dark, despairing features where / Crowned with dark rebellious hair, / Patience wavers just so much as / Mortal grief compels, while touches / Faint and slow, of anger, rise / To smitten cheek and weary eyes."[42]

Comparative studies of the Harlem Renaissance and the BAM gain more depth when we acknowledge the power of anticipation. The musical definition of anticipation, in the epigraph of this chapter, embodies the spirit of the anticipatory flows between the movements. If anticipation is indeed "the early sounding of one or more tones of a succeeding chord to form a temporary dissonance," we need to learn to hear unexpected sounds in the space of improvisation that Fred Moten so aptly calls "in the break."[43] We need to understand the full force of the role of *anticipation* in the improvisation and experimentation that continue to define black aesthetics. Written at the height of the BAM, Amiri Baraka's music theory puts anticipation at the heart of black aesthetics. In the essay "The Changing Same (R&B and New Black Music)" (1966), Baraka explains: "The something you want to hear is the thing you already are or move toward. We feel, Where is the expression going? What will it lead to? What does it characterize? What does it make us feel like? What is its image? Jazz content, of course, is as pregnant."[44] Anticipation is the force of giving birth to expression that has not been named and fully realized, but is nonetheless a part of you the entire time it is being formed. When I was growing up, my mother would warn, "I knew you before you were born." Black aesthetics often has that texture of something that is most known and felt when it seems so elusive (such a "flash of the spirit") that it seems to not be born yet.[45] The word "renaissance" may mislead us with the notion of the rebirth of black aesthetics and culture; the Harlem Renaissance and the BAM are best understood as the *pregnant* state of anticipation. The more militant, anti-assimilation texts of the Harlem Renaissance knew "Black Arts" before it was born.

The Black Arts Movement Anticipation of "Post-Blackness"

The title of Evie Shockley's poetry volume *The New Black* (2011) resonates. The poetry of the BAM performed a rhythm of anticipation that made "black" often mean "new black." Amus Mor, one of the most underrecognized trailblazers of the movement, stages this spirit of anticipation in his "Poem to the Hip Generation" (1972) through the refrain "who are we / where are we going / what are we here for." Spanning eight pages, the poem has jagged-edged margins on the left and right until the final two short stanzas, which have justified margins on the left and a tight compactness that the other open stanzas lack. The beginning stanza introduces David ("he was David" are the closing words of the stanza) by visualizing the "first steps" of both David and "the nation."[46] As the first three lines, following the opening line, are indented, successively, closer and closer to the right margin, the birth of David slowly unfolds. This birth is tied to the biblical creation story, an "electric storm," urban rooftops, soup lines, kitchenettes, and a "nation's first step." This birth is the birth of David's jazz; we learn, in the fourth stanza, that *he* enters the "academy / of Lester the president." The visual steps in the first lines of the poem thus present David's own "first step" toward jazz: "david dug genesis / did not dream / heard the electric storm / that was his intro."[47] The word "dug" is the spectacular vernacular that captures David's love of the biblical story. There is something about the biblical language that makes David begin to move over the rooftops and gain a new self-image. He does not move into the self-enclosure of dreams but rather an open space that feels like "an electric storm," the tumultuous wind that you can only feel on rooftops that are so close to the electrical lines spanning across the city.

The word "dug" also captures David's digging (his anticipatory questioning) throughout the poem, echoed in the repeated words "who are we / where are we going / what are we here for." Mor makes the digging much more than the creation of a metaphysical hole when he ends the poem with answers to these questions: "we are the hipmen / [. . .] where are we going / into the sky / [. . .] why were we sent here / only to love."[48] Just as Sun Ra's response to the Black Power call and response "What time is it? Nation Time" was to declare, "It's Planet Time" (the title of his 1973 album), Mor, in this poem, makes the move to outer space, "going / into the sky," the birth of the black nation. The opening stanza's "first steps of nation" are rewritten in the final stanzas as the first steps into outer space. In this closing part of the poem, when Mor makes hipness, outer space, and love the answer to the cosmic questions about identity, action, and the future, his lines are no longer literally moving across the page with the uneven left margin. In this final stanza, with its left-justified lines, the poet pauses to breathe deeply and rest after the long jazz riff performed throughout the poem. The return to the normative stanza shape is a return to the controlled Black Arts chant after the play with the enchantment of anticipation.

We also hear this power of anticipation in Gwendolyn Brooks's reflection on the sense of futurity that Baraka's poetry made her envision. She writes, "My aim, in my next future, to write poems that will somehow successfully 'call' (see Imamu Baraka's 'SOS') all black people: black people in taverns, black people in alleys, black people in gutters, schools, offices, factories, prisons, the consulate: I wish to reach black people in pulpits, black people in mines, on farms, on thrones."[49] Brooks wrote the BAM-esque "We Real Cool" (1960) before she became a vital member of the BAM and a mentor figure for many of its poets. As opposed to many of the young poets who rejected the sonnets and other "closed" forms of poetry that they viewed as white forms, Brooks, during and after the BAM, continued to write poems that neither took up the typical Black Arts chant rhythm, the common experimentation with line indentation and the visual form of the poem, nor dwelt in any easily recognizable African American vernacular. Nonetheless, after what she describes as her "conversion" during the BAM, Brooks consciously and complexly situates her post-1967 conversion poetry in the "Mecca" of the movement. Her poem "In the Mecca" (1968) places Black Arts poets in the very center of her meditation on searching and being lost in structures (actual buildings as well as poetic structures). The poem tells a story about the lost child "Pepita" in a building that is now part of the "Black Belt" ghetto but used to be an elegant upper-class residence. The diction in the poem, best described as "King's English" becomes, for Brooks, as fluid as the street vernacular of "we real cool."[50]

The chewy language voiced throughout "In the Mecca" starkly opposes the character of the aspiring poet Alfred ("Alfred is un- / talented. Knows"), who makes the art such a stale, highbrow performance. As Alfred quotes Leopold Senghor, he makes the 1930s and 1940s Négritude movement into a type of cultural capital. His posturing makes the speaker think of Senghor the president of Senegal, not Senghor the poet who wanted to own his own words instead of using the colonizing toys. After squeezing herself around Alfred's toxic art of imitation and his attempt to take up too much space (he "who might have been a poet-king"), Brooks calls directly for "Don Lee," who anticipates a "new art and anthem":

> Don Lee wants
> [. . .]
> a physical light that waxes;
> [. . .]
> new art and anthem; will
> want a new music screaming in the sun.[51]

"Don Lee" is also the "slave name" that was discarded in 1973, when its bearer renamed himself Haki Madhubuti. The words in the spiritual "Amazing Grace"—"I was lost, but now I'm found"—capture the way that the speaker feels when she meets Lee in the midst of the Mecca. In this "lost but now found" poetic narrative, Brooks uses the precision of the iambic meter to set up her steady pace through the "black Mecca" literally created by "white flight," the term sociologists use to describe the quick exit, in segregated communities, by white residents once a neighborhood begins to turn "black." The "waxing" Brooks ties to Lee signals that her formalist poetics and the Black Arts free verse meet in the open space created when she, Lee, and the other Black Arts poets she mentored find a black aesthetic that is the outer space of a community's interior (not the internalization of the outer that makes Alfred, the false poet, keep choosing the wrong words).

The BAM poetics of anticipation gains a diasporic reach in the work of Keorapetse "Willie" Kgositsile, a South African exile whose poems are shaped around the broken boundaries between African American and African space. There is a call and response between Brooks's poetry and Kgositsile's. In her introduction to Kgositsile's *My Name Is Afrika* (1971), Brooks offers a poem titled "To Keorapetse Kgositsile" in which she proclaims "MY NAME IS AFRIKA! / —Well, every fella's a Foreign Country. / This Foreign Country speaks to You."[52] Kgositsile's "Exile" (1975) cites Brooks's poem "Kitchenette Building" (1945), but whereas Brooks's poem ends with an image of the shared bathrooms in kitchenette buildings and the lack of enough "lukewarm water," Kgositsile, in his response, begins with the terror of the water during the Middle Passage: "And the ocean, my brother knows, is not our friend."[53] After this invocation of the Middle Passage, Kgositsile anticipates, in the next stanza, the need for a "community alarm" that would resound throughout the "oceans," signaling a "wake up" call that would be local and cosmopolitan. Recalling Brooks's words, "We are things of dry hours and the involuntary plan," the oceanic "community alarm" becomes that which would awaken those who have been "grayed" by the "involuntary plan."[54] Kgositsile depicts this "plan" as colonialism when he writes, "Did you say independence?" and "Lumumba, do you hear us?" Brooks depicts this "plan" as the shackles that continue, after slavery and the Great Migration, to reduce African Americans in the urban landscape to "things." As Kgositsile responds to Brooks's poem, he anticipates the BAM's move to the intersections between the plan of the Middle Passage, the Black Belt neighborhoods in Chicago, and colonialism in Africa. Kgositsile's reshaping of "Kitchenette Building" into "Exile" demonstrates his anticipation of a diasporic dimension to Black Arts poetry even as he appreciates the local specificity of this poetry. Kgositsile, in the penultimate stanza in "Exile," shows that the space of anticipation brings groundedness and searching together: "I stand among my silences / in search of a song to lean on." This simultaneous groundedness and movement is the spirit of black post-blackness.

The Art of Anticipation: The Residual, the Dominant, and the Emergent

Black anticipatory aesthetics is the art of not knowing what blackness will be; it is the art situated within the sustained dissonance of the earlier chords being heard, simultaneously, with the sounds that are just beginning to emerge. Claudia Rankine's signature text of the twenty-first-century wave of African American literature, *Citizen: An American Lyric* (2014), epitomizes the art of anticipation. Even the textual production of *Citizen*, with the cover image of David Hammons's sculpture *In the Hood* (1993), the shiny, heavy (thick) white pages, and the empty white pages, signals the role of anticipation as black post-black art becomes the tension between what Raymond Williams calls the dominant, the residual, and the emergent.[55] *In the Hood* was created nineteen years before the killing of Trayvon Martin and the emergence of Martin's hoodie as an icon of young black men's lack of protection against police brutality. As readers begin reading Rankine's depictions of the everyday life of antiblack racism in the twenty-first century, and her direct meditations on Trayvon Martin, the cover image can easily be misread as twenty-first-century, post–Trayvon Martin art, but Hammons's 1993 sculpture anticipated the power of the twenty-first-century reclamation of the hoodie as a way of raging against a white power structure. *In the Hood* anticipates *Citizen*; Hammons anticipates art that will enter into the presence of black absence—the real force that he produces when he hangs the hoodie on the wall and shapes it, with wire, into a sculptural form of presence as absence. With *In the Hood*, David Hammons evokes black people's escape from the "hood" (city spaces controlled by white power) as the image reminds us of Baraka's 1970 words, in *In Our Terribleness*: "I can take off these clothes and wear some others. I can unchain air held to a stone be myself getting up!" (119). Hammons's use of wire (as he makes the hoodie gain the shape it would have if someone were wearing it) makes us feel the air that cannot be chained and, also, the white power that has been the "stone" chaining black freedom. As the most literal frame (the cover image) of *Citizen*, Hammons's *In the Hood* represents the tension between the dominant (white power), the residual (the clothing of survival), and the emergent (the unchained air) that Rankine explores throughout *Citizen*.

Rankine's meditation on the feelings that surfaced on July 13, 2013, the day the jury declared George Zimmerman not guilty of the murder or manslaughter of Trayvon Martin, is one of the many sections in *Citizen* that zoom in on the entanglement and inseparability of the dominant, the residual, and the emergent. Rankine repeats the words "feeling" and "feelings" in this section, titled "July 13, 2013."[56] She struggles to capture the dissonance of feeling like a black subject who has a right to seize her freedom by recognizing that white supremacy has lost some of its life-shaping force and also feeling like a black subject who cannot pretend that the structure that killed Trayvon Martin is not also imprisoning her. Rankine describes the danger of the the "go-along-to-get-along tongue" (154), of being seduced into being a conciliatory, naïve black citizen, but she also confesses the desire for a "breeze" ("A breeze touches your cheek. As something should" [151]). The breeze signals black people's right to, as Rankine writes earlier in the text, "Feel good. Feel better. Move forward. Let it go" (66). This letting go is figured, throughout *Citizen*, as the black affect that cannot be "known" because there is no grammar to explain the black non-naïve subject's delicate dance between holding on to a consciousness that racism remains real and constantly letting go every time that realism tries to grip and tie the subject down. Rankine writes, "You smile dumbly at the world because you are still feeling if only the feeling could be known and this brings on the moment you recognize as desire" (153).

Rankine's elliptical words "you are still feeling if only the feeling could be known" are a search for language that can explain the power of anticipation when it allows one to feel that which is entirely unknown and illegible within the logic of a dominant power structure. When Rankine attaches the word "desire" to the "moment" of feeling otherworldly as you "smile dumbly at the world," we see that this full meditation on the "moment" (July 13, 2013) of the legal erasure of Trayvon Martin's right to live freely leads Rankine to the role of desire in black freedom struggles. Desire, when mixed with anticipation, is so different from desire that hurts because, as Bob Marley sang, it is just "waiting in vain."

Rankine ends *Citizen* with images of the great difference between waiting and breathing. Waiting is depicted as the pain of just enduring the passage of time when you "don't know how to end what doesn't have an ending" (159). Breathing is figured as that which "creates passages to dreams." This breathing is fully tied to the power of anticipation through the image of the speaker being able to hear the "even breathing" that can only be heard through a stethoscope. "Even breathing" conveys the peace and rhythm that give another, black-optimist meaning to the words "don't know how to end what doesn't have an ending," which can easily be read as Afro-pessimism. Rankine ends *Citizen* with an explicit tension between this pessimistic waiting ("waiting in the car for time to pass") and the temporal confusion of present and future that is created by desire and anticipation. In one of the final lines, Rankine writes, "The sunrise is slow and cloudy, dragging the light in, but barely" (159), as if she is echoing Toomer's words at beginning of *Cane*— "Her skin is like dusk on the eastern horizon, / O cant you see it, O cant you see it."[57] Rankine's and Toomer's words beg comparison to Baraka's words, in *In Our Terribleness*, "I cant say more than that except all the visions and thoughts you've had actually exist."[58]

David Hammons's abstract art is misread every time the wide, record-breaking readership of *Citizen* can only see Trayvon Martin's hoodie and the Black Lives Matter movement on the cover of *Citizen*, and not the power of black abstraction to reenchant black humanity and refuse to reduce blackness to "matter." Black post-blackness is what readers miss when they can't feel the Black Arts Movement echo in Rankine's lines "Who shouted, you?

You [. . .] shouted you, you the murmur in the air, you sometimes / sounding like you, you sometimes saying you" (145). Baraka's signature words "How you sound" echo in these lines. *In Our Terribleness*, like *Citizen*, pivots on the tension between pessimism and optimism and the difference between waiting and anticipation. Baraka's emphasis on the pain of waiting gains most force toward the end of *In Our Terribleness*, when he responds to Fundi Abernathy's photograph of an older black woman waiting for a bus on a Chicago sidewalk. Similar to Rankine's words, "with the patience of a stethoscope," Baraka writes, "When the old sisters get to standing there waitin for us. Been waitin for so long, like that endless patience [. . .] all our souls can be seen."[59] *In Our Terribleness* is a signature BAM textual production of the "black book," with literal black pages and a black cover as opposed to the overwhelming whiteness of the pages and cover of *Citizen*. But these differences fade as Baraka and Rankine meet in the space of a black post-blackness, as both *In Our Terribleness* and *Citizen* foreground the Black Power of "moving on" and the black melancholy of feeling stuck.

In *Don't Let Me Be Lonely* (2004), Rankine anticipates the possible misreading of *Citizen* as her more "optimistic" text that keeps the same subtitle "An American Lyric" but moves from black melancholy to black citizenship. If we remember Rankine's direct critique of American optimism in *Don't Let Me Be Lonely*, we are set up to resist any reading of *Citizen*'s emphasis on "moving on" as American optimism. In *Don't Let Me Be Lonely*, Rankine writes, "The sadness is not really about George W. or our American optimism; the sadness lives in the recognition that a life can not matter. Or, as there are billions of lives, my sadness is alive alongside the recognition that billions of lives never *mattered*. I write this without breaking my heart, without bursting into anything" (italics added).[60] As Rankine anticipates the "burst" of the Black Lives Matter movement, these words become a lucid reflection on black optimism as the need for black sadness to be "live." Leaning on Cornell West, she counsels readers, in the same part of the text, to understand that black "hope is different from American optimism" (21).

In a 2014 interview with Lauren Berlant, Rankine, as she reflects on her twenty-first-century, black post-black text *Citizen*, muses, "The opposite of the surreal dream is the lying down in the stereotypes in an attempt to throw them in relief. Pope.L, Glenn Ligon, Kara Walker, and Jayson Musson, a.k.a. Hennessy Youngman, all do this for me. All their layering and super-imposition and running alongside and multiple utterances render the idea of realism mute when it comes to self-consciousness around race. It's impossible to just see what's there as a single thing or to speak all that you see."[61] Rankine recognizes that realism is rendered "mute" in the layering and superimposition of twenty-first-century black aesthetics. She views experimental contemporary black aesthetics as the practice of "running alongside," which refracts the linear into a new way of thinking about the *motion* of simultaneity and the collective creation of space where blackened subjects can be connected through unbelonging. *Citizen*'s empty, shiny white pages and cover, through the lens of the BAM textual production of the "black book," epitomize a post-BAM sensibility. But Rankine's words in *Citizen* "run alongside" BAM texts such as *In Our Terribleness*. The last words in *In Our Terribleness* are "get up and go." Rankine writes, "Yes, and this is how you are a citizen: Come on. Let it go. Move on" (151). Baraka's words "get up and go" are preceded by the words, "try to see your own face, when you close your eyes." *Citizen*, with Rankine's strategic use of the second person, decenters "I," but *In Our Terribleness* is the immersion in the blackened eye.

Rankine, in *Citizen*, captures the microaggressions that shape being black in America in the twenty-first century. Originally coined in the 1970s by Chester Pierce, an African American psychiatrist at Harvard, the term "microaggression" is now often treated as a way of understanding the performance of antiblackness in the twenty-first century, but it might matter that the term emerged in the field of black psychiatry during the Black Power era. In 1974, Pierce wrote, "The minidisasters accumulate. It is the sum total of multiple microaggressions by whites to blacks that has pervasive effects on the stability and peace of this world."[62] *Citizen* shows how insidious and resilient whiteness is as black wounds become so naturalized that they appear to be unintentional scrapes and accidents. The larger 1970s Black Arts/Black Power theorizing about whiteness produced the very word "microaggression," the word that predominates as people try to explain the everyday, "unintentional" life of antiblack racism in the twenty-first century.

The black radical imagination is profoundly anticipatory. Anticipation opens up a new way of thinking about the relationship between earlier and later cultural movements. The later movements often situate themselves against the earlier ones, but the later flows are actually anticipated by the earlier movements. The "temporary dissonance" between what has already settled into a recognizable movement and what is emerging creates the ongoing flow of black aesthetics. When black aesthetics itself becomes this "temporary dissonance," blackness is an always already unsettled aesthetic mix of the experimental and that which has become so familiar it is no longer recognized as experimental. Through the lens of anticipation, we can rethink the back and forth ("tidalectic") flow of African American literary history and cultural movements.[63] Ralph Ellison's 1952 novel *Invisible Man*, for example, includes the depiction of Ras the Exhorter (and Destroyer) that could easily, if the novel was written in the 1960s, be read as a depiction of Malcolm X, the Black Power muse of the BAM. Larry Neal, in the afterword of *Black Fire*, critiques Ellison's use of the word "invisible" as a way of describing the lived experience of being black in an antiblack world but then later, in "Ellison's Zoot Suit," revels in the fact that Ellison, like the character Rinehart, is a consummate improviser, in the full spirit of BAM improvisation. In his initial critique of *Invisible Man*, Neal writes, "We are not Kafkaesque creatures stumbling through a white light of confusion and absurdity. The light is black (now, get that!) as are most of the meaningful tendencies in the world."[64] We need to remember the 1,369 lightbulbs in the Invisible Man's underground space. The 1,369 lights are 37 squared, the multiplication of the age of Ellison when he wrote the novel (the compounding of the sheer individuality that the underground space represents). But the lights also anticipate the BAM move to "black light." The stolen electricity that Monopolated Light and Power does not know the Invisible Man is using is similar to the "by any means necessary" black self-determination strategies of the BAM's move to "black light" (one of the movement's many ways of theorizing the power of black abstraction).

Gwendolyn Brooks's "Kitchenette Building" remains one of the most resonant poetic expressions of the need to anticipate that which remains abstract, beautiful, and black. As Brooks thinks about the "dry hours and the involuntary plan" (the limits of any worldview that makes it impossible to imagine the unimaginable), she wonders: "But could a dream send up through onion fumes / [. . .] / Even if we were willing to let it in, / Had time to warm it, keep it very clean, / Anticipate a message, let it begin?"[65] On the lowest frequencies, when the most radical art of the BAM and the twenty-first century seizes the power of black experimentation to be a form of black representation (not abstraction for abstraction's sake), we see the power of Brooks's dream of a "message" that would be felt most profoundly as "flutter" and "aria," and not as "the involuntary plan."

2

The Politics of Abstraction

That was the first abstract piece of art that I saw that had
cultural value in it for Black people. I couldn't believe
that piece when I saw it because I didn't think you could
make abstract art with a message.

—David Hammons on Mel Edwards's work

Abstraction didn't cost consciousness.

—A. B. Spellman, "Big Bushy Afros"

How has the strategic abstraction of the 1960s and 1970s Black Arts Movement been misread as strategic essentialism? One of the "lost in the archive" BAM flyers announcing a 1971 Weusi Collective art exhibit (fig. 3)
offers a direct way of rethinking the role of abstraction in the BAM. The
words "We Are One" appear in the middle of an abstract line drawing
that makes the flyer's message "We Are One" seem to be a strategic use of
abstraction, not the strategic use of some imagined, naturalized essence.
As the BAM counseled the meditative closing of the eyes in an attempt to
find a black gaze (as depicted in Amiri Baraka's and Fundi Abernathy's *In
Our Terribleness*), the space of abstraction was a black mirror stage that
was never complete but always in process. How might strategic abstraction be a useful way of understanding the substance of style, the depth of
the flash of the spirit, the inseparability of aesthetics and ideology? When
we hear Baraka's famous words, "Let the world be a Black Poem / And Let
All Black People Speak This Poem / Silently /or LOUD," do we believe that
aesthetics can change how ideology sounds?[1] The strategic abstraction may
be the words that create the magical spell ("Let the world be" . . .) and the
magical new space. The poets of the Black Arts Movement spoke abstraction into existence, and their speech acts partially transformed abstraction
into concreteness. In other words, abstraction may be the starting point of
identity-politics movements. As people begin to break bread together, they

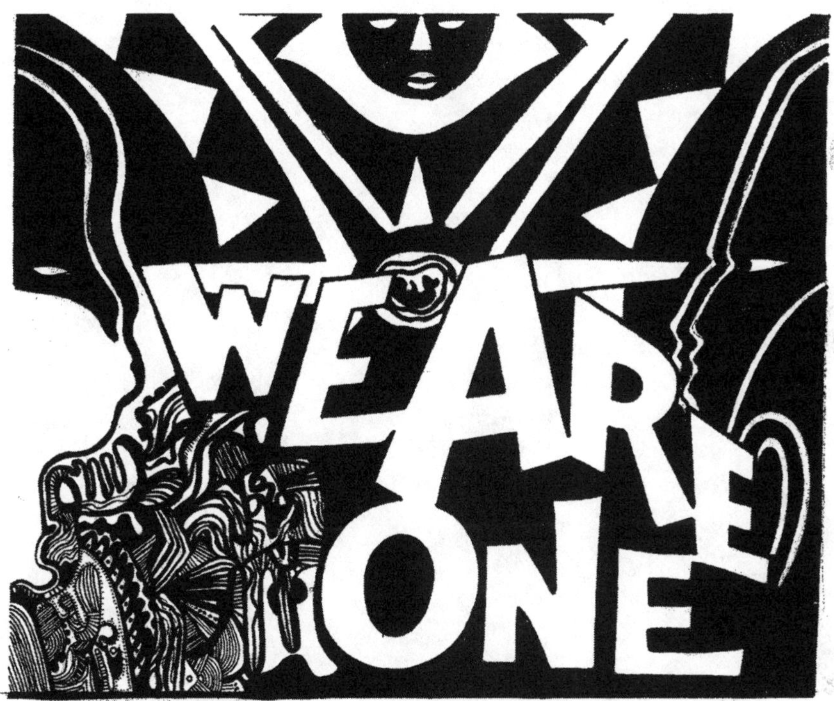

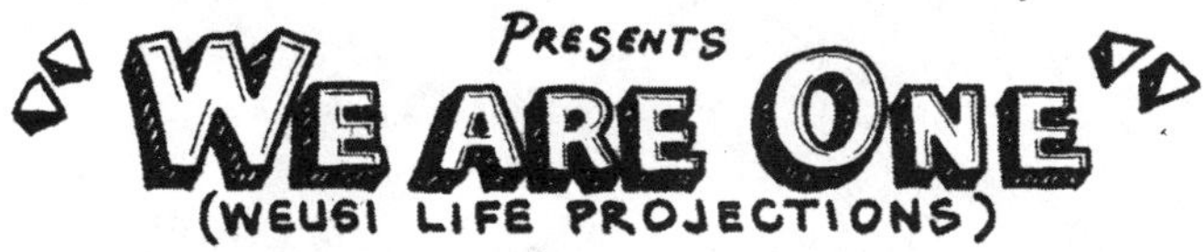

Figure 3. Flyer created by the WEUSI Artist Collective. From the collection of Ademola Olugebefola.

start with the dough. The transformation of the dough into the mimetic forms and recognizable forms is never total.

We need to begin with the common misreading of how the movement used the word "black." A critique of the 1960s political uses of "black" occurs in Raymond Saunders's 1967 pamphlet *Black Is a Color*.[2] At the very moment when the Black Power and Black Arts movements had made "black" into such a powerful, concrete sign of identity, the visual artist Saunders attempts to make people pause to think about the abstract nature of this overdetermined sign. Saunders wanted readers of his self-published pamphlet to reconsider "black" as simply a color and not a way of thinking or a political consciousness. The title of the pamphlet "Black Is a Color" contrasts with "Think Black," the title of Haki Madhubuti's 1966 poetry volume. Saunders insists, "Racial hang-ups are extraneous to art. No artist can afford to let them obscure what runs through all art—the living root and the ever-growing aesthetic record of human spiritual and intellectual experience. Can't we get clear of these degrading limitations, and recognize the wider reality of art, where color is the means and not the end?"[3] The Gap's fall 2014 advertising campaign commercialized the slogan "black is a color" and performed an *innocent, unconscious* post-race erasure of the rhetoric of the Black Power movement. The advertisement included the following words painted on the glass of Gap store entrances: "black is a color / 1969 black denim in a full range of shades and washes." One fall 2014 Twitter response to this ad stated: "Black is not a color; a black object absorbs all the colors of the visible spectrum and reflects none of them to the eyes."[4] This everyday talk about whether or not it makes sense to consider black as a color is tied, unknowingly, to the role of the concrete and the abstract in the use of the word "black" as a way of referring to people of African descent. Raymond Saunders's words "black is a color" can seem much more abstract than the BAM's circulation of slogans such as "Black Is Beautiful" and "Black Power." But just as Saunders insisted that color is too abstract to be contained by racial and political discourse, many BAM writers and visual artists reveled in the abstract, *world-opening* force of the concrete tags such as "Black Is Beautiful" and "Black Power."

The assumption that BAM visual art and literature were *representational* art (not partially abstract, deeply experimental art) is one of the quick and easy approaches to the movement that make post-BAM art appear to be the more nuanced and more playful next step. But the play with abstraction during the BAM was tied to some of the movement's most complex engagements with black post-blackness. The concreteness of feeling black (the feeling that the BAM performs as the exuberant collective performance of "becoming black") is a type of concreteness that is best understood as what the hip-hop artist Q-Tip describes as "this abstract *thing*."[5] The words "abstract thing" gesture to the BAM concreteness and groundedness that was not antithetical to the force and power of black abstraction.

Amiri Baraka's short story "The Man Who Sold Pictures of God" (1960) brings to the surface the BAM's recognition that black abstract art could play a vital role in the movement's liberation struggle. "The Man Who Sold Pictures of God" is a story about a man named Maurice who sells canvases that are entirely white and appear, to the unnamed first-person narrator, to have "absolutely nothing on them."[6] These all-white canvases infuriate the narrator, who is greatly disturbed by Maurice's steady, robotic repetition of the question, "You like the pretty canvases?" Maurice's question becomes violent as the exchange continues, and he grabs the narrator by the shoulder and begins to "scream" the question "into [his] face."[7] Baraka capitalizes the question at this point in the story, so that the repetition of "DO YOU LIKE THE PRETTY CANVASES?" gains the aura of a forced conditioning process, a colonizing of the the mind. As the narrator fights Maurice's assumption that the canvases must be "liked" and seen as "pretty," he eventually (once Maurice is holding his shoulders) regains his ability to speak (after being entirely silenced by Maurice's master discourse). "BUT WHY ARE THEY CANVASES?" are the words he "spits out" as he gains the strength to speak against this dominant ideology.

The emphasis on the possessed nature of Maurice is depicted as his partial transformation into a slot machine with eyes "spinning around like roulette wheels" and "numbers on his eye balls."[8] Maurice, who wears army coveralls with red and white stripes, signifies the power structure that has gambled on white power and won to such an extent that the narrator has to muster all of his own machine-like strength to rage against the words that Maurice shouts. Baraka uses the idea of "electricity in [the] body" as he depicts the bodily current of resistance that the narrator has to pull through his "adam's apple" in order to "spit out" his counter-discourse that refuses to accept Maurice's naturalizing of a white aesthetic. The title of this short story explains the horror of Maurice's canvas salesmanship: he gains capital and profit by convincing people that bare canvases are "pictures of God." Maurice's art of white power needs the blankness; the bewildering blankness helps him program and hypnotize people. The all-consuming whiteness and the shouted word of indoctrination silence resistance. Baraka signals that power is subtle and, sometimes, too abstract to pin down. The oppressed who buy the white canvases really might think that they are only buying a canvas and not an oppressive worldview of white supremacy. Baraka intimates that, in the seeming post–Jim Crow era of no "Whites Only" signs, the signs of naturalized white power may be comparable to signs that reinforce white power while appearing to be as innocent as a blank canvas.

Why might it matter that, in this short story (written on the "edge" of the Black Arts Movement), the canvas of white power contains the epitome of abstraction (the seemingly unmarked space) as opposed to marks and images that represent white people or objects tied to a white power structure? The significance of the abstraction may be Baraka's recognition that whiteness is, as Kalpana Seshadri-Crooks argues, a master signifier without a fixed referent and that, when nonwhite people are forced to assimilate, they are in effect entering into a societal structure that is not named "white," that is a "melting pot" precisely because the whiteness is the final, "neutral" color.[9]

Abstraction, in Wesley Brown's short story "I Was Here but I Disappeared" (1990), is figured as a strategy of white power. The setting is the 1960s. A black male character, who poses as a model for a white painter, is stunned and outraged when he sees that the painter has used his black body as a medium through which he can paint a normative painting of Christ as white. This black male character later learns that the painter is part of a group that believes in minimalism as a way of living, which makes them shut out any societal forces or tensions that make them feel vulnerable. The "Center for Minimalist Living" is described in the following manner: "I discovered that 'minimize' was indeed the crucial word. One evening soon after my talk with Alex, she and Rudy took me to a place called The Center for Minimalist Living. The building was furnished sparsely with folding tables and chairs. The walls were bare except for framed signs, which read CARES AND WORRIES ARE EXPENDABLE and MINIMALISM IS THE ABSENCE OF WHAT YOU NEVER THOUGHT YOU COULD LIVE WITHOUT."[10] The painter who uses a black model as means of reproducing the white Christ is a minimalist and abstractionist when he is not representing white Christ. Brown shows that there can indeed be a dangerous politics to white abstraction—a dangerous white performance of colorblindness that literally minimizes the lived experiences of blackness as excess and hypervisibility.

And yet, Baraka and others discovered that, as they fought white aesthetics, they themselves did not want to only produce art that represents blackness. Baraka and others decided that they also needed to mobilize the power of black abstraction, the power of that which Baraka calls "Black Dada Nihilismus" and Larry Neal calls "Black Boogaloo." In addition to fighting back with images of blackness that would be concrete alternatives to the dominant white images, the movement artists decided that the radicalness of black aesthetics may lie in its opening up of the black interior. Black inner space is a prime image in most BAM literature and visual art. This interiority leads the artists back and forth between the surface of the black mirrors they were

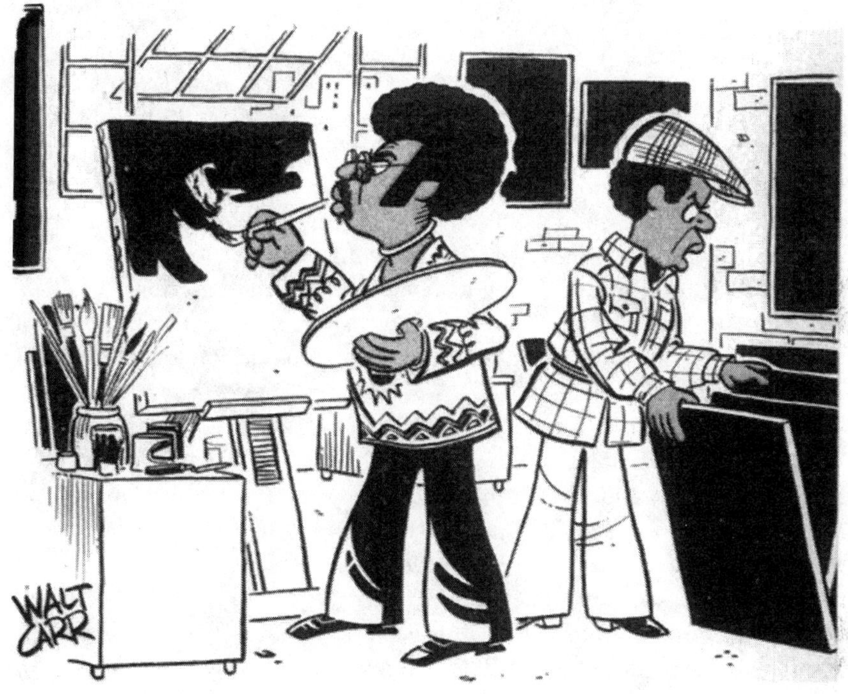

"Hey, man, I agree that Black is beautiful, but,
wow!, isn't this going a bit far?"

Figure 4. Editorial cartoon in *Black World* (December 1974). Walter R. Carr Jr., Artist Collection.

hailing and the depth discovered in their reflections. Getting lost in the black mirrors made the black representational space a smooth passage to the black abstraction. The black mirrors of the movement were a form of strategic essentialism, and this essentialism (this strategy of building community and political solidarity through the call for people to be "black," not "Negro") was a smooth passage to strategic abstraction (the strategy of building community and political solidarity through the call for people to embrace an entirely new cosmology and worldview that would decolonize their minds).

A 1974 editorial cartoon by Walt Carr in *Black World* (fig. 4) is prime evidence of the complex questions about the representation/abstraction tension during the BAM. The focus on the all-black canvas in this cartoon, which was published in the most central BAM journal, begs to be compared to

Baraka's use of the all-white canvas in "The Man Who Sold Pictures of God." Carr contributed to other magazines and journals, such as *Jet*, *Ebony*, and *Playboy*; his work was profiled in the July 1973 issue of *Black World*. In his study of black cartoonists, Charles Johnson describes Carr in the following manner: "Always his compositions were balanced, his lines bold and clean and economical like those of Hank Ketcham ('Dennis the Menace'), with a startlingly effective use of solid black shapes to pull a viewer's eye to his drawing's focal point. A typical Carr cartoon might show a seven-foot, militant, black high school student sitting on the sofa in his parents' home beside a white baffled-looking college recruiter and saying, 'Never mind the $100 a week job, new clothes and car, rent free apartment and job for father—will I get a degree?'"[11]

The 1974 cartoon with the all-black canvases is even more nuanced than what Johnson recognizes as the wit and skilled composition of Carr's typical cartoons. A black man looks through a stack of all-black canvases and asks the black artist who is in the process of creating yet another one, "Hey, man, I agree that Black is beautiful, but wow!, isn't this going a bit far?" The wit in this cartoon works on multiple levels. The gesture to "black is beautiful" being a huge abstraction, a move to the serial production of nothingness, is as much a part of the wit as the more subtle gesture to the idea that, for some people, whose consciousness had been raised by the movement, the full embrace of an alternative worldview was too radical ("going a bit far").

The cartoon stages black aesthetic radicalness as the move to black abstraction. The canvases are black representational space, but, unlike Darby English's sense that abstraction is "outside the confines of black representational space," this cartoon stages the inseparability of black representational space and black abstraction.[12] The all-black canvases may be black representational space, but they may also be black abstraction. The cartoon teaches us how to see black abstraction within black representational space. The all-black canvases only remain identical if we cannot imagine the different textures and brush strokes in each painting. English begins *How to See a Work of Art in Total Darkness* with a compelling analysis of David Hammons's *Concerto in Black and Blue* (2002), an installation piece that demands that spectators use flashlights to find the art (and create the art through their own movements through the room). English is interested in denaturalizing black representational space, in showing that there is no black essence that exists before the flashlights of the black aestheticians appear.[13] But this denaturalizing of black representational space also occurred during the BAM. When A. B. Spellman writes, "some called it mimetic but I thought it was surreal [. . .] a surreal negritudinous dream," he is recognizing that the black representational space was often the space of the surreal and the abstract. The visual arts collective with the name "African Commune of Bad Relevant Artists" (AfriCOBRA) began during the BAM and produced some of the movement's most vivid images of the tension between the representational and the abstract.

Mimesis at Midpoint

In "Perspectives/Commentaries on AfriCobra," Larry Neal described Afri-COBRA's "visual narrative of a Nation asserting its artistic consciousness."[14] In "Ten in Search of a Nation" (1969), Jeff Donaldson proclaims: "Check out the image. The words are an attempt to posit where we are coming from and to introduce how we are going where we are going. Check out the image. Words do not define/describe relevant images. Relevant images define/describe themselves, dig on the image."[15] This insistence on visual relevance that does not need a verbal explanation connects more than we may initially realize with AfriCOBRA's interest in both abstract and representational art. The repetition of the words "check out the image" (even as the power of the words is also emphasized) suggests an interest in words' ability to name and clarify visual images as well as a worry about the need to explain images. AfriCOBRA's assertion of visual power—"Check out the image"—sounds simple in comparison to the collective's descriptions of "mimesis at midpoint":

> Mimesis at midpoint, design that marks the spot where the real and the unreal, the objective and the nonobjective, the plus and the minus meet. A point exactly between absolute abstractions and absolute naturalism.[16]

> Images that mark the spot where the real and the overreal, the plus and the minus, the abstract and the concrete—the real and the replete meet. *Mimesis*.[17]

To fully "check out" the images of AfriCOBRA, the lushness of their aesthetic tenets such as "shine," "expressive awesomeness," and "mimesis at midpoint" must also be grasped.

In addition to deserving an award for the most evocative self-naming ("African Commune of Bad Relevant Artists"), the collective created lush manifestos in which they explored the principles that defined their aesthetic vision. Their vision, in these formative years, was inseparable from the larger mission of the Black Arts Movement, and this visual-art collective played a huge role in shaping the movement. AfriCOBRA continues to thrive as one of the most dynamic visual-art collectives tied to African diasporic aesthetics. The BAM was its launching pad, the originary site of the collective's ongoing aesthetic movement. How did abstraction become a form of black self-determination? That question lingers as we see the BAM roots of AfriCOBRA opening up to the current continued balance, in the collective, between representation and abstraction. Thinking about the name of the collective, we wonder how abstraction remained "Bad" and "Relevant."

The interest and the worry about abstraction during the BAM led writers and visual artists to test the limits of realism and abstraction. "Mimesis at midpoint" was a phrase coined by the collective. When connected to the collective's tenet of "expressive awesomeness," "mimesis at midpoint" cannot be understood as a feeling of frozen ambivalence about the usefulness of art that produces a mirror-image experience. The "expressive awesomeness" of the creation of incomplete mirror images (another way of interpreting "mimesis at midpoint") suggests that AfriCOBRA decided that ambivalence, abstraction, and fractured mirror images could be mobilized as collective experiences of wonder. AfriCOBRA's approach to abstraction is tied to the aesthetic of wonder. The artists "wondered as they wandered" back and forth between the realism of *black* magic (the abstraction that somehow seemed black) and the magic of *black* realism (the mirror images that made the art of delivering messages seem like "expressive awesomeness," not expressive staleness).

When AfriCOBRA committed themselves to depictions of the "real," they were not understanding it as a stable, fixed form. The collective's enactment of realness is similar to the alternative reality so lucidly articulated by the BAM playwright Ed Bullins: "Each individual in the crowd should have his sense of reality confronted, his consciousness assaulted."[18] When realistic art takes the form of assaulting people's sense of reality, the boundary between "representational art" and abstraction dissolves. AfriCOBRA made black approaches to abstraction gain visibility. Abstraction for abstraction's sake may be too easy when people are seeking liberation from an antiblack aesthetic system of power. In a 2012 interview, Nelson Stevens explained that as he produced the *Centennial Vision* mural (1979–80), he was thinking about mimesis at midpoint and was fully aware that there "was always the risk that you could go too far, into total abstraction."[19]

Gerald Williams, one of the cofounders of AfriCOBRA, explained the cryptic concept of mimesis at midpoint as follows:

> It was a puzzle back then, and more puzzling later as I realized that it was little noted in dialogue about the group over the years. I've taken fresh looks

at the work that was produced by members at that time, finding myself to have become more critical. I haven't come to any conclusions yet, but feel as though mimesis was the one principle that should have been more intellectually challenging to pursue. In direct answer to your question, I do not recall how others felt about the concept, and I do not think that most of the work even deals with it. But that begs the question as to what mimesis is and what were we trying to do with it, and how did or do we define it? A point between abstraction and realism, I think, was reached by Africans, Australasians, et cetera, many years ago, but doing the same thing within the environment of the sixties and seventies, or even today, is still a viable endeavor. I'm not sure I fully agree with the sentiment of Spellman's quote ["Abstraction didn't cost consciousness"]. I have to see it within the context of his whole assertion. There are probably some mandates required for black consciousness and probably some universally agreed-upon parameters. Identification with black consciousness has always been a complicated matter for some artists, who may easily find comfort in the contemporary notion of this supposedly post-racial period.[20]

On the one hand, "mimesis at midpoint" may be a simple recognition that all visual art is some type of abstraction, some type of obvious reformulation of the subject being represented. But Williams's musing on the mystery of AfriCOBRA's use of this phrase also suggests that the collective was confronting the mystery of mimesis itself; the collective was puzzled by quick and easy ways of understanding the black mirror stage performed by the BAM. During the Black Power/Black Arts movements, the revolution was always *about* to happen. Change was being hailed, and a sense of urgency was created as people were called upon to help ignite the cultural revolution that was already in motion. "Mimesis at midpoint," on the lower frequencies, sounds like the state of suspension in Baraka's elongated "It's nation time eye ime / It's nation ti eye ime."[21] The powerful tension in this performance poem, "It's Nation Time" (1970), between "I" and "eye" staged the movement's suspension between *self-identification* ("I am") and *looking at others as part of self* (the black gaze and "eyesight").

Mimesis at midpoint was a way that the AfriCOBRA artists paused and anticipated what was at stake in making art that could have a message and remain as free as any abstract or experimental art. Terezita Romo's use of the term "aesthetics of the message" as a way of explaining the art of identity politics is as helpful as the reversal of those words—"the message of the aesthetics."[22] The messages delivered through art can be direct and intentionally political, without canceling out the subjective responses that shape any aesthetic experience. The excess that the art of "mimesis at midpoint" produced was the individual responses that were not predictable. One way to understand the artists' awareness of the necessarily subjective uses of the direct message is to consider the significance of the use of clothing in the art of one of the AfriCOBRA members. Jae Jarrell's "revolutionary suit" and other clothing creations translated the experience of looking at a work of art into the experience of wearing a work of art. This AfriCOBRA artist did not imagine art as an object: she made it into a covering that gains an interior dimension once it is inhabited and embodied. Jarrell's use of collage in *Urban Wall Suit* shows that the cluttered space of representation was literally inhabited as the movement performed what Baraka called the "putting on of new clothes."[23] The transformation of art into clothing shows that AfriCOBRA wanted art to be experienced in a most performative manner.

The AfriCOBRA use of clothing as a means of dramatizing the need to embody and perform art explains Edward Spriggs's use of the sculpture metaphor as a means of explaining AfriCOBRA aesthetics. In the introduction to the catalog of the 1971 AfriCOBRA Studio Museum exhibit, Spriggs writes, "They see 'art' as a movement in-the-round—completing and complementing our bas-relief existence."[24] The notion that African American existence is "bas-relief" is a tremendous way of understanding the interplay of surface and depth that shaped AfriCOBRA's approach to the interplay of the abstract and the concrete. The abstract has a depth that can be experienced quite differently from the aesthetics of the concrete, but the depth and mystery of the abstract are often discovered through powerfully tangible surfaces. When Spriggs frames the 1971 exhibit as an exposition of protruding surfaces (bas-relief), he suggests that the art of AfriCOBRA makes people experience surface as depth. The "movement in-the-round" complicated the presumed two-dimensional quality of representational art. Tracy Vaughn, the curator of Northwestern University's AfriCOBRA exhibit at the Dittmar Gallery in 2010, accentuated this sculpture effect of mimesis at midpoint. In one room of the gallery, she put Jae Jarrell's clothing art on metal headless mannequin posts next to Jeff Donaldson's framed paintings. When Jarrell's *Urban Wall Suit* is juxtaposed with Donaldson's painting *Wives of Shango* (which includes an image of Jarrell's bullet belt and revolutionary suit), the imagined boundary between the image and the real transforms into the powerful doubling of the painted image and the worn image. This curatorial arrangement allows viewers to experience mimesis at midpoint as the in-betweenness of representational art that is not intending to transcend the real people that inspired the art. The headless mannequins have less of a Yinka Shonibare–inspired aura of the colonized and dispossessed and more of an aura of decolonizing bas-relief that protrudes further out than the framed paintings can. The clothing art on the pedestals also inevitably makes viewers think about how they can or cannot imagine themselves wearing the revolutionary clothing. Looking at mannequins in clothing stores, we are either imagining the clothing on our own bodies or encountering the clothing and the mannequin as a pure other. AfriCOBRA was aiming for the former. The curator of the Dittmar Gallery exhibit clearly wanted viewers to walk around the clothing posts and feel the Black Arts Movement's hailing of new clothes and new black self-images.

In this 2010 retrospective at Northwestern University, the curator not only mixed the framed paintings and clothing hung on pedestals; Vaughn also added a purposefully non-flat painting to this mix. Napoleon Jones-Henderson's tapestry *A Few Words from the Prophet Stevie* was hung in a manner that made it appear to be not stuck to the wall. The curator placed it next to a small framed print of the same image. The art of mimesis at mid-point gains the shape of art that is waiting to be used and removed from the gallery wall. The movement in-the-round also has this element of not being tied down and of dislodging any fixed frame. The interplay of words and images, in Jones-Henderson's *A Few Words from the Prophet Stevie*, stages the tension between direct but stunted words (such as "In God We Trust?!," "IF YOU WANT TO HEAR OUR VIEW," and "YOU AINT DONE NOTHING") and images such as a pyramid with the pan-African colors (red, black, and green), a white African mask with red eyes, and profiles of faces with different shades of brown. The use of vibrant color in this tapestry is as striking as the play with the tension between triangular shapes and the shape of layered waves. Shapes are often viewed as metonyms and color as metaphors, but Jones-Henderson's tapestry is an experiment with the color of shapes and the shape of color. Jones-Henderson approaches a counter-literacy that refuses to privilege how something is said over what is being said. If the words in the tapestry seem simple, trite, and too direct, the energized colors and shapes seem to call for new words that will have more music. The colors and shapes must speak; color is rendered an abstract shape, not abstraction for the sake of abstraction. This word and image interplay is another example of how the collective's principle of "mimesis at midpoint" became a blurring of the lines between representation and abstraction.

In a 2010 interview, Gerald Williams explains, "Lettering, or incorporating written messages in the work, was adapted from Barbara Jones, who had used it in some of her pre-AfriCOBRA prints. It was fairly unique in 'pure' painting by African Americans, although several Europeans used it. The graffiti that was ever-present also had a lot to do with it. Of course, not all members used messaging, and some took it to astronomical heights. Lettering also had to do with our discussions about creating posters."[25] The collective believed that poster art would be a type of art that could be widely distributed. In the manifestos and catalog descriptions, they implored "everybody to have some" of this art.[26] Many AfriCOBRA paintings convey a sense of posterized consciousness. The paintings are not posters, and yet the artists capture some elements of the political posters and broadsides that were circulating as a main engine of the Black Arts and the larger Black Power movements. When Emory Douglas's iconic Black Panther party posters are compared to AfriCOBRA paintings, it is clear that AfriCOBRA was thinking deeply about the power of using painting as a way to interpret, document, and expand the posterized consciousness that circulated in the streets. AfriCOBRA's move to screen-printing collaborations and collective printing sessions is clearly one way of understanding their poster aesthetic, but paintings such as Gerald Williams's *Nation Time* (1969) unsettle any notion that a painting is not a reproduction of an original. This painting of an outdoor mural is impossible to not read as a creative reproduction of the 1967 *Wall of Respect* mural. The poster art that was circulating in forms such as outdoor murals, rally announcements, poetry broadsides, and Black Panther party newspapers was the "original" that the AfriCOBRA paintings were reproducing and reinterpreting. The collective's great interest in poster art may have reflected a desire to redefine normative assumptions of the relation between an original work of art and a reproduction. AfriCOBRA artists located the "original" in the black freedom struggle that became their muse.

Like the principle of "lettering," the collective's theory of "shine" adds new dimensions to their interest in mimesis at midpoint. In the AfriCOBRA manifesto written by Barbara Jones-Hogu, "shine" is described as being both "literal and figurative": "Luminosity, 'shine,' literal and figurative, as seen in the dress and personal grooming of shoes, hair (process or Afro), laminated furniture, face, knees, or skin."[27] Jones-Hogu connects the literal shine of hair and shoes to a more abstract type of shine that Jeff Donaldson captures when he writes, "ad shineum! [. . .] Color color Color color that shines."[28] In "AFRICOBRA: The First Twenty Years" (1990), the abstract power of shine is described by Nubai Kai as "the visible reflection of an inner affinity for the 'shine' of spiritual effulgence."[29] The concrete shine, attached to bodies and objects, suggests a clear move away from the dullness that Gwendolyn Brooks laments in "Kitchenette Building": "We are things of dry hours and the involuntary plan, / Grayed in, and gray."[30] The aesthetic of shine was a bold refusal of the "gray." The literally shiny things in AfriCOBRA visual art allowed viewers to feel the larger, more abstract, emotional state of "color color color."

The excessiveness of shine is an apt image of the 1960s mobilization of blackness as a unifying concept that fought against the tactics of divide and conquer. This political mobilization of blackness made it more than any of the divisions (of light or dark skin, of economic status, of location in the African diaspora). AfriCOBRA's aesthetic of shine was an overshadowing of the divisions. The civil-rights refrain "This little light of mine / I'm gonna let it shine" is the soundtrack we should remember as we appreciate the power of the collective's use of "shine." Jeff Donaldson thinks directly about the role of shine in the black freedom struggle when he writes, "The Shine who escaped the Titanic, the 'li'l light of mine.'"[31] AfriCOBRA celebrated the transformation of the acts of individuals (the "little light") into the power of collective action (the "shine"). The words "this little light of mine / I'm gonna let it shine" pivot on the midpoint—the word "mine." The process of turning individual light into collective shine was the process of creating mirrors that could be shared. The words "mimesis at midpoint," when connected to "shine," gain this new inflection of the individual force that is in the process of becoming a collective force.

The movement from the singular point of consciousness to the collective consciousness sheds light on AfriCOBRA's use of the phrase "ten in search of a nation" in multiple catalogs and manifestos. One of the most striking usages of these words appears in a map of Africa that includes a group photograph of the collective and small reproductions of some of the collective's works of art. This image is framed by the same focus on nationalism as a search process that appears in the 1973 catalog of the AfriCOBRA exhibit at University of Massachusetts at Amherst. The penultimate page of this catalog is black, with the following words in white typeface: "It is Nation time and we are searching." This imaging of black nationalism as a search for a nation is a powerful depiction of black aesthetics itself as a process of looking (not a fixed way of seeing). The deepest meaning of "mimesis at midpoint" may be the aesthetics of motion and stillness, the aesthetics of wandering in order to find a sense of rootedness. The aesthetic joy of this search mission is what we see when Nelson Stevens, in the mural *Work to Unify African People* (1973, fig. 5), pairs the words "Work to unify African people" with two kaleidoscopic faces in a manner that makes this art of unification become the art of *unification through fragmentation*. The "Ten in Search of a Nation" map of Africa also dramatizes this creation of a shape through fragmented,

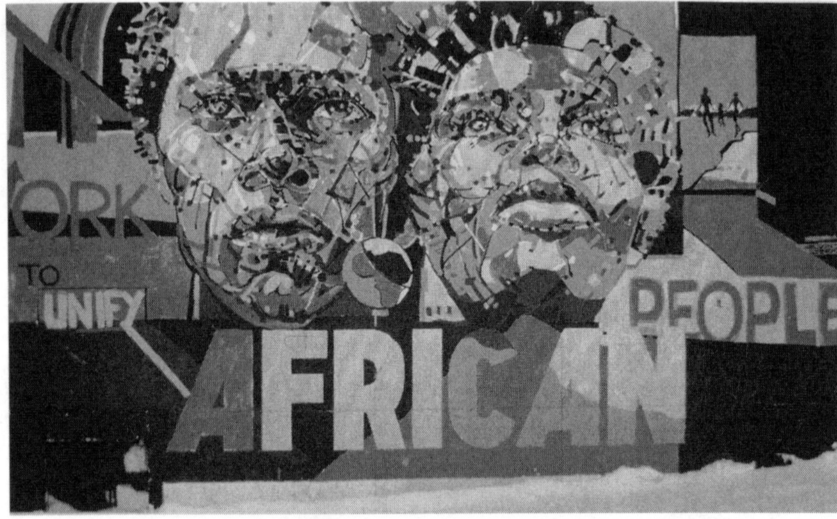

Figure 5. Nelson Stevens (with Howard McKaleb), *Work to Unify African People*, 1973. Mural, United Community Construction Workers Labor Temple, Boston. Photograph by Nelson Stevens.

multiple images. This map of Africa *and* the art of AfriCOBRA make the art the liminal nation-state of this African American nationalism. The art in the map is figured as the substance of the search, which makes a process of becoming feel like an actual location, not a dislocation.

AfriCOBRA and other movement artists made people feel the exuberance of the means being the end (one way of understanding the value of a cultural revolution). In *The Autobiography of LeRoi Jones*, Amiri Baraka remembers the feeling that the revolution was about to happen. He describes the small distance between the cultural revolution and the "real revolution" as a pivot around a corner. He also explains that when he first heard the circulation of the words "Black Power" and felt the movement growing, he would draw the image of a Black Power fist on abandoned buildings and sidewalks. Like the AfriCOBRA artists' use of the map of Africa, Baraka was drawn, in the first stages of his art of nationalism, to images that would reclaim these unlikely nation-spaces such as abandoned buildings, sidewalks, and fragile outlines of Africa. In his autobiography, Baraka describes this tagging, on the streets of Newark, as a "stenciling." The process of spraypainting over a cut-out form in order to reproduce the stencil on the underlying surface captures another tension of mimesis at midpoint—the relation of cultural nationalism and revolutionary nationalism (the cultural revolution and the "real revolution").

We might rush to think that the underlying surface is the real revolution, but the cut-out form is a more apt image of the artist-activists' use of the template of the "real revolution" to create art that made blackened people feel free. The real revolution is the cut-out dream that actually seemed to be "around the corner" due to the artist-activists' creation of very material *impressions* of that dream and very real struggle. The stenciling, however, is more than a metaphor when connected to the Black Arts Movement's registers of mimetic mirrors and transparency, but also depth and contradictions. The stenciling impulse is the first stage of black consciousness-raising—the reproduction of signs with a transparent meaning. The stenciled Black Power fist was a transparent call for raised fists of resistance. But the next step, the more abstract art, is the layering of signs, points, and midpoints. AfriCOBRA embodied both of these strategies of liberation.

Reading Black Arts Poetry as Strategic Abstraction

Larry Neal's poem "The Narrative of the Black Magicians" (written, as he states at the end of the poem, in "Spring—1965 / a painful season") is an ideal starting point for an analysis of the role of abstraction in BAM poetry. The call for "form" in "The Narrative of the Black Magicians" is one of the most lucid examples of the BAM's understanding of form as the antiformulaic. Neal chants, "form child. form in the rush of war. / form child. form in the taking of life. / form child. form in the sun's explosion."[32] Sound, for Neal, becomes a prime way of breaking the boundary between form and formlessness. BAM poetry connects with the AfriCOBRA visual artists' theory of mimesis at midpoint. The "form of formlessness" was the poets' version of the debate that the visual artists were framing as the tension between abstraction and representation. Purposeful plays with poetic formlessness become one way of representing the "free jazz" of blackness. The seeming formlessness of the poetry was tied to a black aesthetic. The didacticism of the poetry sometimes makes us forget the role of abstraction and nonrepresentational form in this poetry.

We need to reconsider the concrete abstractions of "teeth or trees or lemons" in the beginning of Baraka's "Black Art" and consider the poetry of the BAM as a staging of a version of mimesis at midpoint that is not entirely different from the paintings of Jeff Donaldson and the murals of Nelson Stevens. Baraka's sense that non-grounded poetry is useless leads him, in this iconic BAM poem, to images that are concrete and also abstract. The BAM needed the abstract as Black Power was being performed. The politics of strategic abstraction have been overshadowed by our focus on strategic essentialism. The difference between strategic abstraction and strategic essentialism may be the difference between the more experimental and less experimental artists of the movement. The more experimental ones embraced the challenge of finding space within a collectivity rather than taking the easier route of abandoning the collective vision. The power of black abstraction, for these strategic abstractionists, was the power of discovering, as A. B. Spellman explains, that "abstraction didn't cost consciousness," that some of the most liberating black aesthetic experiences would be the ones that make one feel that one is falling in love with something that remains unknown, something that remains too abstract to fix.[33]

Some BAM poems are concrete poetry that must be viewed as well as read; the illegible parts of the poems can produce an experience similar to looking at an abstract painting. In *Mouth on Paper* (1977), the interplay of Mel Edwards's images and Jayne Cortez's words is a prime example of the word-and-image approach to the counter-literacy of strategic abstraction. Edwards's drawings and Cortez's poems speak directly to each other, exploring the ability of lines to form shapes. The lines of poetry and the lines in the drawings gain a sculptural dimension. Edwards is a sculptor who draws, and Cortez is a poet who sculpts. Indeed, sculpture may be the best way to understand the *matter* of abstraction.

The title of Neal's poetry volume *Black Boogaloo* (1969) signals the movement's blackening of the abstract. Baraka's preface adds emphasis on the blackening of sound as the most abstract feature of the movement's representational space. In *Black Boogaloo* and *Hoodoo Hollerin' Bebop Ghosts* (1974), Neal shows that sound is abstract because it does not fully settle into objects or words. Ed Roberson uses this idea of the pre-settling in his foreword to the post–Black Arts word-and-image text *Seismosis* (2006). Roberson wonders "what we see before our field of observation settles or finalizes into an object or its word."[34] This foreword parallels Baraka's focus on process and "presettlement" in his preface to *Black Boogaloo*. The most meaningful thread between the BAM and post-BAM cultural productions is the presettlement emphasis on process, becoming, and experimentation. Through the lens of what Baraka, in his introduction to Neal's *Black Boogaloo*, calls the "sound for sounding" ethos of the BAM, Roberson's question is reshaped into, "What do we hear before sound settles or finalizes into an object or word[?]." Black Arts poetry dramatizes this question. In *Black Boogaloo* and *Hoodoo Hollerin' Bebop Ghosts*, Neal suspends readers/listeners in this presettlement zone of sound. These Black Arts poetry volumes fully show how the movement experimented with different ways of depicting contained and uncontained sound. *Black Boogaloo* is the volume that is most closely tied to the sound that has not yet settled. Neal sets up each section as a jazz set (set 1, set 2, . . .), but the poetry does not reflect a predictable approach to jazz poetry. Each jazz set is an experimentation with pushing poetry out of its normative form.

Neal's use of "Boogaloo" is similar to the BAM's use of the word "soul." In Barbara Simmons's poem "Soul," in *Black Fire*, soul is depicted as more of an affect than a feeling or an emotion. If, as Eric Shouse explains, "The power of affect lies in the fact that it is unformed and unstructured," as opposed to the more formed nature of feelings and emotions, the word "soul" became one of the BAM's ways of situating blackness in the boundary between the conscious and the automatic (the physiological).[35] In Simmons's poem, "soul" is described in multiple images that convey this notion of the space in between the conscious and the physiological. In her litany of definitions of soul, Simmons includes the following images that shape it into something akin to a blush, something that happens to the body without being in the control of an individual: "and you feel it when it moves ya / [. . .] Heard a man say, / 'I laughed all the breath out my body.' / Now that's Soul."[36] The poem unveils the BAM's use of the word "soul" as a means of finding a space where blackness is experienced bodily and also as a collective sensorium that no individual can own (what Baraka describes when he writes "we are parts of one body").[37] This shared space of abstraction was a principal element of the politics of the movement's black abstraction. The BAM resituated black abstraction as black affect, and this move to the automatic, bodily nature of affect made the cultural movement vibrate more widely, as poems like Simmons's "Soul" spread the idea that the abstract can have a bodily dimension.

To understand the deeper registers of the BAM use of the color black as it mobilized the power of black abstraction, the confluence and conflict between Faith Ringgold's *Black Light* paintings and Ad Reinhardt's black paintings must be examined. Through this study of "black painting," in and outside the BAM, the core question of black abstraction emerges: how can art be experimental, open, and still black? The BAM's performance of black post-blackness can be understood as the recognition, as Richard Iton argues, that the words "black fantastic" are a pleonasm.[38] In a similar sense, the BAM made the words "black abstraction" redundant.

The Black Light Paintings

The tangible vibration of black abstraction is foregrounded in Faith Ringgold's 1967–69 *Black Light* paintings. This series has a political resonance that sets it apart from Ad Reinhardt's black painting series (1954–67). In "The Case of Blackness," Fred Moten argues that Reinhardt saw black as the "absence and negation of color."[39] In contrast to Reinhardt's black absence, Ringgold uses the larger BAM concept of "black light" to discover the plenitude of dark colors that can only be seen when the color black shines and becomes much more than "blackout." Moten's critique of Reinhardt becomes a larger critique of the racial "playing in the dark" that makes Theodor Adorno see blackness as the negation that the (white) abstractionists were aiming for. Moten writes:

> For Adorno, "the ideal of blackness with regard to content is one of the deepest impulses of abstraction." Moreover, "there is an impoverishment entailed by the idea of black," according to Adorno, to which "trifling with sound and color effects" is a mere reaction. It is, however, precisely through a consideration of the unstable zone between the lived experience of the black and the fact of blackness, between the color black and what it absorbs and reflects, what it takes in and pours out, that we can begin to see how it is possible to mistake impossibility or impoverishment for absence or eradication.[40]

In the *Black Light* paintings, Ringgold unveils the explosive sounds and colors in the color black. Her approach is fundamentally different from Adorno's theory of the "ideal of blackness [as absence]" in abstraction. Ringgold's mix of black abstraction and black representational space shows what Moten aptly identifies as the "unstable zone" that emerges when Ringgold darkens the color palette and makes the color black become a mirror that both reflects and absorbs. When Ringgold and other BAM writers and visual artists produce black mirror images, they hail subjects who will enter into black representational space (this entrance is performed in a most literal sense when readers open *In Our Terribleness* and see their own face in the full mirror title page).

Ringgold's most direct mirror image is the painting *Woman Looking in a Mirror* (1966). The curation of a 2011 exhibit of the *Black Light* images placed this mirror image in conversation with Ringgold's *Black Light* images. This exhibit was titled "American People, Black Light: Faith Ringgold's Painting of the 1960s" and was organized by the Neuberger Museum of Art and curated by Thom Collins, director of the Miami Art Museum, and Tracy Fitzpatrick, the curator of the Neuberger Museum of Art. The curators arranged the exhibit as a smooth progression from representational paintings such as *Woman Looking in a Mirror* to the some of the more abstract paintings in the *Black Light* series. The black mirror stage is framed as a first step that leads to the mix of representational and abstract paintings in the series. The wall text, seen when viewers first entered the exhibit, used Ringgold's own words as a means of explaining black light: "As she observed, 'In art school no one could ever teach me how to paint black skin.' Here, Ringgold relied on black rather than white to create the 'light' in her paintings as she experimented with the tonal ranges of black flesh." As Ringgold embraced this BAM mission of "black light" (what Larry Neal, in the afterword to *Black Fire*, announced as a new epistemology of light when he proclaimed, "The Light is Black, now get that"), she began with abstractions of faces. She saw these abstractions as similar to the abstraction of physical traits in African masks. As she attempted to teach herself what "no one could ever teach me" ("how to paint black skin"), she drew upon African masks and, also, the removal of the color white. The curators of the Neuberger exhibit explain, "The images seem to emanate light without the use of the color white." Ringgold produced this alternative light through her mix of browns, blacks, reds, yellows, blues, and greens. The *Black Light* paintings that play with different hues of the color black fully energize the idea of black light. Blackness is reclaimed as a non-monolithic color, a kaleidoscopic color that denaturalizes the notion that darkness does not contain shades and a type of light that cannot be separated from the sparkling nature of the darkness.

This new epistemology of light is a visual-art approach to the larger Black Power movement's use of black as a unifying concept that inveighed against the divide-and-conquer that used antiblack ideology to make lighter skin ("high yellow," light brown, etc.) a form of social currency for some. As the movement called for "Negroes" to become "black," a process of counter-interpellation relied on the power of counter-aesthetics. The movement's mantra "black is beautiful" was inseparable from the other mantra, "Black Power." When viewers of Ringgold's art began to see the possibility of black light, Ringgold was disrupting the most ingrained aesthetic foundations of antiblack racism (a metaphysics of light that aestheticizes white skin) and the racial self-hatred created when the *white light* of antiblack racism is internalized.

The search for black light led Ringgold to the creation of paintings that include words. As she played with this alternative way of experiencing light, the interplay between words and images allowed her to perform the BAM word-and-image counter-literacy (analyzed in chapter 3). For Ringgold, this word-and-image counter-literacy, like her approach to black abstraction, is a search for art that can "say something" and have the freedom and play tied to abstraction. Her use of words in some of the *Black Light* paintings prepared the way for her move, in the 1970s, to poster art, which was the final work in the Neuberger exhibit. The curators, in the wall text, framed the poster art as the culmination of her 1960s art. The exhibit's seamless move from

Black Light art to the poster art would leave viewers with a sense, as they left the exhibit, of any gallery space's inability to fully contain Ringgold's black consciousness-raising art. The concept of "black light" is an abstraction that Ringgold tried to concretize. Just as AfriCOBRA adopted the principle of mimesis at midpoint (the halfway point between representation and abstraction), Ringgold's particular use of the larger BAM concept of black light pivoted on making something abstract *appear*. Baraka's words, "What you see actually exists" and "Try to see your own face when you close your eyes," in *In Our Terribleness*, illuminate Ringgold's mission to show that black light actually exists (that black gazes can create the *realism* of what A. B. Spellman refers to as the "surreal Negritudinous dream").[41]

Afrofuturism and Black Abstraction

When we remember that Sun Ra, the iconic figure of black outer space, was deeply involved in the BAM, we gain a fuller sense of the movement's understanding of the realism of abstraction. Sun Ra's performances at BARTS (Black Arts Repertory Theater School) and on BARTS's jazz mobile, his inclusion in *Black Fire*, the use of his music in BAM plays, and the constant references to him as the muse of BAM poetry open up the role of abstraction in the BAM. In a 2011 interview with Sala Udin, Baraka explains, "We brought artists from all over the area uptown, some of the great musicians of the time. We brought Sun Ra into the community. People were saying Sun Ra's too out there for the people. But people thought it was dance music, they started dancing to it."[42] Sun Ra's Afrofuturism epitomizes the black post-blackness that shaped the most nuanced parts of the BAM. A *New York Times* article on the 2013 Afrofuturism exhibit at the Studio Museum reveals why Sun Ra's involvement in black cultural nationalism is so important to rediscover. In "Going beyond Blackness, into the Starry Skies," Holland Cotter writes, "Beyond Black is an important part of Afrofuturism, and of this show. [. . .] The Studio Museum, which coined the much-debated term 'post-black' more than a decade ago, has been stretching at its own ethnically specific boundaries ever since." Cotter fails to grasp Sun Ra's black post-blackness. His discussion of the glory of moving "beyond blackness" cannot account for the Studio Museum's "stretching" within and against the boundaries of blackness.

Cotter's inability to recognize the black post-blackness of Sun Ra and his emphasis on the Studio Museum's coining of "post-black" draws attention to what he does not say about Glenn Ligon, one of the two coiners of the term. Glenn Ligon's recent work on Sun Ra and Ayé Aton defies the notion that blackness and "beyond blackness" cannot coexist. As Ligon revels in the power of the shared vision between Aton's murals and Sun Ra's music and otherworldly style, he uncovers a literal black interior to Afrofuturism. Aton's interior wall murals dramatize his ability, like Sun Ra's, to situate himself fully inside the black aesthetic movement without losing the ability to stretch. In "Sound and Vision," the foreword to *Sun Ra + Ayé Aton: Space, Interiors and Exteriors, 1972,*[43] Ligon uncovers Sun Ra and Aton's embrace of that which does not exist (the wildly fantastical) as a means of uncovering the black oppression that *does* exist. When Ligon connects his aesthetics to Aton and Sun Ra, we see that this co-originator of the term "post-black" is tied, like Aton and Sun Ra, to black post-blackness.

Afrofuturist aesthetics are what Jacques Ranciere, in *The Politics of Aesthetics*, refers to as the aesthetics of the "community to come."[44] Black post-blackness can be aptly described as the "community to come." Fred Moten's question, "What will blackness be?" is an Afrofuturistic inquiry. Moten writes, in the epigraph to *In the Break,* "What is the edge of this event? [. . .] What is the beautiful? What will blackness be?"[45] As visual artists and poets of the BAM drew upon abstraction and found room for black abstraction, they were at the edge that the AfriCOBRA painter and muralist Nelson Stevens describes as the "risk of going too far into abstraction."[46] Going too far, for BAM cultural workers, would mean losing relevancy in grassroots black communities. But Sun Ra did go "too far" and remain relevant; his "far out" movement into outer space is what enchanted his BAM devotees.

Sun Ra's performance in the youth-community-center scene in *Space Is the Place* (1974) captures the larger way in which his black post-blackness enchanted the BAM as a whole. *Space Is the Place* has many aspects that make it seem like another 1970s Blaxploitation film, but the power of the film's depiction of black cultural nationalism emerges with such force in the scene when Sun Ra (who acted in and codirected the film) suddenly appears in a youth community center and says, "Greetings, black youth, planet Earth. I am Sun Ra, ambassador from the intergalactic regions of the Council of Outer Space." As the black teenagers look at Sun Ra's otherworldly clothing and shoes, initially they are simply amused, and one asks, "Is he for real?" Sun Ra tells the teenagers, "I'm not real. I'm just like you. You don't exist in society. If you did, your people would not be seeking equal rights. [. . .] You're not real. If you were, you'd have some status among the nations of the world. I come to you as a myth. Because that's what black people are. Myths." As he speaks, the black youth begin to nod and listen hard, and they are transported to the state of freedom that Sun Ra's dress embodies and the background music signals. As the scene ends, the lyrics "We're living in a space age" punctuate the transition to the next scene. Black aesthetics might be reclaimed, in the twenty-first century, as particular ways of visualizing, hearing, or somehow experiencing an abstract "flash of the spirit" that bridges the gap between *black* and *post-black*, being and becoming, the past and the future.

Just as it matters that Glenn Ligon, one of the unintentional architects of the post-black inquiries, recognizes Sun Ra's outer-space presence in the BAM, it also matters that, in the essay "Black Light: David Hammons and the Poetics of Emptiness" (2004), Ligon develops a theory of black light (as he analyzes David Hammons's art) that begs to be compared to the use of the words "black light" during the BAM. Ligon does not mention the BAM's direct focus on this new epistemology of light, which circulated throughout the movement as the words "black light" spread. In BAM essays, poetry, photography, and other visual art, the words and the concept "black light" become the core aesthetic energy of the movement. When Ligon discovers the concept of black light through his deep engagement with David Hammons's art, he unknowingly uncovers the BAM roots of the twenty-first-century innovations made by Hammons.

As Ligon develops his twenty-first-century approach to black light, he draws inspiration from Hammons's sheer delight as he thinks about the possibility that African American artists might find the means to produce art that is truly "on a different wavelength" and still, somehow, "very black."[47] Ligon moves to the possibility of black light as he ponders the following moment in a 1991 interview of David Hammons by Robert Storr. Hammons states, "Turrell [the artist James Turrell, who deftly explores light and space], he's on a different wavelength. He's got a completely different vision. Different than mine, but it's beautiful to see people who have a vision that has nothing to do with presentation in a gallery. I wish I could make art like that, but we're too oppressed for me to be dabbling out there. . . . I would love to do that because that also could be very black. You know, as a black artist, dealing just with light."[48] Ligon lets this language lead him as he develops his interpretation of the "black light" in Hammons's *Concerto in Black and Blue*. He interprets this installation art as the performance of people as they shine their tiny flashlights into the dark room, experiencing blackness as what we construct (what we bring) as opposed to a blackness that is always already *there*.

The approach to black light in Baraka and Fundi's *In Our Terribleness* reveals what is at stake in the difference between Hammons's sense of "dealing just with light" and the BAM inclination to usually include images of black bodies in their enactments of black light. A key passage in *In Our Terribleness* begs to be compared to the use of the tiny flashlights in Hammons's *Concerto in Black and Blue*. Baraka responds to Fundi's photograph of two young African American men walking down a sidewalk, as one of the men points at something that we cannot see, as if he sees something remarkable not too far from them. The young man's pointing gesture is captured in Baraka's words, "Good God I'm black and fast as life itself. / (pointing in dark. At YOU)."[49] Whereas Hammons's installation art makes people "point in the dark" without a targeted object (as Ligon explains, they point in the dark and bring, through their gestures of aimless pointing, whatever black light might exist in the installation room), the pointing in *In Our Terribleness* is tied directly to the words "Good God I'm black and fast as life itself." Black light, as figured during the BAM, is a rethinking of what it means to become a subject. Instead of the subject entering into light (imagined as whiteness), the movement imagines subjects entering into illuminated darkness (imagined as blackness). Hammons's installation art imagines a flash entering darkness in order to create a black light that is much more than the racial categories of blackness or whiteness. Hammons's black light is not "Good God I'm black" but rather "Good God I'm looking for black light." This wonder and surprise (over the very possibility that light could be so disembodied and still be somehow tied to a black aesthetic) is also a part of the black-light discourse in *In Our Terribleness*. We need to be able to hear the mystical flash that connects Baraka's "Good God I'm Black" and Hammons's "Good God I'm looking for black light."

The relation between Ligon's text paintings and BAM text paintings shows how the BAM discourse of "Good God I'm black" merges with something much more mystical and difficult to pin down. The text paintings of Glenn Ligon unknowingly build on Edward Christmas's 1967 painting of Amiri Baraka's poem "SOS" on *The Wall of Respect* BAM mural (fig. 6). In 1991, Ligon created an oil painting (fig. 7) of the opening words of *Invisible Man*. This passage includes the sentence in which Ellison asserts the nonbiological state of his invisibility ("I am a man of substance, of flesh and bone"). Ligon literally defamiliarizes the trope of invisibility as illegibility (the idea that the hypervisible, antiblack marking of the body makes the full humanity illegible) by smudging Ellison's words until the familiar opening of this canonical novel approaches the unspeakable and the unreadable. This smudging and making-illegible of what has been taken for granted as canonical African American literature is one way to understand the post-black impulse of twenty-first-century black aesthetics.

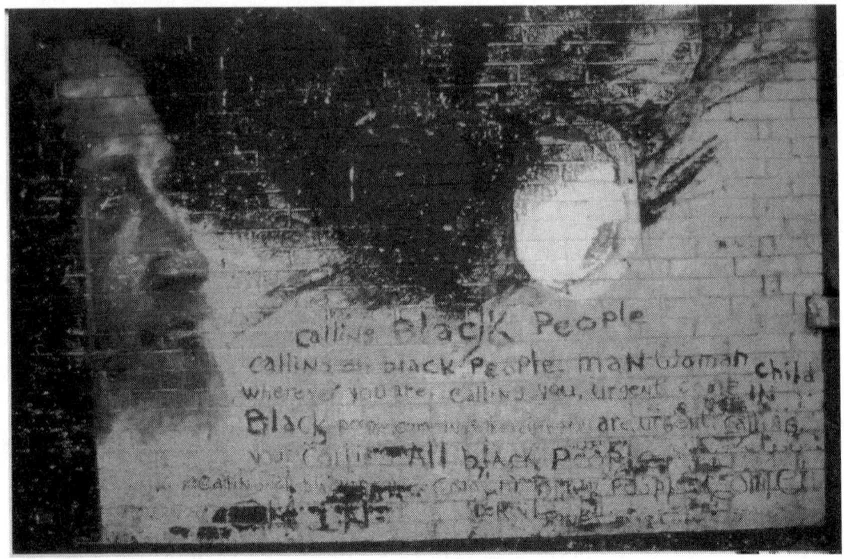

Figure 6. Detail from the *Wall of Respect* mural. Photograph by Bob Crawford, 1969, Artist Collection.

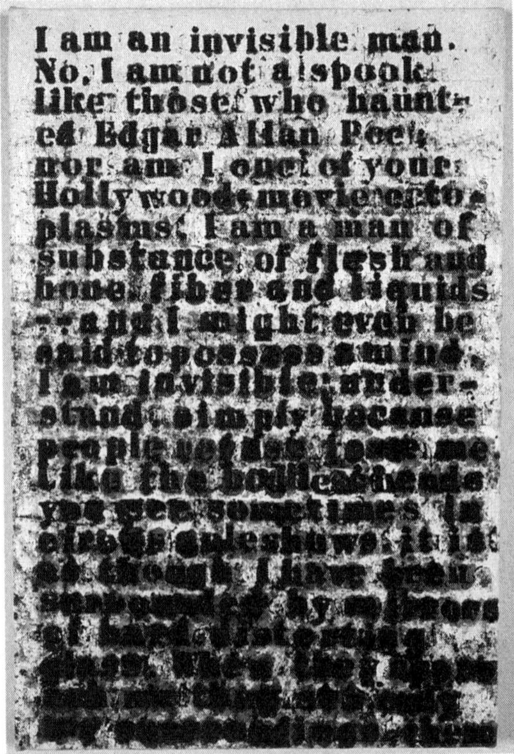

Figure 7. Glenn Ligon, *Untitled (I Am an Invisible Man)*, 1991. Oil stick on canvas, 24 × 15.5 in. (60.96 × 39.37 cm.). © Glenn Ligon, Courtesy of the artist, Luhring Augustine, New York, Regen Projects, Los Angeles, and Thomas Dane Gallery, London.

The smudging is a strategic abstraction that also shapes the BAM text painting of "SOS." When Baraka's poem and Ellison's fictional words are rendered partially illegible, the value of the opaque emerges—and, as Edouard Glissant argues, there is a violence when people lose their right to be opaque.[50] This productive opacity is at the core of the strategic abstraction in the BAM. When the words in "SOS" are painted on *The Wall of Respect* as if they should not be read but experienced as a visual blur that signals the need to literally find the depth of blackness in the surfaces that keep erasing it, the opaque becomes a part of the Black Power/Black Arts mission. Making blackness lose its transparency allowed the movement to hail black opaque subjects who could meet in the zone of inscrutable blackness.

Rereading *Erasure* and *The Intuitionist* as Black Abstraction

The opaque and the abstract are also a huge part of twenty-first-century black aesthetics, and they play a crucial role in Percival Everett's *Erasure* (2001), the novel that has brought the most attention to the role of satire in twenty-first-century black aesthetics. Everett foregrounds the abstract when he uses the very word in the first pages of the novel, as he sets up the protagonist Thelonious Ellison's inability to fit into his sister's perspective on black accountability (her sense that black people must do something that is helping other black people):

> I was too flighty for her, lived in a swirl of abstracts, removed from the *real world*. While she had struggled through medical school, I had somehow, apparently, breezed through college "without cracking a book." A falsehood, but a belief to which she held fast. While she was risking her life daily by crossing picket lines to offer poor women health care which included abortions if they wanted, I was fishing, sawing wood, or writing dense, obscure novels or teaching a bunch of green California intellects about Russian formalism. But if she was cool to me, she was frozen to my brother; the high rolling plastic surgeon in Scottsdale, Arizona. Bill had a wife and two kids, but we all knew he was gay. Lisa didn't dislike Bill because of his sexuality, but because he practiced medicine for no reason other than the accumulation of great wealth.[51]

Throughout the novel, Thelonious remains obsessed with "sawing wood." His woodcutting, in his sister's eyes, is, like fishing and novel writing, "a swirl of abstracts." Everett mixes Thelonious's meditations on wood with the other purposefully fragmented parts of the novel. The sections that present this meditation on wood have the texture of an aside that disrupts any possibility of linear narration in this deeply fragmented novel that includes more than one "novel within the novel." I read these meditations on wood as strategic abstraction that allows Everett to situate his novel, outside of all of the play and satire, as a serious reflection on how the black eccentric's hands-on desire to create whatever he or she is drawn to create is misread as what Thelonious's sister views as "swirls of abstracts removed from the *real world*."

When read carefully, Everett's quick jolts from the more linear narrative to the short passages describing Thelonious's woodworking offer a way of understanding the the complexity of black abstraction. One of the meditations on wood includes the following language: "I considered my woodworking and why I did it. In my writing my instinct was to defy form, but I very much sought in defying it to affirm it, an irony that was difficult enough to articulate, much less defend. But the wood, the feel of it, the smell of it, the weight of it. It was so much more real than words. The wood was so simple. Damnit, a table was a table was a table" (139). The first layer of this passage (the notion of the form of formlessness) is stunningly similar to the language used in a *Black World* essay on Ed Bullins's drama. The *Black World* critic responds to a white critic's assessment of Bullins's drama as "shapeless." As the white critic performs a hostility toward the experimentation in the BAM, he wonders, "What is the shape of shapelessness?" In the *Black World* essay, the "shape of shapelessness" takes on an entirely new meaning as the critic argues that the seeming shapelessness in BAM drama actually has a shape.[52] The belief in the shape of the shapelessness, during the BAM, explains the investment in free-verse poetry and free jazz and also the movement's counterintuitive depictions of blackness as both the shapeless process of becoming black and the actual shape (the actual identity) of the process—as Everett says, "a table was a table was a table" (139). Thelonious realizes that his woodworking is different from the writing that the lens of black accountability (tied to his sister) considers too "obscure" (or too abstract). He realizes that he needs the woodworking as much as he needs to write obscure novels. The woodworking is not, like the novels, a play with defying form in order to affirm form; Thelonious sees it as much more concrete action. The notion of "defying [form] to affirm [form]" is the spirit of black abstraction. Everett's use of this language, as he creates a character writing about his own novels, makes it impossible to not connect this character's theory of his novels to Everett's own novel *Erasure*. Black post-blackness is the ethos of *Erasure*; the character Thelonious "defies" blackness in order to "affirm" that "there is blackness," as Fred Moten writes in his poem that has a title with these same three definitive words.[53]

Thelonious is not post-black; he is black post-black. He asserts that he does not "believe in race" and therefore cannot wear his blackness tightly, but he does not repudiate blackness. He wears it loosely, to gain more breathing room. His woodworking connects him, in a *loose* manner, to the approach to art in the BAM. One of his meditations on wood explains his love of "heartwood" in trees. It is easy to connect his musing on the importance of heartwood to his woodwork and the BAM ideal of making art that has a commitment to black people at its core. Everett does not name the heartwood "black"; he depicts the commitment to being grounded and making art that has a clear function without explicitly connecting this commitment to blackness. The meditations on woodworking are Everett's way of talking about the need for relevance without assuming that "black eccentrics" like Thelonious do not also need access, sometimes, to this relevance. Everett seems to tell us that we should not assume that the black eccentric does not worry about being too "obscure" (as Thelonious fears his sister views him).

When the role of the black eccentric in the BAM is erased, we fail to appreciate how the movement gave black eccentrics the opportunity to be relevant and create a collective enterprise of black eccentricity. It is no surprise that "weird" is one of the words used most frequently by Larry Neal, the coeditor of *Black Fire*, the most pivotal anthology of the movement. As Neal opens up the power of black eccentricity in *Hoodoo Hollerin' Bebop Ghosts*, the word "weird" abounds. The "weirdness" of the meditations on woodworking, in *Erasure*, is their ability to make us feel the nitty-gritty concreteness of Baraka's call, in his famous poem "Black Art," for art that is not aiming to be abstract, and also their ability to make us see how the concrete can easily gain the texture of the abstract and the poetic. The power of strategic abstraction is its ability to shape concrete political and collective missions around that which remains poetic and abstract in an unadulterated sense. Everett writes, "A table is a table is a table," but we still hear the abstract poetry of "You always want the heartwood" (13). Baraka, in "Black Art," writes, "We want a black poem. And a / Black World," but we still hear the abstract poetry embedded in the second and third lines of the poem: "teeth or trees or lemons piled / on a step."[54]

In the full spirit of black post-blackness, even as Everett allows us to feel these strong ties between his twenty-first-century experimental writing and BAM experimental writing, he also gestures to nonblack texts. It is hard to read these woodworking meditations and not think about William Faulkner's use of woodworking in the novel *As I Lay Dying* (1930). Like the woodwork of Everett's character Thelonious, the carpentry of Faulkner's character Cash is depicted as the product of straightforward thinking. But just as Thelonious cannot escape abstraction as he muses on his woodworking, Cash's famous list of the steps of making a coffin slips away from the concrete when number six in the list is the single word "Except." Black post-blackness has the force of this qualifier. "Black post-blackness" is a sign of the new vocabulary we need in discussions of race.

Colson Whitehead's end-of-the-century novel *The Intuitionist* (1999) finds this nonrepresentational new vocabulary in elevators (the theme of the novel). As Whitehead subtly depicts the problems with racially inflected, linear notions of progress, a black identity crisis is always *on the verge* of becoming the theme of the novel. Whitehead never lets this theme take up more space than the theme of the politics of the elevator industry and the two competing philosophies of vertical transport (Empiricism) and horizontal movement (Intuitionism). The protagonist, Lila Mae Watson, who is the only black female elevator inspector, decides that the founder of the Intuitionist understanding of elevators created the theory of Intuitionism as a "joke," an effort to counter the dominant discourse of Empiricism. After his death, it is discovered that the founder of Intuitionism (James Fulton) has notebooks with a hieroglyphic code that explains a Black Box, a type of elevator that would revolutionize the world of transport. Since Fulton passed for white, his secret notes about the revolutionary elevator gain a racial inflection (the black secret), but just as the white Empiricists are not disturbed when they learn that Fulton was black, since they simply want the Black Box, the reader of the novel is never led to think of the Black Box as a racial designation.

Whitehead includes a stunning focus on how abstraction shapes black people's everyday life and the black radical imagination. Early in the novel, as he introduces the focus on elevators, he writes: "The lumpy, pitted texture of the cab's door tells her that management has painted it over a few times, but Lila Mae still recognizes the unusually wide dimensions of an Arbo Smooth Glide door. Taking their cue from the early days of passenger-response criticism, Arbo equipped their newest model with an oversized door to foster the illusion of space, to distract the passenger from what every passenger feels acutely about elevators. That they ride in a box on a rope in a pit."[55] These last words—"a box on a rope in a pit"—are tied to the practice of black abstraction as the novel progresses and Lila Mae is hailed by Fulton, the founder of the Intuitionist school of elevator theory, to complete his work in progress that, like his other texts, is only abstractly about race and blackness.

Whitehead connects abstraction and intuition as he foregrounds Lila Mae's bodily interactions with the elevator that she is inspecting. Lila Mae does not study the elevators; her sensorium interacts with the elevators. In the descriptions of her body leaning into the elevator and being massaged by its vibrations, Whitehead dramatizes Lila Mae's "communication with what is not-[her]." He defines Intuitionism as "communication with what is not-you" (241). It becomes most clear that Lila Mae is an abstractionist when she is described as someone who "always had a thing for geometric forms" (6). In the novel's final passages, Whitehead shapes Lila Mae's aesthetics of abstraction into questions about the future. She is figured as a "citizen of the city to come," and she is the "keeper" of that which is described as abstractly as "this thing he's writing" (253). At the end of the novel, Lila Mae is filling in the gaps in this "thing he wrote." She is imitating Fulton's handwriting and following the instructions left by him, but she is also aware that she has to make room for "world changes" that he could not foresee. The novel ends with Lila Mae's guided improvisation and a sense of words being "pulled into the future" (253).

This novel is set in the pre–Black Power era, when the use of the word "colored" was still a norm. As Whitehead makes abstraction and intuition matter more than the empirical, the repeated use of the word "colored" reminds us that the word "black" as a new norm will emerge with force as the years pass and Lila Mae enters into the era of Black Power. The most Black Power/Black Arts–sounding passage in the novel is the question Mrs. Rogers asks Lila Mae, "Was it worth it? All the stuff they put on you?" (92). In this novel that stands on the edge of the twenty-first-century post-black discourse, Whitehead makes room for questions about the post-colored sensibility that will be as "black" as the BAM purging of the dominant white "stuff" that was "put on," and also as "post-black" as the words "citizens of the city to come" sound. *The Intuitionist* is a literary representation of black abstraction that, like BAM abstract art, shows that abstraction can be the space where the vibrations of black post-blackness can be most intuited.

The Intuitionist illuminates the Black Arts Movement and turn-of-the-century post-black play. The empiricism, for example, in Stephen Henderson's Black Arts manifesto "Saturation: Progress Report on a Theory of Black Poetry" (1975) constantly contends with an intuitionism that takes the form of mystical references to the outer-space dimensions of the black aesthetic.[56] Henderson adopts a structuralist approach to explaining "saturated blackness," as he reads particular BAM poems; but, throughout this BAM manifesto, there are moments when he cannot fully explain this saturated blackness. At these moments, when his essentialism is based on a feeling (not what he presents as the textual evidence in the poetry), the black aesthetic shows the limits of structuralism. It is beyond language. When the strategic essentialism of this movement led artists to gesture beyond language, the counter-interpellation at the core of the movement worked language for its most material possibilities as well as its most mystical possibilities. The materiality of mysticism and the empiricism that needs intuition are exemplified in the photograph of sculpture and books that appeared in the main advertisement for *Negro Digest/Black World*, the Black Arts magazine edited by Hoyt Fuller. This image evokes mysticism through the African sculpture that sits without scrutiny, but the pile of books is not only the empirical pile that signals the man's discovery of the "black world" of ideas. The pile of books can also be experienced as an abstract form, strategically placed by the photographer at the edge of the table to evoke the sculpture in-the-round (the free-standing sculpture) effect of blackness. Like the photographer's strategic placement of these books so that they look as much like sculpture as the actual piece of sculpture, the strategic abstraction of black post-blackness gains its power from making what something *really is* constantly shift to what it could be, if we look again. Black post-blackness is the inseparability of *what is* and *what could be*.

Twenty-First-Century Black Visual Abstraction

Kerry James Marshall's 2012 paintings *Who's Afraid of Red, Black, and Green* illuminate what is at stake when art of the BAM and the twenty-first century pivots on that which remains intensely abstract and also intensely black. The title of this painting series begs to be compared to Touré's *Who's Afraid of Post-Blackness? What It Means to Be Black Now* (2011). Touré's investment in calling complex blackness "post-black," and his investment in the space-clearing gesture of the word "post-black," differs greatly from Marshall's sense that we need to realize that "a Black consciousness fluctuates between overt and subtextual manifestations."[57] Marshall makes this claim about the expansiveness of black consciousness in a 2012 interview that also includes his lucid words, "black power has not gone far enough."[58] When he returns, in the twenty-first century, to the black-nationalist colors (red, black, and green) that first became a sign of black nation building during Marcus Garvey's 1920s United Negro Improvement Association movement and then were reenergized during the Black Power movement, Marshall aims to "stretch out" the Black Power that he feels "has not gone far enough." He re-invokes 1960s and 1970s black consciousness-raising in the twenty-first century and shows how generative black nationalism was. In the paintings

Who's Afraid of Red, Black, and Green, his reinvocation of black nationalism opens up the role of abstraction in black nationalism. The paintings force us to move past the literal meaning of the colors in the red, black, and green black-nationalist flag that Garvey unveiled in 1920 (the red is the "color of blood which men must shed for their redemption and liberty," the black is "the color of the noble and distinguished race to which we belong," and the green is "for the luxuriant vegetation of our Motherland").[59] Marshall names the three paintings in this series *Red*, *Black*, and *Green*, and the paintings compel viewers to wrestle with the political possibilities embedded in something as abstract as color.

In "The New Danger of the Pure Idea," Rael Jero Salley analyzes these paintings as the play with colors and ideas. He argues that Marshall "transform[s] colors into ideas and shift[s] ideas into colors."[60] The notion of an idea becoming as abstract as color opens up the role of black abstraction as black nationalism becomes the everyday practice that Wahneema Lubiano refers to as "black common sense."[61] When black nationalism becomes a part of the practice of everyday life, pro-black alliances and rejection of white dominant culture become less of an idea or a doctrine and more of a way of moving through the world. As an abstraction, black nationalism is not a straitjacket (as it is often depicted in contemporary repudiations of it as a backward and ridiculous desire for separatism) but a way of feeling black without the need to explain or justify this feeling. Marshall's painting *Black*, in the *Who's Afraid of Red, Black, and Green* series, offers one way of understanding the abstract nature of feeling black. The painting is partially an abstract rendering of shades of black, but it also includes images of the American flag and the Chicago flag and what appears to be the black-nationalist, pan-African flag of red, black, and green. The tilted X shape of this red, black, and green flag, in relation to the other flags with more recognizable flag shapes, should make us wonder how abstractions become so normative that they can become flags of identity and nation. The painting's title pushes us to question the relation between *feeling* black (hovering like the tilted X flag in a state of liminality that is blackness) and *being* black. How do abstract feelings become the stuff that social movements like the BAM are made of? How do abstractions gain the ability to hail concrete action?

In Marshall's painting *Red (If They Come in the Morning)* (fig. 8), there is a literal call for a reading of an urgent political message and warning *within* the openness of abstraction (the openness of what initially appears to be Marshall's abstract play with different shades of red). The words "If They Come in the Morning" are literally *in* the abstraction. With these words, Marshall directly conveys the politics of this abstract painting, this play with the shades of the color red. Marshall's twenty-first-century art reenergizes these famous words from James Baldwin's 1971 letter to Angela Davis, as Marshall reminds his twenty-first-century viewers that the urgency of Baldwin's message ("If they take you in the morning, they will be coming for us that night") lingers. In the twenty-first century, for many (but not all) African Americans, racism is more subtle (more abstract), but Marshall reminds us not to flatten the Black Power movement and to remember that, just as racism can take abstract forms, resistance to racism can also take the form of strategically abstract art.

Marshall's words—"If They Come in the Morning"—are a literal subtext that enables his abstraction to gain a political resonance while remaining abstract. Ben Jones's 2010 painting *Malcolm and Fanny Lou—Freedom Warriors* (fig. 9) also includes a literal subtext that makes the politics of the abstraction legible. Jones paints over a wallpaper of Frederick Douglass's 1857 address "On West Indian Emancipation," delivered in Canandaigua, New York, on August 4, 1857. In a 2016 interview, Jones explained that, in his wallpaper images, he wanted to use the "decorative designs that repeat themselves" in wallpaper as a means of thinking about the everyday, interior spaces of black consciousness-raising.[62] In this same interview, he identifies *Malcolm and Fanny Lou—Freedom Warriors* as an example of what he calls the "back and forth" work of the "figurative and abstract." His words "back and forth" (and his BAM roots and desire to hold on to the movement as a continued foundation for his twenty-first-century art) exemplify black post-blackness.

His use of the drip-drop technique while painting over the text of Douglass's address adds new dimensions to the key question animating black

Figure 8. Kerry James Marshall, *Untitled, Red (If They Come in the Morning)*, 2011. Acrylic on canvas, 96 × 214 in. © Kerry James Marshall. Courtesy of the artist and Jack Shainman Gallery, New York.

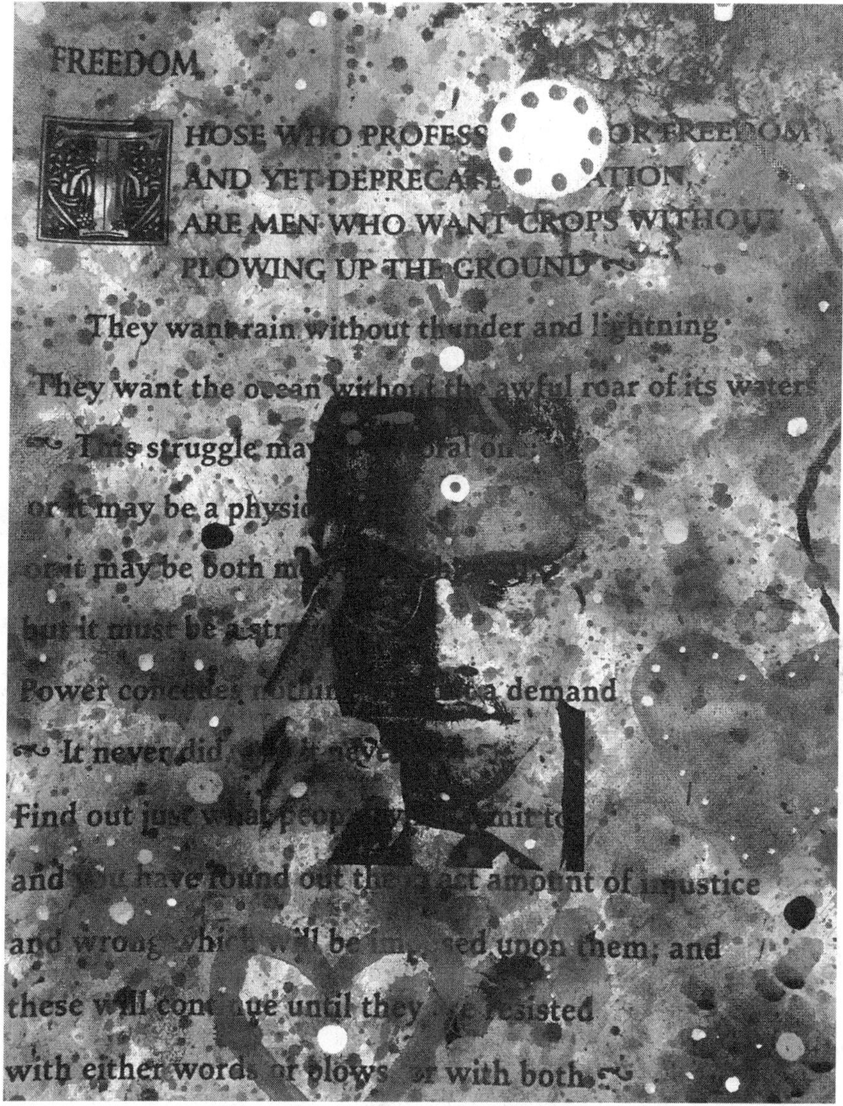

Figure 9. Detail from *Malcolm and Fannie Lou—Freedom Warriors*, 2010. Acrylic on canvas—86 by 48 in. Ben Jones, Artist Collection.

abstraction—if it's abstract, what makes it black? For Jones, the question becomes: Since my subtext is overtly political, how can I "drip drop" until I discover the form and color within the direct political message expressed in Douglass's address? Jones's wallpaper subtext is one paragraph in Douglass's speech, the paragraph that begins with the following words: "This struggle may be a moral one, or it may be a physical one, and it may be both moral and physical, but it must be a struggle. Power concedes nothing without a demand. It never did and it never will." Jones emphasizes that his use of red paint as the predominant color in his drip-drop technique was overdetermined by his desire to let red signal struggle and woundedness, but also love and kinship. The word "struggle" in the wallpaper subtext representation of Douglass's speech resonates as Jones's struggle to create room, in this painting, for the expression of tremendous love and tremendous rage. The heart shape in this painting is the whimsical surprise. We don't expect to see that lightness in the midst of the "bleeding" (the trauma) that the red paint also evokes. Jones creates a heavy lightness that makes us re-see the photographs of Malcolm X and Fannie Lou Hamer that are a part of the wallpaper subtext. Jones emphasizes how "natural" abstraction is, as opposed to the unnatural attempt to "imitate the camera." As Jones refuses to imitate the camera, black abstraction in this painting becomes a refusal to document the black struggle. His aim was to conjure up the feeling of an "altar" through the wallpaper repetitive images of Malcolm X and Fannie Lou Hamer. His use of the word "altar" reveals the potentially healing nature of abstraction. If the painting was not the mix of the abstract and the representational, we would not feel its release and grip (the sense of the letting go of black woundedness *and* holding on to black rage and black love).

Barbara Chase-Riboud leans into the politics of abstraction when she returns to the Black Power movement in her twenty-first-century art. In 2003, she returned to her Malcolm X series begun in 1969. This abstract sculpture from the *Malcolm X* series (fig. 10), which was created between 1969 and 2008, is a stunning play with softness and hardness. Each sculpture in the series combines cast bronze and silk fibers. In a public interview at the 2014 *Callaloo* conference at Emory University, Chase-Riboud explained that when she made these Malcolm X sculptures she was thinking about the fact that public monuments, memorializing heroic historical figures, are somehow not supposed to be abstract. Public monuments are supposed to embody the urgency of representation and the need to remember. But Chase-Riboud uses the texture of the cast-bronze abstractions to express the concrete work of the visionary Malcolm X. Her explanation, in "The *Malcolm* Steles and the Silenced X," of the "third materiality" that "took abstraction in a new and entirely original direction" offers a lucid theory of the destruction of binaries that can be achieved through black abstraction.[63] In the foreword to the 2007 edition of *Black Fire*, Baraka develops a similar theory of black abstraction as the overcoming of binaries: "In that emotional spontaneity there was not an advanced enough unity to maintain the eclectic entity that 'Black' had brought together."[64] As Chase-Riboud explains her process of

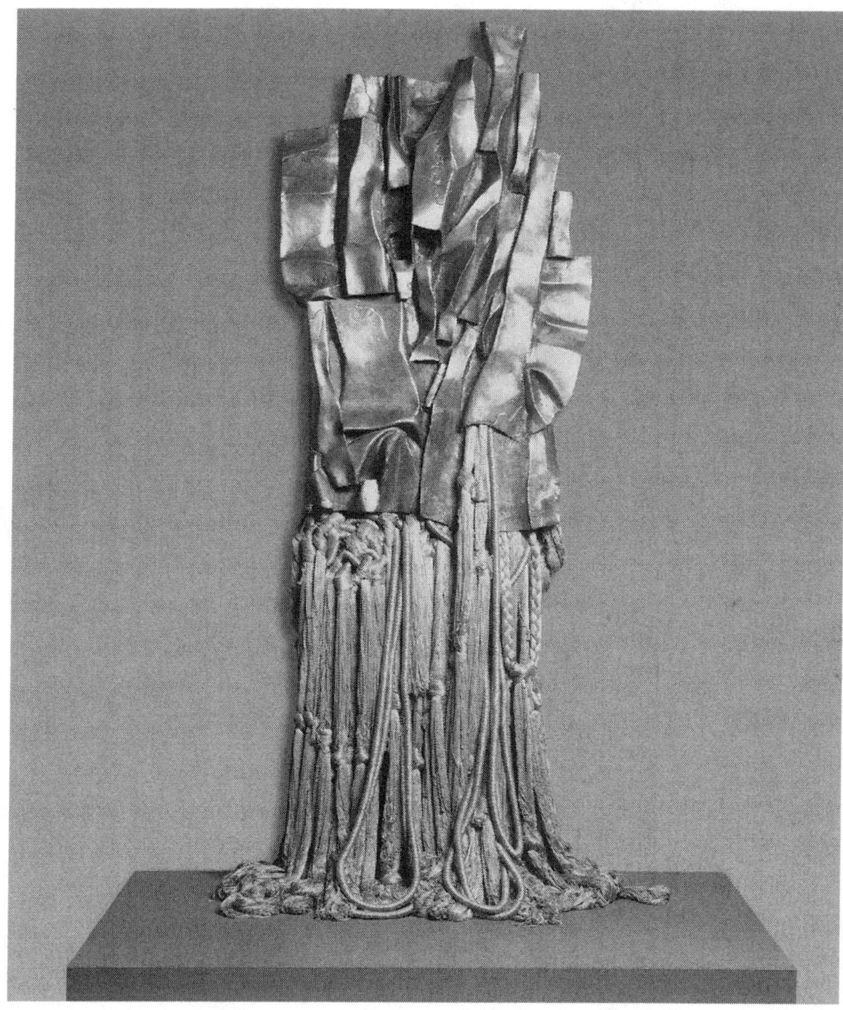

Figure 10. Barbara Chase-Riboud, *Malcolm X #3*, 1969. Polished bronze, rayon, and cotton, 8 ft. 6½ in. × 3 ft. 1 in. × 2 ft. 8 in. (260.4 × 94 × 81.3 cm.). Philadelphia Museum of Art Object Number 2001-92-1. Philadelphia Museum of Art 125th Anniversary Acquisition. Purchased with funds contributed by Regina and Ragan A. Henry, and with funds raised in honor of the 125th Anniversary of the Museum and in celebration of African American art, 2001.

creating the *Malcolm* steles, it is clear that "X" became what Baraka refers to as the "eclectic entity that 'Black' had brought together."

On the meta-level, Chase-Riboud's full description of her process of making the steles is an explanation of the theory and practice of black abstraction. In "The *Malcolm* Steles and the Silenced X," she writes:

A word about the metamorphosis of the "soft" silk into solidity and the "hard" bronze into fluidity. In the collage of these materials, there occurs the alchemy of metamorphosis, as the British painter Frank Bowling would put it—a celebration of the impure coalescence or collision of materials that can both signify and undermine time-honored ideas about abstraction. The first time it happened, I was astounded. Then I realized it would happen every time if I was careful—and that this phenomenon had revelatory importance to the sculpture and what I was trying to do. The combination of these elements took abstraction in a new and entirely original direction. The transformation of the materiality of the two opposing elements had produced a third materiality neither hard nor soft, black nor white, male nor female, totally visual nor totally literary.[65]

Why does she name this abstract, third materiality "Malcolm X" and grant it all the "blackness" that this leader of the Black Power movement hailed and inspired? When she first named this work, in 1969, she seemed to anticipate the spirit of black post-blackness—the need to almost make blackness itself the soft silk that needs solidity and the hard bronze that needs more fluidity.

Her *Malcolm X* sculpture allows Malcolm X to remain a visionary as she guides viewers to learn to honor the amorphous, unfinished work of social movements. Her return, in the twenty-first century, to this late 1960s and 1970s sculpture, suggests that she wants her twenty-first-century Malcolm X sculpture to be a *space-opening* gesture (not the *space-clearing* gesture of too many formulations of the "post"). In this space-opening sculpture that bridges the gap between the 1960s and the twenty-first century, Malcolm X (the constant muse of so many BAM writers) emerges as an abstraction with a political message that can only be known if we enter into Chase-Riboud's entanglement of the hard and the soft (what blackness was and what blackness will be). A. B. Spellman, in "Big Bushy Afros," his 1998 retrospective on the BAM, writes, "Abstraction did not cost consciousness," as he remembers the refusal to let go of the political in the more abstract art produced during the movement.[66]

The twenty-first-century approach to black abstraction of certain post-BAM visual artists, such as Kevin Cole and Adrienne Gaither, holds onto this BAM belief in the political work of black abstraction. Gaither's use of abstraction as a means of critiquing the twenty-first-century rhetoric of colorblindness is one of the most powerful usages of black abstraction as a way of "lay[ing] bare the structures of a racial caste system alive and well in the age of colorblindness." In *The New Jim Crow: Mass Incarceration in the Age of Colorblindness*, Michelle Alexander uses this language of going "beneath the political surfaces" and "laying bare" the violence of colorblindness.[67]

Gaither's paintings *Eye Don't See Color* (2016) and *Black, Brown, and Beige* (2016, fig. 11) are squares divided into solid colors. The length and width are both three columns. The paintings evoke a color-test chart, as if Gaither is testing our ability to see shades of tan approaching brown (in *Eye Don't See Color*) and the starker contrast of beige, off-white, light yellow, deep browns, and black (in *Black, Brown, and Beige*). The center square, in *Black, Brown, and Beige*, is a pronounced black that sets the browns and beiges apart. The black center square is almost the visual benchmark that grants the other squares their relative lightness or darkness. Through the play with the arrangement of these squares of different colors, Gaither makes people see the blackness that remains the hypervisibility projected onto those who remain vulnerable to antiblack racism in spite of the discourse of colorblindness. Adia Harvey Wingfield encapsulates the critique of colorblindness when she writes, "They argue that as the mechanisms that reproduce racial inequality have become more covert and obscure than they were during the era of open, legal segregation, the language of explicit racism has given way to a discourse of colorblindness. But they fear that the refusal to take public note

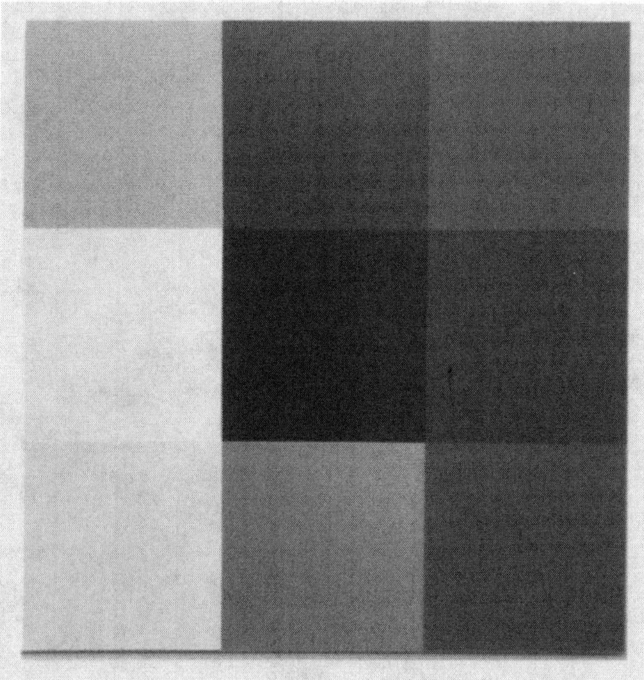

Figure 11. Adrienne Gaither, *Black, Brown, and Beige*, 2016. Collection of the Artist.

of race actually allows people to ignore manifestations of persistent discrimination."[68] Through the sheer play with color as an abstraction that has been racialized, Adrienne Gaither critiques colorblindness's erasure of the materiality of race—the fanciful treatment of racial difference as an abstraction.

Kevin Cole's post-BAM approach to black abstraction is as innovative as Gaither's. In 2006, Cole joined AfriCOBRA; he is too young to have been a part of the BAM but is directly tied to the movement's energy that continues to inspire AfriCOBRA. In Keith Morrison's interview with the painter Sam Gilliam, Cole's black abstraction is described as a "merging [of] painting and sculpture in free space." The free space that Cole achieves is black post-blackness. Gilliam uses the idea of the "post" as he explains the significance of Cole's steady use of neckties in his free-space merging of painting and sculpture: "He [Kevin Cole] uses neckties as parts of his imagery a lot. [. . .] His necktie work reminds me of the ones Wayne Thiebaud did in the sixties. [. . .] There are allusions in his neckties that are ironic: the festive symbol but also, in the African American experience, a euphemism for lynching. Lynching yes, but post lynching also. The works are responsive to memory; it is a dream that is about light and change. A gritty purpose prevails in the way that the work is made."[69] Cole's bringing together of the "dream" of "light and change" and the "gritty purpose" is tremendous. In *3am Sunrise Wings for TC* (2009, fig. 12), the painted wood gains the lightness of silken fabric as

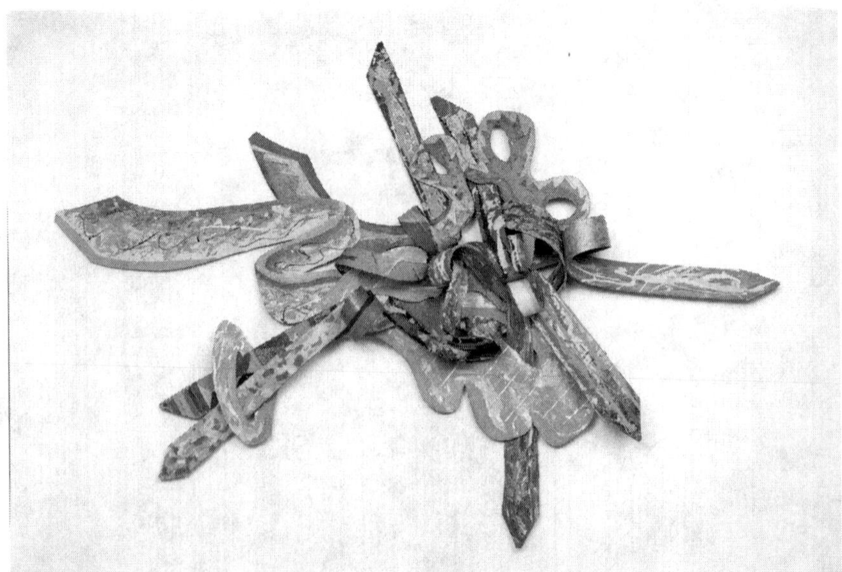

Figure 12. Kevin Cole, *3am Sunrise Wings for TC*, 2009. Collection of the Artist.

he evokes the neckties of African American historical trauma that still choke and hurt so much and, also, the twists, turns, and loops that can set us free. In "The Black Artist as Activist and Transformative Agent," Brenda Greene explains that "when Kevin Cole turned eighteen years old, his grandfather stressed the importance of voting by taking him to a tree where he was told that African-Americans were lynched by their neckties on their way to vote."[70] Cole's *3am Sunrise Wings for TC* evokes the horror of this lynching even as it remains powerfully abstract. The "gritty purpose" of his dream of "light and change" demonstrates that black abstraction breaks down any imagined difference between the reality of black struggle and the dreaminess of black freedom. As Phillip Brian Harper's eye-opening *Abstractionist Aesthetics: Artistic Form and Social Critique in African American Culture* (2015) signals, this undoing (and unseeing) of realism as the black-aesthetic *master* lens is the pulse of black abstraction.[71]

3

The Counter-Literacy of Black Mixed Media

How did the Black Arts Movement stage a mixed-media aesthetic that brought together poetry, music, photography, painting, illustration, dance, and sculpture? How do twenty-first-century black aesthetics take mixed media for granted in the same way that mixed media was a necessity during the BAM? How does the mixed media become an ongoing form of black counter-literacy that privileges the ephemeral and the process-oriented over the bound and fixed nature of a "text"? In this chapter, I explore these questions by zooming in on the BAM and then moving to the twenty-first century.

The notion of counter-literacy emerges when we recognize that some of the BAM poetry and visual-image mixed-media texts were primers and handbooks, such as *In Our Terribleness* (1970), with the subtitle *Some Elements and Meaning in Black Style,* and Stephen Henderson's pedagogical essay "Saturation: Progress Report on a Theory of Black Poetry" (1975).[1] Some of the BAM mixed-media texts are young-adult and children's books. The artists who created this mixed media were a part of a larger attempt to teach a certain type of alternative *feeling.* In *Where I Must Go* (2009), Angela Jackson crystallizes this feeling that mixed media can produce: "A body: it is a mosaic made of colors, shapes, designs, textural arrangements, symmetries, studies in contrasts that collide, oils and water that hug like sweat. At last, I am all these forms meshed so fine, so skillfully, that I am feeling."[2] Jackson offers a lucid explanation of the effect of black aesthetic mixed media—the production of "feeling," where feeling is understood, as explained in the next passages in this novel, as a "forgotten geometry of fusion" that allows Magdalena to understand herself as a "creature husky with history, caresses, and mad with aromas."[3] Jackson's theory that mixed media produces a heightened zone of feeling that is a "forgotten geometry of fusion" explains the real work being done during the BAM, when black aesthetics were grounded in the mixing of forms. Consider the title of Haki Madhubuti's *Think Black* (1967) as not so different from Apple's "Think Different" marketing language. The mixed media of the BAM made "Think Black" into a call for the imagining of different interactive forms of art that would not be highbrow and inaccessible to the black masses. The mixed-media, interactive technology of Apple is advertised with the words "Think Different." As the BAM *thought differently*, it mixed words and images to teach people how to begin to become literate in *black aesthetics unbound*.

In African American studies, the role of orality in creating an alternative African American literacy is now a very familiar idea, but the BAM performed a counter-literacy that was as closely tied to the visual as the oral. BAM counter-literacy was the movement's privileging of what Zora Neale Hurston, during the Harlem Renaissance, recognized as "word pictures" and "hieroglyphics."[4] Hurston's sense that the "Negro speaks in word pictures" is her recognition that "cheque words" (the language that she views as a literal type of currency) are tied to white power. The BAM's direct critique of white power included a full critique of the privileging of written language over orality, visual images, and action. During the BAM, the mixed media that accentuates the flows *and* ruptures between the visual, sonic, and the written staged a meta-language (a language that all of the subjects being hailed by the movement as "black" would understand).

The counter-literacy project's pedagogical mission was the muse that inspired many of the children's books written by artists directly tied to the BAM, as well as those who felt the vibrations of the movement while they were situated on the edge of it (neither outside of it, nor completely absorbed by it). The great interest, during the BAM, in the study of the relation between mental pictures and language enlarges the scope of the children's coloring books produced during the movement.[5] The movement's pedagogical mission was the revolutionary attempt to teach children and black subjects at large how to begin the process of imagining a black space in which they were not oppressed minorities.

The Stillness and Motion of Counter-Literacy

When one is reading a word-and-image book, pages are turned more slowly as the words fail to frame the images—the relation between the words and the pictures makes the reading move forward, backward, and sometimes pause as one lingers in the state of suspension where the purpose, the effect, of the multimedia remains to be seen, or unseen (if the multimedia effect privileges the limits of the visual). The forward and backward motion, in BAM word-and-image books, is as important as the books' production of stillness. At a 2010 performance-studies conference, Hortense Spillers responded to Harvey Young's study of stillness in daguerreotypes of enslaved Africans, speaking of the uncanny relation between motion and stillness (the fact that, in these daguerrotypes, that which is still is *about to move*). Tensions between motion and stillness overdetermine social movements. Consider the call for stillness in the civil-rights movement slogan "We shall not be moved."

In *In Our Terribleness*, there is a great emphasis on stillness in the midst of collective motion. Subjects photographed by Fundi Abernathy pause on street corners and evoke a sense of melancholy even as Baraka's words signal the collective performance of freedom and the vulnerability that creates the "terribleness" of the photographed subjects. The motion and stillness that Abernathy and Baraka create is a play with the difference between photography and cinema. The hailing of black subjects, as invoked by the mirror at the beginning of this text, becomes the impossible task of creating movement within still-life frames, an apt description of the tension in this text between the photographic and the cinematic. Baraka refers to the book as a "long image story in motion."[6] Words are set in motion in this text as the cinematic flow of words and images becomes the counter-literacy that pushes against the bound book. The cinematic flow is created by the movement of pages turning, but there are key moments throughout *In Our Terribleness* when Baraka makes the counter-literacy of cinematic words and images morph into the counter-literacy of arrested motion and the performance of the temporary end or suspension of the reading and viewing process.

At one of these moments of pause, Baraka signs his name. The signature, as Derrida argues in "Signature, Event, Context," testifies to the presentness of the text but also the past.[7] Baraka writes, "And now the contact is broken," as he performs the role of the hypnotist who is leading black people to discover the black gaze, black aesthetics, and a black world. When the signature appears, when the "contact is broken" and the state of ecstatic trance breaks, Baraka troubles the framing device of the slave narrative, which includes the signature of the former slave certifying that he or she has written the text. Given the illegality of black literacy during slavery, the powerful mission of the slave narratives is the force of people literally writing themselves into existence. But Baraka and the BAM as a whole search for a counter-literacy that cannot be rendered legitimate by a signature of the author. Baraka places the signature in the middle of the book, not on the first page. When we consider Baraka's signature as a riff on the framing of slave narratives, the words "written by himself" and "written by herself," in the paratext of slave narratives, transmute into the BAM ethos of the writing and visual-art production that cannot be produced if one remains a soloist. Before the "contact is broken," Baraka is leading a group session of counter-hypnotism. When the collective spell breaks, he is the soloist who can only sign his name and wait for the resumption of the collective spell that will be the redemption (the overcoming of the melancholy of the black soloist).

The tension between motion and stillness, in this word-and-image text, is the tension between being a part of a movement and losing "contact" and waiting to join again (waiting to see "what will blackness be").[8] The future tense is a core part of the BAM's mobilization of counter-literacy. As Ben Sidran explains, in *Black Talk* (a 1970s analysis of black music as alternative literacy), "Literacy freezes concepts."[9] Baraka, in *In Our Terribleness*, is terrified that the ideal (black) subjects he is hailing will be frozen once they heed his call and become trapped in his own gaze or the gaze of those who are not a part of the Black Power mission. The BAM's determination to create art that would not freeze blackness led to the multimedia of the counter-literacy project.

In *Who Look at Me* (1969), June Jordan uses the dramatic texture of pages with huge amounts of blank space to signal that, in her multimedia text, word-and-image interplays produce gaps, gestures, and openings that are the antithesis of the frozen, closed texts that make us forget that, before and after the literacy of American slavery's systematic creation of black illiteracy, there were other forms of literacy. Jordan plays with the illegible as she gestures, in the blank spaces and pages, to something not yet here. The blank spaces are half of a page in some cases and entire pages when she wants the reader to linger longer in the blankness that screams "do something" and "create something else." Jordon selected visual images from Milton Meltzer's collection as she created this word-and-image text. In 1956, Meltzer coauthored, with Langston Hughes, *A Pictorial History of the Negro in America*. The images were collected by Meltzer while he was traveling for his job as a public-relations executive in a pharmaceutical company. Dennis Hevesi explains, "While traveling the country for the drug company, he did research at historical societies, local archives and museums and collected nearly 1,000 illustrations."[10]

The BAM insisted on the black collection of blackness, to resist what the movement saw as the ongoing white power that always already frames blackness and makes it into a fixed and contained object of study. When *Who Look at Me* is compared to *In Our Terribleness*, the influences of the BAM on Jordan become clear. Jordan's re-collection of Meltzer's images of African Americans is a version of the black collection of blackness that the BAM was demanding. Most importantly, in *Who Look at Me*, Jordan performs the stillness and motion of words and images in a manner that is very similar to Baraka and Fundi's use of stillness and motion in *In Our Terribleness*. The black counter-literacy, in both books, emerges from the textual performance of the uncontainable nature of black aesthetics (the material reading and viewing experience produced as the pages are held and turned).

Like the reading and viewing experience produced by *In Our Terribleness*—of a "long image story in motion," punctuated by profound stillness—the word-and-image interplay in *Who Look at Me* produces an exhilarating cinematic flow of moving pictures and a melancholic stillness. This sadness and the wonder of furious movement reflects the cultural mood of the early 1970s black post-blackness of the BAM. In *Who Look at Me*, melancholy is everywhere, but a post-melancholy possibility emerges each time the reader turns one of the pages that leads to a page with partial or complete blank space. The blank spaces are not simply the space of post-melancholy. Like the circular entanglement of black post-blackness, the possibility of post-melancholy never escapes the sadness. Melancholic post-melancholy is the most apt description of the aura of *Who Look at Me* and *In Our Terribleness*.

When readers first open *Who Look at Me*, the tone of melancholic post-melancholy is heard before the first visual images appear. The question, "Who would paint a people / black or white?" appears in the upper right corner of the otherwise blank page.[11] When the page is turned, the following words appear in the upper left-hand corner:

> For my own I have held
> where nothing showed me how
> where finally I left alone
> to trace another destination. (2)

As in *His Own Where* (1971), one of Jordan's other BAM-era texts of counter-literacy, there is a play with the vagueness of "where." Jordan makes "where" the point of necessary departure, and yet it is also a point of necessary holding-on to a self that is under assault by the dominant societal structure that "would paint a people black or white." The tension in these opening lines between the power of collective "holding on" ("For my own I have held") and the power of "finally" leaving alone in order to begin to create his or her "own where" does not situate individuality as a repudiation of collectivity; individuality is produced in the collective. In the line "For my own I have held," the missing word "people" allows Jordan to entangle the speaker's grip on self and her grip on other black people. Margaret Walker's iconic, pre-BAM poem "For My People" (1942) echoes in the line, but does not cancel out other sounds we might hear.

This first entrance into *Who Look at Me* begs to be compared to the dramatic textual production of the entrance into a mirror in *In Our Terribleness*. When the reader opens *In Our Terribleness* and sees his or her face in the mirror transparency, the text becomes an entrance into a black mirror stage that aims to create wholeness from brutal fragmentation, the literal tearing apart of African Americans that Baraka underscores when he proclaims, "But look at it. We were brought here slaves and survived that. Now we are trying literally to get our selves back together."[12] Melancholic post-melancholy is introduced in passages such as: "Pray that we are not part of the Western / Empire, in soul. / We know we are not. / In Our Terribleness."[13] These words gesture to Fundi's photograph of a sign on the New Macedonia church, where the times given for prayer meetings are condensed in the following manner: "Pray, M.T.Wed. 7:30 P.M." The hodgepodge of letters, alternating with no seeming reason from bold to regular print and from capital to lowercase letters, signals the reclamation of language itself at the heart of the Black Arts mission. This photograph of linguistic signs is the only one that does not include bodily depictions of the black subjects being hailed. This moment of prayer in this "long image story in motion" is the quietest moment of introspection and disembodiment, as Baraka's prayer frames the call for prayer in the church sign.

Jordan does not include any visual images in *Who Look at Me* until the fifth page. Charles Alston's painting *Manchild* (a painting that troubles any impulse to separate black representational art and black abstraction) appears when the reader turns the third page and sees the following words in the upper left corner and Alston's painting on the next page: "Is that how we look to you / a partial nothing clearly real?" (4). This word-and-image interplay shows that Jordan is using the visual images as much more than captions. Alston's painting defies this gaze that renders black people "a partial nothing."

The most striking part of this painting is the face that looks "partially" like an abstract piece of African sculpture and "partially" like an actual face. Alston uses a patchwork background of colors that highlights a play with the abstract, open, and free quality of color itself. This background, like the partially abstract face, makes the force of the painting the tension between abstraction and what is "clearly real." The mood of the painting can be described as "black is subdued and beautiful." The painting is portraiture defying a gaze that renders black subjects into primitive mask-like objects, but it is also a quiet painting that makes viewers think about the private, interior self-reflection and self-imaging that might make African Americans see a fleeting connection between their faces and African sculpture. The painting almost has a bas-relief effect; the man's face seems to extend off the flat canvas. Jordan gestures to sculpture through the mixed media of words and paintings. She also gestures to a pop-up book as she calls upon the three-dimensional quality of sculpture and joins the BAM in their use of mixed media as a means of creating non-matrixed, non-enclosed, forms of art. The exact language "non-matrixed" is used by James Stewart in the opening essay in *Black Fire*.

The movement's interest in the non-enclosed quality of black aesthetics is related, more than we may realize, to the BAM's melancholy as they performed a black collection of blackness. The gestures to the open book were recognitions that dominant fixed books and dominant archives cannot contain the *live*.[14] In the BAM signature poem "Black Art," Baraka calls for "live words of the hip world live flesh & coursing blood."[15] The black book, in the BAM imagination, was a peculiar, open container of "live words."

Textual Productions of the Black Book

BAM remains the first African American cultural movement that performed the production of books written specifically for black people. To gain a fuller grasp of the role of textual production in the creation of the literary traditions that are understood as "African American," we must appreciate the BAM's explicit framing of the book as "black." Even the covers of Black Arts literary texts were often black. The founding of black-owned publishing presses was a vital part of this production of the black book. Dudley Randall founded Broadside Press in 1965, when he created a broadside of his poem "Ballad of Birmingham" that responded to the 1963 church bombing that killed four young African American girls. Third World Press (which remains the largest independent black press) began in Chicago in 1967, when the poets Haki Madhubuti (Don L. Lee), Johari Amini, and Carolyn Rodgers created the first publication with a used mimeograph machine. Madhubuti, the editor of Third World Press and one of the main architects of the BAM, has asserted that black nationalism "means publishing our own books."[16]

How did the BAM understand the idea of the black book? The movement made the black book a type of counterpublic, a particular type of public space that aimed to offer a privacy for the ideal black reader.[17] The movement hailed ideal readers and created desire to "think black" (the title of one of Madhubuti's poetry volumes). One of the movement's most dramatic examples of the hailing of ideal black readers was the textual production of Baraka and Abernathy's *In Our Terribleness*. The book begins with a full-page mirror image that demands that readers see their face, and the title "In Our Terribleness" is inscribed on the face, as readers enter this "long image story in motion." Readers enter black, urban, South Side Chicago in the 1960s. The "black book," during this movement's reenergizing of black urban space, was the textual production of African Americans' reclamation of the city as their intimate dwelling place. Toward the beginning of *In Our Terribleness*, Baraka shapes the book into a guide for ideal black readers' new way of moving through the city: "Who inhabits the cities possesses the thrust of life to power. [. . .] Man woman child in a house is a nation. More than them we become large cities that shd have, domes, spires, spirals, pyramids, you need somethin flashy man. Some red and bright green or yr black self. The cities the cities our dominion."[18] As Baraka's words interact with Fundi's photographs, there are "domes" and "spirals" of words becoming more concretely visual and photographs gaining more abstract dimensions. The book itself becomes the binding, bursting at its seams, trying to hold this large "dominion" of black urban style. This book's interplay of words and images is framed specifically as a "black book" mission in a letter that Abernathy sent to Baraka as they were struggling to expedite Bobbs-Merrill's publication of *In Our Terribleness*. Abernathy met Baraka when he and his wife Laina temporarily left Chicago to be a part of the Spirit House collective in Newark, New Jersey. After Abernathy was back in Chicago and he and Baraka had already completed the manuscript for *In Our Terribleness*, he sent Baraka this letter expressing his frustration with the publishing press Bobbs-Merrill and his commitment to the "black book."

Like many Black Arts poems, the letter works written language for its most visual and oral possibilities. The full letter reads:

                    TO
                 IMAMU
          DIG
             TO SUE BOBBS-MERRILL
             NO MATTER WHAT
             GON DO THAT BOOK
             AND FINISH IT CLEAN
             NO MATTER IT MEANS
          LATER FOR ANY SLOW-MOTION
                    ideas
                       of any bodies
          THE BLACK ARTIST MOVE SPEEDY
             DOING WHATSINEVER is
                       NEEDY

          FAST PASS PAST MOVIN METEORITE
          BLINDING THE PACE OF LITE
          WE GO   WE OUT   O SIGHT
          WE BLACK BLACK & RIGHT
          WE GIT TA GETHER GIT OUR GAME UPTIGHT
          WE SUE WE SUE WE SUE
          & do &   do the SACRED BOOK
          WITH OR WITHOUT ANYBODY YOU DIG!
          & ITS CREATION WILL SIGNAL THE WORLD
          ITS GREATEST BIRTH BEGINNING—A NATION
                    SO BLACK
       A NEW WORLD OF IMAMU AMEER BARAKA'S
             BEAUTIFUL BLACK CONCEPTION A WORLD
             BLACK ART FILLED BLACK WORLD
             YOU CAN DIG IT
                ITS REAL
                Our BLACK BOOK WILL BE THE
       WORLD'S GREATEST CREATION
             FOR BLACKNESS
                MIND   MIRROR   MAGIC
       the Hypnotic force of BLACK LOVE will
                conquer UGLINESS AND endure for sure as
                do sue do sue do sue do sue do do do do
                MASTERS sue due do due sue we we we WEEEEEEEEEE
                BANG! BANG! BANG! Love (Billy Abernathy) Fundi May 5 1969[19]

This letter is similar to the performance poems and broadsides created during this movement, and, like these Black Arts poetic and visual texts, the letter includes a play with the atypical arrangement of words on the page and the use of capital letters that make the words approach poster art, one of the tenets of the central BAM visual-arts collective AfriCOBRA. Abernathy's emphasis on the mirror and "hypnotic" effect of the "black book" explains why he and Baraka decided to frame this book with a full-page mirror. The opening title page of the book includes a silver mirror surface (that appears to be pasted in an intentionally homemade manner) with the words "In Our Terribleness" engraved in the center. The BAM shaped the reading of the black book into ideal black readers' process of imagining that they were look-ing into a counter-mirror, a mirror that countered a dominant, hegemonic lens—the white gaze. Instead of the slave-narrative paratext (the documents that authenticate that the narrative "was written by himself" or "written by herself"), this BAM paratext replaces the slave narrative's opening certificate of the slave's literacy with the mirror certification that an actual face is read-ing a book, that the reading process has a materiality.

This materiality is also dramatized in Toni Morrison's preface to the leg-endary African American text that was given the name "The Black Book." This text, published in 1974 by Random House, is a collection of words and images that explain the historical trauma and the cultural production of African Americans. Henry Louis Gates has aptly referred to it as the "the ultimate treasure chest of the black experience."[20] What matters most about *The Black Book* is the framing of a specifically black book as an archive, which creates the "treasure chest" effect described by Gates. *The Black Book* is a surreal collection of slave-auction ads, folklore, song lyrics, photographs, minstrelsy posters, a huge range of newspaper stories, color photographs of quilts and other examples of art created by enslaved Africans, and many other texts and images. In the preface to *The Black Book* (the original preface that also appears in the 2009 edition), Morrison begins with the words "I am the Black Book" and ends with the words, "I am not complete here; there is much more, / but there is no more time and no more space . . . and I have journeys to take, / ships to name, and crews."[21]

With these last words, Morrison channels the words of the slain BAM poet Henry Dumas. Six years after his murder by a white police officer, Morrison makes his poetic words the beginning and the end of *The Black Book*. His words are not only the final words in the preface; they are also the final words framing (on the last page of the book) an untitled, undated photograph of an elderly African American man, wearing a tattered suit, sitting on a porch chair, and looking at the camera with an expression that is difficult to read:

is it contempt, expectation, or is it simply unknowable? The unreadability of this facial expression performs the lack of closure of *The Black Book*. Morrison's prefatory words linger—"I am not complete here." The BAM "black book" also has this lack of closure. Consider the final words in *In Our Terribleness*: "Now get up and go." It matters that *The Black Book* was published as the BAM was ending; the editors collected words and images that define the black experience. The BAM was invested in a similar collection process and also in black collection of blackness, as opposed to what the movement saw as the dominant (white) culture's collection of African American culture. The black books produced by the BAM were the textual performance of the antitext, the performance of writing and producing books that would be too action-oriented to be held as a precious object of highbrow capital.

Unless we remember the word-and-image interplays in the Black Arts books, we forget the role of process-oriented conceptual art in these books that were performing antitextuality. The inclusion of the images allowed the BAM to dramatize the pictures embedded in words and words-as-pictures, as the movement attempted to situate black aesthetics as the inseparable mixture of image and text that W. J. T. Mitchell refers to as the "imagetext."[22] When AfriCOBRA made mimesis at midpoint one of their prime tenets, in addition to lettering (the need to add words to murals and other visual art), the movement was conceptualizing the hybrid form of the imagetext as the collective mission of creating an alternative understanding of text.[23] The use of the mirror at the beginning of *In Our Terribleness* makes readers see themselves as a part of the black book. The black book incorporates the black body. We see this same emphasis on the intertwining of book and body when Baraka writes the word "gesture" on the right-hand margin of one page. The word appears at the very edge of the page, where readers would turn it. The black book not only hails black readers; it also incorporates the bodily gestures of readers. The open text produced by readers is dramatized in BAM children's coloring books. These alternative coloring books (published by BAM presses, such as Third World Press) emblematize the call for counter-literacy and echo Morrison's words in *The Black Book*, "I am not complete here."

The Counter-Literacy of Broadsides and Murals

The 1968 Third World Press broadside of Don L. Lee's poem "for black people (and negroes too): a poetic statement on black existence in America with a view of tomorrow" sheds light on other dimensions of this counter-literacy work. The cover of this broadside (fig. 13) was designed by the AfriCOBRA

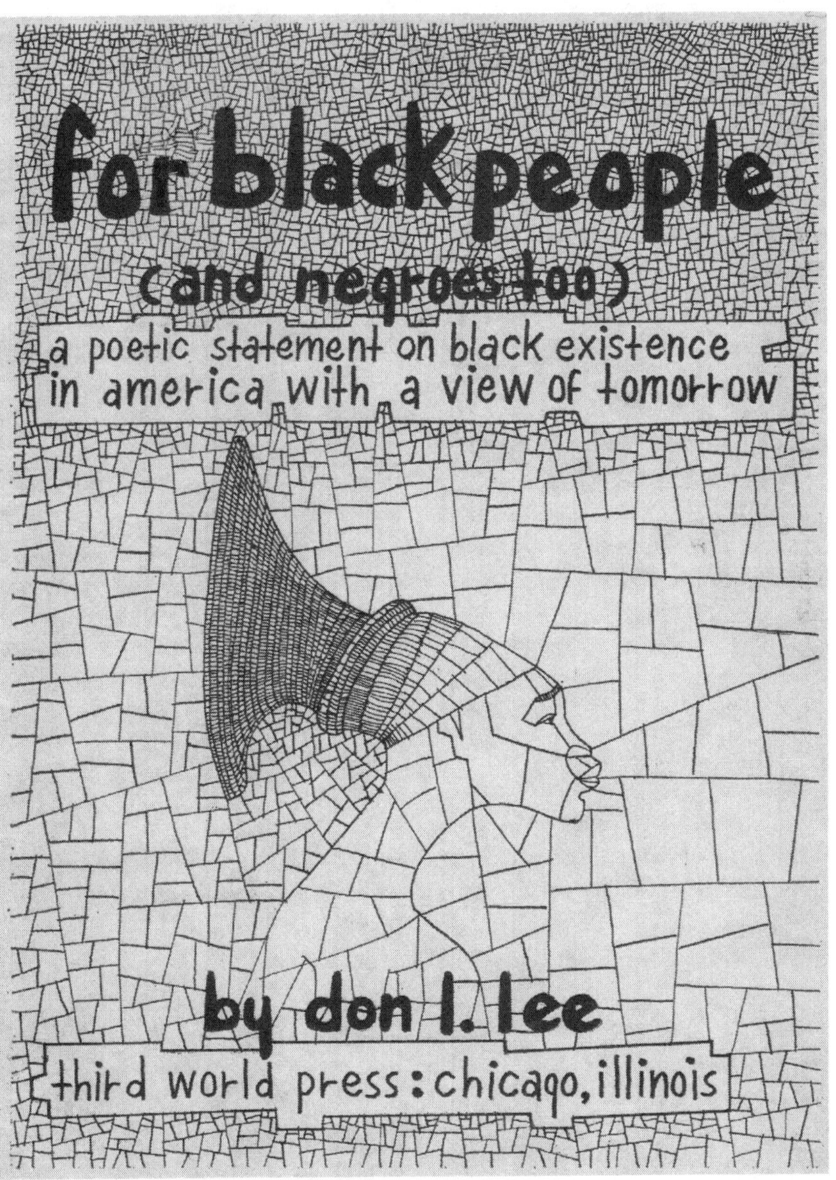

Figure 13. Word-and-image cover of Haki Madhubuti's broadside "for black people (and negroes too): a poetic statement on black existence in america with a view of tomorrow" (Chicago: Third World Press, 1968).

artist Omar Lama. The cover image is a profile of a woman; geometric shapes (an array of lines) form the profile and the area surrounding the profile. The force of this drawing is the artist's ability to create the aura of stained glass without using any colors other than black lines and the white paper. This thick paper broadside is folded so that the cover image opens up to two pages of Lee's poetry. Like many Black Arts performances, the poem performs the purging of the dominant ideology that the movement ties to whiteness. When the poem is framed by Lama's drawing, its "view of tomorrow" may seem much more concrete than the abstract geometric forms in the drawing. If the drawing is comparable to a precoloring template for a stained-glass design, Lee's poem delivers concrete words that aim to shatter the glass of Catholicism (and the whiteness it signifies in the poem). Lee's worrying of the lines of the Catholic prayer "Hail Mary" into "Hell Mary" drains the color out of the stained-glass Catholic church image, and the form discovered after the purging can be visualized through the broadside cover image of the *pre-stain*. When connected to the drawing, the poem's "view of tomorrow" is a shape waiting to be colored, the BAM hailing of more lines that can enclose areas and create space. Half of the woman's profile (the darker part of the image) is foregrounded, but the other half merges with the background. The profile could tilt outward or inward, away from or deeper into the background of geometric forms. The tilt to the left would make the real face emerge, outside of the abstract forms. The tilt to the right would make the real face become entirely abstract. Lama was practicing the AfriCOBRA aesthetic principle of mimesis at midpoint.

As the BAM made "black" into such a powerful sign, it became an abstract sign, like the shape of a stop sign that can be recognized in the distance even if its color and words cannot be seen when visibility is poor. Signs become abstract shapes when they are silhouetted in order to make the shape of the sign matter more than the details in the interior. In Nelson Stevens's 1973 mural *Work to Unify African People*, the map of Africa is the abstract sign that is the center of the mural.[24] The northeast part of this map is a black silhouette, and the rest of the map is red. Like Lama, Stevens was an AfriCOBRA member. His depiction of mimesis at midpoint is a stunning coloring of the black-and-white "stained glass" in Lama's drawing. Lama shows the woman's profile that is a realistic sign tilted as if it is in the process of entering the outer space of the abstract (that which the AfriCOBRA manifestos describe as "superreal"). Stevens shows what might appear when the profile turns into the full facial view. The two faces painted by Stevens are realistic and abstract: the clear facial features are the signs of realism, but the explosion of colors (red, light blue, yellow, green) are signs of the abstract. The color black is most prominent around the hairline and the eyes. The mural captures the tension between black as a sign of race and black as an abstract sign (the "koolaid colors" embraced by the AfriCOBRA collective). The faces in the mural depict the mimesis at midpoint. The circle with the map of Africa is painted in between the faces. The aspects of realism in the faces are not only under siege by the nonblack "koolaid colors"; the realism is also under siege by the partial silhouette of the map of Africa. This circle makes viewers focus on the abstract shape of Africa as they contemplate the message in the painted words "Work to Unify African People."

Abstract shapes become powerful signs when they deliver a message without the need for words. Nelson Stevens's inclusion of the words follows the AfriCOBRA rule of lettering (the collective's decision to make the message explicit through words), but Stevens's multicolor painting of some of the letters underscores that the letters, like the image of Africa, are shapes.[25] The movement pivoted on an investment in words as images; the new literacy was a performance of word pictures. The movement needed word pictures because words that were not treated as images would have been too private. The public language that the movement demanded was an insular blackness made public. The word pictures were tied to AfriCOBRA's mimesis at midpoint in the sense that they were public like graffiti (literally in the painting of the outdoor murals) and private like coded hieroglyphics. The flow, layering, and rupture that Tricia Rose ties to the graffiti of hip-hop also explains the graffiti of this earlier movement—the BAM outdoor murals and the symbolic writing on the "walls and in the streets" of the entire cultural movement.[26] The BAM writing "on the walls and in the streets" was the flow, layering, and rupture of visual and poetic lines.

Ted Joans's poetry volume *Afrodisia* (1970) highlights the BAM word pictures' conversation with the larger 1960s conceptual art movement. This poetry volume intersects in complicated ways with the word-and-sign (and word-as-sign) layer of the 1960s conceptual art movement as well as the experimental-typography layer of conceptual art. Joans mixes the pages of poems with pages of collages of cut-out photography and other images (what he called "outagraphy"). Some of the cut-out parts of photographs are used as silhouettes. The cover image is a collage that includes a cut-out silhouette image of a phallus. The boldface black letters also have this cut-out silhouette effect. Joans's word-and-image collages and the collages without words (placed on a separate page after particular poems) are conceptual art in the sense that Joans makes readers/viewers think more about the *process* of cutting and creating the collage of word and image, as opposed to readers/ viewers encountering the poems or collages as fully formed or complete. Joans's term "outagraph" signals that his poems and collages are an acting *out*, a type of conceptual art poetry.

This peculiar form of conceptual poetry is even more dramatic in the "neglphics" section of Larry Neal's *Black Boogaloo: Notes on Liberation* (1969). In "Neglphics: Or Graffetti Made Respectable," Neal lists propositions (such as "Bird Lives!!!" and "Black Power/Every Hour") that could be spraypainted as graffiti. The propositions are separated by short lines of asterisks.[27] After two pages with these graffiti tags, Neal then, in the next three pages, creates conceptual poetry that gives instructions for black poets, painters, and musicians. These conceptual poems have the shape of prose poems in progress. The conscious engagement with conceptual art is most apparent when Neal includes a marginal note, after the "Notes for Black Painters," titled "Idea for a Mural."[28] This same focus on the idea for a work, and not the completion of a work, shapes Neal's manifesto "Some Reflections on the Black Aesthetic." In the first edition of *The Black Aesthetic* (1971), which includes this manifesto, the following words preface this most visual verbal manifesto: "This outline below is a rough overview of some categories and elements that constituted a 'Black Aesthetic' outlook. All of these categories need further elaboration, so I am working on a larger essay that will tie them all together."[29] This manifesto is printed in such a manner that readers must twist the book and read this work *in process* from the bottom to the top of the page, with an entirely different gaze from the reading of the other "completed" essays in the volume. When we consider "Some Reflections" as conceptual art, the "idea," the black aesthetic, emerges as pure assemblage. Neal shows that one vital layer of the movement was the commitment to not textualizing the ephemeral.

In *Iconology: Image, Text, Ideology*, as W. J. T. Mitchell emphasizes that we need more study of how images continue to be experienced as *what really is*, he revels in the possibility that a "reprocessing" of dominant images and ideology can occur once there is a greater understanding of our deep conditioning to see pictures as having a tie to the "real" that words do not have. The BAM was also very invested in pictures' ability to make people feel a connection to the real. In the classic BAM words-and-image text *In Our Terribleness*, the insistence on the pictorial connection to the real makes Baraka exclaim, as he responds to one of Fundi's photographs, "Not represents. But is." Baraka ends the text with, first, the call for stillness and meditation, and then a call for motion: "Now, sit (mama) and meditate . . . try to see your own face, when you close your eyes. Now call that name, of the figure you see, call that name the real sound your substance is. Call it deep inside yourself. The beginning. We all need to do the same. Then get your hat i.e., get up and go."[30] Even as he assumes the position of the hypnotist leading others to his vision of the collective black body, he worries ultimately that the ideal (black) readers/viewers of the text will not realize that the assumption of a new way of seeing themselves is a personal journey that should not be appropriated by others; hence, the need to "get up and go" once this new vision is achieved (since remaining still may lead to being further objectified by others). Part of the enactment of terribleness is the framing of words such as "Visualize yr own face, when you close yr eyes" as injunctions.[31] As Baraka *commands* the ideal (black) readers to be free, Abernathy's photographs, within this "long image story in motion," are placed in a manner that creates particular moments of pause during which the commands fizzle out into a quiet yearning. When the incessant prose poetry with cinematic photography is punctuated in this manner (sometimes literally with a definitive period mark), Baraka yearns to not order the assumption of this black aesthetic but to simply be able to point toward (gesture at) the terrible black urban style that is already a part of his ideal (black) readers. He wants to hold up a type of mirror that would defy the very need for any external mirrors. He wants these ideal (black) readers/viewers to hail themselves and be the subject and the object of this reconditioning process.

The Black Arts/Post–Black Arts Novel

Angela Jackson's *Where I Must Go* (2009) is a liminal BAM and post-BAM novel about a seventeen-year old-girl's coming of age during the Black Power movement. *Where I Must Go* is literally both a post-BAM novel and a BAM novel, since Jackson began working on the novel in 1969 and completed it in the twenty-first century. The novel embodies the tension of black post-blackness. Jackson's poetry gained its wings during the movement, and she was recognized, in multiple *Black World* issues, as one of the most dynamic emerging new voices. Jackson was one of the younger members of the Organization of Black American Culture (OBAC) and developed strong ties to Jeff Donaldson, Haki Madhubuti, and other framers of the Chicago BAM. Her deep immersion in the BAM and her status as one of the younger new wave of OBAC writers explains the dramatizing in *Where I Must Go* of the seventeen-year-old protagonist's state of suspension as she waits to see (as she is unsettled in the point of departure, as she waits to leave the university, Eden) what type of cultural work she can accomplish with the newfound black consciousness. She fully embraces this Black Power consciousness (as a powerful process of resistance that she and her black peers learned collectively), but she also does not know her next steps as she continues her journey.

Jackson imagines a teenager who wants to draw and paint images that reflect a new black consciousness. The protagonist is drawn to the poetry of the movement but feels an even greater affinity to visual images. Jackson depicts herself in this partial autobiography as an aspiring visual artist, not a writer. In order to rediscover the power of the linking of word and image during this movement, Jackson writes a novel that constantly reminds readers of the visual aspirations of the protagonist Magdalena and the limits of words when they are not working in conjunction with visual images. Jackson depicts the power of coming of age during the BAM as the power of a seventeen-year-old trying to figure out how she can somehow make her visual art a part of a movement. When Magdalena learns about the outdoor mural *The Wall of Respect*, she gains a new sense of the *movement* work that visual artists can do. As Jackson includes references to Jeff Donaldson's painting *Aunt Jemima and the Pillsbury Doughboy*, Romare Bearden, Charles White, and Hale Woodruff, she makes African American visual art a roadmap of Magdalena's journey through the first year in the overwhelmingly white university Eden and a roadmap of her journey to the radical black consciousness that she and the other black undergraduates gain (the journey that leads to their taking over Eden University's finance building). Visual pictures are never seen outside of words in *Where I Must Go*, but Jackson, steadily throughout the novel, gestures to the visual as the place "where Magdalena must go" (echoing the title). The black radical movement that hails Magdalena is "where she must go," and Magdalena's visual art will be the medium she uses as she finds her own place in this movement. In this novel, counter-literacy is the constant gesture to the visual that the words can describe but not fully *show*. In the BAM, counter-literacy is a mixed-media approach to black aesthetics.

The professor and mentor of Magdalena (and the other students who discover the BAM when they leave the Eden campus) is enchanted with the history of the translation of Egyptian hieroglyphics as other African languages are created. This professor knows that Magdalena is an aspiring visual artist and tells her that paintings are a type of language. Jackson uses this professor (who encourages the students to rebel and connect their studies to the Black Power movement happening outside the walls of Eden) to dramatize the reasons why the BAM was drawn to the counter-literacy of mixed media. The mixing of forms created the community cultural centers. The BAM itself was a national (and transnational) community cultural center that decentered the singular objects of poetry, drama, photography, painting, and sculpture and centralized the power of black aesthetics unbound.

Since Magdalena's sense of wonder, at the end of the novel, about the next steps in her Black Power journey is inseparable from her sense of wonder about the type of visual art she will produce, the invocation of particular images created by BAM visual artists and other African American painters, throughout the novel, is Jackson's means of gesturing to the future frames of black aesthetics that cannot be fully seen yet. The text literally gestures to the visual as Jackson makes Magdalena's musing about certain visual artists and images a central aspect of the novel. Gesture is a key part of the black counter-literary produced by the BAM. When the word "gesture" is written on the margin of one of the pages of *In Our Terribleness*, Baraka makes readers think about the gesture of turning to the next page of this word-and-photography text. Gesture is also Baraka's means of signaling that the words are not explaining the photographs—that words and images do not produce a one-to-one correspondence. For words to have the connection to the real that we have been conditioned to believe pictures have, they must escape the page—they must not be contained by the system of dominant (white) literacy that makes art into a product as opposed to a process. Black counter-literacy, for the BAM, is the power of multimedia that refuses to be a fixed or stable work of art. This unstable, black multimedia is black aesthetics unbound; it is black post-blackness.

Jackson began writing *Where I Must Go* in 1969, the same year that June Jordan published *Who Look at Me*. Jordan includes images by many of the artists whose work is described by Magdalena, as Jackson grounds her novel in the presence of the absence of the visual images described but not seen. Sculpture is where we begin in *Where I Must Go*: "I am a sculpture made of clay gathered from impoverished resourceful earths of a big womb, with eyes."[32] The beginning of the novel is the only part that describes Magdalena after she leaves Eden (the final scene of the novel). Magdalena has a lover (which she never had at Eden), but this lover wants to change her name, to help her discard her "slave" name. Magdalena refuses to be renamed (explaining that she has been Magdalena too long), and sculpted form is Jackson's way of depicting the love that Magdalena and her lover, Treemont Stone, can share once they learn to be a part of the dynamic Black Power movement without losing the ability to sculpt their own identities. Jackson writes, "A man wants to change my name. I tell him I been too long to come by this. He lifts me up in laughter. I am myself. I can see myself." In this extended passage, Jackson presents the notion of the mixed media *feeling*, the "forgotten geometry of fusion."[33] This entire BAM/post-BAM novel makes words matter, even as the novel is about the young woman's desire to create her own visual images that will be as powerful as the *Wall of Respect* and the other black visual art that inspires her.

Counter-Literacy in Twenty-First-Century Black Aesthetics

In *Condition Report* (2000, fig. 14), Glenn Ligon visually performs a similar process of uncovering the *feeling* that has been lost when the full mixed media of black aesthetics is not recognized. Ligon uncovers and dissects that which is usually not recognized as a mark that has meaning. Mixed media, for Ligon in this poster art, becomes the meshing of recognized, legible marks and illegible marks. Ligon's relation to the BAM project of counter-literacy complicates quick and easy attempts to read his direct tie to the earliest mobilizations of "post-black" as a repudiation of the BAM. The use of the "I Am a Man" signs, in the 1968 Memphis Sanitation workers' strike, is the collective act of black resistance that Ligon rechannels in his text painting. He adds words in the margins that identify each mark and tear on the sign. Some of these words are "Hairline crack," "Brown smudge," "Feather crack," "fingerprint," and "loss at edge." This text painting makes viewers think about the unique texture of each individual sign as opposed to the focus on the power of the collective signs in the iconic photographs of the striking sanitation workers. Whereas Charles Johnson contends, in "The End of the Black American Narrative" (2008), that we need an "end" to what he deems a too familiar narrative,[34] Ligon looks for the close-up marks that are the "loss at [the] edge" of the African American narrative unless we learn to look more closely and to rearrange the iconic signs that (given the surreal nature of African American experience) have always been decentered, off-kilter, and experimental.

Glenn Ligon's interest in words and images builds on the use of words in BAM paintings and murals. One of the AfriCOBRA collective's manifestos explained the value of word-and-image interplay in the following manner: "The subject matter must be completely understood by the viewer, therefore lettering would be used to extend and clarify the visual statement. The lettering was to be incorporated into the composition as a part of the visual statement and not as a headline." But BAM murals created by AfriCOBRA members, such as those created by Nelson Stevens, use words in a manner that far exceeds the imperative to "clarify the visual statement." Their painted words often fail to "clarify" or pin down the visual (as the AfriCOBRA artists unconsciously defy their own tenet). When we compare Ligon's word-and-image work to that of Nelson Stevens, we see that the twenty-first-century work of counter-literacy is a continuation of the BAM's play with the unsettled and the uncontainable.

Stevens's 1973 mural *Work to Unify African People* forces us to see letters as colors (to not only read them), and this synesthesia allows the power of black aesthetics unbound to deepen. This mural performs color-graphemic synesthesia, a condition that makes people see colors while reading letters (for example, the letter "b" might be read as light blue). Stevens's depiction of seeing colors while reading highlights the movement's interest in alternative pedagogy and alternative ways of reading. Learning to read with color (and in color) is Steven's expression of the movement's desire to make art that makes sense by calling upon multiple senses and thereby producing the feeling of black aesthetics unbound.

The sensory-overload approach to black aesthetics is what Ligon builds on and also dissects in *Condition Report*, as he makes viewers squint to see the barely visible marks on the sign. Ligon makes the sensory overload of synesthesia morph into a sensory denuding (the stripping tied to being unable to feel and know everything that has settled on the signs carried in the black freedom struggle). This move from the overload of synesthesia to the bareness of the lines connecting word and images is the power of *Seismosis* (2006), with John Keene's words and Christopher Stackhouse's line drawings. When we enter this very experimental twenty-first-century word-and-image text through the lens of the BAM mixed-media approach to counter-literacy, we gain a heightened appreciation of the aesthetic and ideological conundrums that Keene and Stackhouse are exploring.

In the spirit of Baraka's use of his signature in *In Our Terribleness*, Keene uses the word "signature" throughout *Seismosis*. In *In Our Terribleness*, the signature occurs when the "contact is broken," when Baraka attempts to mark "self" precisely because self's communion with his audience is temporarily lost; the signature is an attempt to hold on to the communion even in this state of suspension. In *Seismosis*, Keene and Stackhouse use signature as a means of conveying the difficulty of holding on to "self" when one is drawing lines that break any boundaries between self and the "folds" that gather. Keene writes, "Whom will I gather, gather into these folds."[35] The complexity of this gathering process is also the dilemma performed in *In Our Terribleness*. Like Keene and Stackhouse, Baraka worries about "self's" disruption of the process of collaboration. When Baraka insists that his readers "get up and go," he warns them to run away from his direction of their liberation processes. In *Seismosis*, Keene warns, "In the end, refuse signature."[36] To refuse signature is to refuse to let self fully define the art that one has produced.

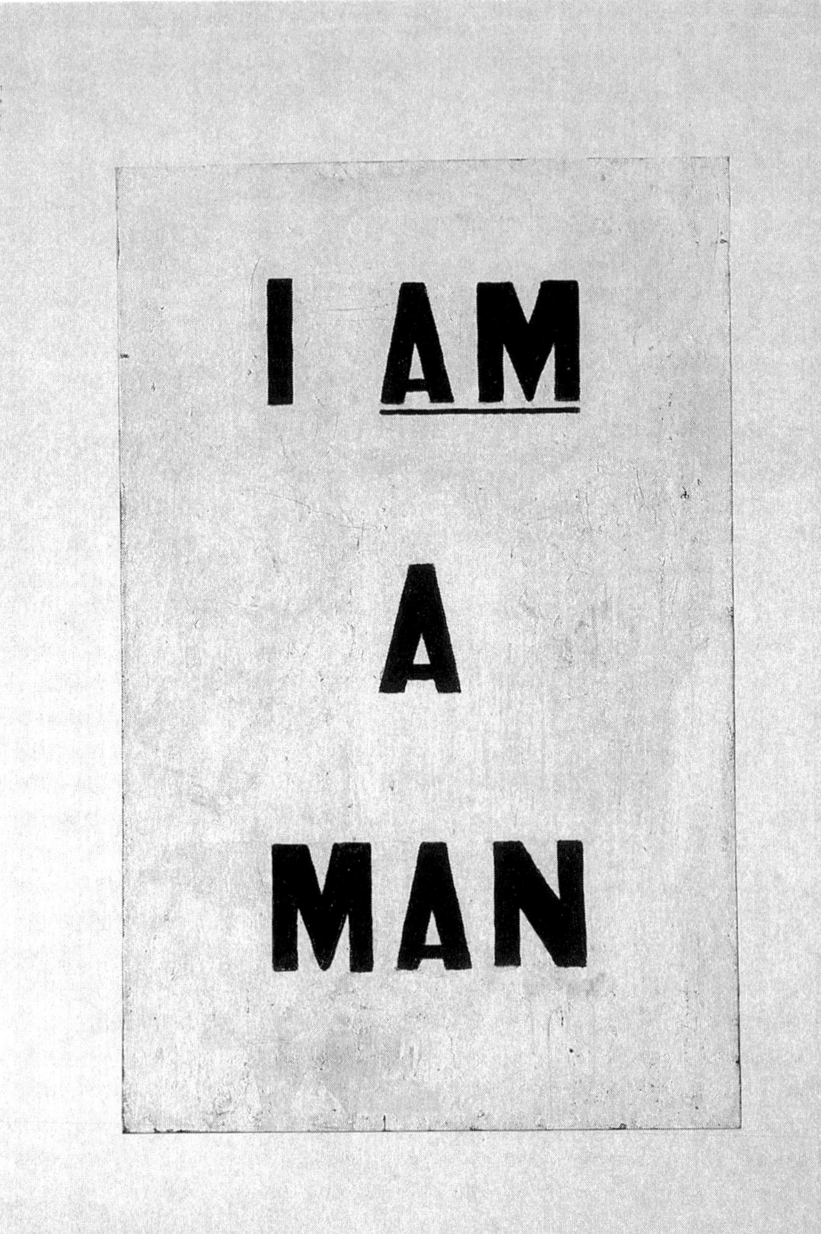

Figure 14. Glenn Ligon, *Condition Report*, 2000. Iris print and iris print with serigraph, two p[anels,] each 32 × 22.75 in. (81.3 × 57.8 cm.). © Glenn Ligon, Courtesy of the artist, Luhring Augustine, [New] York, Regen Projects, Los Angeles, and Thomas Dane Gallery, London.

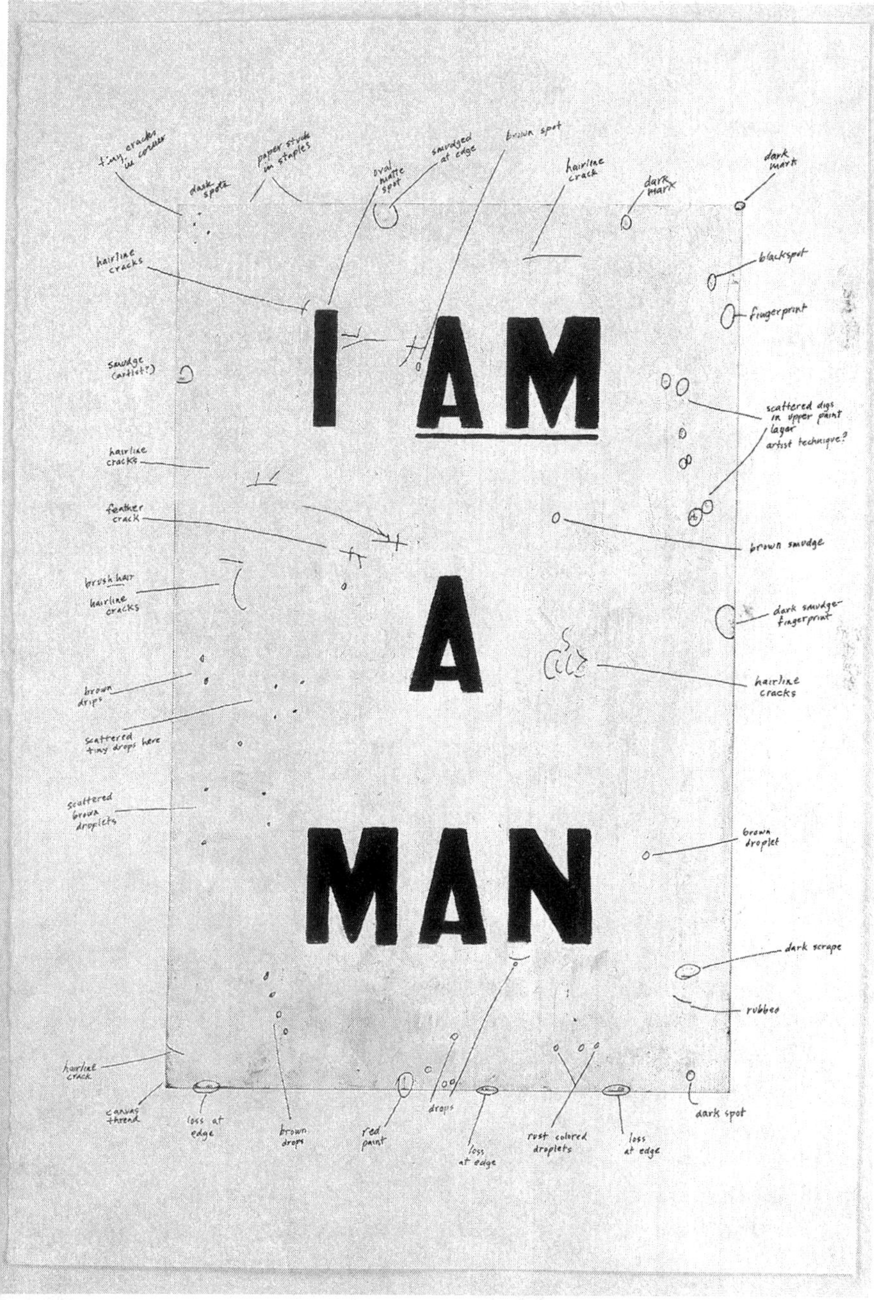

Figure 14 (*continued*)

BAM counter-literacy yearned for art that could be more than self. As Keene and Stackhouse collaborate, they approach a similar opening up of art. Art, for Keene and Stackhouse, is tied to self, and yet it must be more. We hear this post-self emphasis in Ed Roberson's foreword, when he wonders, "What is drawing's *word* for 'self'?"[37] But the most explosive move, in *Seismosis*, to the issue of self and post-self emerges in the poem simply titled "SELF."

Keene's opening words in "SELF" are "Self, black self, is there another label?" (19). These words encapsulate the full force of black post-blackness. This is the only poem in the text that includes the word "black." Keene makes blackness matter by not mattering, by appearing in one *signature* poem that teaches readers how to understand the entire experimental text. In this signature poem that refuses to sign without also letting go of the sign, Keene helps readers understand the final words in the text, the one-line poem "Process": "In the mark, we choose and lose signature" (103). The strange power of choosing blackness and losing blackness is the power of black post-blackness. In "SELF," Keene describes this simultaneous choice and loss as a process of using "black images to shore up [the] parameters" of "all configurations, positionalities, and momenta" (19). The BAM relied on the constant foregrounding of black images that extend to a black universe that is too large to be contained as "black," but Keene, in *Seismosis*, does not foreground "black images." Keene includes this one poem that unconsciously explains the mission of the BAM and, most importantly, makes it impossible to read *Seismosis* as post-black.

We also cannot view the drawings in this book as post-black. Two of Stackhouse's line drawings appear alongside Keene's signature "black post-black" poem "SELF." Keene's use of the word "selving," in the poem, takes readers back to Roberson's question in the foreword about "drawing's *word* for 'self.'" One of the two drawings that accompany the poem includes a profile of a face in the midst of a web of lines that lead to no recognizable shapes. Stackhouse refuses to privilege the formation of recognizable forms over the flow of lines that remain marks that cannot be treated as shapes. The mark-versus-shape tension is a profound way to explore the tension between "self" and "black self" (the opening words in the accompanying poem "SELF"). "Black self" is a shape, and "self" is what Keene describes, in the accompanying poem, as a "layer[ing] in sleeves into which identity presses" (19). This image of the formation of identity as a filling in of clothes adds another spin to Baraka's call, in *In Our Terribleness*, for the putting on of new clothes. Baraka makes the new clothing signal the putting on of new identities of black self-determination, but Keene's image of filling in clothes signals the potential for the clothing (any "shape" that determines self) to become oppressive. Stackhouse's accompanying line drawing also troubles the investment in "shapes"; the deep web of lines literally decenters the profile of the face by making the person remain prone in a horizontal position, as if Stackhouse is showing that the lines that mark and keep marking do not need to be read as a final formation of recognizable shapes.

The opening words in *Seismosis* are, "In the mark event, you enter your signature" (1). The tension between mark and shape is the tension between the "mark event," the process of signing ("enter[ing] your signature"), and the "shape event" that assigns labels to *process*. *Seismosis* begins and ends with the poems titled "Process." Keene and Stackhouse revel in a post-object aesthetic that is as propelled by the power of uncontainable movement as the BAM's reclamation of the "black book" as the open book that resists the transformation of culture (process) into capital (product). The deepest connections between the BAM counter-literary mission and this twenty-first-century black experimentation emerge when Haki Madhubuti's grid poem "Awareness" (1966) is compared to Keene's grid poem "Geodesy." On the surface, the poems appear to be dramatically different from one another. Madhubuti uses the horizontal and vertical columns to shape the poem into a visual poster that exclaims the same message, in all different directions, as if the play in the poem is Madhubuti's experimentation with maximizing the number of statements that can be made with the three words "Black," "People," and "Think."

Black	People	Think
People	Black	People
Think	People	Think
Black	People	Think
Think	Black[38]	

Keene's grid poems in *Seismosis* build on this BAM interest in concrete poetry (poetry that accentuates the visual texture of words), but "Geodesy" and other grid poems in *Seismosis* use the form of concrete poetry as a means of expressing the abstract. "Geodesy" can be read as a play with the thoughts that "Awareness" is hailing but unable to contain. Keene writes:

invisible	skin	shatters	manual	diffusion
machine	merges	psychic	sub-planar	tears
node	bounding	shadows	subjective	dynamics
serpentine	prisms	refract	metaphor	consciousness
interior	wave	curtaining	seismic	effect
billowing	perforation	spans	metamorphic	position (33)

When we read Madhubuti's poem with Keene's "Geodesy," what is most no-ticeable is the difference between the visual compression in Madhubuti's block poem versus the stretching out that is expressed visually and verbally in "Geodesy" through the longer rows and the words such as "shatters" and "bounding." Geodesy is the science of "accurately measuring and under-standing the earth's geometric shape, orientation in space, and gravity field."[39] Groundbreaking texts such as *Black on Earth: African American Ecoliterary Traditions* (2010) and *Black Nature: Four Centuries of African American Nature Poetry* (2009) have opened up the field of black environmental lit-erature.[40] If the typical black eco-literary approach is a focus on the ecol-ogy of slavery or the natural (and social) disasters that affect black life in particular ways due to the afterlife of slavery, Keene swerves in "Geodesy," suggesting, with words such as "billowing perforation," that when the earth itself becomes the subject of black aesthetics, the steam, the smoke, and the bursting out cannot be contained. This "billowing perforation" is the move-ment of black post-blackness, and we can only fully grasp this movement when we break the boundaries between the counter-literacy of the BAM and the counter-literacy of the twenty-first-century black aesthetics embodied in texts such as *Seismosis*.

4

The Local and the Global
BLKARTSOUTH and Callaloo

In "A Post-Racial Anthology?" (2013), Amiri Baraka critiques the choices Charles Rowell, the editor of *Callaloo* (one of the most acclaimed twenty-first-century journals of African diasporic literature and criticism), made as he edited *Angles of Ascent: A Norton Anthology of Contemporary African American Poetry* (2013).[1] In Rowell's introduction, the titles of the anthology's sections, and the arrangement of the selected poetry, Baraka sees a repudiation of the Black Arts Movement (a framing of the "angles of ascent" around the transcendence of the BAM). The BAM connections to *Callaloo* are not well known. When *Callaloo* was first founded in 1976, there were three editors (Charles Rowell, Tom Dent, and Jerry Ward). Dent and Ward had deep ties to the BAM, and Dent was the coeditor of the BAM journal *Nkombo* (which means "gumbo" in Bantu and has a direct connection to the "gumbo" meaning of the name "Callaloo").

In Rowell's introduction to *Angles of Ascent,* he sets up a divide between the innovation of the post-BAM poets and what he views as the programmatic nature of BAM poetry. Amiri Baraka's critque of Rowell's framing of the BAM matches Kalamu ya Salaam's direct critique of Rowell's dismissal of the nuances of the BAM. In a 2013 interview, Salaam (the coeditor of *Nkombo*) argues, "Rowell acts like he is just talking about craft, but it's not about craft. It's about censorship. In *Nkombo,* we were making room for everyone, but those in the academy who are now controlling the output while making it not look like censorship, are doing what I call 'picking the cotton of craft.'"[2]

After the founding of *Callaloo* in 1976, *Callaloo* lost two of its editors (Tom Dent and Jerry Ward) after the journal gained a university affiliation. Once

Figure 15. Announcement of first issue of *Callaloo*. Tom Dent papers, box 40, folder 29, Amistad Research Center, New Orleans.

Charles Rowell was the sole editor, *Callaloo* blossomed and became what it is now—one of the two most acclaimed journals of African American and black diasporic literature. Rowell's mentorship of younger scholars and creative writers has been tremendous. The *Callaloo* conferences, moving widely from places like Atlanta, Providence, and New Orleans to Addis Ababa and Oxford, have been as pivotal as the journal in the shaping of black diasporic literature and literary criticism. Clearly, Rowell would not be critiqued if his editorial leadership in twenty-first-century black diasporic literature did not shine so clearly. Salaam argues that "by 1976, there were no more nationally distributed black literary journals that did not cater to the academy. *Negro Digest, Black Dialogue*, et cetera, were gone. Almost all the funding for independent black work disappeared. You had to be a part of existing institutions and the lack of independence meant that limitations on the art were set, whereas before there were no limitations."[3]

Angles of Ascent frames the BAM as a narrow place that had to be repudiated as the "ascent" occurred. Baraka's critique of this framing created as much of a stir as Helen Vendler's critique of Rita Dove's framing of twentieth-century American poetry in *The Penguin Anthology of Twentieth-Century American Poetry* (2011).[4] Vendler ironically accuses Dove (who, in her earlier work, has been quite critical of the BAM) of including too much BAM poetry. Dove's critique of the BAM is not a simple repudiation. Her poem "Upon Meeting Don L. Lee, in a Dream" (1980) shows her refusal to flatten the BAM. Lee's "fists clenched," in this poem, have the tightness and rigidity that is set apart from the poem's final image of the women's "brown paper wings."[5] The lightness of the wings made of brown paper might conjure images of brown paper bags that have been reshaped, in a type of resourceful origami, into angelic wings. The image of this delicate reconstruction is as resonant as the image of Lee's "lashless eyes." The lush word "lashless" makes us feel the presence of the absence. Dove creates a delicate balance between the push against the BAM and her lean into a certain mysterious and seductive part of the movement that remains as opaque as Lee's "lashless eyes." She stages this entire mysterious encounter as a "dream." The dreamlike nature of the black male revolutionary imagination is engaged as a containment of black women's "wings" and also as a mystery that cannot be entirely known or contained by anyone who does not enter into the "dream." The cultural nationalism of the BAM was a dream of an other world, and the dreamers had big eyes and many blindspots.

An anecdote told by Jerry Ward shows how the BAM has been flattened. In a 2013 interview, Ward explained that he was at a celebration of Robert Hayden at the University of Michigan in 1969 when a group of "young blacker-than-thou brothers try to chastise him [Hayden]." Ward and a friend defended Hayden by telling the "young brothers," "You don't even know him."[6] As opposed to Baraka's emphasis on the tension between the BAM mission and Hayden's investment in not being pigeonholed as a "black poet," Ward insists on the impulse, felt by some in the movement, to "not put down other black writers."[7] Baraka writes, in "A Post-Racial Anthology?", "Back in 1966 I was invited to Fisk University, where Hayden and Rowell taught. I had been invited by Nikki Giovanni, who was still a student at Fisk. Gwen Brooks was there. Hayden and I got into it when he said he was first an artist and then he was Black. I challenged that with the newly-emerging ideas that we had raised at the Black Arts Repertory Theatre School in Harlem in 1965, just after Malcolm X's assassination."[8] The black-solidarity impulse to not judge is not recorded in the movement manifestos, but Baraka's "Hayden story" is not the same as Ward's. Ward's story shows that some black artists who were deeply tied to the BAM cannot be caricatured as simply performing "blacker than thou." As he told this story, Ward explained, "Hayden was so appreciative. He was so pleased to hear two black voices defending him. He invited us to his apartment and talked to us for an hour."[9]

In this same interview, Ward remembered the young Charles Rowell as "very interested in Black Arts writers" and "in synch with many of us who saw the function as encouraging everyone, not just those who have a name." Ward, like Baraka, views Rowell's framing of *Angles of Ascent* as an elitist erasure of the black solidarity that shaped the BAM.[10] When we remember the flow from *Nkombo* and BLKARTSOUTH to Charles Rowell's cofounding of *Callaloo*, with Dent and Ward, we may be hesitant to view any of Rowell's three "post-1960s waves" of African American poetry as an "ascent"—a progress narrative that entails the repudiation of the BAM. When we refuse to accept this narrative of ascent, we see the power of African American poetry as the power of what is deemed illegitimate insisting on its right to flourish in full gumbo fashion with no predetermined form. Indeed, Jerry Ward, in his introduction to Tom Dent's poetry volume *Blue Lights and River Songs*, describes this gumbo poetry as "the unfinished revolution of African-American letters."[11]

Remembering *Nkombo*

The opening of *Free Southerm Theater by Free Southern Theater* (1969) presents the "unsettled and the unfinished" as the productive tension that gave shape to the BAM in the South. The first words in the preface are: "This book is not about a finished theater. The FST is not finished—washed up; nor is it finished—a fully realized project."[12] The editors then explain, "This is a book about many starts, many ideas, many individuals. We were all joined in a single project—freedom. We tried, and some of us are still trying, to make an art about freedom, a freedom through art."[13] Tom Dent and Kalamu ya Salaam were the coeditors of *Nkombo*, the journal of BLKARTSOUTH, the post-integrationist stage of the Free Southern Theater, which, as Kalamu ya Salaam explains in *The Magic of Juju*, was "all black" by 1969.[14] The full nitty-gritty textual production of *Nkombo* testifies to the profound role of the "not yet finished" during the BAM. The black aesthetic of this movement was tied to the "not yet finished" in a manner that scholars have failed to recognize. Zooming in on the intricacies of the production of *Nkombo* is one way to uncover the depth of the process-oriented vision, the textual production of the entanglement of individuality and collectivity, and the unsettled nature of the BAM as it moved through the different regions of the United States and the transnational sites of pan-Africanism.

BLKARTSOUTH started as a workshop that grew out of the civil-rights-era Free Southern Theater (fig. 16) and then became the name that lingers as the final manifestation of the Free Southern Theater. We hear the force of the need to add more to the northern BAM when Tom Dent, in a 1969 letter to Calvin Hernton, writes, "In other words what I'm driving for now

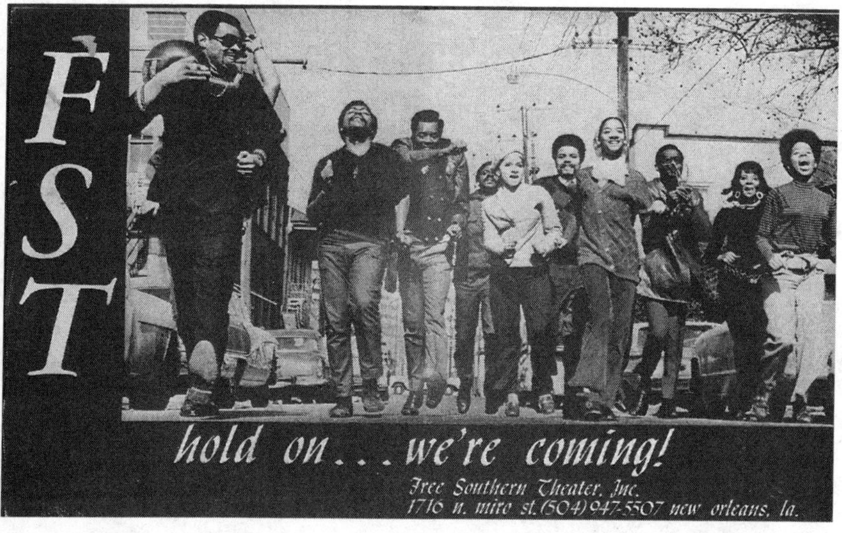

Figure 16. Free Southern Theater Poster of Northern BAM artists who joined the Southern BAM (French Quarter, New Orleans). Tom Dent papers, Amistad Research Center, New Orleans.

is a sort of Black Arts South, localized, centralized in New O . . . which will among other things produce material for the touring company and other black companies and bring to the whole fucking black arts concept a southern orientation, a source of material coming from the South."[15] Dent's exhaustion with a certain fixed notion of "Black Arts" propelled him to add "South" to "Black Arts"; the concept of Black Arts had new energy when it gained the southern "orientation." While Dent and Salaam edited *Nkombo*, they made the journal a powerful extension of the grassroots theater work of the collective. The gumbo-like mix of visual images, poetry, prose poetry, plays, essays, and other liminal genres in *Nkombo* performed the gradual move from the integrationist energy of the Free Southern Theater to the Black Power of BLKARTSOUTH. As Dent and Salaam produced this journal they gave the FST creative-writing workshop a new orientation, a mix of forms that could not be integrated and that had to be understood as the collective gumbo that took a Black Arts concept and shaped it into a BLKARTSOUTH orientation.

Dent's focus on adding the South to "Black Arts" is yet another way of understanding the role of black post-blackness during the movement. Dent's fatigue with the "whole fucking black arts concept" leads him to coin the name "BLKARTSOUTH" as a space-clearing gesture that does not become a gesture of erasure. The black post-blackness of BLKARTSOUTH takes many shapes in the nine issues of *Nkombo*. One of Dent's poetic meditations on the legacy of Marcus Garvey is a direct depiction of the power and urgency of black post-blackness (the power and urgency of movements that allow black consciousness-raising and black cultural nationalism to be fully necessary and, also, not enough). In "For the Southern Univ. in New Orleans Students Arrested Attempting to Raise the BLK Flag of Liberation," Dent evokes Garvey's "rotten ships" but also emphasizes that these ships, these lingering post-movement signs, "still haven't sunk." As Dent connects the BAM and the 1920s Garvey era of black nationalism, he uses the image of a "legacy of flags" "yearning to fly high" to convey the idea that the BAM is raising that which is in the process of sinking. The BAM is black post-blackness when it rescues that which is always already vulnerable (always already in the process of "rotting"). Dent writes:

> You left a
> Legacy
> Of blk & green flags
> Yearning to fly high
> . . . .

Garvey,
All yr rotten
Ships
Still haven't sunk,
There must have been something
Beautiful
In yr fiery eyes
That
Grows larger
Each
Day
Of the rising
Sun.
Up, you mighty flag.[16]

Dent rewrites Garvey's famous words, "Up you mighty people, you can accomplish what you will." "What you will" evokes a vulnerable futurity, the possibility of action or inaction, that echoes BAM images of the black cultural revolution as what will happen and also, sometimes, as what has happened already. When the cultural revolution is depicted as that which is unfolding now, the next stage after the cultural revolution is always a question.

One of BLKARTSOUTH's workshop invitations included Keith Ferdinand's drawing of a map of Africa that is created out of many faces that are almost bursting out of the map and refusing to be contained by any geographical space. The Swahili words "Watu Weusi" (black people) appear next to the map of faces. The crowdedness and the excess evoked by the faces twisting and turning in Ferdinand's image make these words "Watu Weusi" signal sheer linguistic motion (as opposed to any fixing of blackness).

Kalamu ya Salaam, as the coeditor of *Nkombo*, asserts, in one of his 1969 "Food for Thought" prefaces, that "blk poetics is / motion" and "nothing is concrete, blk lives are in a constant state of flux."[17] The unfolding of the nine issues of *Nkombo* can be read as the textual performance of black being as collected motion; turning the pages of these journal issues reminds us of Zora Neale Hurston's words, "folklore is not as easy to collect *as it sounds*" (italics mine).[18] Collected motion is an impossibility; the "constant state of flux" referrred to by Salaam cannot be captured in the journal issues. As the editors attempt to textually produce this "constant state of flux," they actually produce a steady "stop and go" tension as the poems and other genres blend into each other but also remain contained. The voices are separate

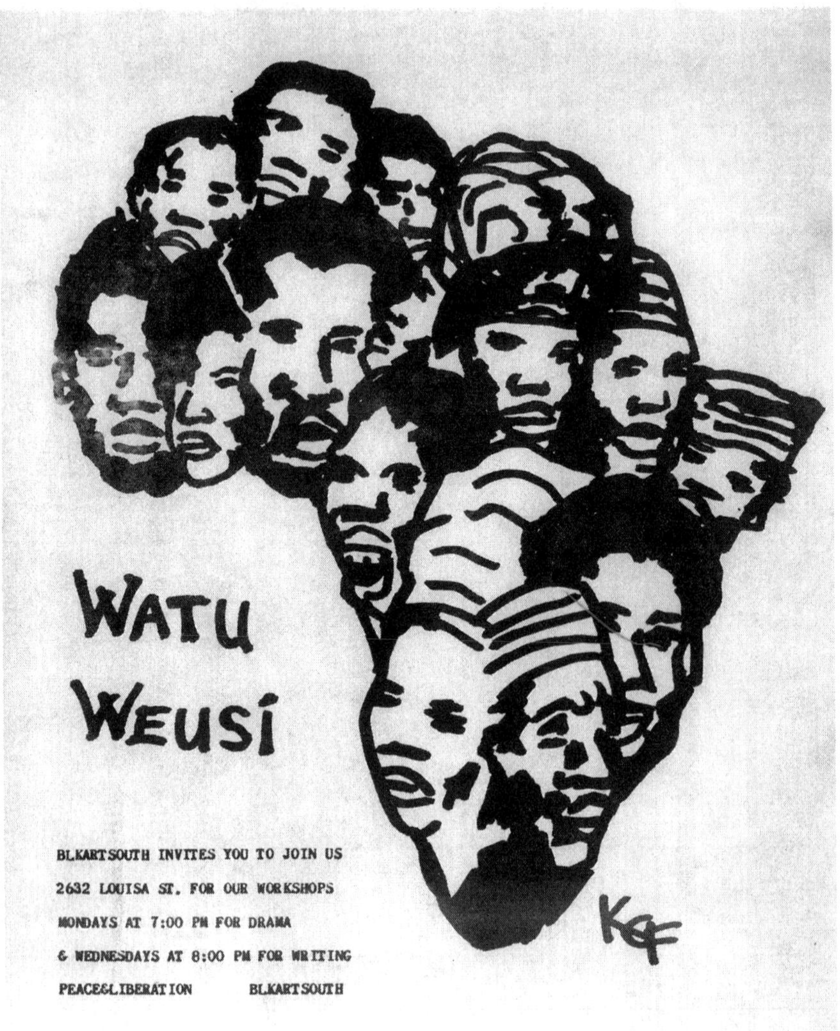

Figure 17. Back cover image of *Nkombo* 2.2 (1969), *Nkombo* papers, Amistad Research Center, New Orleans.

and connected. In the first issue, the initials of the authors appear after each poem, but as the issues progress these initials (these marks of distinction) disappear. Without the initials, the pauses in the reading process are less pronounced, since some of the poems, ending with no author credit, flow quickly into the next piece written by a different uncredited author. Looking at the table of contents is the only way of identifying who wrote what. There are no clustered, multiple pieces written by the same author. In the later issues that do not have the authors' initials in the text proper, the table of contents names the writers and visual artists that create the particular moments of pause and resumption of flow. The table of contents is comparable to a program received at the beginning of a performance; it is only before or after watching the performance that the audience will carefully read the names of the actors. When the editors, in their opening statements, emphasize that the collected work is a part of the ongoing BLKARTSOUTH performance tours, it becomes clear that we should understand the journal as a staging of text and image, a flash of the spirit. The editors do not want to translate the flashes of black aesthetics into a permanent published imprint.

The first issue of *Nkombo* was published in 1968 (when the name of the journal was *Echoes from the Gumbo*, with a subtitle *Nkombo* on the second page with the copyright information). This end-of-the-1960s moment matters; an Ed Bullins essay collected in Tom Dent's papers describes this moment as the "recently left behind sixties."[19] The mood of the 1970s BAM is a complicated post-movement sensibility, the mood of black post-blackness. Bullins, in this essay "Black Theatre: The 70's Evolutionary Changes" (1971), explains the difference between those in the 1960s black cultural revolution, who were only claiming blackness, versus those who were making black art. For Bullins, the 1970s BAM is the time to pause and assess the difference between simple identifications with blackness and the "altered consciousness" of black art (and black theater, which, for Bullins, is the energizing, "altering" force of black art). Bullins writes: "A handful of these 'revolutionaries' evolved into what can best be described as 'Black Artists,' using the tired and wasted Western theatre form as a medium to effect the most profound changes in black people here in America, that process termed 'altering consciousness,' at the same time revitalizing the form aesthetically and literally through attacking the intellectual and ideological premises of Western civilization, while shaping their models for future Black conceptualization through the evolutionary struggle of creative practice, to bring a confrontation with reality to be what is now known as Black Theatre."[20] In *Nkombo*, the altered consciousness takes on the affect of the "just left behind," post-1960s style merging with the opening affect of the "not yet finished" in *Free Southern Theater by Free Southern Theater.*

What is the gumbo mix of "just left" and "still there"? In a 1969 issue of *Nkombo*, this mix gains clear shape in Nayo Ola's poem "today, tomorrow, sister." The limbo between "just left" and "still there" is staged as the talking between "two nationalist sisters" that occurs as they "sip coffee."[21] The sipping is figured as a lack of action, a paralysis that happens once the women have fully absorbed the style and discourse of cultural nationalism: "we have refused for some time / to paint our faces and cook our hair / our clothing reflects / the taste of our ancestors." As the sixties are "left behind," the poet, like the speaker in the poem, is "sipping" as she remains "still there" in a cultural movement that she hopes is approaching a next stage. The poem ends with a call for the next step after the "sipping": "something / my nationalist sister / and me / should be doing."[22] On the cusp of the 1970s, this reflection (and many similar ones) on the need for action more than style shows that, as the BAM progressed, some of the 1960s performances were critiqued. This self-critique reenergized black consciousness-raising. The focus on the future of black consciousness-raising, in poems such as "today, tomorrow, sister," differs greatly from the "no future" sensibility of some of the twenty-first-century mobilizations of post-blackness. The end of the 1960s BAM affect of black post-blackness is performed in *Nkombo*, as many of the poems and images become flashes of black aesthetics that are immediately recognizable as Black Arts poesis and also slightly different from what we expect to see and hear in performances of black cultural nationalism.

"The Unfinished Poem," by Adam Weber, appearing immediately after "today, tomorrow, sister," dramatizes the role of the unfinished in producing the energy of the turn-of-the-decade, second wave of the movement. The idea that the poem will be finished when poetry is no longer necessary suggests that the unfinished poem is battling the dominant cultural power tied to the "finished" poem. This poem sheds light on black post-blackness by emphasizing that there is a politics tied to the unfinished; the black cultural revolution will continue to have a circular, unfinished nature (black-post-black-black . . .) until the finished, stable nature of global white supremacy is undone.

Where Was Black Arts Going?

One of the *Nkombo* writers, Quo Vadis Gex-Breaux, makes unheard black sounds entirely coexist with the sounds of deep immersion in the movement's black aesthetic warfare. In the flow of the *Nkombo* issues, Gex-Breaux provides flashes of whimsical images such as God riding a tricycle and, also, flashes of unadulterated black aesthetic rage. Her birth name, the latin words "Quo Vadis," is itself a swerve from the expected sounds of the movement. We expect to hear the adopted African names, not the Latin phrase for "where are you going?" or the equally evocative meanings of the word "Quo" (to which place, to what place, whither, where). Her name dramatizes the Creole and Catholic background of this poet who joined BLKARTSOUTH when she was very young (a high school student). Her edge-of-the-twenty-first-century, post–Black Arts poetry appears in a 1998 anthology that frames her as a "Louisiana poet," not a black poet. This anthology has the delightful title *Uncommonplace:An Anthology of Contemporary Louisiana Poets.*[23] The word "uncommonplace" makes place into a common ground *and* a common disorientation, that which Fred Moten, in his poem "There Is Blackness," calls "a particular embraced affinity of veering."[24] Just as Moten describes blackness as a common veering, Gex-Breaux's poetry, during and after the BAM, is a profoundly black *uncommonplace.* Her poems in *Uncommonplace* may not be framed by the editor as "black," but, when we read them alongside her BLKARTSOUTH poems, the power of black uncommonplace explodes.

In "Jazz Rain," one of the *Uncommonplace* poems, Gex-Breaux gives us a metanarrative of tbe black post-blackness that is entirely lost in the framing of the anthology as simply "Louisiana poets." Her poems in *Uncommonplace* have the force of poetic manifestos that explain the deeper connections between the most experimental flows of the BAM and the most experimental flows of edge-of-the-twenty-first-century black aesthetics. In "Jazz Rain," Gex-Breaux locates a sonic explanation of what she describes as a "wet, unfinished song."[25] In this poem about a woman whose style is not legible to others ("a kind of classy coarsesness / like raw silk" and "a kind of open earthiness / without being dirt"), Gex-Breaux develops a character who is not unlike the opening description of herself in her BLKARTSOUTH poetry volume, *Dark Waters* (1969). In this introducton, Kalamu ya Salaam describes Gex in the following manner:

> Quo is quiet, tranquil
> and strong, all the attributes that a woman should have
> i introduce by way of saying she is not hard to understand,
> she speaks in the alto flute range, seldom heard but beau-
> tiful when recognized
>
> . . . .
>
> Quo is of creole background, a strange rendering not noted
> for its blackness, i once thot her an escapee from some ca-
> tholic cathedral but in fact she is just like all of the
> rest of us—growing blacker by the minute, the next words
> you read will be/ will be/a/u
> ti-ful/will/we/we will/will
> Quo/YES!
> PEACE&LIBERATION[26]

Even though this male gaze reduces her to womanhood ("all the attributes that a woman should have"), this description of her "black uncommonplace" is strikingly similar to the image of the "classy coarse" music maker in "Jazz Rain." The "wet, unfinished song" described in "Jazz Rain" can easily be interpreted as Gex's post-BLKARTSOUTH continued recognition that the "unfinished" is not an aesthetic problem but rather a way of understanding the power of art to enable people to refuse to live life as a series of dead ends and points of closure. The power of the not-yet-finished emerges as this poet, who gained her wings while in BLKARTSOUTH, meditates on a type of "scat between life's drops" that cannot be easily taught.[27]

Black aesthetics, for Gex-Breaux, before and after the BAM, remains *scat*. The final lines of "Jazz Rain" suggest that she understands black aesthetics as a play with forms that are not fully legible in a dominant aesthetic structure: "hers was too cloistered an intellect / [...] / she glistened, spontaneous, evolving / defined by blues bridges / a wet, unfinished song."[28] Quo Vadis Gex may have been a soloist not only after BLKARTSOUTH but during it. The lack of authors' names after the poems in *Nkombo* should not be read as the collective's refusal of the possibility of solo performances. Fred Moten's theory of the multiplicity that energizes the soloist is the best way to understand the type of soloist that, as Gex depicts in "Jazz Rain," is "defined by blues bridges."

This kind of soloist—in what James Baldwin, in "Sonny's Blues," calls the "deep water"—is, according to Moten's theory, a "black study group."[29] Moten explains: "Like an autoethnographic soundcatcher, driven and enabled by eccentric, hesitant, sociopoetic social logic—a radical empiricism that avoids the spirit of empirical system—[Anthony] Braxton collates and collects what is beyond category and reveals how solo performance comes to be the field in which multiplicity is studied and performed."[30] Moten emphasizes that the "soloist is unalone; the soloist is not (all) one," precisely because "solitude is haunted, crowded."[31] This crowded solitude is what the woman soloist described in "Jazz Rain" knows too well. Moten's idea of the soloist as "a black study group" opens up the most meaningful bridge between the BAM and the more productive zones of post-black performances. The black study groups, epitomized by BLKARTSOUTH and the many other BAM collectives, pivot on the power of collectivity, but this working together was never something that could be completely untangled from the "crowded solitude" that we hear in so many of the melancholy poems and plays of the movement. "Jazz Rain" dramatizes Moten's theory of the power of the "unalone" soloist. The image of the "cloistered intellect" may initially make us think of a mind caught in an elitist shelter, but Gex-Breaux wants us to imagine the type of shelter that holds ideas, sounds, and colors that the organic intellectual has absorbed.

This type of shelter is not very different from the deeper resonances tied to the omnipresent word "nation" in BAM literature. As the cultural workers of the movement found shelter in their black conciousness-raising, they were transported to an imagined black nation. Much of the aesthetic warfare was tied to finding that alternative "nation within a nation," but some of the movement artists, the unalone soloists, were *scatting* within a (soloist) nation within a (black) nation within a (white) nation. Gex-Breaux's sense of the "overdubbing" ("Solo she sang her own harmonies / overdubbed") conjures up this image of the layering of the soloist nation within a black nation within a white nation. The notion of black post-blackness also conjures up the over-dubbing technique of listening to a previously recorded performance and creating a new performance *with* it, not *against* it—as Baraka insists when he begins his poem "Black Dada Nihilismus" with the impossible punctuation, ".Against what light."[32]

As the black soloist Quo Vadis Gex-Breaux continues, in her post-BAM work, to overdub (working *with* and not against), she builds on the overdubbing and scatting with the same sense of purpose that shaped her art in *Nkombo*. One of her *Uncommonplace* poems, "The Long and Short of It," is a direct return to the gumbo reference embedded in the title of the *Nkombo* journal. In this poem, after Gex-Breaux indulges in the metaphor of food as a way of emphasizing the resilience of New Orleans black culture, she ends with a less familiar twist—a focus on how the constant "spice" created through resistance and struggle transforms the culture that "blackened" people assume they know (because they have lived it) into a culture that they are "aching / to get to know." The final lines of the poem are: "to change that thing / you once recognized / into something you're aching / to get to know."[33] The art in *Nkombo* accomplishes what this poem describes. Taking Gex-Breaux's lead, we can reread her art (and that of her BLKARTSOUTH comrades) as a performance of blackness not as something known but as something that these young poets, during the late period of the BAM (the early 1970s), were defamiliarizing (knowing and not knowing) through their conscious attempt to "get to know" the "Black Arts concept" through the lens of their "southern orientation."[34]

BLKARTSOUTH'S "SOS"

Part of this defamiliarizing process included the purposeful repetition with a difference, in *Nkombo*, of some of the mid-1960s iconic Black Arts poetry. An untitled poem written by Dara Ebun Ola (fig. 18) ends with the words "BLACK

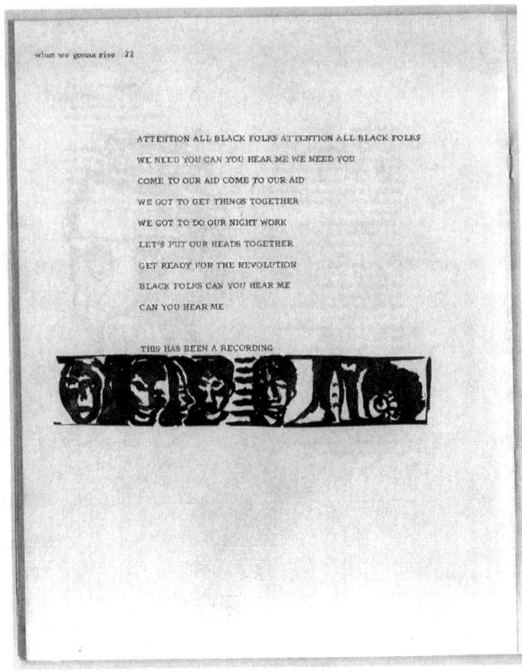

Figure 18. Untitled poem, Dara Ebun Ola. Drawing by Keith Ferdinand. *Nkombo* 2.3 (1969): 22. *Nkombo* papers, Amistad Research Center, New Orleans.

FOLKS CAN YOU HEAR ME / CAN YOU HEAR ME"—an echo of Baraka's poem "SOS," with its resonant words, "calling all black people [...] / Wherever you are" and the plea for these hailed subjects to simply "come / on in."[35] But, in *Nkombo*, this BLKARTSOUTH version of the hailing of black people includes a drawing by Keith Ferdinand (Kalamu ya Salaam's brother) that suggests a strip of negatives that could be blown up into full-size pictures. The simulation (through line drawings done with markers) of the process of developing prints in a darkroom takes us to the edge (the strip) between the stubborn referent of photography and the power of producing all of the new images that will be produced as global black consciousness continues to *develop*.

The cookbook form of *Nkombo* (fig. 19) was tied to this aesthetic of the power of collective process. But, as Catherine Michna explains in "We Are Black Mind Jockeys: Tom Dent, the Free Southern Theater, and the Search for a Second-Line Literary Aesthetic in New Orleans" (2011), the use of the cookbook form was a swerve from the typical shape of BAM journals.[36] The black consciousness-raising text that shared this cookbook form was Vertamae Smart-Grosvenor's *Vibration Cooking: Or the Travel Notes of a Geechee Girl* (1970). Smart-Grosvenor explains in her introduction, "The

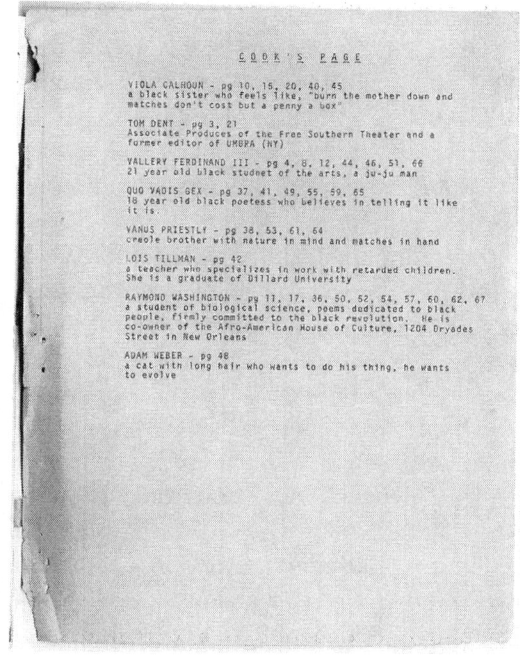

Figure 19. Back page of *Echoes from the Gumbo, Nkombo* 1.1 (1968). *Nkombo* papers, Amistad Research Center, New Orleans.

Demystification of Food," that she "cook[s] by vibration," not strict or fixed recipes.[37] *Nkombo* is a similar type of cookbook, one that is best understood as BLKARTSOUTH's desire to create a journal that was more liquid than solid— a text that would treat the poems and the other works as "ingredients," not as the final dish. These food metaphors reveal the movement's performance of black consumption of blackness and, also, the movement's performance of a "feeding" process, one echoed in the New Orleans poet Mona Lisa Savoy's image of "feeding pages": "I feed pages / words until they speak / the lives I've seen or heard of."[38] The first issue of *Nkombo, Echoes from the Gumbo* (1968), has the explicit form of a cookbook. We might not expect two male editors to decide to use the cookbook form, and the gendered dynamic of the framing of the journal is even more important to consider when we appreciate Quo Vadis Gex's memory of being a "sixteen- or seventeen-year-old girl with these grisly guys and having them kinda influence and change my voice."[39] The cookbook form may signal a partial undoing of the patriarchal discourse of the BAM, but it also may remind us that the decision to name the journal after the Bantu word for gumbo could have simply been based on the "southern orientation" to which Tom Dent refers (the male editors' identification with New Orleans culture).

The role of drama in the the Deep South BAM emerges, in *Nkombo*, when Dent refers, in the preface to the first issue, to the "emerging black stage." The coeditorship of the journal by Salaam and Dent made this "black stage" a breaking of boundaries between the black middle class and the black majority, as art became a means of overcoming the class divide and forging blackness as a unifying concept. Tom Dent, before he betrayed his class position, was set up to be a part of the most privileged African American class in New Orleans. His father was the president of Dillard University. When he returned home after his work with *Umbra* and his graduate studies at Syracuse, he found a new home in the Free Southern Theater and then the BAM. He and Kalamu ya Salaam first met in a Free Southern Theater meeting. Salaam was not running away from a privileged class position; both Dent and Salaam were running with the currents of a social movement. In 1965, as the civil-rights movement flowed into the Black Power movement, they were both, as Salaam writes about Quo Vadis Gex-Breaux, "growing blacker by the minute." "Growing blacker by the minute," for both editors (or "chefs," as they are called in the first issue of *Nkombo*), was a process of growing more and more committed to local and global freedom struggles. It was also a process of making and editing art that was "growing blacker by the minute." The *cooks*, the BLKARTSOUTH writers listed after the chefs in the first issue of *Nkombo*, included men and women, but the women cooks such as Quo Vadis Gex-Breaux were directed by two male chefs whose process of getting "blacker by the minute" was a male-oriented production of taste. In a 2013 interview, Quo Vadis Gex-Breaux explained, "Kalamu gave me a new name, Laini, but it didn't stick. I remained Quo Vadis. My mother made me promise not to change my name."[40] As BLKARTSOUTH's cookbook journal staged the production of taste, some aspects of the chefs' "taste" stuck in the cooks' poems; but many of the poems show that the cultural workers in the movement were not naïve about the subjectivity of taste. A common taste was performed but never entirely achieved. The gumbo of black aesthetics could never become one taste. *Nkombo*, more than many BAM journals, displays the writers' awareness of the different tastes that shaped their production of a collective black aesthetic.

The double layering, in each *Nkombo* issue, of Dent's opening "From the Kitchen" introduction, immediately followed by Salaam's "Food for Thought" introduction, includes many lucid examples of BLKARTSOUTH's strategic mixture of taste, as they created an overarching aesthetic that was much too closely tied to a larger political agenda to be reduced to any individual taste. In one of the double-voiced frames, Dent begins with a full focus on the groundedness of BLKARTSOUTH: "This marks the third issue of NKOMBO. A project now here to stay. The group which produces the magazine is also here to stay, and has widened its activities into what we now call BLKARTSOUTH of the Free Southern Theater."[41] An image of a tree branch shaped like a sun follows the words "Toward Blk unity!" at the end of this introduction. The tone of Kalamu ya Salaam's next editioral move in "Food for Thought" (after Dent's celebratory tone) is explosive. The page is turned and the tree branch shaped like a sun unravels into flames: "[I]t is becoming increasingly difficult to identify what the task of the black writer is other than to write, black artists are highly tuned to and aware of the terrible smell of destruction rampant in this land, black artists know and recognize the terrible oppression daily mounting against our people, it is a difficult task to keep writing, it is difficult to not run into the streets & shoot every white face you see, it is difficult to not become an apathetic nigger who doesn't give a damn about nothing but at the same time it is very beautiful to be alive in these times."[42] Dent's calm and optimistic call for black unity slides without any resistance into Salaam's opening words—"our lives have exploded." The movement between the calm hopefulness and fierce rage is as present in the iconic, signature poem of the movement, Baraka's "Black Art." After the rage, Baraka moves to what sounds like a calm plea: "Poem scream poison gas on beasts in green berets / Clean out the world for virtue and love."[43] As the coeditors shape a politics and aesthetics around rage, pain, love, and pleasure, the issues of *Nkombo* show that identity politics and black aesthetic warfare do not necessarily fix black subjects in a prelapsarian state of woundedness; they can also gesture toward the shifting ground and unreadability of black everyday life. The *Nkombo* issues gain the most depth when they gesture toward the full range of what Nikki Giovanni, in her 1968 poetry volume, calls "Black feeling" (the excessiveness of the mix of black rage, black love, black pain, black humor, black being).[44] This "Black feeling" is not entirely legible in the civil rights–oriented, integrationist Free Southern Theater work but emerges when the Free Southern Theater slides into the Black Power work of BLKARTSOUTH.

Tom Dent announces this need for "black feeling" at the end of *Free Southern Theater by Free Southern Theater*, as he critiques the first stage of the FST's reliance on northern and nonblack scripts in their Deep South performances. Dent ends the book with the call for the very work that BLKARTSOUTH created: "To bring Broadway, off-Broadway, even radical white theater as it exists today in America, to the black community is most irrelevant. It is a statement of negation, if taken too seriously. [I]t is saying, 'What you have ain't shit. If you want to be 'cultured' you got to dig *Godot*.' Well, I say goodbye *Godot*, we'll stick with Otis."[45] Salaam, in *The Magic of Juju*, echoes this call for the post-integrationist work of black self-determination: "One can easily imagine the bemused, if not confused, reaction of sharecroppers in the Mississippi Delta to the [FST's] 1964 production of Samuel Beckett's *Waiting For Godot*. By 1969 FST was all Black and those same Mississippi Delta viewers were literally and profoundly 'moved' by a pre–New York performance of LeRoi Jones' *Slave Ship*. The audience was aroused to militant action. There were actual civil disturbances following the production. Moving its audience to action was an intended goal of this play and of BAM."[46] The Salaam/Dent coeditorshop of *Nkombo* was a vital part of this post-1969 wave of the FST. *Nkombo* was a "post-waiting" move to the textual production of a black cultural revolution.

The Mystical and the Ideological

As the issues of *Nkombo* progress, Dent's voice becomes less subdued. In a 2013 interview, Quo Vadis Gex-Breaux remembers the evolution of Dent's poetry performances. She explains that initially his performances lacked the "rhythm and lyricism in the poems he was reading," but he "grew and became a wonderful reader."[47] The emergence of his voice as *Nkombo* unfolds is a fascinating way to understand the complexity of the class, race, and sexuality entanglements that he was working through as he became one of the core orchestrators of BLKARTSOUTH. In a 1968 letter, Dent performs a self-analysis that shows his own awareness that his decision to dive into black cultural nationalism is overdetermined by these entanglements:

> So often I could see myself drifting into the image of me New Orleans Negroes see: "he's Al Dent's son, rebelling, but that's all he'll ever be." Then the sexual problems start. West Point was so invigorating because they didn't know I was Al Dent's son, if they did they didn't care. [. . .] Sometimes the attacks go like this: "Who are you to presume to have anything to say? You who have been given everything?" Sometimes like this: "You can never be a black writer like the great black writers because they come from nothing into something, their life had a consistent arch upward, you came from money and not poverty, you can never be a part of the 'folk,' only a fakir." [. . .] This kind of stuff brings on sexual and every other kind of trouble.[48]

This letter is written to Dr. Thomas Brayboy, a black psychiatrist who counseled Dent and was a pioneer in 1970s analyses of the effect of oppression on

African American mental health. The "trouble" that Dent refers to without elaborating is a sense of disorientation that makes him feel that "always my search for identity goes on, like a bubbling organism just below the surface occasionally bubbling over."[49] The "search for identity" never stopped; the blackness he embraced during the BAM allowed this "bubbling organism" of identity formation to "bubble over" the surface.

In this same lucid letter, Dent describes his "stronger affinity for black people" as a process of "believing and accepting ideas [he] had merely mouthed before," after his return to New Orleans once his *Umbra* editorial work was finished. He insists that this process of becoming tied to blackness was "mystical," not "ideological": "I say mystically because it was not an ideological development, it happened apart from that without the dedication or resolve of reason. Of course being in New Orleans helped. That is I could *see* again how I had developed, how my esteem for things white, for non-African hair, for non-Negro culture had developed so firmly in New Orleans. It was as if I was coming to an acceptance of myself that was not possible before, a part of my reality."[50] Dent shows that we have failed to recognize that, in the midst of insidious antiblackness, becoming black is a mystical experience, an *unreasonable* new eyesight that cannot be fully explained as a counter-belief system. Returning to the South (and New Orleans in particular) from the North makes an upper middle-class black person discover, in the mid-1960s, a newfound connection with black people. As Dent assumed a prime leadership role in the BAM in the South, he wrote and edited southern BAM literature that is overdetermined by the tension betweeen the mystical experiences of becoming black and an ideological understanding of blackness. He and the southern BAM writers he edited and organized in the BLKART-SOUTH workshops gave a new spin to Toomer's opening words in *Cane* (his "swansong to the South"): "O cant you see it / O cant you see it."[51] They shaped their sense of the black aesthetic around the southern ground that Amiri Baraka, in reference to slavery, has called "the scene of the crime."[52] Form sounds so mystical when Dent writes about the BLKARTSOUTH need to "attempt to fill in vast, unpainted canvases," but he also develops, in his essays, a theory of the transformation of that which seems mystical into an "ideological dimension." He writes, it is "not so much introducing an art form, but of formalizing and reshaping traditions in black culture already present so that they take on an ideological dimension."[53]

In *Nkombo*, the tension between *mystical* black aesthetics and the ideological is dramatized in Salaam's shift, in his "Food for Thought" prefaces, from pro-formlessness proclamations to the idea that what black writers need is control over form, not formlessness. The call for control over form is a call for an understanding of art not as simply political and necessarily ideological, but rather an understanding of the art of Black Power as the mystical transformation and control of the dominant culture forms. The first issue of *Nkombo* included Salaam's poetic tribute to Baraka that situates black people as the *form* that BLKARTSOUTH should use. The full poem, written in 1968, is:

> LEROI
> IS SO TOGETHER
> THAT WHEN HE WRITES
> HE DOES NOT USE A PEN
> HE USES US
> NO PAGES, NO WORDS
> THE STREETS AND SCREAMS
> OF BLACK FOLK ARE THIS
> GREAT POET'S LIBRARY.[54]

This poem is a signature version of the movement's interest in the art of cultural work, life as a work of art. The movement set up a certain type of conceptual art that could be defined as the art of *use*, where use is the performance of ideas that, since they are being *used*, do not settle into the normative object of art. Salaam's tribute to Baraka makes "using us" entirely positive; this call for more "use" sounds like Bill Withers's 1972 song "Use Me": "I want to spread the news / That if it feels this good getting used / Oh, you just keep on using me / Until you use me up."[55]

The Everyday Use of Blackness

Alice Walker's short story "Everyday Use" (1973) explains the power of this *art of use* to critique the art of cultural capital. Walker's role as one of the fiction collectors for *Nkombo* and her correspondence with Tom Dent makes this canonical African American short story a direct way of uncovering the role of BLKARTSOUTH in the larger mobilization of a critique of any collection of black culture that crushes the art of "everyday use." Walker signed her letters to Dent, "Alice in Da Palace." The "palace" was Harvard (where she had a fellow position at the Radcliffe Institute), but the "palace" was also that zone of high-art privilege that Larry Neal simply called "the white thing."[56] Like Salaam's emphasis on an alternative type of library tied to "THE STREETS AND SCREAMS / OF BLACK FOLK," Walker's "Everyday Use" is a critique of the dominant instititions that collect blackness and shape it into a type of cultural capital divorced from the "streets and screams of Black folk." *Nkombo* is the journal that aims to not be the "trunk" that the college-educated sister, in "Everyday Use," "rifles through" as she tries to collect the quilt and other material that only becomes beautiful and black, for her, when it is removed from the inner black home space and framed by the new black consciousness that her mother and sister, in her estimation, fail to understand.[57] Walker's use of the words "rifling through" signals the violence of the black bourgeois cultural-nationalist appropriation of black southern folk material.

One year after the publication of "Everday Use," Walker's poetry became a part of the "use of us" gumbo that Salaam and Dent created in *Nkombo*. Her poem "The Labels Slip Sometimes" was published in the final issue of *Nkombo*. Like Dent and Salaam, Walker was committed to collecting the art of the black South. In her letters to Dent, she expresses her excitement about BLKARTSOUTH and her role as a collector for the planned fiction issue. When she submitted "The Labels Slip Sometimes," she asked Dent to publish the poem if he could "believe" it.[58] Their fondness for each other is clear in their correspondence. Dent sent his feedback on *The Third Life of Grange Copeland*, and Walker's response shows that she saw Dent as an ideal reader.[59] The poem, and its inclusion in *Nkombo*, offers a fascinating way of thinking about the role, during the BAM, of black skepticism about the usefulness of the names and labels used to mobilize collective black consciousness. This skepticism does not only surface after the movement. Walker's "The Labels Slip Sometimes," like other poems in *Nkombo*, shapes skepticism into much more than a post-black sentiment. Skepticism leads Walker to see pro-blackness in subjects who, on the surface, seem to be counterrevolutionary. Walker's gathering of each example of the performances that are hard to label, after the opening lines "The labels slip / Sometimes," are linked by her repetition of the word "and."[60] The poem creates a sense of the addition that cannot lead to closure. Walker asks Dent in one of her letters, "What are you collecting?"[61] The wonder of the collection process (with all the optimism, skepticism, pleasure, and frustration that shape the process of collecting what remains *unknown*) connects Walker, Dent, and Salaam when their missions converge in BLKARTSOUTH.

These collectors understood the power of "cut interpellation"—Fred Moten's term, for the type of assemblage in which the process of "frames cutting frames" does not create a fixed frame but rather a process of more cutting.[62] In the final issue of *Nkombo*, Dent and Salaam's prefaces announce the ending of BLKARTSOUTH, a revisiting of the goals of the collective, and an opening up of space. Dent explains this opening up of space as, partially, the opening up of space for black writers in anthologies not focused on the South (anthologies that reprinted poems that originally appeared in *Nkombo*). The opening up of space can also be seen in the placement of a series of Quo Vadis Gex-Breaux's poems at the very beginning of this final issue. Dent emphasizes (in "From the Kitchen") that Quo Vadis Gex-Breaux is one of the poets who should be more well known. In the first of her poems in this final issue, "Song to Be Sung for Poets," Gex-Breaux writes, "Poets have to be word motions, / i mean be living words / blk life is not about paper."[63] This antitextual emphasis is one of the most insightful BAM descriptions of black conceptual art (art that is more concerned with process and ideas than being an actual "work of art"). If "blk life is not about paper," the black poem becomes a push beyond the limits of the "paper," an antitext push that takes Gex-Breaux to the mysticism that Dent describes when he explains that his post-*Umbra* falling in love with blackness was not ideological but mystical. Gex-Breaux captures this mysticism by referring, as Larry Neal often did, to the weirdness of the black aesthetic.[64] Toward the end of the poem, Gex-Breaux writes, "Ain't it strange the things / we decide that words must be / hammers to the brain / walking shoes for the lame / blood thru the veins / man what a shame."[65] These words—"Ain't it strange the things / we decide words must do"—become the refrain in the final three stanzas. This direct focus on the strangeness of the black aesthetic movement, in the opening poem in the final issue of *Nkombo*, testifies to the winking (the productive playfulness) in the BAM. The winking effect hovers when we hear the speaker wondering how exactly would words leap off the page and become the concrete objects she lists—the hammers, walking shoes, and blood. "The wonder, the wonder" are the subtextual words, the affect the poem produces.

Immediately following this poem, on the same page, there is an abstract drawing by the Ethiopian artist Skunder Boghossian, who was deeply involved in BLKARTSOUTH. The sense of wonder embedded in the poem leads Gex-Breaux to the abstraction that she calls "word motion." She ends the poem with a chant: "But poets must be word motions / poets must be word motions." The abstraction in the drawing also has a clear sense of motion as Skunder's lines gesture toward the idea of a person bending down and flexing her or his muscles in a downward position that makes the hands almost reach the feet, which look more like hands. The drawing is too abstract to be only understood in this manner. The possibility of the flexing of the muscles can be seen as easily as we can see the rounded arms that, instead of a flexing of the muscles, could be an embrace. And the hands are holding uprooted vegetation: the rhizome, the web of roots, may be the most strikingly delicate part of this drawing. The open space between the ground and the uplifted roots could be read as AfriCOBRA's principle of mimesis at midpoint (as the drawing blends the abstract and the representational).

The sense of wonder that this drawing and Gex's poem "Song to be Sung for Poets" evokes is a fitting frame for the mixing of forms that shape this entire final issue. As BLKARTSOUTH ends, Dent and Salaam make the mixing of forms matter much more than it does in the earlier issues. Poetry, in this final issue, cannot be separated from drawings, photography, short stories, and journal entries. This opening up of the meaning of poetry shows that the BAM was, as Greg Thomas argues, "redefining poetry as a generic name for 'Art' or creativity itself [. . .] Poesis, not poetry narrowly construed."[66] *Nkombo*'s final issue is a full celebration of the power of poetry to expand into black conceptual art with the force of what in the larger conceptual art movement, in one of the Fluxus manifestos, is described as the "revolutionary flood and tide in art" that "promote living art, anti-art [. . .] NON ART REALITY to be fully grasped by all peoples, not only critics, dilettantes and professionals."[67] The use of photography by Roy Lewis and Larry Songy, in this final issue, pushes the poems and the other written literature to this level of the *real*. But the photographs convey a certain sense of the real that makes people experience "non-art reality" as the "revolutionary flood" of the black aesthetic experience. Larry Songy's photograph, on the back cover, of a trumpet player holding his instrument in his lap makes the not playing, the resting between sets, into a poetic interlude. This image of silence is not silent. The sense of suspension takes us back to the AfriCOBRA principle of mimesis at midpoint. The representational force of the photograph is the stubborn referent of the hands that are holding the trumpet in such a loving, anticipatory manner. In Songy's photograph, the move to a partial type of abstraction is the unknown nature of the sound that will be made once the hands lift the trumpet. The abstract drawing on the front cover of this final issue (fig. 20) is the co-framing image that makes this photograph seem more tied to abstraction than most photography. The editors' opening up of poetry from a bourgeois understanding of art as an object of cultural capital makes the abstract blend into the representational. The mixing of poetry, prose, and visual images make the amorphous gumbo into a representational force, not a mixing for mixing's sake.

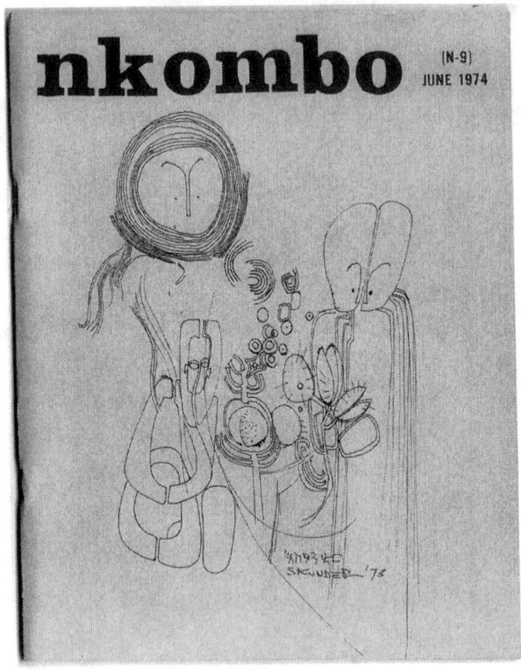

Figure 20. Cover of *Nkombo* 9 (1974). *Nkombo* papers, Amistad Research Center, New Orleans.

Living as Form

At the very end of this final issue, David Henderson's "Jass Funeral" (1967), a prose-poem journal entry on a New Orleans jazz funeral, shares a two-page spread with a photograph of a second line, taken by Larry Songy (fig. 21). This word-and-image interplay embodies the full spirit of the process-oriented, anti-object art that Dent and Salaam set in motion in *Nkombo*. Henderson, in the closing sentence of the prose poem, describes two people dancing and shaking as they take photographs of a New Orleans second line—a jazz funeral procession. The photographers cannot produce the work of art (the photographs) without being a part of this living art form. Henderson writes: "We followed the parade for about a mile. Bob and Yvette joined the parade with their cameras taking pictures of the jiggers and jigging and shaking as they took the pictures as if they were second lining on the other side of a mirror."[68] Second lines are communal processions that often gain new dancers, walkers, and shakers as the procession continues—an apt symbol of the power of the not-yet-finished, the power that Dent and Salaam foregrounded as they made the *Nkombo* issues so closely tied to process and collaboration. Henderson's image of the two-way mirror captures the BAM

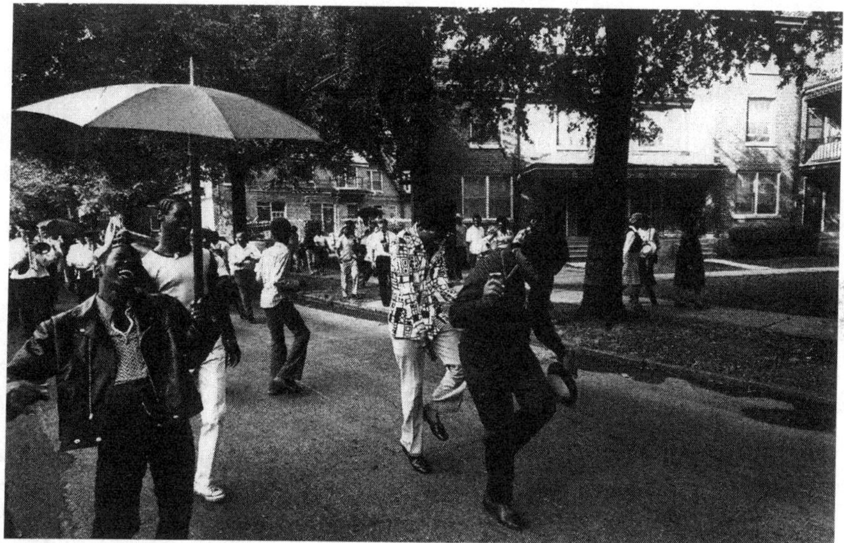

Figure 21. Photograph of a second line, by Larry Songy, ca. 1975. Tom Dent papers, Amistad Research Center, New Orleans.

struggle to find a type of art that would not create a distance between black artists and black "folk."

When Dent and Salaam allow the frame of David Henderson's words to "cut the frame" of Larry Songy's photographs, so much is produced in the break. Like the photographers Henderson describes, Songy seems to be "jigging and shaking as [he] took the pictures." It is hard to look at the photographs and not feel that the bodily gestures and movements arrested by the camera's lens actually exceed the lens and that art (whether photography or literature or mixed forms) really can be "living art." As Henderson describes the "beautiful happy feeling exud[ing] from the procession," his ethnography of the second-line funeral procession becomes a powerful recognition that the second liners reshaped the dead form of a funeral into a living form. Henderson's repetition of the words "Tom tells me" situates Tom Dent as Henderson's guide to black New Orleans, the native informant who pulls this northerner into BLKARTSOUTH. "Jass Funeral" is Henderson's recognition that the art of this southern movement had an everyday performative, living dimension that was even more heightened than the performance edge of other BAM circles. In this prose poem, the embrace of life in the very zone of death is comparable to Dent and Salaam's determination in all of the *Nkombo* issues, and especially this last one, to make poetry a living form that cannot be deadened through any attempt to separate the more formalist poems from the more experimental, seemingly less crafted ones. The range of poetic styles included in this final issue makes it clear that, as Salaam explained in a 2013 interview, they "were trying to make room for everyone."[69]

When we view the art of black consciousness-raising as an attempt to "make room" in the category "art" for all forms and styles, the power of black aesthetics is then the power of letting the range of expression unsettle the category to such an extent that a core idea ("blackness") that animates the art is just as important as, if not more important than, the form of the particular work of art. In other words, in the process of opening up the poetry so that it becomes poesis, the BLKARTSOUTH members discovered black conceptual art. The last issue of *Nkombo* performs this black conceptual art through a focus on the concept of the second line. In the final pages of this final issue of *Nkombo*, as the poetry lines move to Larry Songy's photograph of a second line, the editors produce a second-line effect of black aesthetics—the idea that black aesthetic tradition invites people to join a moving, bouncing, and bending formation. Songy's photograph of second-line dancing makes the dance through the New Orleans streets appear to be a dancing out of the frame of the camera's lens. The next dancing moves of the second liners look like they will make these photographed subjects break out of the photograph, the art object, in order to become a most alive form. This movement out of the art objects into the "art of living as form"[70] also explains the editors' interest in including Henderson's journal entries (the prose poems such as "Jass Funeral"). The prose poetry of the journal entries, more than the poetry, the short stories, and interviews, embodies the spirit of living as form. Henderson's 1967 experiences in New Orleans become a part of the BLKARTSOUTH's production of the gumbo of black aesthetics.

In the listing of the contributors' biographies on the final page, Henderson is described as "the Berkeley poet, author of DE MAYOR OF HARLEM." The biographical note then explains, "These sketches were written in 1967 when he was in New Orleans. They are previously unpublished." As Dent emphasizes in his opening "From the Kitchen," Nkombo gave many writers a new visibility, but it also gave writers like David Henderson a new black southern audience. When this last issue was published, Henderson was the editor in chief of *Umbra* and an established writer, but *Nkombo*'s publication of these "sketches" made him, and other non-southern black writers, the unsettled voices that moved *through* the southern landscape of the BAM and left work that actually marked and shaped the regional specificity of the BAM southern movement.

The Black Arts Global South

In 1974, as Dent and Salaam were editing the final issue of *Nkombo*, David Henderson was editing the "Latin Soul" issue of *Umbra*. The simultaneity of these journal productions of the southern and Latin Soul orientations of the BAM underscores that, by the 1970s, the movement was reshaping "It's Nation Time" into these more specific spaces of consciousness—"It was *Latin Soul* timee" and "It was *Black South* time." Henderson's involvement in both the 1974 issue of *Nkombo* and the 1974 issue of *Umbra* accentuates the ties to *Umbra* that Dent never lost. After Dent's 1962–65 period of being one of the founders of *Umbra*, he did not simply abandon the New York scene and gain the southern Black Arts orientation. The avant-garde energy of his *Umbra* years stayed with him, and his ongoing ties with Henderson are one way of understanding the multidirectional flow between the New York/California *Umbra* energy and the New Orleans scene. The blackening of *Umbra* as the 1960s progressed (the move from the interracial avant-garde energy to a more heightened focus on black aesthetics) parallels the blackening of Free Southern Theatre that led to the use of the name "BLKARTSOUTH." When the two 1974 journal issues are compared, the common ground is the feeling of a collection process that is bursting at the seams (the sense that both the art of "Black South" and the art of "Latin Soul" dislodge any fixed frame).

Nkombo was a cookbook approach to the gumbo of the BAM in the South, and the thick "Latin Soul" issue of *Umbra* was a gumbo that made blackness inseparable from the "Latin." The "soul," in the issue's title was the *mixing* force that allowed Henderson to do what Kalamu ya Salaam posits as the goal of *Nkombo*—to "make room for everything." The Global South dimension of this *Umbra* issue, when compared to the U.S. black South dimension of *Nkombo*, does not seem entirely different. Both issues show the groundedness (the embrace of the local) and also the expansiveness (the global dimensions) of the BAM. Dent's desire (as expressed in his 1969 letter to Calvin Hernton) to "add a southern orientation" to the "Black Arts concept" makes his editing of *Nkombo* a work of local cosmopolitanism. Henderson's image, in "Jass Funeral," of a visiting, non-southern black artist "jigging with the jigging," as his camera creates art about the black South second-line dancers, shows that local cosmopolitanism and Edouard Glissant's "rooted wandering" guided the BAM practice of moving frames (literally the trembling hands on the cameras). Rooted wandering (jigging *with* the jiggers, not making a museum exhibit out of the jigging) is the editorial practice that makes Tom Dent's early years as an editor of *Umbra* flow into his later editorial work with *Nkombo* and into Henderson's editing of *Umbra*.

The editors' use of word-and-image interplays makes the simultaneous 1974 publication of the final issue of *Nkombo* and the "Latin Soul" issue of *Umbra* become the textual production of global black aesthetics as that which is produced through a gumbo that makes photography, line drawings, poetry, and prose blend into the open space of black conceptual (process-oriented) art. Throughout the *Nkombo* final issue, the tension between the line drawings and the photographs is a constant experimentation with worrying the lines between what has been seen, captured, and understood and what remains to be known, what remains outside the lines of any attempt to contain black aesthetics. In The "Latin Soul" *Umbra* issue, a poem by Sam Cornish, "Marcus," has the weight of an aesthetic manifesto theorizing black aesthetic counter-literacy. The subtitle of the poem is "A Student Who Writes Backwards and Sits Close to Me Even If I Am Reading Dr. Seuss." This poem dramatizes the trauma and insight of a black child, who, while watching a teacher read and point to a book's visual images, yearns to find language that would enable black people to live fuller lives. The poem makes the word-and-image interplay signal the move from language for language's sake to language as action. The child tries to speak into existence the pictures to which the teacher points, but he cannot produce any sounds. The teacher who feels this closeness to the child, with the aphasia and seeming illiteracy, looks at his eyes and thinks that "he seems to say how do people live like this."[71] The child has an urgent need to find a counter-literacy (he writes backwards, as the subtitle tells us). In the "Latin Soul" special issue and the final issue of *Nkombo*, the counter-literacy of words mixing with images is the editors' means of dramatizing the counter-literacy of global black consciousness.

The Global South community of black aesthetics that *Nkombo* and Umbra imagined was not a textual production of community that fully coincided with the direct affiliation of individual writers with the BAM. The journal issues' textual production of a community of writers *in* the movement included some who were not in the movement in the manner that the editors were. Sam Cornish, for example, was not, like Dent, Salaam, and Henderson, a part of the leadership of organizations and journals directly tied to the BAM, and his later explanations of his role in the BAM signal that he was in the movement but not *of* it. Although his work is included in *Black Fire*, the signature anthology of the movement, and he is now often described as one of the most underappreciated writers of the movement, his own retrospective view of the movement sees it as too narrow to include poetry like his. When we do not look through this quick and easy way of seeing the movement, we discover the real value of the gumbo that the journals produced. Just as, in the final issue of *Nkombo*, Dent and Salaam place Henderson's experimental prose poetry alongside much less experimental poems such as Richard Haley's "To My Son on His Twelfth Birthday," which immediately follows "Jass Funeral," Henderson's own *Umbra* editorial practice juxtaposes Cornish's work with poems that perform the black rage from which Cornish separates himself in the twenty-first century.

Cecil Brown's untitled poem, for example, appears a few pages before Cornish's poem "After Teaching My Students Fill Me with Images." Brown's poem performs a direct message about the need for black power and calls for "black words." The notion of "black words" is an example of the rhetoric that seemingly represents the BAM's overdetermined political use of art. But this poem about "black words," when compared to Cornish's poem, is much more complicated than it appears on the surface. The call for "black words" becomes not only a call for black power; the poem is also a reclamation of "black words" as a type of sustenance. The rage in this poem is less pronounced than the emphasis on the need for words that can "fill one up." In "After Teaching My Students Fill Me with Images," Cornish's meditation on students is a similar recognition that the art of black consciousness-raising feeds a certain hunger and a need to feel grounded (in the midst of the black homelessness that global white supremacy creates). But the gumbo of black aesthetics, in *Nkombo* and "Latin Soul" *Umbra*, feeds this hunger in different ways. Cornish may not now see his work as being tied to this gumbo, but it is as tied to the black aesthetic gumbo as the movement poetry that he critiques as too reactionary.

The early issues of *Umbra* are a prelude to the BAM (the Umbra workshop was one of the roots of the BAM), but the 1974 "Latin Soul" issue is a full-fledged BAM production that is only on the edge of the movement if we fail to see how *Umbra*'s pre-BAM avant-garde energy evolved into *Umbra*'s avant-garde approach to the BAM. The focus on the black Global South in these issues seems to push the editors to a recognition of that which cannot be captured; the global dimension overwhelmed and produced a heightened sense of the ineffable. Victor Hernandez Cruz's poem "Walking Faces" is the gem that shines brightest in the "Latin Soul" issue, as a meditation on the unknowability that shapes the power of the global black consciousness of these issues of *Nkombo* and *Umbra*. For readers who do not know Cruz's poem "African Things" (1973), it may be difficult to read "Walking Faces" as a reflection on the role of Africanness in Latino/a identity and cultural formation.[72] When read slant-wise with "African Things," the word "it" in "Walking Faces" is a vague pronoun that gestures to Africa: "It comes here now / and sits beside me / This old thing that I once knew / We stare at each other." "African Things," with its direct reference to the "black & shiny / grandmother" who is being asked to "speak to me & tell me of african things" and "dance & tell me black african things," performs the intentional work of excavating "black african things." But "Walking Faces" is the work of living with an "old thing that I once knew." Cruz does not make it easy for us to name this "old thing that I once knew" as the "black african things" in the poem "African Things," but Henderson's inclusion of "Walking Faces" in *Umbra* encourages readers to interpret the references to the unknowable as subtle gestures to the lived, everyday experience of the unknowable that can produce the deepest, most sensitive registers of feeling Afro-Latino/a or feeling black.

In Baraka's introduction to David Henderson's 1967 poetry volume *Felix of the Silent Forest*, he describes "Black Poetry" in the following manner: "The sensitive collect and carry. [. . .] The Black Poetry is a sensitivity to the world total, to the American total. It is *about*, or *is* feeling(s). Even governmental structures are made the way people *feel* they should be made."[73] With these words, Baraka captures the reason why the "collection" of black art in *Nkombo* and *Umbra* should not be separated from the "collection" process that *Callaloo* continues in the twenty-first century.

Charles Rowell's interviews with BAM writers in *Callaloo* are some of the most "sensitive" collections we have of the BAM. In *Angles of Ascent*, Rowell sets the younger, "post-1960s" poets apart from the BAM, but this framing of BAM poetics (as that which twenty-first-century black poetics aspires *not* to be) belies the feeling of sensitivity that can "collect and carry" forward, without any *insensitve* repudiation. Baraka's notion of "sensitivity" that can "collect and carry" forward is the spirit of black post-blackness. Any framing of the BAM must acknowledge the depth of the editorial practices that produced black aesthetics as the power of the not yet finished. This aesthetic of the unfinished was the spirit of *Nkombo* and the original collaborative, BAM-inspired editing of the first issue of *Callaloo*, and it is the spirit of Rowell's twenty-first-century editing of *Callaloo*, as this thriving, prominent journal continues to gather some of the most innovative diasporic literature that is black post-black.

5

The Satire of Black Post-Blackness

You're dealing with a silly man.

—Malcolm X

Satire and what Ralph Ellison described as the "extravagance of laughter" is defining twenty-first-century African American literature and visual art.[1] Writers such as Percival Everett, Paul Beatty, Mat Johnson, and Colson Whitehead are producing as much satire and unexpected, blasphemous laughter as visual artists such as Glenn Ligon, Kara Walker, Kerry James Marshall, and Mickalene Thomas. But this extravagance of laughter also shaped the Black Arts Movement. The satire of the 1970s second wave of the BAM anticipated much of the satirical play with imagining the unimaginable and unnaming that shapes twenty-first-century black aesthetics. In *Laughter: Notes on a Passion* (2010), Anca Parvulescu writes, "Laughter is a response to hailing, raising crucial questions about the very notion of response. For what is a response? What does it mean to respond, and especially to respond properly?"[2] The *response* of laughter in the BAM and twenty-first-century black aesthetics is closely tied to the dodging of seemingly inevitable hailing processes that cancel out the sheer pleasure of the simultaneity of feeling black and post-black.

In "The Path Cleared by Amiri Baraka" (2014), Jelani Cobb states, "Reading these lines [from *Home*, Baraka's 1966 essay collection] now, in an era defined by a black Presidency, the kill-whitey rhetoric has an almost comic undertone."[3] The "kill-whitey rhetoric" of the BAM was partially comical even during the BAM itself. The satire in Ishmael Reed's *Mumbo Jumbo* (a text that clings to the BAM without becoming a BAM novel) builds on the satire in many BAM poems and plays. Through the lens of *Mumbo Jumbo*, we can rediscover the lost, often unrecognized satire in the BAM. After my analysis of *Mumbo Jumbo*'s connection to BAM satire, I compare Paul Beatty's twenty-first-century *Slumberland*, Percival Everett's twenty-first-century *Percival Everett by Virgil Russell*, and a range of BAM satire and BAM-inspired satire, as I uncover satire as one of the most expressive forms for the difficult task of making black post-blackness legible.

In Ishmael Reed's novel *Mumbo Jumbo* (1972), the narrator describes the movement of Jes Grew, the plague that can upset Western Civilization as it spreads an alternative way of being, a way of dancing and a larger counter-aesthetic that the "Atonists" and the "Wallflower Order" struggle to contain. The character Papa LaBas explains: "Jes Grew which began in New Orleans has reached Chicago. They are calling it a plague when in fact it is an anti-plague. I know what it's after; it has no definite route yet but the configuration it is forming indicates it will settle in New York. It won't stop until it cohabits with what it's after. Then it will be a pandemic and you will really see something. And then *they* will be finished."[4] Reed never defines Jes Grew as black aesthetics; he leaves it undefined, as if he is suggesting that blackness itself cannot de pinned down. In *The Signifying Monkey: A Theory of African American Literary Criticism*, Henry Louis Gates reminds readers that *Mumbo Jumbo* has been read as an "allegory of the Black Arts Movement," but the novel is more aptly read as a satire of the fear of black aesthetics unbound and of any attempt (whether by white external forces or the less motion-oriented forces in the BAM) to freeze the jazz of black aesthetics unbound.[5]

Reed ends *Mumbo Jumbo* with an image of the "pendulum" that connects the 1920s and the 1970s. The 1960s era of the BAM is separated from the early 1970s era of the BAM, as Reed imagines the different responses each decade gives to the Harlem Renaissance lecture that Papa LaBas continues to deliver. Reed writes, "People in the sixties said they couldn't follow him. [. . .] In the 20s they knew. And the 20s were back again. Better. Arna Bontemps was correct in his new introduction to *Black Thunder*. Time is a pendulum. Not a river. More akin to what goes around comes around" (218). The pendulum swing between the 1920s and the 1970s produces what Baraka, in the poem "Return of the Native," calls the "BangClash" of "vicious modernism."[6] In *Mumbo Jumbo*, the earliest decade of the BAM is depicted as the "Black bangclash," whereas the 1970s (and its 1920s swing backward) is the blackness that "jes grew" before and after the bangclash. The imaging of the first wave (1960s) of the BAM is encapsulated in the following passage: "A new generation is coming on the scene. They will use terms like 'nitty gritty,' 'for real,' 'where's it at,' and use words like 'basic' and 'really' with telling emphasis. They will extend the letter and the meaning of the word 'bad.' [. . .] They will shout loudly about soul because they will have lost it. And their protests will be a shriek. A panic sound. [. . .] No, he will get it across. And he will be known as the man who 'got it across'" (39). Reed, from the vantage point of the early 1970s, looks back at the 1960s BAM. The 1920s character Abdul Hamid anticipates the arrival of this "new generation" and anticipates the language of "post-soul" that emerges in the 1990s as a way of describing the period after the civil-rights movement. Reed describes the BAM participants as "post-soul," as those who "shout loudly about soul because they have lost it." In this post-soul movement imagined by Reed, the loss of soul propels the movement's determination to claim their soulfulness. This Soul Power movement is figured as the insistence on soul in spite of a post-soul condition. This formulation of the soulful post-soul is very similar to Reed's description of the unnamed blackness of Jes Grew as that which "won't stop until it cohabits with what it's after" (25). Blackness "just grows" into what comes after it; blackness cannot stop moving until it gains its own afterlife. Blackness needs a future in order to have a present. Jes Grew is an "anti-plague" because it does not kill; it allows blackness to be a state of cohabitation (the cohabitation of *being* and *becoming*).

Lurking Late in *Mumbo Jumbo*

When Ishmael Reed ends *Mumbo Jumbo* with the reading of the 1970s as a better version of the Harlem Renaissance, what he calls "Afro Satire" (words used in *Mumbo Jumbo* itself) becomes a particular form of black laughter that "lurks late," that holds on to the anticipation that shaped the awakening of black aesthetics in the Harlem Renaissance (the anticipation tied to doing something sneaky and subversive).[7] Gwendolyn Brooks's words "we lurk late" in the poem "We Real Cool" capture this *sneaky* second-wave BAM satire. The 1970s wave of the BAM differs from the 1960s BAM, as a kind of post-prelude. The mood of the 1970s is a heightened sense of black post-blackness, and this mood of being in the middle of the second wave is depicted, at the end of *Mumbo Jumbo*, as being similar to the mood of anticipation in the 1920s. When Reed sees the 1970s as a better version of the 1920s, he is realizing that after the 1960s testing ground of black aesthetics, people were "waiting" for the next step. They were "lurking late," as they began to lean into the unbound nature of black aesthetics, the way that blackness consolidates and also keeps moving.

Reed's inclusion of a photograph of Black Panthers in motion is one of the most vivid depictions, in *Mumbo Jumbo*, of the militancy of "lurking late" (the way in which the mood of "lurking late" makes the satire in *Mumbo Jumbo* much more than the laughter that aims to simply entertain). In the passage that includes the words "Afro satire," Reed draws out this militant black wit. He writes, "They [the European colonists satirized by the African artists] did not realize that the joke was on them. After all, how could 'primitive' people possess wit" (97). In a 1973 essay in *Black World*, titled "The Sardonic Vision: Wit and Irony in Militant Black Poetry," Ruthe Sheffey situates this militant wit as a core part of the BAM ethos. Sheffey poses the question, "Can satire be put to revolutionary use?"[8] Hoyt Fuller's inclusion of this essay in *Black World* signals that he, like Sheffey, recognized that satire was at the core of the most complex dynamics of BAM literature. The BAM satirizing of whiteness was a crucial part of the movement's attempt to weaken its hypnotic spell and create room for black people to discover the power of the black gaze.

When Reed satirizes Harlem Renaissance poetry in *Mumbo Jumbo*, he opens up a way of reading BAM poetry as revolutionary satire. The BAM satirized whiteness and also black style without substance. Reed's depiction of the white character "Safecracker" performing the poem "Harlem Tom Toms" in blackface (to a "high society" black audience) foregrounds the BAM focus on black people needing to recover their own faces underneath the layers of blackface. The structural layers in *Mumbo Jumbo* (the hodgepodge mixing of fragmented narratives and images) can be read as the layers that we would have to learn to read through in order to find the lecture that PaPa LaBas waits to deliver to the "classroom that knew what he was talking about" (218). The lecture is about the Harlem Renaissance (the unnameable force of "Jes Grew") and is the face, the dance, and mumbo jumbo underneath the layers of blackface text. The lecture waiting to be delivered is the text that LaBas realizes must be stolen from those who stole the archives. Learning to see the satire in BAM poetry is comparable to the process of learning to read the blackface poem "Harlem Tom Toms" not as satirizing black aesthetics but as mocking the white, "safe-cracker" attempt to tame radical black sound. Many BAM poems gain the energy of revolutionary satire when they make people *face* blackness and recognize the blackface of white power. The interiority of blackness emerges as the extravagance and depth of black laughter. In many BAM satirical poems, the tension of facing blackness in the midst of ongoing blackface is deeply connected, as it is in *Mumbo Jumbo*, to a radical anticipation of a *post-white* world that remains to be seen—a lurking late that Baraka performs with the clearest vision when he chants, "It's Nation Tiiiiieyeime," after insisting "Get up Santa Claus," in his iconic BAM poem "It's Nation Time" (1970).[9] In *Mumbo Jumbo*, post-whiteness is figured as the real effect of Jes Grew if it is not contained. The satire of whiteness in "It's Nation Time" is the call for Santa Claus "to get up." Baraka chants, "Get up Santa Claus Get up. . . . It's Nation Time." The humor of the Santa Claus reference produces action (getting up).

This note of furious anticipation of the next movement ("Nation Time") is the final note of *Mumbo Jumbo*. Another conciliatory "Santa Claus" figure wants PaPa LaBas to teach the classics and "come clean with those students" (217). This conservative figure has great ambivalence about Jes Grew. He cannot embrace the post-whiteness that allows PaPa LaBas, as he thinks about his lecture, to lean on *Black Thunder*, Arna Bontemps's book that reminds LaBas that the time of black aesthetics is "what goes around comes around," a dialectic of black post-blackness that constantly produces more and more of the Jes Grew. LaBas is "lurking late," but the "old man" is lurking "scared" about the young people's lack of the knowledge of Western classics (217). In *Digging: The Afro-American Soul of American Classical Music*, Baraka declares that jazz is black classical music; like Papa LaBas, he has no need to hold on to Western Civilization. Like the *Mu'tafikah* depicted in *Mumbo Jumbo*, Baraka is ready to seize the stolen goods from the Western museums and build the counter-archive Reed builds in his mixing and sampling throughout *Mumbo Jumbo*.

The satirizing of whiteness in BAM poetry is also tied to this readiness to let whiteness go. The purging gains a new force when connected to Frantz Fanon's description, in *The Wretched of the Earth*, of the laughter that can vomit up what black colonized people have been forced to swallow: "The violence with which the supremacy of white values is affirmed and the aggressiveness which has permeated the victory of these values over the ways of life and of thought of the native mean that, in revenge, the native laughs in mockery when Western values are mentioned in front of him. In the colonial context the settler only ends his work of breaking in the native when the latter admits loudly and intelligibly the supremacy of the white man's values. In the period of decolonization, the colonized masses mock at these very values, insult them, and vomit them up."[10] According to Fanon, laughter that is tied to decolonizing the mind makes white supremacy visible in a way that other forms of expression cannot. In the most viciously satiric BAM poems, this subversive laughter unveils the "mumbo jumbo" that masquerades as white superiority.

The satirizing of whiteness also leads to a satirizing of blackness, which is not only a satire of black people performing whiteness but also a satire of some performances of blackness that fail to locate a black interior. In the anthology *The Black Seventies* (1970), Larry Neal argues:

We reversed the Manichean dualism that placed the symbolism of Blackness on the side of Evil, and whiteness on the side of Good.

This was a necessary reversal. But it led to some contradictions, the most important of which was that our nationalism could not exist primarily in contra-distinction to white nationalism. We could never hope to develop a viable concept of self, if that concept were purely based on hating crackers. We had to really dig each other, for each other, on our own terms and on the basis of the common emotional history and identity that we shared. The primary focus of our emotional energies would have to be black people. [. . .] Black people know how to relate to white people; that part of the survival kit is cooled out. But us relating to each other, that's another thing.[11]

The 1970s BAM satirizing of blackness is best understood through the lens that Neal offers. This anthology shows that, by the early 1970s, people in the movement were thinking deeply about the new wave; they wanted the 1970s to take the BAM to a greater focus on moving away from whiteness to the black interior. Neal uses the term "nation" as he explains that, by the 1970s, it was clear to the most committed and liberation-seeking people in the movement that "nation," not only a reclamation of blackness, had to be the focus. When Neal explains that in the "black seventies" the lingering work was black people learning how to "relate to each other," the emphasis on "nation-building" (in this same essay) then becomes Neal's call for a black "emotional" interior and, also, a focus on the political realities of a need for a nation (as opposed to remaining in the state of black oppression that the movement often referred to as the "black colony").

Laughter may be a powerful way in which black people move to the black emotional interior, which can, as Neal proposes, make us see the larger political work of actual black empowerment (the political and economic power that the words "black nation" captured in BAM rhetoric). Neal's sense that the "black seventies" is the time of the BAM moving to another stage (where the focus is on black people trying to learn to know each other) begs to be compared to the description, in *Mumbo Jumbo*, of black people in the 1970s having more insight than in the 1960s. Like Neal, Reed envisions the 1970s as a "new space" (Neal's words) that is deeper than the 1960s black consciousness-raising. But Reed's imaging of these matters adds a different dimension to Neal's essay. Reed adds the 1920s and 1970s connection, as he shapes the "new space" of the 1970s around the 1920s. The Harlem Renaissance emerges as the "old space" that Reed foregrounds in order to make *Mumbo Jumbo* pivot on a theory of blackness as that which has coalesced and also has yet to coalesce, as a looking back and a looking forward.

The revolutionary nature of the black satire that Reed sets up is the novel's ultimate privileging of the uncontainable nature of Jes Grew. In a similar sense, when we read Ed Bullins's short play *The Theme Is Blackness* (1966) as satire, the laughter produced when blackness is announced by the speaker but does not appear (at least in a bodily form) recognizes the uncontainable nature of blackness.[12] When we read this play through the lens of the "lurking late," 1970s mood, the play gains a new dimension: the waiting for blackness to arrive is a full focus on the anticipation of an arrival that will be more than what people expect to see, the sense that blackness is going to be harder to pin down or even experience in a visual sense. The move to the sonic (the free jazz used in the first performances of the play) is a move not only to that which seems to be less containable than words or the visual; the use of sound in the play's space of anticipation is also a move to sound as a particular way of making people experience black post-blackness. If the "theme" is blackness, the "sound" is black post-blackness—that which can never be as concrete and fixed as a "theme." When blackness is treated as a sonic experience—in this play and other BAM texts, such as Baraka's introduction to Larry Neal's *Black Boogaloo* and Reed's "on the edge of the BAM" *Mumbo Jumbo*—the unboundedness of blackness fully emerges.[13] When Baraka, in the introduction to the 2007 edition of *Black Fire*, explains that that the BAM was bound to end because "black" is not an ideology, he implies that the most progressive post-BAM maneuvers would be a movement that added an "ideology" (a theory of resistance) to black cultural nationalism.[14] For Baraka, that next step was what he called "Third World Marxism." When Baraka, in some of his last writings, such as "A Post-Racial Anthology?" (2013), continued to rage against attempts to read the BAM as a movement that did not produce meaningful art, his post-BAM stage of Third World Marxism was built on his investment in radical black aesthetics.[15] The satire that took Baraka and other BAM writers to critiques of blackness being treated as something that can be as pinned down as an ideology is similar to the satirical spirit of twenty-first-century African American literature.

Satirizing the End of Blackness

Paul Beatty's novel *Slumberland* (2008) begins with an announcement of the end of blackness: "blackness has officially been declared passé."[16] The narrator is a DJ and musician who creates sounds that signal this "official" end of blackness. Sound, not the legal structure implied by the language of the "official," is the posterizing or space-clearing gesture. For Beatty, sound is the force that can disrupt the visual logic of race.

Just as Baraka, in his introduction to Neal's *Black Boogaloo*, asserts that "sound is what we deal in," Beatty finds that playing with what makes sound seem black or not black is an ideal frame for a satire of the end of blackness.[17] In one passage, Beatty connects the end of blackness to sounds that seem to have an "indeterminate blackness." These words capture the seriousness beneath the raging humor in this novel. Beatty wants to open up space for black people's occasional desire for unknown or indeterminate blackness (not desire for lighter skin or a racially ambiguous appearance, since the narrator enjoys going to tanning salons). Beatty foregrounds black people's boredom with known blackness and "blackened" people's desire to be more than the "charade of blackness." The novel's opening words are: "You would think they'd be used to me by now. I mean, don't they know that after fourteen hundred years the charade of blackness is over? [. . .] The Negro is now officially human" (3). This depiction of exhaustion with blackness does not lead to a final celebration of the end of blackness. Instead, Beatty, throughout and most dramatically at the end of the novel, dramatizes the complex reasons why African Americans who are exhausted and bored by the mundaneness of race still do not necessarily stop *feeling* black.

This focus on why, in an era in which blackness is "passé," people still feel black is most heightened at the end of the novel, when the narrator believes he has met a kindred spirit who shares his phonographic memory that defies the ocularcentrism of race. When this woman lets him hear the full beauty of her phonographic memory but then rushes back to the safe zone of racist oculacentricism, DJ Darky feels most black. Immediately after the woman lets him share a wondrous soundscape with her and imagine an end of whiteness (the end of white people's objectification of black bodies), she rushes back to a racial dissection of his body that is the final note of the novel. The novel ends with the reiteration of racial discourse and loops back to the beginning emphasis on the end of blackness. Ellison's words in *Invisible Man*—"the end is in the beginning"—capture the circular nature of this ending and beginning of the novel. The woman touches his face as her gaze objectifies him. She makes him literally *feel* black as her touch, gaze, and words pin him down. Beatty begins the novel with the narrative of a cultural mood of post-blackness and ends with this emphasis on an individual black body being molded into an object of a white gaze.

During the BAM (in the interior of the movement), the cultural mood was blackness, not post-blackness, of course. But, just as Beatty shows that the cultural mood of post-blackness makes individuals *feel* most black when assaulted by oppressive white gazes, the cultural mood of blackness, in the inner zones of the BAM, made individuals *feel* most post-black when assaulted by the "blacker than thou" forces. The shift from the phonographic memory to the reinstatement of racial ocularcentrism at the end of *Slumberland* adds more weight to Baraka's words, "sound is what we deal in." One of the deepest differences between the BAM and *Slumberland* is the move from the BAM's investment in black sound to *Slumberland's* focus on the sound that is post-black. The connection between the BAM and *Slumberland* is the shared focus on uncontained sound. The BAM connected being black to this uncontained sound; *Slumberland* frames this uncontained sound as an exhaustion with the container "black." But the satire of blackness in *Slumberland* is an extension of the satirizing of blackness that happened during the BAM itself. When the BAM satirized "blacker than thou" performances, the movement refused to see "black" as a container and insisted on the uncontained possibility of black post-blackness.

It matters that *Slumberland* is about the experiences of an African American in Berlin. Beatty's interest in the satirical point of view that emerges when African Americans are outside of the United States parallels the BAM-era satire of Carlene Hatcher Polite's *Sister X and the Victims of Foul Play* (1975). Beatty's focus on blackened people's desire to be more than black is also a core theme in *Sister X*. In this deeply BAM-influenced novel, the desire to be more than black is figured as being literally worn out with the constant reference to everything in the world needing to be black:

> One of the most beautiful Black Men whom a Black Woman and a Black Man ever brought into this World stepped away from a closet with an armful of clothes.
>
> From a black suitcase (which looked as if it had seen better days), the beautiful Black Man took out some colored underwear. His beautiful black body he rubbed down with an oil and citrus cologne an ex-girlfriend had turned him on to back in 1956, down in Oriente Province. Santiago de Cuba, to tell the truth about the place.
>
> Next, the beautiful Black Man put on some fine black pants, tailored for him by Kalik Shabazz, a Temple #1 Brother from Black Bottom.[18]

Polite was living in Paris when she wrote *Sister X*. Her engagement with the BAM had the texture of "in it but not of it." Polite uses signs and symbols throughout the novel that cannot be pronounced. Her interest in sound extends to what cannot be heard. In this quasi-detective novel, Polite retains mystery by not clarifying these parts with playful graphics and punctuation. As Ishmael Reed, on the back of the first edition of *Sister X*, describes the novel as the first arrival of "jazz writing," he considers it a "long alto saxophone solo." Polite's play with punctuation such as "!?!?!?!?!?!?!?!?!?" that is not tied to particular sounds was a part of her experimental "long jazz solo."

In the first pages of the novel, the repetition of the ampersand appears in an indented passage with the following graphic layout:

> Walkin' "that" Walk (which only a Black Man from the United States of America can . . .), the beautiful Black Man strolled on down the hotel hallway, caught the elevator, strided clean 'cross the lobby, exchanged a few light words with the desk clerk, took out his black address book, and picked up a black phone.
>
> &&&&&&&&&&&&&&&& (6)

The dialogue between Abyssinia and Black Will appears after this play with symbols. The hidden meaning may be the call for the BAM's need to pause, to recognize that all of the references to blackness have produced a collective impasse that is comparable to a "black address book" that no longer has any useful directions or phone numbers. The play with unconventional graphic symbols in *Sister X* explodes as signs of Black Power in the final chapter, in which Polite dramatizes the full meaning of the reference in the first chapter to the "Moment of Silence" as the "the more radical, therefore the more subjective, the better" (31). The use of graphic symbols in this chapter is a direct gesture to a radical break-out of the language that makes white power make sense and a radical implosion into an alternative black *sign* language. When Beatty ends *Slumberland* with the white kindred spirit who has phonographic memory but lapses, finally, into the visual memory of race, he, like Polite, ends the novel with a direct critique of the sign-making that keeps white power in place. When the white woman touches DJ Darky's skin, Beatty ends with the white power of forced intimacy that refuses to give black subjects any distance from the white gaze. Critical distance from the external white gaze is exactly what the BAM-inspired satirists of whiteness demand. Beatty's novel is not so different from the BAM-inspired satirists.

At the end of *Slumberland*, the phonographic memory of the would-be kindred spirit is a depiction of the possibility of a way out of white power, the possibility of a shared (post-white, post-black) consciousness that is a space of a negotiated, difficult universalism, not a celebratory, easy universalism. Satire becomes an ideal way of representing the move from uninterrogated blackness to the negotiated, difficult space of a universalism that opens up blackness, instead of repudiating it. *Sister X and the Victims of Foul Play* is a stunning depiction of black satire's ability to show how the more radical forms of black nationalism were a push away from known blackness to the unimaginable and fantastic. There is a core passage in the novel that brings to the surface this rethinking of radical black nationalism as the critical, conceptual distance that allows a new understanding of *nation* as the "brand-new" (the unimaginable). The following rethinking of the meaning of nation in the black radical imagination occurs after Abyssinia asks Black Will, "Say, Homes, tell me quick now, where in this World haven't you been yet?" (105):

> "Careful now, 'ssinia," he said, making her slow her road. "There you go, slipping back into the Dead World. Listen, pay attention to what you've just said. Where I have 'not' been is stone insignificant. Dig it? Where we are 'now' going is what's goin' on. One of these days soon now we are going to have a Going Back to the Roots trip. We are going home, not back to America either, because that would mean that we are going backward, retrogressing. We are getting back to the Nation which will be our brand-new world, our original world. That means that we are going straight ahead, stone right on!
>
> "We are not turning to the right, nor are we turning to the left. We are having no more detours, thank you. Perhaps that new Nation will be on American soil. Who knows? [. . .] We are in need of the Sea. Light will find us out, soon now. The light has begun falling on the Path. We are hooking up, lining up together, readying ourselves for the long walk. We are going to make it down to the Shore. Once we are out to Sea, we will no longer squabble among ourselves or consider ourselves strangers long lost." (105–7)

The "brand-new" world evoked in this passage is Polite's imaging of the freedom that the Black Power movement has allowed these characters to envision. Polite begins the novel with the satirical depiction of Black Will's superficial investment in objects and clothing that are literally black and make his blackness seem entirely visible, commodified, and known. But Polite, in this "brand-new world" passage, uncovers the Afrofuturism that propels the more dynamic parts of black cultural nationalism. The temporal dimension of Black Will's nationalism signals Polite's interest in black post-blackness. Black Will is focused on "going straight ahead," but he is also insisting, to Abyssinia, that this Nation work is about "going home" and "getting back to the Nation." His theory of the black nation is not backward motion; it is *indigenous* motion, what Edouard Glissant describes, in *Poetics of Relation*, as "rooted wandering."[19] Black Will makes it clear that there are no "detours," that this Nation work is about forward movement, even though it makes home (the past) and the future inseparable. Polite refuses to make Black Will's theory of Nation a source of humor. Unlike the many other humorous elements in the novel, Polite grants a seriousness to Abyssinia and Black Will's dialogue about Nation. Black Will's theory makes multidirectional movement (moving back home and forward to a brand-new space) a way of being black and post-black.

Setting the novel in Paris allows Polite to think literally about the characters' critical distance from 1960s U.S. black cultural nationalism. Black Will and Abysssinia are enamored of the black liberation struggle in "America," and they are also set apart from it. They are African American exiles, but Polite emphasizes that their shared exile and their pro-blackness has produced an "inwardness" that keeps them tied to African Americans at large, figures such as Malcolm X, and the fight against obvious and subtle white power. Abyssinia and Will's decolonization of their minds is depicted as an inwardness. Polite writes, for example, "And they huffed and they puffed and they blew their minds in" (109).

The Black Inwardness of BAM Satire

The role of satire in this creation of black inwardness is most vivid in Sharon Stockard Martin's play *Edifying Further Elaborations on the Mentality of a Chore* (1969). Martin entered the BAM through her participation in the Free Southern Theater collective and BLKARTSOUTH. In the BLKARTSOUTH archive at Tulane University, this play makes you pause—an example of the satire that has been "lost in the archives" as people fail to appreciate the role of humor in the BAM. The play's focus on the *moment* of becoming beautiful satirizes the before-and-after texture of black consciousness-raising. But Martin's satire of the newness of "black is beautiful" does not make black consciousness-raising into a joke; she uses this satire as a means of thinking through the disorientation and exhaustion that the collective, urgent performance of a new aesthetic created.

The word "yesterday" resonates throughout this play.[20] Esol tells Aswa, in the opening dialogue, "It was only yesterday that we were ugly."[21] Martin later makes it clear that the question about "yesterday" is a question about "tomorrow":

> *He closes his eyes and kisses her.*
> ESOL: And let's hope that tomorrow we'll still be beautiful, sweet, and
>   refined.
> ASWA: Wouldn't want to turn back tomorrow. Not for the world which
>   is ours also.
> ESOL: It would be a drag.
> ASWA: Definitely.

ASWA: Esol.

ESOL: What?

ASWA: Do you think they'll like us more now that we're no longer considered ugly? (67)

For Aswa and Esol, pre–"black is beautiful" is always as close as "yesterday,"
and post-"black is beautiful" is always as close as "tomorrow." This play is
one of the most lucid reflections of the BAM's heightened awareness that the
new black consciousness they were speaking (and, sometimes, screaming)
into existence would only continue to exist if the collective "speaking it into
existence" continued. Martin depicts Esol and Aswa's commitment to the
collective performance and also their exhaustion (their need to, as the final
words state, "shut up" and find a black inwardness that is not overdetermined
by the external, collective performances).

The power of the play is its ability to fully inhabit the BAM ethos even as
the collective performance of "black is beautiful" is depicted as an exhausting
"chore." The title is purposefully unwieldy. Martin's words "the mentality of
a chore" evoke the idea that black consciousness-raising created, for "conscious" black women, the type of double labor that, in black feminist theory,
has been named "double jeopardy." The double labor of fighting the antiblack
"ugliness" and the silliness of male black nationalists' investment in black
women's bodies (another spin on Malcolm X's words "you're dealing with a
silly man") made the "power of the new mentality" inseparable, for gender-
and race-conscious black women, from the mentality of a chore. The mood
of exhaustion steadily evokes the need for a next step. Black post-blackness
is the full mood of the constant dialogue between Aswa and Esol about the
terror of the very recent past ("yesterday"), the tiring commitment to adding
their voices to the voices of the counter-discourse that will only exist if it is
spoken (the depiction of "today" in this play), and the need for inwardness
(the final move to "shutting up" and Martin's depiction of "tomorrow" as
post-chore blackness).

The inwardness takes on a heightened dimension as the exhausting repetition of "black is beautiful" leads Aswa and Esol, in the final scene, to the
bare inward truth of "black only is." These simple words are Martin's final
offering of a black self-sufficiency that is inseparable from a black openness
(in this case, the literal openness of the incomplete sentence). The words "further elaborations" in the title of the play offer another way of understanding
Martin's final foregrounding of this incomplete sentence. The "elaborations"
remain to be seen; black is a launching pad, and it only becomes a "chore"

when its ability to push people forward disappears. Martin also depicts the love that Esol and Aswa share as a chore. The core tension in the play is Esol and Aswa's desire to move from the chore of black love to a love that is deeper than what they discuss as their mutual "admiration" of their commitment to the revolution. Martin satirizes the BAM's framing of love as a political act. If love is only a political act, the play insists, then how deep is that love? Would actual "revolutionary" love be unconditional? Unconditional love is figured in the play as the love that is deeper than the artifice tied to black cultural nationalism. Martin depicts the undressing of the layers upon layers of Aswa's "African" clothing. When one robe is taken off, another robe appears:

> ESOL: (*Grabbing her African garb by the waist and unraveling it, spinning her away from it like a top*) There. It's done.
> (*She's wearing an identical one underneath.*)
> ASWA: It took me all day to get that dress together.
> ESOL: I've been waiting all day to take that dress apart.
> ASWA: Don't be ridiculous. In front of all these people.
> ESOL: Ridiculous. Ridiculous? She says ridiculous. I've been working all day like a slave. I've been bent over drawing little lines on a white page. I look at the pages so long that they blur and the lines always become your face. In everything I see, I see you. I spend half of every day erasing mistakes that I make from thinking about your face that sits in my mind behind my eyes and sees me.
> ASWA: Nonsense.
> ESOL: It wasn't that long ago that everything was different.
> ASWA: It wasn't that long ago that I was different.
> ESOL: Yeah. Waking up every morning like you was in some kind of hell. Living in a world that wasn't even meant for you. Clothes weren't even made for you. Food was for somebody else. And even though everything you did had to be done twice as hard, twice as good, it still didn't make any difference. Nothing made any difference. Everything and everyday just added up to trying and dying.
> (71)

Getting to the unadorned body that signals the unconditional love of "black only is" encapsulates this play's approach to black post-blackness. Martin, situated within the BAM (not as a critical outsider), satirizes the movement's love affair with blackness in order to reveal the deeper love that people found as "black is beautiful" opened up the space for the freedom of the erotic and other self-expressions that could never be contained by the category of the political. Esol's words—"clothes weren't even made for you"—capture this BAM play's ability to press against Baraka's sense, in *In Our Terribleness*, that "you can put on new clothes." Martin shows that the "old" oppressive, antiblack clothing was clearly not made for black subjects and that the "new" BAM clothing can also never contain the excessiveness and ephemerality of black affect and style. Martin uses the trope of BAM "clothing" and the layers and layers of Aswa's clothing to satirize the masculinist traps that sometimes needed the overdetermined "can't be naked" black female body.

The most unpredictable aspect of BAM satire may be the complex depiction of an interracial orgy in William Melvin Kelley's novel *dem* (1967). This novel has recently come back into print as a part of Coffee House Press's BAM series. The packaging of it as a BAM novel can also be seen in Willie Abraham's introduction to the first 1967 edition: "Some public narcissism on the part of the black man is called for in all of this. Black is indeed beautiful in *dem*. The black person is sweet and reasonable and does no wrong without cause. The Black Arts Movement itself can be seen as a concerted effort to portray and enhance the beauty, strength, pain, and prophetic inspiration of blackness in America, not exclusively as an intuition but also as psychic ballast for the black man if his equality is not to mean his neurotic assimilation."[22] Readers of this introduction may wonder what exactly makes black "beautiful" in this novel. Abraham situates the novel firmly in the BAM and also in what Abraham refers to as "racelessness": "William Melvin Kelley's novel, *dem*, almost falls within the tradition of the black 'raceless' novel of America, in which explicit judgment is avoided on issues concerning race."[23] Abraham anticipates twenty-first-century post-black sentiments that express a certain boredom with talking about the oppression of black people. Abraham creates a balance between the "racelessness" of the novel and its tie to the BAM; this balance fully evokes the spirit of black post-blackness.

The orgy is the part of the novel that shows BAM satire's ability to use what is seemingly "counter-revolutionary" in a manner that deepens our sense of what it would mean for African Americans to really be free. While writing *dem*, William Melvin Kelley (like Carlene Hatcher Polite) was an expatriate in Paris: literal distance shaped the critical distance of his BAM satire. In the orgy scene and in the final scene of the novel, Kelley's use of satire to "undress" white bodies and black bodies becomes most clear. He uses literal images of undressing as a means of imagining skin dissolving into flesh and creating a post-skin state of excessive flesh and uncontained erotic energy. In the scene of the orgy, both white and black bodies are depicted as this "post-skin" flesh. The black character Cooley is described as having "white flesh oozing between his fingers," and the excessive flesh of Glora is described as "her breasts hanging like water-heavy brown paper sacks."[24] This language conveys the sense that whiteness and blackness are always bursting out and experienced as liquid spaces. Categorizing *dem* as a BAM novel only makes sense when we recognize the black post-blackness in the BAM itself. The novel's (and the BAM"s) black post-blackness is its movement from a whiteness that only hurts to a whiteness that also bores black people to death and takes up too much room in black lives precisely because of its banality. Boredom with whiteness (not boredom with blackness) is one way to grasp black post-blackness. When whiteness controls the meaning of blackness, it makes blackness a dead end. The move to post-whiteness is a move to making blackness mean more than the reaction to racial terror. *Dem* removes the focus on the racial terror that whiteness produces and makes white power seem more ridiculous than frightening.

In *Slumberland*, Beatty stages black boredom as a certain investment in blackness that makes blackness as boring as the whiteness that Kelley depicts in *dem*. For Beatty, the radicalism of black satire is its ability to help younger black people tell new stories that do not lock them into the stories that older black generations tell and also do not repudiate the more familiar stories. The words "my healthy hatred of self" are one example of Beatty's attempt to produce new stories without repudiating the older tutelage. Beatty describes the narrator's sense that he is a very unusual DJ as follows: "Acute left-handedness, a fear of crowds, and what I consider to be my healthy hatred of self make for a catchy stage name, DJ Darky" (23). The notion of a "healthy hatred of self" is on the surface antithetical to the self-love that the BAM championed, but the "narcissism" (Abraham's word in his introduction to *dem*) in the BAM was a *collective* narcissism that was a healthy distance from self. Abraham writes, "Some public narcissism on the part of the black man is called for." The hatred of self that Beatty explores is the healthy move to a reckoning with self that is heightened once black people like Beatty, born in the 1960s, have lived their entire life with the collective black identities produced during 1960s black consciousness-raising. These post–Black Power children inherit the collective formations of blackness and turn to self, through the lenses of older people, because they have lost a commitment to creating art that is not for individual advancement. But the twenty-first-century turn to self by the artists who were born in the 1960s can also be a turn to what Beatty describes as "the search for identity and a sense of place" as "both process and result" (22). How does a focus on self become more than narcissism? If self is a process, then a "healthy hatred of self" is the awareness that any black consciousness-raising that limits the process of self-transformation is a dead end. DJ Darky's "healthy hatred of self" is productive; it makes him want to have a jam session with the Schwa and be more than a soloist. As he jams with the Schwa, he feels that the Schwa is daring him to deal with black sound and break out of his belief that blackness is "passé."

The Schwa (Charles Stone) is depicted as a musical genius who decides to re-create the Berlin Wall as a "wall of sound." Beatty imagines this rebuilding of the wall as DJ Darky's "rebuilding" of his relation with blackness. His jam session with the Schwa teaches him that "you can play with blackness"; DJ Darky learns black post-blackness from the Schwa. With the depiction of DJ Darky's obsession with any clocks that show the stoppage and resetting of time (such as the stoppage caused by power outages), Beatty brings to the surface the play with change and continuity at the core of the black post-blackness that shapes twenty-first-century black aesthetics. The stop-and-start aspect of black post-blackness is what Souleymane Bachir Diagne describes, in his work on *négritude,* as the "weaving during the day that is then unwoven at night."[25] This description of the creation that depends on re-creation captures the full spirit of black post-blackness.

Charles Johnson's *Black Humor* and Hoyt Fuller's *Black World*

Ironically, the words "black post-blackness" are the type of new vocabulary that Charles Johnson calls for in his essay "The End of the Black American Narrative" (2008). Johnson, in this essay, performs a post-blackness that, on the surface, differs greatly from black post-blackness but shares, in the deeper registers, black post-blackness's investment in the provisional. Johnson asserts:

> In the 21st century, we need new and better stories, new concepts, and new vocabularies and grammar based not on the past but on the dangerous, exciting, and unexplored present, with the understanding that each is, at best, a provisional reading of reality, a single phenomenological profile that one day is likely to be revised, if not completely *overturned.* These will be narratives that do not claim to be absolute truth, but instead more humbly present themselves as a very tentative thesis that must be tested every day in the depths of our own experience and by all the reliable evidence we have available, as limited as that might be. (Italics added)[26]

Black post-blackness is an "overturning" of fixed blackness; like Johnson's sense of the "tentative thesis," black post-blackness is the aesthetics of improvisatory revision. Johnson's repudiation, however, of the "black American narrative" differs fundamentally from the work of black post-blackness. Johnson views the "black American narrative" as an outdated discourse that situates black Americans as eternal victims. Black post-blackness holds onto blackness even as it keeps updating it.

The title of one of Johnson's satirical books of editorial cartoons is *Half-Past Nation Time*.[27] This collection of comic art, with his words and his drawings, was published in 1972, two years after another cartoon collection, *Black Humor*. In both texts, we see the young Charles Johnson wrestling with the rhetoric and iconography of the Black Power movement. Johnson is deeply interested in the Black Power discourse, and his interest is tempered by an intriguing suspicion that never allows him, in these word-and-image texts, to approach the type of "skepticism from within" that we see in the editorial cartoons that Hoyt Fuller included in every issue of *Black World*, as he, through this pivotal journal, became one of the prime architects of the BAM. This "skepticism from within" takes the shape, in *Black World*, of satirical editorial cartoons that make fun of the signs of the rhetoric and style of Black Power without erasing the possibility that there is a lingering substance to the rhetoric and style after the satire has exposed the intensely performative nature of this black consciousness-raising. In the full spirit of Johnson's own title, *Half-Past Nation Time*, Fuller makes "skepticism from within" signal a questioning of what happens "post–nation time." How does the rhetoric and new image-making itself become a type of action? What are the world-opening possibilities and the limitations of these performative acts? These questions that animate the cartoons in *Black World* are foreclosed in those produced by Johnson at the same time that Fuller was directing the shape of the BAM through his editing of *Black World*.

Johnson's images, in *Half-Past Nation Time*, of a middle finger waving and trying to resist the conformity of the Black Power fist (fig. 22) is one example of the book's less nuanced satire that would shut down the substance of Black Power style. There is sequence of four frames in this editorial cartoon: in the first two frames, the index finger tells the middle finger (that is first pointing upward, potentially creating the "fuck you" gesture and then, in the next frame, waving and wiggling around), "Hey, you! Get down here with the rest of us!" In the third frame, the middle finger continues to bend and twist, and the index finger says, "C'mon, you heard me!" In the final frame, the middle finger has settled down and joined the other fingers folded in the Black Power fist, and the index finger sighs, "There—isn't that better?!" Johnson implies that conformity

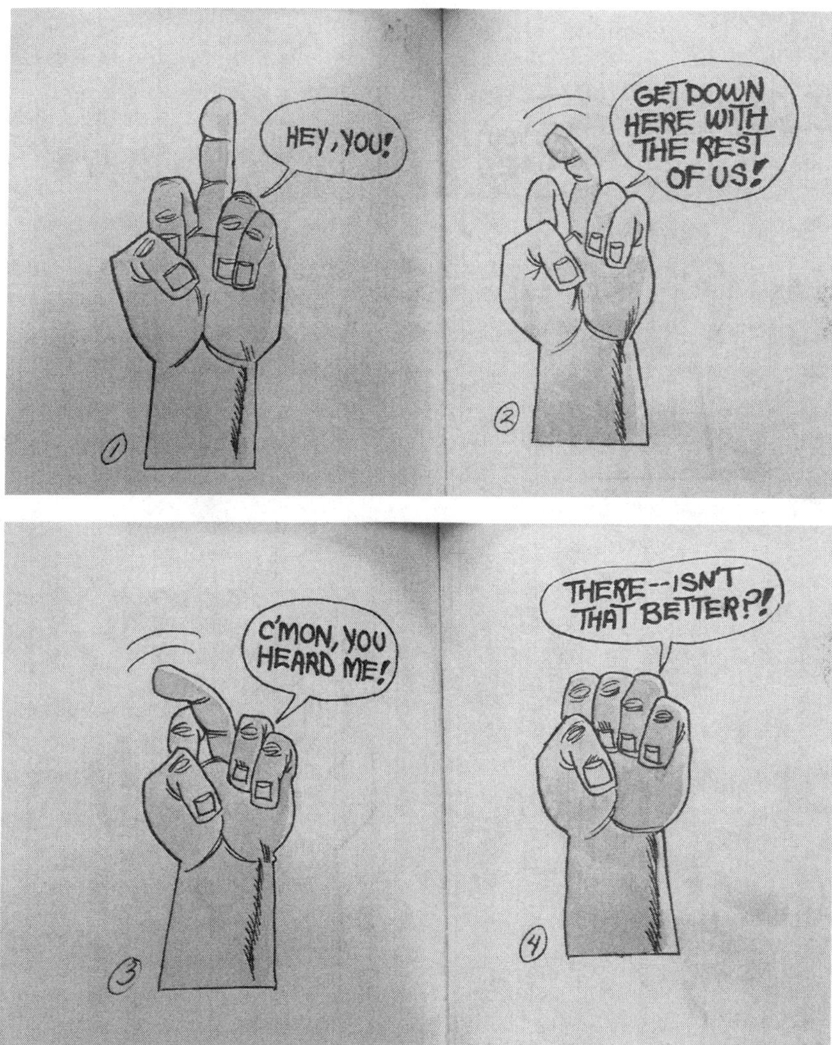

Figure 22. Charles Johnson, editorial cartoon in *Half-Past Nation Time* (1972). Copyright © 1972 by Charles Johnson. Reprinted by permission of Georges Borchardt, Inc., on behalf of the author.

has been achieved once the rebellious middle finger loses its individuality and is hailed ("Hey, you!) by the forces of Black Power that depend on a togetherness that is stifling ("Get down here with the rest of us!"). But the sequence of frames also shows the power of gestures, like the Black Power fist, to create solidarity out of individual quirkiness. Without the words, the sequence can be viewed as a move from the quirky actions of the individual to the pause and rest of a collective black solidarity created out of the weird, individual wiggling and squirming. Johnson's words reduce the complexity of the gestures in his own drawings and the complexity of the relation between individuality and collectivity during the Black Power movement. Ben Jones's sculpture *Black Face and Arm Unit* (1971, fig. 23), like Johnson's editorial cartoon, dramatizes the role of gesture during the BAM. The fantastically multicolored plaster-cast arms and hands twist and turn in all directions. The bent, curved, and stretched-out motion of the fingers conveys a full sense of choreographed quirkiness. Jones shows the power of the BAM hailing of quirkiness as a necessary part of any black collective. *Black Face and Arm Unit* does produce a sense of wandering and skepticism about the formation of any "unit," but Jones shapes this black collective quirkiness into a skepticism from *within* the black interior (a skepticism that does not pivot on the impulse to not trust and believe in the power of black radical imaginations).

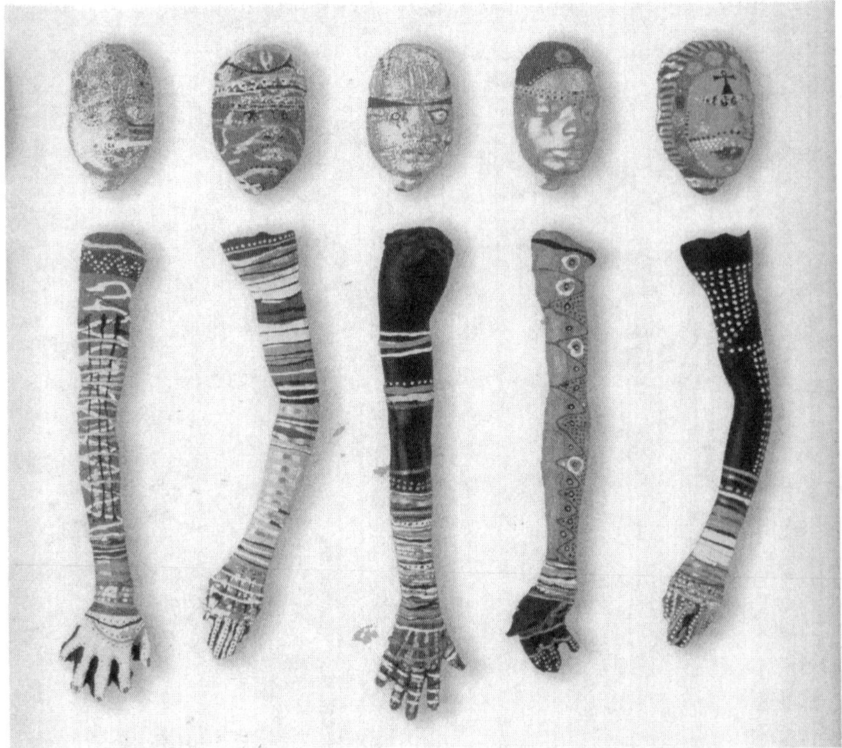

Figure 23. Detail from Ben Jones, *Black Face and Arm Unit*, 1971. Acrylic on Lifesize Plaster Casts.

A comparison of Walt Carr's *Black World* cartoon, with the serial production of the all-black canvas (discussed in chapter 2), and Johnson's cartoon in *Black Humor* (1970, fig. 24) of a similar all-black canvas highlights the foreclosing of skepticism from within (of the very possibility of black post-blackness) that begins to grow in Johnson's *early* cartoon work and shows up again, in later years in the form of the emblematic post-black essay "The End of the Black American Narrative." Johnson's version of the all-black canvas is similar and yet so different from Walt Carr's editorial cartoon. The all-black canvas in Johnson's cartoon is a sign of emptiness (the black subject's despair over being so black and empty). A black artist stands next to a canvas that is painted entirely black and tells a white male observer, "It's life as I see it."[28] In Carr's cartoon, the serial reproduction of the all-black canvas signals that resumption is the redemption—a changing same is in effect. Carr suggests that although there is reason to laugh at the outrageousness of the literal move to that which is all-black, there is no reason to despair. Johnson was not as able to see the power of the outrageous. In Carr's *Black World* cartoon, the power of the outrageous is the sheer possibility that (echoing the caption) black aesthetics really could

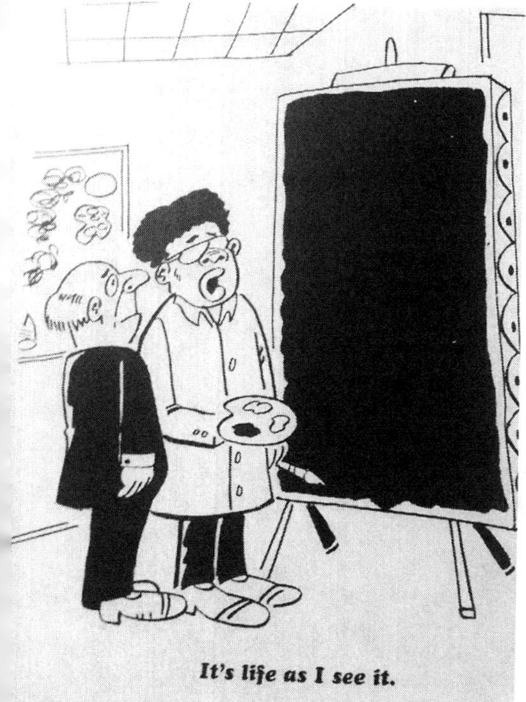

Figure 24. Charles Johnson, editorial cartoon in *Black Humor*. Copyright © 1970 by Charles Johnson. Reprinted by permission of Georges Borchardt, Inc., on behalf of the author.

"go too far" and create an alternative (an elsewhere) that would be much more than a reaction to the dominant "white" canvases. The skepticism from within (literally within the main journal of the BAM) is productive; it produces the investment in the "black elsewhere." In contrast, Johnson's cartoon produces the dead end of racial self-hatred.

Johnson's editorial cartoons show that the post-black satire performed by him and others during the BAM era is significantly different from the black post-black satire performed by Hoyt Fuller and others who were situated firmly within the BAM. The difference between post-black satire and black post-black satire is the difference between feeling frustrated with being born black and feeling that "I am still being born"—the feeling depicted in Carolyn Rodgers's 1971 *Black World* essay "Uh Nat'chal Thang—The WHOLE TRUTH—US." Rodgers describes this feeling of "still being born" as she recounts her own struggle (after years of believing that "BLACK IS BEAUTIFUL") to recover from a sickness that made her feel "not so beautiful" and made her begin "to realize how the real black/negro Nation feels."[29] The black post-black satire of many of the editorial cartoons in *Black World* taps into what Rodgers depicts as the confusion of the everyday *black person in pain* who struggles to pretend to be "well enough" to fully believe the messages of the BAM. Rodgers writes:

> The proclamation. The Declaration of beauty. Literally overnight. From super ugly Black to Super Black Beauty. [. . .] Then I got sick. Really sick. Hospitalized, then bedridden, away from the recorded messages. And I grew back into my old self. [. . .] My record was jammed. I was stuck. Stuck in bed on sick, ugly, Black and helpless. And not so beautiful. That's when I began to realize, relate, to how the real black/negro Nation feels.
>
> Now I am growing well. It did not happen overnight. It took nine long months. Birth ritual. Birth operation. Dissection. Examination. I am still not Black and Beautiful. I am still being born and it is pain. Perhaps one day I will be REALLY BLACK AND BEAUTIFUL. I will not be a recorded message. I will be me. For after all, before Black is anything, Black is human. Record THAT message.[30]

Some of the *Black World* editorial cartoons do "record THAT message," this feeling of "I am still not Black and Beautiful" (this desire to make room for the post-"black and beautiful" state of questioning the "new" identity, the new "proclamation").

One of the *Black World* editorial cartoons that gives shape to this state of blackness "still being born" is an image of a man standing on a street pointing both index fingers and moving his arms up and down in a whirlwind of different directions (fig. 25). Three other men stand on the corner and stare at the man; they stand close together as if they are afraid of the "man who is pointing fingers." The stillness and tense, tight bodies and mouths of the men who stare are dramatically set apart from the uncontrollable motion of the arms of the man who points. The caption reads: "What part of town you from . . . man?" Charles Boyce, the cartoonist, plays with the idea that the man who points is so lost that he is insane, but the cartoon also suggests that the man who points is so lost that he, not the onlookers, is the most sane. He is the one who, like Carolyn Rodgers, feels "stuck" in the middle of the Black Power movement. His body is too still to have arms that are moving so wildly. He is a bird trying to fly; he is a subject hailed and reborn by the Black Power movement who suffers, like Rodgers, the pain of incomplete birth.

The "proclamation" (the interpellation by the BAM) creates incomplete birth (not subjecthood). This notion of incomplete birth is yet another way that we can grasp the elliptical work of black post-blackness; "black," in this formulation, signals that which is still being born. After becoming "black" during the first part of the movement in the 1960s (what Rodgers, in "Uh Nat'chal Thang," depicts as "ten years of rhetoric, of desire, of need to believe," which she also says "is hardly enough to cancel out 400 years of denial of self, destructiveness, apathy, and inertia"), some people, like Rodgers, had to figure out how to live within a state of incomplete hailing (what Rodgers

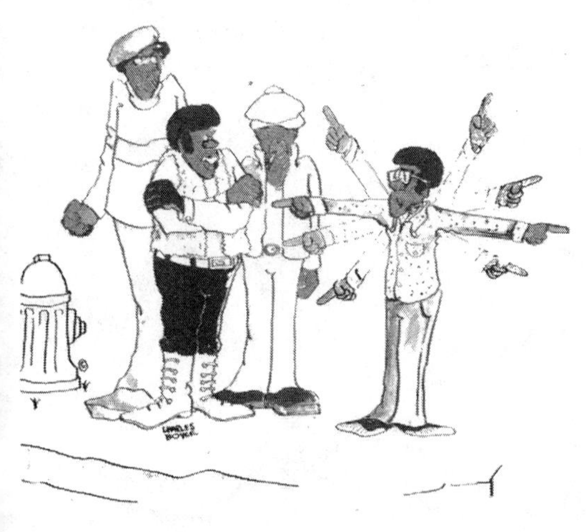

Figure 25. Charles Boyce, editorial cartoon in *Black World* 24.3 (January 1975). Charles Boyce, Artist Collection.

describes as the "black/negro" double consciousness).[31] Satire was a perfect form for the expression of this incomplete birth; BAM satirists in the 1970s show how absurd the state of incomplete (or "stuck," as Rodgers depicts it) blackness can be. Like Rodgers, they rage against "recorded messages" that cancel out the pain and reality of their incomplete blackness—recorded messages such as Maulana Ron Karenga's 1967 black-cultural-nationalist maxim, "You were black before you were born."[32]

The image of being stuck in the movement's "jammed records" (Rodgers's lucid way of thinking about the second wave of the BAM) is captured in all of its pain in one of the *Black World* editorial cartoons created by the artist named "HAM." This cartoon makes it impossible to escape the pain of the incomplete birth; it makes us remember Rodgers's own insistence on pain—"I am still being born and it is pain." HAM's drawing includes an image of a man's body half eaten by a caged lion in a zoo. The sign on the cage states, "Do not feed the animals." The man's legs (the only part of the body that is not in the lion's mouth) are pulled by the black guard at the zoo, who is trying to save the half-eaten man. The caption reads, "Damnit, man! . . . Can't you read?" The half-eaten man is a heavy reversal of Rodgers's "I am still being born" mantra for "incomplete blackness." "I am still dying because my humanity has been distorted to such an extent that I feel like a caged animal" is the sad message of this satirical editorial cartoon. HAM subtly implies that the man identified with the caged animal and wanted to help him without realizing he was risking his life. The guard trying to save his life is pulling on the "jammed body" (the body of a person who, after the BAM "recorded messages" of reclaimed black humanity, still feels shut up from his full humanity).

These 1970s *Black World* images of feeling stuck (even after the 1960s "proclamations" of freedom) convey skepticism about the BAM and a sense of an ongoing process of "working it out," of pulling harder to save the body from the lion's mouth and waving arms with pointing index fingers until some type of flight and identification of a destination must occur. Charles Johnson's editorial cartoons in *Black Humor* lack any comparable sense of a skepticism from within (a skepticism that is not so cynical about the Black Power movement that the possibility of black gazes and the black interior disappears). In one of Johnson's *Black Humor* cartoons, a black man is nailing more and more signs of the Black Power movement on his office wall as his white boss and coworkers look on with dismay. The signs are: "THINK BLACK," "LOOK BLACK," "LOVE BLACK," "ACT BLACK," "WALK BLACK," "WORK BLACK," and "TALK BLACK." The man is in the process of hammering the nail for the sign "ACT BLACK," as he turns around to look at his boss upon hearing the words in the caption—"Jackson, when you find the time, I'd like to see you in my office." Jackson is in a state of suspension that will only be resolved once he talks to the white boss. The black interior hailed by the signs is belied by the white superiority that his boss represents. The pain of this editorial cartoon, through the lens of the BAM, is the fact that there is no way in this white space to "ACT BLACK." The satirical wit in this cartoon is the sense that the signs are style without substance, empty gestures that mean nothing.

The satire of black post-blackness in the *Black World* cartoons is the satire of a post-blackness that can be readily assumed by the frustrated black subject who has never accepted the hailing of "black is beautiful." Johnson shows the angst of those black subjects who saw the Black Power movement happen but never entered into it and never understood it enough to grasp the black post-blackness that it produced in the late style of its 1970s waves. Carolyn Rodgers, one of the most acclaimed poets of the BAM, made readers of *Black World* pause, in 1971, and think about the reasons why the BAM performance of transforming the Negro into a black person sometimes produced an incomplete transformation that made people feel like they were stuck between being hailed as black and being hailed to begin the more quiet work that has no proclamations—the work of seizing black people's right to be human. When Rodgers insists on a new recorded BAM message, "black is human," she makes room in the BAM for an inseparability of black and post-black, as if the power of black post-blackness is really its ability, during both the BAM and in our current twenty-first-century moment, to make people experience that which Souleymane Bachir Diagne describes as a "negotiated universalism," a post-blackness that can only be felt when one is in the throes of blackness, not outside of it.[33] Rodgers's move to "black is human" is the feeling that we need to recover as the most liberating zone of the BAM's satirical play with black post-blackness.

Satirizing Themselves: Amiri Baraka, Percival Everett, and Mat Johnson

Baraka's *Tales of the Out and the Gone* (2007) brings together his mid-1970s prose and his science fiction of the 1980s, 1990s, and 2000s. In the introduction to this volume, he states, "The smashing of the Black Nationalist paradigm of the 60s happened in a number of ways, obvious and un."[34] *Tales of the Out and the Gone* helps us see the *smashing* of black nationalism in these "obvious and un-obvious ways." In this volume, Baraka's satirical wit abounds as he puts together the "smashed" pieces of 1960s radical black nationalism. The first story in *Tales of the Out and the Gone* evokes this sense that, during the movement itself, people knew that "something brought together" was always falling apart and falling back together in the space of the "out and gone."[35] This first story, "New & Old," is about the character Conrad's affection for and worry about a former kindred spirit's loss of an ability to "speak 'people'" (22). Baraka writes, "But Conrad, looking from the back of the truck where he stood waiting to speak, was wondering what Pander and the young white revolutionary Gruen had explained to their people. At the point of the police attack, they shouted to nobody and everybody, 'Let's get outta here, we ain't gonna get killed' and sped away in their three and four year old cars" (22). Conrad is "out," and this outness is tied to his ability to "speak 'people'": "Conrad swallowed and got ready to speak 'people'" (22). In *Tales of the Out and the Gone*, Baraka keeps *swallowing*. As he explains in the introduction, these tales reveal the "interior of a social movement"—the space of "speaking people," what Baraka describes as "co-babbling" in another story, "Retrospection." "Co-babbling w/ the host" are the final words in this short story written at the beginning of the twenty-first century (213). As Baraka puts together the "smashed" pieces of radical black nationalism, he makes "Retrospection" an "unobvious" return to the "out" and the "gone" in his BAM texts. It is hard to read "Retrospection" and not remember the "outness" of his most experimental 1960s texts (such as *The System of Dante's Hell*, *In Our Terribleness*, and the beginning of the play *A Slave*).

One key passage in "Retrospection" captures the experimental and satirical ethos of Baraka's *Tales of the Out and the Gone*. In this passage, Baraka uses some of the same words as *In Our Terribleness* but satirizes himself, as he literally tears apart his earlier words when he writes, "head beat ing of under standing," as if he is suggesting that the BAM attempt to decolonize minds (to "beat some sense" into colonized minds) was both absurd and laudable (213). The full passage reads: "And him, still flat, trying to remember the touching interior of why he before was other than this Thating flat. A search. A quest lit with reality—terrible name, this place. Sound thrown as chance, head beat ing of under standing. Get up then. Blow that note. Be its endless substance. An us" (213). "Get up" and "substance" are the keywords that stand out in the resonant ending of *In Our Terribleness*, as Baraka urges his readers to believe in "an us" and begin the process of seeing themselves with their own eyes: "Now call that name, of the figure you see, call that name the real sound your substance is. Call it deep inside yourself. [. . .] Then get your hat, i.e., get up and go."[36] When Baraka, in 2000, returns to this BAM language and names this story "Retrospection," it is clear that he is thinking about the lingering significance of Black Power decolonization practices in the twenty-first century. The humor of the words "this Thating flat" is tied to frustration. Baraka seems to be wondering why black people are still "falling flat," as he plays with the word "flat" throughout the story. The satirical wit emerges most acutely through his image of "flattened" people still imagining that they have access to some type of interior (the "touching interior"). The humor (laughter instead of tears) in the first lines of this passage blends with the seriousness of the final words, "Be its endless substance. An us."

Before this passage, he explains that the "flat" is that which is "kicked to the curb" (211). It is hard to read the full playful but serious description of the flat without remembering his discussion, in the introduction, of the flattening (the "smashing") of black nationalism. The full description of the flat is: "Flat. Like they say, 'Kicked to the curb.' But now, even worse, to roll, or been thrust off & flattened. Not flat across the street, arms akimbo, like the imaginary dead" (211). The image of "arms akimbo" captures the indignant stance of Baraka and others of his generation who witness the twenty-first-century flattening of the black consciousness-raising they mobilized in the 1960s. Baraka also makes this story a metanarrative about his own writing as he uncovers a self-criticism that is as tender and honest as the self-criticism in *In Our Terribleness*:

> My man Morris wd say, "And then, so what?" A challenge.
>
> The question remains. Remains, like stays, longer a verb. Hold to that. (Can *that* be a verb? *That*? That it sticks—what about *Thating*?) Yeh, he was down there Thating. (211)

Baraka's unabashed move to experimental language recalls his experimentation with nonstandard spelling in his BAM texts, but his twenty-first-century experimental language also takes us back to the experimental language in his pre-BAM texts (his Beat-period texts). The BAM experimental language is, in some cases, less outrageously experimental than his Beat literature and his twenty-first-century literature. The BAM gave Baraka an anchor for his experimentation; the movement made his bohemianism legible as he found other kindred spirits who were looking for a "way out and gone." But Baraka's holding on to the words from *In Our Terribleness* in his twenty-first-century text "Retrospection" shows that the BAM remained the pulse of his experimental urges. The BAM remained, over the years, the "reason for the season" of experimentation (the movement that made him see that experimentation and improvisation could be relevant, grounded, and politically useful).

Tales of the Out and the Gone holds on to the BAM discourse but adds even more satire and humor than we see in some of Baraka's BAM texts. In a similar (but different) sense, in Percival Everett's 2014 novel *Percival Everett by Virgil Russell*, we see a holding on to an interest in black consciousness-raising even as the direct centering of the tension between an older black man and his younger son and the layers of satire, humor, pure play and experimentation make it easy to read this novel as "post-black." The novel's black post-blackness becomes more clear when Everett's satirical urges are connected to Baraka's satire in *Tales of the Out and the Gone*.

The opening anecdote in *Percival Everett by Virgil Russell* is full of Baraka-esque humor. The novel begins with the following satire of the post-race logic imagined during the era of the first black president of the United States: "Let me tell you about my dream, my father said. Two black men walk into a bar and the rosy-faced white barkeep says we don't serve niggers in here and one of the men points to the other and says but he's the president and the barkeep says that's his problem. So the president walks over and gives the barkeep a box and says these are Chilmark chocolates and the barkeep says thank you and reaches over to shake the president's hand. The president jumps back, says what's that? And the barkeep says it's a hand buzzer, a gag, get used to it, asshole."[37] The humor of this portrayal of entrenched antiblack racism and the naivete of African Americans who still aspire to assimilation has the texture of Baraka's wit in his most humorous twenty-first-century texts, such as *Un Poco Low Coup* (2004). Everett's anecdote has a wit that is not that different from Baraka's story "Adventures in Negrossity": "Negro tried to cash hisself for Money at a bank . . . / Got arrested as a counterfeit Nickel!"[38]

Baraka's notion of "co-babbling" is a perfect description of the intentionally frustrating form of *Percival Everett by Virgil Russell*. Everett frames the novel as shared storytelling by a father and son, a cowriting that constantly pivots on the blurred boundaries between the father's voice and the son's voice. This "co-babbling" gains the texture of black post-blackness when Everett, after the opening anecdote about the lingering racism in the age of Obama, makes issues of blackness matter and not matter in this exchange between father and son. Issues of blackness emerge in the narrative about the censoring of militant language in a draft of a SNCC speech, in the narrative about a son witnessing a father being attacked by KKK and having to take his father's advice and run away to save his own life, and in the narrative that imagines Nat Turner reversing history and becoming the one who writes the narrative of William Styron. Everett does not make race a core theme in this novel, but he somehow makes race matter even as he moves beyond "black representational space."

In the narrative about the censoring of the SNCC speech, Everett approaches the "up against the wall motherfucker" language of some BAM poetry. Everett's narrator imagines that this language ("*If the dogs of the South continue unchained, then we will bite back, we will move on those tender parts that bleed so readily, that bleed so profusely* [. . .] *We say fuck the administration that still walks hand in hand with Jim Crow*") was probably too crude, but he still feels that other parts of the speech should not be removed (45). He still feels that the expurgation of parts of his speech violates his right to express himself freely. This worry about the flattening of black rage takes us back to Baraka's worry about the "smashing" of black nationalism in "obvious" and "unobvious ways." Both *Tales of the Out and the Gone* and *Percival Everett by Virgil Russell* move from this worry about the purging of black rage to the layers and layers of experimental language. Both Baraka and Everett play with language itself in these texts, as if the play and satire is a form of resistance that may be most effective when it is not labeled as resistance. "You can't catch me" is the state of nonromanticized freedom that the son running from the KKK achieves. The riotous word play and satire of Baraka and Everett also convey this feeling of "you can't catch me."

The surprising connections between Everett's twenty-first-century self-satirizing in *Percival Everett by Virgil Russell* and Baraka's self-satirizing in *Tales of the Out and the Gone* reveal a complex tie to blackness that lurks late in many twenty-first-century novels and can, in a quick and easy fashion, be read as not being concerned with blackness. The BAM centered blackness as a worldview and aesthetic; twenty-first-century African American satirists such as Everett decenter blackness and "tell it slant." This slantwise view leads to insights about the dynamics of race and resistance to racial terror that are not always that different from the BAM discourse of black consciousness-raising and black self-determination. For example, in Mat Johnson's highly satirical 2011 novel *Pym*, an unpacking of the root of African American frustration with white privilege emerges in the midst of the depictions of the absurdity of the African American hunt for a "lost African tribe" (as professor Chris Jaynes seeks to prove the reality of the remote island of unadulterated blackness in Edgar Allan Poe's *The Narrative of Arthur Gordon Pym of Nantucket*). The slantwise interest in black suffering and white privilege in twenty-first-century African American satirical novels sometimes enables writers like Johnson and Everett to uncover the deepest wounds that make post-race a twenty-first-century impossibility. This turn to the deepest wounds is what we hear Johnson processing in *Pym*, when he writes: "This is a black American thing: to wish to be in the majority within a nation you could call your own, to wish for the complete power of that state behind you."[39] Without ever mentioning the BAM or the black nationalism it embodied, Johnson, in this passage, crystallizes the BAM call for a "nation within a nation" (the very name of the most acclaimed biography of Amiri Baraka).

We also hear slantwise echoes of BAM poetics in *Pym*, when Jaynes describes the blackness of the inhabitants of Poe's Tsalal. Johnson writes: "These brothers are black. These brothers are so black they wear only the skins of animals that are black. The only wood they carry is darker than ebony. These brothers are so black, we eventually find out, that even their teeth are black."[40] When this passage is compared to Baraka's call in his signature poem "Black Art" for a "black world," it is clear that younger writers like Johnson are both laughing at and absorbing and holding on to the consciousness-raising that the Black Power movement produced. Black post-black satire is the holding on and letting go that Baraka himself performs in the prologue of the play *The Slave* when Walker Vessels, dressed as an "old field slave," addresses the audience from the space of "before" and "beyond" as he prepares for his role, in the play proper, as an angry, militant black nationalist. The "old man" in the prologue becomes as beyond fixed blackness as any twenty-first-century "post-black" satirist, making statements such as "but figure, still, that you might not be right" and, "your brown is not my brown, et cetera, that is, we need, ahem, a meta-language," before the lights dim and turn on again with the "old man" now, in act 1, becoming the younger black nationalist Walker Vessels.[41] Baraka's stage directions describe how the actor playing Walker must morph into the younger man through bodily and sonic expressions of an exhausted discourse moving into another exhausted discourse, revealing the need for what Walker calls a "meta-language"—some type of motion that allows black subjects to inhabit the past, present, and future at the same time. This motion of black post-blackness produces the slippery "shift in an instant" labor that Baraka calls for in the stage directions: "Running down, growing anxiously less articulate, more 'field hand' sounding, blankly lyrical, shuffles slowly around, across the stage, as the lights dim and he enters the set proper and assumes the position he will have when the play starts."[42] The satirical impulse to "figure, still, that you might not be right" reflects a heightened awareness, in both the BAM and twenty-first-century African American literature, of the necessity to "shift in an instant." The temporal dimension of black post-black satire is this shift in an instant in both the direction of "black" and "post-black," as these texts satirize blackness and post-blackness.

6

Black Inside/Out

Public Interiority and Black Aesthetics

Volunteer to call yourself to this interior scar outside
—Fred Moten, "There Is Blackness"

In 2007, the collective Otabenga Jones and Associates produced an art installation (fig. 26) that captures the flattening of the BAM and the Black Power movement itself. This collective of artists (who are too young to have participated in the Black Arts or Black Power movements) arranged objects in a glass museum case that evoke the full flow of the text, sound, and style of Black Power. The objects include one part of a broken trumpet, Eldridge Cleaver's *Soul on Ice*, a small handgun, a bound pile of very dusty and worn papers, Stokely Carmichael and Charles Hamilton's *Black Power*, and a Muhammad Ali toy figure. All of these objects are placed flat on the shelves. One of the action figures (which appears to be a black wrestler) is placed with its legs suspended above the glass shelf and its arms raised high, as if the black male toy figure with a muscular unclothed chest is begging to be lifted up and restored to an upright position.

This installation conveys the sense that Black Power has been reduced to objects in a museum. In *From Storefront to Monument: Tracing the Public History of the Black Museum Movement* (2013), Andrea Burns argues that we need to link the Black Power movement with the black museum movement of the 1960s and 1970s. The Black Arts Movement was calling for art that could not be treated like a museum exhibit (too bold and radical to cater to a white, dominant art establishment). The call for a black interior and the call for the *black* collection of blackness, during the BAM, shaped the movement's anti-museum ethos. This same ethos also shapes some twenty-first-century black visual art. Indeed, some of the visual artists who are defining twenty-first-century black aesthetics are engaging directly with the problem

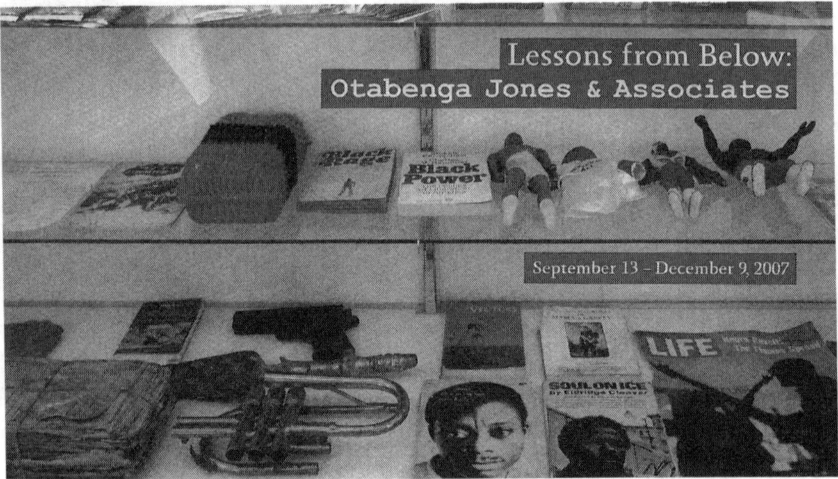

Figure 26. Cover of exhibition catalog, *Lessons from Below: Otabenga Jones and Associates*, September 13–December 9, 2007. Photo Courtesy of the Menil Collection

that the BAM underscored: what can blackness be when it is not treated like an object in a museum?

The BAM embraced public art (outdoor murals, grassroots-oriented performance poetry, agitprop drama), and the movement's call for public art was also a call for inward art—what Baraka calls for when he pleads "come on in" at the end of his iconic poem "SOS." Beneath the movement's privileging of public art was its investment in what we might best understand as "public interiority." This public interiority—art that is public and tied to the black interior—was a deep part of the BAM's mission, and this public interiority is also a principal part of some of the twenty-first-century art that has been named "post-black." The notion of "*not* airing dirty laundry in public" encapsulates some of the critiques of contemporary black art that exposes the intraracial strife and ambivalence about blackness that usually remains hidden in the black interior. The BAM did not often use this "airing dirty laundry" approach to public interiority; the power of black people meeting *publicly* in a collective black *interior* was the movement's typical approach.

The desire, in the most radical zones of BAM and twenty-first-century black aesthetics, to work black inner space and black public space for their most freedom-inspiring possibilities is most evident when black public interiority emerges. When the BAM outdoor mural movement is brought into conversation with twenty-first-century installation art and the interiority of the letter writing in BAM archives, the power and complexity of black public interiority becomes clear. The words "black collectivity" were used during the Black Power Movement as a means of expressing the collective wounds created by white power and the collective resistance forged to fight white power.[1] I offer the idea of "black public interiority" as a means of capturing the individuality that was never erased by the collective wounding and the individuality that gains a public, collective dimension during social movements like the BAM.

How Can Interiority Be Public?

The BAM was constantly performing ways in which the personal could be collective and inner mental space could be shared as people deconditioned their minds together. When Quo Vadis Gex of BLKARTSOUTH explains that sometimes, during the BAM, "introversion was viewed as elitism," she captures the difficult work that this black public interiority had to accomplish; the collective, public identities could not cancel out the power and force of that which is remarkably private and personal.[2]

We take it for granted that the personal is political, but there was difficult work being done by some artists in the BAM to make sure that the personal was not effaced. As Quo Vadis Gex asserts, in the same interview where she emphasizes that introversion was sometimes assumed to be elitism: "It's not about you; it's about my mind."[3] Some of the twenty-first-century African American art that has been viewed as post-black is also insisting on a greater recognition that introversion can be powerfully black.

In *Tales of the Out and the Gone* (2007), when Amiri Baraka remembers the role of "the out and gone" in the BAM, we gain a new way of understanding the force of introversion and black eccentricity that is made public: "The out is out, even if in plain sight. Though it would not have to be. The 'Gone' could be seen or unseen or obscene. But even farther 'Out,' crazier, wilder, deeper, a 'heavier' metaphor, a deeper parable. We'd say that's 'way out.' (At Howard we were so hip we wd say, 'That's way,' meaning 'That's way too much,' exceedingly hip, super wise.)"[4] One way to read "out is out, even if in plain sight" is to recognize that introversion can remain wild and free even if it is made public. This public interiority was created when black inner space was mobilized, during the BAM, through outdoor murals. The 1967 *Wall of Respect* mural in Chicago (which functioned as an outdoor art gallery) needs to be remembered as we gain a fuller sense of the interior spaces of individuality and artistic freedom that can be created in the outdoor spaces of collectivity and artistic ensembles. *The Wall of Respect* was the transformation of a simple wall of an abandoned building into an outdoor community center of poetry readings, political speeches, dance, jazz, and drama.

The installation piece *I've Always Wanted a [Doll] House* (2013), by the Kenyan artist Arlene Wandera, dramatizes this issue of creating a revolutionary interior in the *outside* space of collective resistance. The artist makes the white house a sign of interior space that signals privilege; getting into this inner space requires acrobatic, "by any means necessary" maneuvers. But Wandera's images of the outside maneuvers might make us forget that the goal of these guerrilla tactics is to get inside. The grace of one of the sculptural figures on the outside creates a sense of being grounded in the air; this figure has outstretched arms that are partially framed by an arched window. One of the arms is almost inside the window space (almost inside the house). Wandera, with this figure, counters the trauma of the other figures struggling to get in and, in one case, hanging upside down in the outside space of disempowerment. This graceful figure with outstretched arms is partially in the house; this figure is not shut out from the interior but has also found a way of being outdoors that breaks the boundaries between the inside and the outside.

I saw this installation piece in the 2014 DAKART Biennale. The gallery space had two levels, and this piece was on a balcony-like partial enclosure. When seen in a gallery space, this piece might lead viewers to think about the inside space of the gallery and how it relates to the outside of the gallery. During the BAM, artists were directly fighting power structures' attempts to contain art produced by "the people." The focus on a black interior was one way that the movement fought against the inside space of dominant cultural power that transformed what Baraka refers to as the "out" and "gone" into the "safe," the contained, and the nonthreatening. In the BAM anthology *Black Fire*, incredibly didactic poetry is followed by the Outness, the abstraction, of Sun Ra's poetry. In liner notes to the 1974 reissue of the album *Super Sonic Sounds*, Sun Ra explains his abstract sound: "This is the music of greater transition / To the invisible irresistible space age. [. . .] Outer space is big and real and compelling."[5] The tension between the inner and the outer galvanized the style of black cultural nationalism.

The BAM muralist Gary Rickson imagined an "outdoor museum" that became black space. Rickson used this term as he explained his mural work in Boston. In his artistic statement in the 1969 groundbreaking text *Black Artists on Art*, Rickson states, "The mural, done in what I call black expressionist technique [. . .] is there to counteract the lack of black art in the Museum of Fine Arts in Boston and to create an out-door museum of functional art."[6]

In a 2010 interview, Nelson Stevens, one of the principal BAM muralists, recalled city officials often trying to stop the inclusion of words on outdoor murals.[7] As the murals were in the process of being completed, Stevens explained, city officials were most nervous about the words that might be in them. When I asked him to respond to critics of the BAM need to attach definitive words to images, he insisted, "I always used the words to control the interpretation. I wanted to make sure the image was delivering the message I wanted."[8] In his Boston mural *Work to Unify African People* (1973), the words indeed lead viewers to see a unity in spite of fragmentation as opposed to what could be viewed, without the words, as a fragmentation that defies that unity. In the same interview, Stevens explained that many BAM muralists would only paint on smooth walls, but William Walker would paint on rough walls "brick by brick." The uneven bricks are comparable to the uncontained outer space that Sun Ra brought to the BAM. The "out" art of the BAM was working through uneven surfaces to create a "smooth" delivery of a collective agenda. The uneven surfaces are comparable to the individuality of the artists (their different flows); the smoothing out of the uneven brick is comparable to the power of the collective that A. B. Spellman remembers as the "sensuality of a collective consciousness that declared itself on sight."[9]

In 2010, the architectural journal *Interstices* issued a call for papers for a special issue on "unsettled containers—aspects of interiority" with the question, "When is a set of walls an interior, when is an object a container, and when is a container a world?"[10] In a similar manner, Baraka insists, in "Black Art," that "We want a black poem. And a / Black World. / Let the world be a Black Poem."[11] This probing of the difference between the object that is a container and the container that opens up to a "world" explains the BAM rage against reproducing books of highbrow capital and the BAM belief in books that would (like the outdoor art gallery) unsettle boundaries between inner and outer space. The resonant question posed by the editors of *Interstices*—"When is a set of walls an interior?"—captures the BAM's production of inner black space as a wondrous container of outer space that was as large as the dream of a "Black World."

The category "outsider art" is often viewed as a more progressive term than "folk art" or "naïve art." The BAM gave a new spin to "outsider art." When we use this term as a way of thinking about this movement, the outsider element does not pivot on the tension between folk and highbrow, but on the tension between the art of Black Power and the art of assimilation. Malcolm X's death in Harlem, for example, had a particularly formative role in the aesthetic warfare that was created in Harlem during the BAM. Harlem was reclaimed as "black space" during the BAM, in contrast to the Harlem Renaissance depictions of the breaking of the color-line boundaries as white people gained a complicated intimacy with blackness. The 1969 African American protest of the documentary exhibit *Harlem on My Mind* at the Metropolitan Museum of Art was closely tied to the BAM's call for outsider art that enables a black interior. The inside/out dynamic of the BAM (the movement's refusal to enclose black art even as it hailed a black interior) is very different from some of the twenty-first-century African American visual art that gains its value, in the highbrow art industry, by being different from that which is recognizably tied to black aesthetics. The creation of distance from recognizable black aesthetics by some twenty-first-century black visual artists makes blackness the exterior that enables access to the highbrow interior.

From BAM Murals to Twenty-First-Century Installation Art

In 1997, Kara Walker created a watercolor and colored-pencil word-and-image interplay that mocks a lineage connecting twenty-first-century African American women artists and the BAM. This soft, playful, "fake" advertisement (titled "Do You Like Creme in Your Coffee and Chocolate in Your Milk?") is her response to the bold colors of the BAM. The words painted in watercolor are: "Toward a Positively Affirmative Portrayal of African American Womanhood in the 21st century [. . .] By ~~Kara E. Walker~~ [. . .] A Collage of Thought Provoking Text and Images in the Tradition of the Black Arts Movement."[12] The artist's name is defaced with a horizontal line. The image implies that "Kara E. Walker" cannot exist in the "tradition of the Black Arts Movement." Walker's repudiation of the BAM draws more attention to the difference between her featureless silhouette interiors and the BAM black interior.

The silhouette mattered in the art criticism of the BAM. The relation between the silhouette and the line was explored in the 1968 catalog of the Thirty-ninth Arts Festival Exhibition of the Fisk University Art Gallery. As the artist and critic Keith Morrison examines the "outside the BAM" sculpture of Richard Hunt, he thinks about Hunt's careful use of the silhouette within his line-oriented sculpture. He wonders if the pitfall of many predictable uses of the silhouette is the drama of the negative space (the area outside the dark form enclosed in the silhouette) when it is experienced as an actual shape, as opposed to "air space." Morrison deliberates Hunt's desire, in his sculpture, to foreground "air space" over "shape." In the exhibit catalog, he states: "Hunt also uses the flat shape or silhouette; but he does so more as a way of relieving the possible monotony of his ever uncoiling linear grace than as a final sculptural concept in itself. Whereas the silhouette compartmentalizes negative space or itself takes on a character by being a distinctive positive shape, the line, on the other hand, is not only a shape but a movement, a direction whose trajectory describes an area of air space."[13] This language subtly crystallizes a question at the core of comparisons of the BAM and Kara Walker's post-BAM aesthetics: when does the forming of lines create movement and "air space," and when does it create the compartmentalized space of individual expression? Morrison's sense that the "line is not only a shape but a movement" offers a lucid way of understanding why the BAM obsession with lines of solidarity and collective movement differs greatly from Walker's signature use (as her art gained a critical spotlight in discussions of post-blackness) of the silhouette as a shape that does not seem to move, that signals a state of suspension and arrested motion. The art historian Kirsten Buick shapes her critique of Walker's silhouette approach to American slavery around the issue of public space and antiblack racial terror: "What really does Kara Walker's work have to do with the historical and contemporary fact of enslavement? Nothing. She just yells 'NIGGER!' in a crowded theater, and rather than stampeding out, we are forced to sit and listen and burn."[14] Buick taps into the black interior wounds from antiblack racism that make some people critique the public spotlight on Walker's parodic, playful images of slavery.

The complexity of public interiority emerged in Walker's 2014 installation (fig. 27) of a massive sugar-coated sculpture that appeared to be both a sphinx and a "mammy" image of a black woman. The outdoor display, painted on the exterior wall of the building that contained the installation, was a painting of words that evoked BAM outdoor murals. The painted words were:

A SUBTLETY
OR THE
MARVELOUS SUGAR BABY
AN HOMAGE TO THE UNPAID AND
OVERWORKED ARTISANS WHO HAVE
REFINED OUR SWEET TASTES FROM
THE CANE FIELDS TO THE KITCHENS
OF THE NEW WORLD ON THE
OCCASION OF THE DEMOLITION OF
THE DOMINO SUGAR REFINING PLANT

The site-specificity of this installation art was very different from the sites of the BAM murals. Walker was commissioned to create *A Subtlety* on the

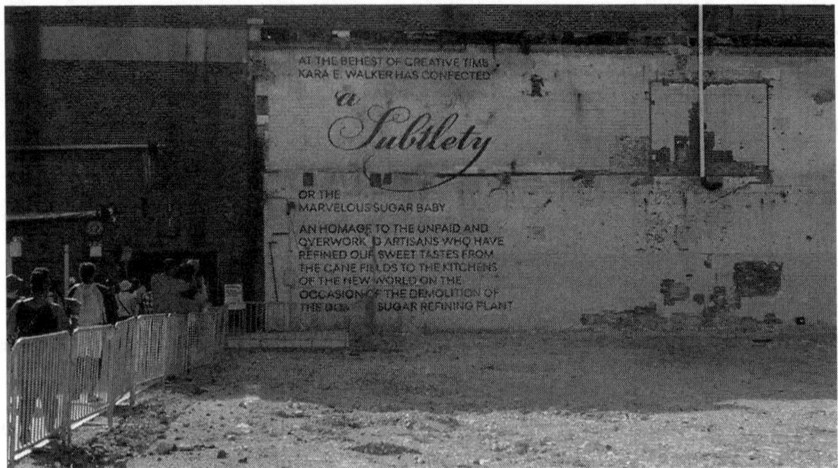

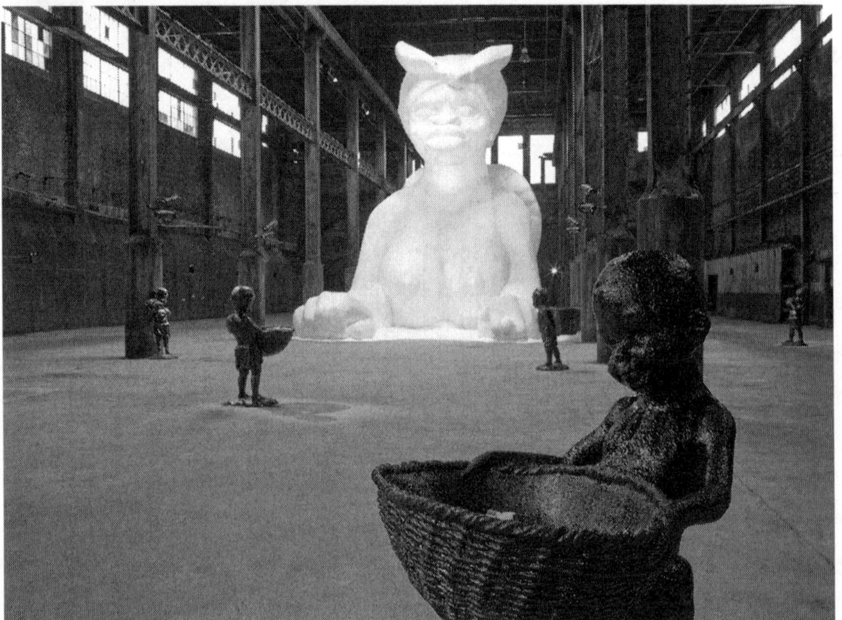

Figure 27. Installation view: Kara Walker, *At the Behest of Creative Time Kara E. Walker Has Confected: A Subtlety, or the Marvelous Sugar Baby, an Homage to the Unpaid and Overworked Artisans Who Have Refined Our Sweet Tastes from the Cane Fields to the Kitchens of the New World on the Occasion of the Demolition of the Domino Sugar Refining Plant.* A project of Creative Time. Domino Sugar Refinery, Brooklyn, N.Y., May 10–July 6, 2014. Photo: Jason Wyche. Artwork © Kara Walker, courtesy of Sikkema Jenkins and Co., New York.

"occasion of the demolition" of a Brooklyn sugar plant that had been bought by investors aiming to convert the space into a condominium building. In contrast, the BAM *Wall of Truth* (1969, Chicago) contained a sign that read, "We the People of This Community Claim This Building in Order to Preserve What Is Ours." As opposed to the *Wall of Truth*'s "claim" of an abandoned building, *A Subtlety* represents a witnessing of the "occasion of the demolition." Instead of seizing a space, *A Subtlety* (like the ephemeral nature of the sugar, which melted within two months) was a letting-go of a space. When the sugar plant is demolished, apartments will be built in the site of *A Subtlety*.

The nonsubtle issues of racial gentrification hover around the edges of this art. Williamsburg, Brooklyn, is one of the most glaring examples of a pernicious type of gentrification that pushes black people out of neighborhoods that used to be home. The predominance of nonblack viewers of *A Subtlety* gathered attention once many of them began posting online "selfies" of themselves and different body parts of this massive "nude" sphinx. One website invites people to use the site's camera to take a "selfie" even if they were unable to visit the installation. The website reads, "CANT MAKE IT TO THE DOMINIO FACTORY TO TAKE PICTURES OF YOURSELF IN FRONT OF KARA WALKER'S SUGAR BABY?? YOUR FRIENDS AND FAMILY NEED NOT KNOW!! REALISTIC SELFIE GENERATOR!!! ITS LIKE YOU ARE REALLY THERE!!!!"[15] The words "selfie generator" are almost a caricature of the BAM generation's view of younger black artists who put individual affirmation before commitment to a conscious desire to engage with black audiences and communities. The desire of white and other nonblack people to pose in front of "Kara Walker's Sugar Baby" can easily be read as the inability of some nonblack people to understand the pain that this image of such an excessive, oversexualized, half-human version of a black woman evokes for many people whose relation to blackness is not produced by a "selfie generator" website. Nonblack people's desire to take selfies in front of the "Sugar Baby" also draws attention to the larger phenomenon of people's desire to see themselves in certain public spaces (to have an image that proclaims "I was there").

The BAM's mobilization of a public black inner space was the mobilization of a tight, safe space that would not allow the white (dominant power structure) intrusion. But this tight black safe space also included the policing that made Hoyt Fuller tell his dear kindred spirit (Carolyn Rodgers) that she should not "unnecessarily bar[e] [her] bones" and "expos[e] [her] most vulnerable self."[16] Like Rodgers, Walker has every right to "bare her bones" and produce art that is "vulnerable." The power and danger of making black pain and vulnerability public is that there is no safe space. The BAM call for black self-determination was most radical when it let go of the reliance on a safe space (the space that cancels out vulnerability). More than any of her BAM poetry, the title of Sonia Sanchez's *Does Your House Have Lions?* captures the spirit of vulnerable blackness that the BAM sometimes embraced. This vulnerable blackness, this sense of the home that is troubled (not simply glorified), makes Baraka's use of the word "terrible" so powerful in *In Our Terribleness*. Kara Walker also uses the word "terrible." In *Kara Walker: Narratives of a Negress* (2007), index cards with Walker's typed words are reproduced throughout the book. One reads, "But I am a terrible people." At the bottom of this same card, Walker types, "that is why I cushion my words."[17] The cushioned words that stem from the terribleness is precisely the type of safe space that Walker rejects. The vulnerable terribleness of *A Subtlety* is embodied in the melting sugar.

Walker makes public a black-woman vulnerability that is not entirely different from the "black-woman strength" that is made public in Nelson Stevens's BAM mural (1974), which includes a painting of Mari Evans's poem "I Am a Black Woman" (1970). One photograph of this mural shows how BAM art (like the reshapings of Walker's *A Subtlety* in the selfies) becomes vulnerable, once it is in the public space that makes a gallery out of that which is not normally considered a gallery, to reshapings that would not occur in less open gallery and museum spaces. Just as some of the selfies taken with Walker's *A Subtlety* seemed to enact a certain type of violence against the heaviness of the black sphinx-woman figure, this photograph of Stevens's mural includes cars in front of it. The cars add a new spin to the painted poem. The parked cars face the mural and drain the poem's words "look on me and be renewed" of their power. The parked cars create a sense of stasis that defies the renewal called for in the painted poem.

Both the selfies taken with Walker's work and the photograph of Stevens's mural turn the art in its original form inside out. The art of Black Power and the art of the post-black play (in Walker's art) are different approaches to the use of public space to open up a vulnerable, "terrible" interior. Evans's poem is much more than a tribute to black women's strength. The word "assailed" makes it hard to read the other words of celebration without thinking about the price of that strength. The vulnerability of the woman who is "tall as a cypress" is signaled in the words "strong / beyond all definition." In this line, Evans moves to the unknowable that we can also see in the fractured prisms that shape each face painted by Stevens (on both sides of the painted poem). In one of the fractured faces, Stevens includes a small circle with the pan-African colors (red, black, and green). In this very public art painted on the side of an apartment building, this tag of pan-Africanism and black nationalism (in a painting of a quintessential BAM women-authored poem) reminds us that the public interiority heralded by the BAM was linked to the alternative nation-building of the movement.

When post-black art such as Walker's *A Subtlety* is compared to this art of nation-building, one key difference is the post-black art's letting go of an investment in tagging artistic inspiration as "African." The black urban space that the BAM was connecting to Africa was the reclamation of outer space as inner space. The tag of black, red, and green marks the side of a building as a site of black alternative nation-building. Walker's skepticism about this alternative nation-building is registered, subtly but clearly, in the poetic interlude on the first page of *Narratives of a Negress*. In this opening, there is a reproduction of an index card with the following words typed on it:

African
African't
[...]
Africould've
Africould.[18]

It matters that the word "African" opens this entire book (which Walker carefully constructs as much more substantial than a catalog of an exhibit). Walker is aware that her work is a space-clearing gesture between black aesthetics that consciously identifies itself as African-inspired and art created by black artists who cannot fully situate the "roots" of their art. Walker might begin with this play between "can't, couldn't, shouldn't, could've, and could" in order to frame the art in the book as art that "can't" be viewed as African aesthetics but "could" (through some possible, not yet imaginable way of understanding African aesthetics) be a part of African aesthetics. Walker's art, unlike the BAM nation-building, is the art of space-clearing. But the nation-building of the BAM was also, sometimes, a space-clearing move to the unimaginable. Walker's collage inspiration for *A Subtlety* (which she has shared with the public, along with a few preliminary sketches) is a play with the superimposition of the Egyptian pyramids and sphinx over the head of a tattooed body of a black woman only wearing a bra, underwear, and socks. The collage, if used in the black popular-culture dissemination of Afrocentrism that proclaims that African American women are the lost African queens, would be a critique of the lowering of the African queen to the lowly state of the sexually demeaned.

In the BAM imagination, this collage would be read as an image of how global white supremacy has made the black woman literally "lose her mind" and how black consciousness-raising can save her by allowing her to see herself through another (decolonizing) lens. Walker's *A Subtlety* is more "subtle" than this collage. She does not use it as a blueprint; it seems to be an inspiration and also a launching pad for a less legible type of art that she wants to create. When this less legible art is compared to the collage, the most striking difference is the insertion of what many will read as the stereotypical Aunt Jemima face in the space that, in the collage, is occupied by the Egyptian sphinx and pyramid.

In *From Storefront to Monument: Tracing the Public History of the Black Museum Movement*, Andrea Burns cites the DuSable Museum director Margaret Burroughs's impetus for creating a museum that could be a black space. She cites Burroughs's frustration (when she was teaching high school students) with the actual "walls" of the high school that became a physical embodiment of the forces that were limiting the ways that black history and aesthetics could be taught. Burroughs states, "For years I had been 'bootlegging' such information [black culture and black history] to my DuSable High School art students, after discovering how dangerous it could be to talk about black history around walls that could 'grow ears.'"[19] This vivid image of walls so confining that they seem to grow the ears of the oppressors captures the tense, complex race and class relations that shape the site-specific cultural production of Walker's play with this sexualized image of Aunt Jemima in a condemned building.

Walking into the condemned building, visitors were asked to sign a form releasing Creative Time, the organization that commissioned the art, and the owners of the condemned building from any liability if visitors became sick from any chemicals or suffered any injuries. Entering into a condemned building as a site of art has a radicalness that is quickly contained when the legal discourse frames the first moment of this radical art entrance. This post-BAM art does not pretend to be dangerous art; Walker is fully aware that her art has the safety tied to its currency within the dominant (white-dominated) art world. The BAM desire to be outside of the white establishment clearly differs from her secure position in the contemporary highbrow art world. But the most important difference between her installation in a condemned building and the *Wall of Truth* sign on the abandoned Chicago building—which states, "We the people of this community claim this building to preserve what is ours"—may be the gentrified Williamsburg area that is the site of Walker's *A Subtlety* versus the entirely black Chicago South Side neighborhood (Forty-third and Langley) that is the site of the *Wall of*

Truth and its legendary counterpart, *The Wall of Respect*. Gentrification is the power of people with more money than those who are being supplanted to give the words in the *Wall of Truth* sign a different twist. The unspoken violence of the gentrification is: "We the people with greater money claim this building and this inner city space." *A Subtlety* was staged in the gentrified space that accentuated the issues of property, class, and race that made some black people feel violated by some nonblack people's responses to Walker's massive image of what some saw as simply a nude black woman kneeling with her buttocks and labia exposed.

In the midst of the critics and defenders of *A Subtlety*, the BAM's legacy of defining black art as black space looms large as one way to understand the deeper dimensions of what is at stake when some post-BAM artists seize the freedom to depict whatever they choose in any space they choose. As opposed to black art as black space, *A Subtlety* made some black people feel that Walker was enabling white people to invade black space. On June 22, 2014, a group of people of color that called itself "We Are Here" staged a collective viewing of *A Subtlety*. On Facebook, they asked people "to invite your friends—and your friends' friends—so that we can experience this space as the majority."[20] One of the responses handwritten on the response board outside the installation directly accuses Walker of turning brownness into whiteness. The respondent wrote:

> I didn't know
> that the purpose
> of <u>REFINING</u> sugar
> is to turn it from
> BROWN to WHITE
>
> Thanks Kara.[21]

The BAM aimed to produce art that would make black people feel empowered to fight white supremacy. When Walker's art makes this respondent feel that *A Subtlety* privileges whiteness over brownness, the respondent may feel that Walker allows a voyeuristic gaze to dilute the horror of the oppression that is emphasized by Walker herself on the outside wall of the site of the installation. In this large painting of boldface words over the brick exterior of the building, Walker describes *A Subtlety* as "an homage to unpaid and overworked artisans who have refined our sweet tastes from the cane fields to the kitchens of the new world." The respondent who feels that the work turns brown into white may be worried about Walker's decision to make the "marvelous sugar baby" white as opposed to brown. The respondent may also worry that the "whiteness" of the artistic production is built into the lack of some curation (subtle or not) that would make evident the historical pain and trauma that makes this "larger than life" exposure of black women's body parts more than a laughing affair or a pleasurable sight.

Unlike Walker's art, the BAM often insisted on a message. AfriCOBRA included "lettering" as one of its principles in order to make the message of the art more clear. As its title implies, Walker's *A Subtlety* does not have a message; it is the type of open art that aims to produce disorientation and ambivalence. The less didactic art of the BAM cleared a space for art to be open but was still tied to a liberation mission. In spite of the fact that the artist Betye Saar has been at the forefront of critiques of Kara Walker, Saar's BAM-inspired *The Liberation of Aunt Jemima* (1972) is an assemblage that begs to be compared to *A Subtlety*. Both works address the ingrained images of Mammy and Aunt Jemima, and both make many viewers think about the price of the "sweetness" that has been produced through the suffering of oppressed black women. Walker's *A Subtlety* (in the estimation of the "We Are Here" participant who thanks Walker for turning brown to white) is so open to different interpretations that it produces ambivalence for the sake of ambivalence and creates a space that is more comfortable for nonblack people than black people. The message (calling for the empowerment of black women) in *The Liberation of Aunt Jemima* is similar to the message in the collage that Walker shared with the public as her preliminary (blueprint) collage and inspiration for *A Subtlety*.[22] The pyramid (placed over the head of the black woman kneeling in a vulnerable, seemingly disempowered position) in Walker's preliminary collage, like the Black Power fist in the center of Saar's assemblage, conveys a message of black women's empowerment. Even though Walker created the watercolor image-collage that makes a parody out of the BAM and performs the literal erasure of "Kara E. Walker" (in this BAM tradition), the similarity between Saar's work and her model for *A Subtlety* shows that the BAM reverberates even when it is being repudiated.

Through the lens of *A Subtlety*, we can see the more subtle aspects of the art of the BAM. And through the lens of the art of the BAM, we can see the less subtle reasons why Walker's embrace of an artist's fiercely free space makes an older generation of African American artists (many of them BAM-influenced) want to echo Gwendolyn Brooks's words at the 1967 BAM Fisk University conference: "Can someone please tell me what is going on?"[23] Brooks is the older poet who was initially disoriented by the BAM and then, once she became a key mentor for the Chicago movement, *reoriented* by the energy of the movement. But Walker's *A Subtlety* made some older and younger black people feel the disorientation of people who have been shut out from the very images that are yoked (through no choice of their own) with their own black bodies. When the letter on the response board ends with "Thanks Kara," after the emphasis on what the letter-writer sees as a peculiar "refining" of brown to create whiteness, the frustrated viewer seems to wonder why Walker contributes to the ongoing pain of black women needing to either dodge or accept the images, like the face of *A Subtlety*, that have visually named black women.

Just as Toni Morrison, in *A Mercy* (2008), asks, "Can you read?" as she begins the novel's play with the "ad hoc territory" of racial formations and power relations that have not entirely settled and solidified (in this seventeenth-century, "pre-race" world), Walker makes viewers doubt their literacy as she makes black historical trauma only matter (and only really be felt) when it is melting away.[24] Saar's BAM-inspired *The Liberation of Aunt Jemima*, like the Black Power fist in its center, is a clinch that holds on to the reality of black women's oppression. Walker's *A Subtlety* is an opening up of the fist in a middle of a gentrified, "white-friendly" space that the BAM would easily "condemn." The BAM had a direct focus on the danger of white space (whiteness as physical spaces and an ideological space). Betye Saar's play, in her window assemblages, with the inner space that becomes outside space is the type of BAM-inspired art of public interiority, like the BAM outdoor murals, that has the tension of a blackness that creates its inwardness *out in the open*. Walker's collage inspiration for *A Subtlety* is an image of a black woman kneeling "out in the open." Unlike the actual installation, this inspirational blueprint has no roof but rather a pyramidal shape that signals the uncontainable horizon of possibilities for black women. The actual site of the installation, the condemned former sugar plant in gentrified Brooklyn, greatly shaped the production of *A Subtlety*. If the massive white sugar baby had been outdoor public art in a black neighborhood, would the open art have created a sense of black space opening up without becoming white space? The BAM would have insisted on the use of brown or black, not white, as the exterior of this massive sculpture.

But Walker's choice of the white face with black features may force us to see black and post-black simultaneously. The black post-blackness of *A Subtlety* can be understood as Walker's invocation of blackness even as she makes it impossible to pin down the "marvelous sugar baby" as necessarily black or, even, as entirely human. The BAM-inspired, black post-blackness of Saar's *Liberation of Aunt Jemima* may be the use of the Black Power fist as the sign of the force that needs to crush the stereotypical images of blackness and create a new space of liberation. The *crushing* that will be accomplished by the Black Power fist is the unknown that Saar can only gesture to. Baraka's famous words "Clean out the world for virtue and love," in "Black Art," could easily be the caption that explains Saar's decision to make Aunt Jemima hold a broom in addition to a rifle.[25] Saar links domestic space to the exterior zones of war.

From 1967 Chicago to 2015 Baltimore

Ernest Shaw's 2015 outdoor mural in Baltimore of Nina Simone, Malcolm X, and James Baldwin testifies to the legacy of the BAM creation of black inner space through outdoor murals. Like the quintessential BAM mural, the Chicago 1967 *Wall of Respect* (fig. 28), Shaw's mural (fig. 29) is painted on a wall of a building that has a bay window. Simone's face is painted, with blue, yellow, and green tints, between a large bay window and a smaller window with an air conditioner protruding outward. Simone was one of the prime sonic muses of BAM poets and one of the heroes painted by Jeff Donaldson in the jazz category of *The Wall of Respect*. Simone visited *The Wall of Respect* once the mural became a veritable outdoor gallery and performance space. Simone's face is painted in a manner that makes it appear to be a bas-relief, like sculpture hanging on the wall. The effect is an outside wall that seems, almost, to be an interior wall. Just as *The Wall of Respect* created this sense of public interiority through the hanging of framed photographs, Shaw's mural creates a strong sense of black public, yet inner, space. The bay windows, in both Shaw's mural and *The Wall of Respect*, signal the complex architecture of the very notion of black public interiority. In architecture, according to the Oxford English Dictionary, a bay is "the space between architectural elements, or a recess or compartment." The word comes from Old French "baee," meaning "an opening or hole." Black public interiority situates us in the openings between the public and the private that are always risky, that can always transform black private pain into public spectacle. Shaw, for this reason, may have decided to paint Simone looking down, with lush eyelashes that make us want to see the movement of the eyes opening up but remain so pleased to see the surprise of the yellow eye shadow on one eye.

It matters that this mural (which holds on, so generatively, to the BAM legacy of outdoor mural making) is in inner-city Baltimore. Simone's song "Baltimore" still resonates, and the lyrics include a profound meditation on collective hiding as resistance, the collective shutting of the eyes from the outside gazes that hurt: "And the people hide their faces / And they hide their eyes / 'Cause the city's dyin' / And they don't know why / Oh, Baltimore / Ain't it hard just to live?"[26] Shaw's twenty-first-century outdoor mural, like

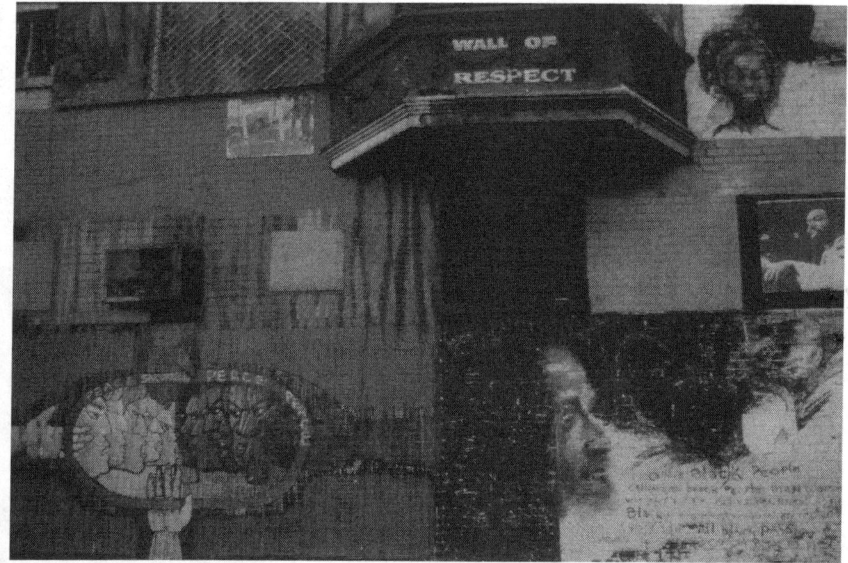

Figure 28. *Wall of Respect* mural, Forty-third Street and Langley Avenue, Chicago (original version, 1967). Photo: Bob Crawford, 1969.

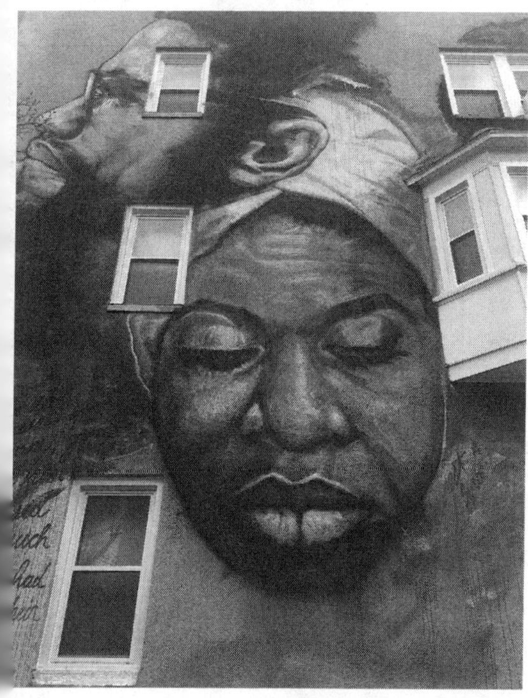

Figure 29. Ernest Shaw, 2015 outdoor mural, 401 E. Lafayette Street, Baltimore. Photo: Margo Natalie Crawford, 2016.

The Wall of Respect, hails people who will feel the power of black public inner space as they realize, "We have our own eyes," as Esther Terry succinctly stated while musing on the real force of the BAM.[27]

In a 2016 interview, Ernest Shaw explained that, before studying with Andrew Pisacane (also known as "Gaia"), he "was a mural maker but not an outdoor artist." As Gaia trained him in street-art techniques and introduced him to spray paint, Shaw discovered that "spray is just another form of brush" (Shaw's own description of his revelation as he made the shift to outdoor public art). These words are a lucid description of the evaporation of any felt difference in scale, as painting on the wall of a building begins to almost feel as "hands-on" as brushstrokes on a canvas. In this same interview, when asked, "Do you feel that in your paintings you have more control of what you are producing as opposed to a lack of control in outdoors mural spray painting?" Shaw insisted, "There is no difference other than scale. Outdoor mural painting is more demanding physically, but simply larger."[28]

The Public Interiority of Letter Writing

The complexity of black public interiority can also be discovered in one of the most interior zones of the BAM: the letter writing between artists in the movement. Reading the Hoyt Fuller papers in the Atlanta University library archives provides a different understanding of the complexity of the black public interiority that the BAM embraced. The public can now read the letters between Hoyt Fuller, the editor of *Negro Digest/Black World*, and Carolyn Rodgers, one of the most significant BAM poets. The letters contain a direct meditation on the BAM's simultaneous call for a black public space of shared feelings and its lapse into restricting the feelings of some artists.

Fuller was one of the main architects of the Black Arts Movement. His editing of *Negro Digest* and *Black World* gave shape to the movement as he used the journal as a means of making writers, visual artists, musicians, and performers see themselves as part of a complex, steadily evolving movement. Fuller understood that one type of Black Power was the power achieved when African Americans put themselves in the position of the curator, as opposed to those who are arranged and collected by nonblack appropriators or mediators. *Negro Digest/Black World* was Hoyt Fuller's seizure of black collection of blackness as a decolonizing strategy.

The letters between Fuller and Rodgers have a tenderness; it is clear that they had a deep respect for each other. The letters also show an interiority of the movement's gender dynamics (black male control of black women's self-determination). In a 1969 inscription at the end of her broadside *2 Love*

Raps, Rodgers writes, "To Hoyt, the sweetest smartest bestest Black man of 'em all."[29] Trust and deep respect enable Rodgers and Fuller to find the private space in their letters to express the power and the problems of the public black inner space that the movement depended on. In these letters, Rodgers and Fuller talk about what cannot be expressed in the movement's public inner space, and they find room to think about those in the movement who seem, in the words of Fuller, to be "hustlers and the poseurs and the phonies."[30] The most meaningful part of their correspondence may be their processing of Rodgers's seeming breakdown (which is a break *out* of the blackness framed by the "hustlers and poseurs and phonies"). Her breakdown and "break out" is an unromantic enactment of black post-blackness. Rodgers was feeling worn out by the movement that had produced her; as Fuller offers advice, he confesses that he is exhausted even though he remains committed to the movement. Exhaustion shapes the mood of black post-blackness in these letters.

In one letter, Fuller responds to Rodgers's seeming frustration with the "public" attention that some poets were receiving: "But you are one of the Special Ones. Yours is a rare gift. Trust it. Be secure in it. There will be those who will have more public (and more fleeting) notice and fame; that is the way life is; but you must never be thrown off-track by that. If there are those recognizably inferior to you in talent who nevertheless get more attention, don't let it faze you."[31] The "public notice and fame" is very different from the publicizing of the movement itself that Hoyt Fuller orchestrated as he edited *Negro Digest* and *Black World*. Fuller and the other leaders of the movement wanted the movement to gain the attention of a black diasporic public. In one of the movement's signature poems, "Black Art," Baraka calls for a "Black World"; this poem ends with this notion of the "Black World" after it stages the infamous purging encapsulated in the words, "Clean out the world for virtue and love."[32] This cleaning out allows the oppressed black subjects to imagine liberated minds (a black interior). When the words "collective consciousness" are used by Baraka in *In Our Terribleness*, and by many other people in the movement, the interiority of the liberated mind is imagined as a public interiority.

In one exchange of letters, Rodgers and Fuller confront the problems of some of the performances of this black collective consciousness. Fuller writes, "We used to talk a lot in the Sixties about 'unity' and 'brotherhood' and 'blackness,' and all that, and not many of us meant what we said. In the name of 'blackness,' we exploit our own people, our own colleagues, our own friends."[33] In order to "mean what [was] said," Fuller recognized that there had to be a more sincere commitment to group solidarity. As Rodgers shared her "breakdown" with Fuller, she refused to sugarcoat her frustration with men in the movement who had, in her opinion, exploited her by not giving her the credit she deserved. When Rodgers shares this frustration with Fuller, he seems to really try to understand her concerns, but he finally rushes back to reminding her that she must take care of her "interior" and that she should not expose her "most vulnerable self." Fuller writes: "At the beginning of this letter, I said that I was sorry not to have been at your book party 'in a way.' In another way, I was glad I was not there. I think you went about the whole affair in a typically clumsy, embarrassing way, unnecessarily baring your bones, regretfully exposing your most vulnerable self."[34] This letter captures the gender dynamics of the black interior celebrated in so many issues of *Black World* that Fuller edited and carefully framed. The radical black woman's interior, when it moves radically out of the endorsed frames, is rendered pathological. But the revolutionary nature of the decolonizing of the mind is always a radical "baring of the bones," and any public, collective use of inner consciousness must entail the exposure of the "vulnerable self." The fear of this "most vulnerable self" may have been heightened when black women, like Rodgers, were approaching the "black interior" not as an orderly zone of a process of decolonizing the mind, but rather as the disorderly zone of the exhausted person daring to express that which seems unimaginable in the most dominant zones of the movement.

As Rodgers dares to share her "most vulnerable" interior with Fuller, she writes: "For I am breaking the holiest rules that I am free enough to."[35] Rodgers wants Fuller as a friend and mentor to see the freedom she can tap into when she exposes her "most vulnerable self." She feels so free, in this vulnerable state, that she feels that she is performing a type of blasphemy. Fuller confesses, again and again, that he cannot understand Rodgers and that she needs to act more rationally. In one letter, he writes, "And we need to resist fantasy and face reality: life is hard and unsentimental."[36] This classic example of the male mentor who aids the irrational woman is also a reminder that the BAM's collectivizing of the black interior sometimes erased the "vulnerability of the self" as individual fantasies were hardened by collective realism. The correspondence between Rodgers and Fuller shows that some BAM writers were deeply aware of this problem and were, like some of the artists defining twenty-first-century black aesthetics, insisting on the power and need of fantasy and vulnerability.

One of Rodgers's poems, "For H. W. Fuller" (1969), shows the connection between her BAM poetry and her correspondence with Fuller. Rodgers imagines a man "standing in the shadows of a / white marble building" and "using the shadows to shield him" as he slowly, through many years, "chips at the foundation" and makes the building fall. Rodgers gives the BAM call for a black interior a new spin in this poem. The man "grows inside the shadows" (the shadows represent the power of the black interior), but this black interior is a shadow of a building; this black interior is located outside. When Rodgers writes, "the man who becomes the dark shadow of a / white marble building," she is not describing the man's defeat; she is describing the power of the man to make the building fall. The poem ends with a visual break from the horizontal stanzas of the rest of the poem to the vertical drop created by the following one-word lines:

the
building
will
fall[37]

The shadows in the poem are, finally, the "black space" that dismantles the white power structure. The shadows are a prime symbol of black public interiority. Rodgers honors Fuller as she imagines that he is a man who can create black public space that allows black people to "grow inside the shadows." The inner space signals black self-determination, and Rodgers seems to see Fuller's work as editor of *Black World* as the work of giving this inner space such a vast, public forum.

When Fuller, in spite of his affection for Rodgers, diminishes her right to express her full "inner space," he flattens what she refers to, in the poem "Black against the Muthafuckas," as the "prism of blackness."[38] What he cannot imagine in the letters that pathologize her exposure of her "vulnerability" is the fact that she, like her image of Fuller in her poetic tribute to him, is "using the shadows to shield" herself.[39] Her "shadows" (her black interior) are denied a public forum. But in Fuller's 1968 introduction to Rodgers's volume *Paper Soul*, he honors her riotous interior: "Her perspective, both sharp and sweeping, encompasses the broad regions of what is and also the clear image of what might be; and her language, honed with bitterness and tipped with grace, swaggers along the brutal street and prances into parlors: it does not know its bounds."[40] Rodgers's unboundedness sometimes frightened Fuller, and it also made Fuller and Rodgers kindred spirits. The black public interiority that Rodgers and Fuller embraced (their commitment to the BAM's seizure of social and mental space as black space) broke walls between them and also accentuated the walls created by male, often unconscious, control of black women's expression.

Stripping Wallpaper

In the movie *Night Catches Us* (2010), the image of stripping wallpaper is used as a symbol of the work needed to really remember the Black Arts Movement (and the larger Black Power movement) and understand its use of interiority to mobilize collective and public resistance.[41] This movie is one of the most vivid depictions of the post–Black Power work of fighting against the tendency to make a caricature of the movement. As the director Tanya Hamilton insists on visualizing the literal layers of the movement (through the symbol of a child tearing wallpaper off a wall), she reminds viewers that the FBI created literal caricatures (cartoons) that they circulated as Black Panther party coloring books in an attempt to encourage more young black people to become violent (and be trapped in the racist prison-industrial complex). In this film, Iris, the ten-year-old daughter of a man who has been killed by white police officers, lives in the house where he was shot. Iris grows up not knowing the full details of her father's death until she asks her mother why they have never moved. When her mother fails to explain everything to her, Iris leaves her mother's room and begins to rip the loose wallpaper off a living-room wall.

As Iris rips this wallpaper, she sees blood stains from bullets on the exposed walls, and, as the walls of the house gain the texture of outdoor walls, a montage of images of the Black Panthers asserting their public presence are mixed with images of state violence against this revolutionary black community-empowerment organization. The interior of the house opens up, and when the mother sees that her daughter has torn the wallpaper off the wall, she knows that she must tell her the entire story of her father's fury when two Panther members were killed by white police officers, his participation in a "revenge" killing of a white officer, and the subsequent police murder of her father in their home. The mother also tries to tell Iris that she was forced to give the police department information about the killing of the white officer in order to keep custody of her and prevent the department from putting her in a foster home.

When she says, "The night they caught me," the parallel between the racial terror of the police state and the unspeakable terror faced by runaway slaves is evoked subtly but powerfully. Before Patricia can tell the full story to Iris, Marcus, the mother's new lover, tries to protect her from having to tell her daughter that the information she gave the police officers led to the killing of her father. Marcus tells Iris that he was the one who told the police what they wanted to know (in order to protect the lives of Patricia and Iris). Iris must somehow cope with the fact that her mother and Marcus (whom she also loves) did not know that her father would be killed but did tell the police what her father did.

When the film stages the street scenes that seem to burst through the walls as the child tears the wallpaper, there is a striking dramatization of the homes and interior spaces that African Americans have created in spite of the fact that "there is no protection," as Toni Morrison writes in *A Mercy*. The film suggests that a calm and safe black interior is, for many African Americans, one layer of wallpaper away from an overwhelming traumatic outside. The pensiveness of the child makes her introspection matter throughout the film. What she is thinking is never fully revealed, but her pensive expressions foreground the legitimacy of black inner space and introspection. In the scene immediately following her mother's explanation of her father's death, Iris tells Marcus, "They're all around us. Ghosts. They're everywhere."

The film ends with Marcus asking Patricia to leave the haunted house and allow him to build a new life with her and Iris. Patricia then says, "We're never going to be happy now here, are we? I can't go with you." His reply is, "I can't stay." After her husband is killed, Patricia gets a law degree and becomes a community lawyer (defending black men who have been arrested or convicted), and she also feeds children in the neighborhood by providing nutritious food and making her house a community gathering place on certain days. Her commitment to the community is as clear as her numb state of not knowing why she is doing what she is doing and her inability to realize how much her daughter is hurting and how much her daughter needs to leave the "scene of the crime." Iris tells her mother, in one scene, "Why do we stay here? It's not normal." The power of this film is the fact that staying (Patricia's position) and leaving (Marcus's position) are both rendered viable options made by two kindred spirits (two lovers who both love Iris deeply and want the children of the Black Power movement to thrive). The film ends with a vision of black post-blackness as the emotional link between staying in the site of the movement and leaving the site of the movement. As Marcus walks away from the house, he and Patricia remain tied to each other. And, like Marcus, Iris will leave at some point, but she will be grounded; she will understand black post-blackness.

Making Doodles Public

The visual and performance artist William Pope.L's essay "Some Notes on the Ocean . . ." (2009) is a lucid manifesto of the elusive black post-blackness that is as present in the BAM as it is in twenty-first-century black aesthetics. His emphasis on the making and remaking of blackness is one of the many formulations in this essay that set up a neverending circular play between black and post-black. He writes, "To be black today is a choice that has to be made and re-made like a cake or a bed or a contract or a promise or a solar system."[42] The essay is shaped around "notions" that seem to be private thoughts made public. This essay is the introduction in *Black People Are Cropped*, a collection of Pope.L's drawings that seem like private doodles made public.

A doodle is a drawing made while a person is supposed to be listening to or doing something else. It is the art of boredom or, sometimes, simply the art of the hand that wanders even if the mind is trying to pay attention to the expected, conscious task at hand. In the *Skin Set Drawings* in *Black People Are Cropped*, Pope.L suggests that blackness, for many *blackened* subjects, is comparable to a doodle. It is what is processed, most freely, when there is a private space that will not be judged. Pope.L stages the sharing (the making public) of the private doodles, and this performance gains a new dimension when it is connected to the doodles that appear in some of the archives of the BAM. The interiority of the BAM archives have margins and edges that show people doodling their way to a type of free sign-making that is remarkably similar to the sign-making in Pope.L's doodles.

One of the doodles in the FST (Free Southern Theater) papers at Tulane University is a line drawing done on a letter to John O'Neal, one of the co-founders of FST.[43] The doodle turns into stationery decoration. The drawing includes a black woman's face in the right corner of the letter and a line pattern around the edges of the letter that looks like a pattern on African cloth. This artistic frame of the letter is an everyday type of art created by the artist Albert Bostick who unconsciously wanted the letter to be more than a letter. The letter writer is unconsciously aiming for a larger, more public audience. In a similar sense, Pope.L's *Skin Set Drawings* in *Black People Are Cropped* are performances of a private doodling type of sign-making that unconsciously desires a larger viewing. Pope.L's *Skin Set Drawings* are eccentric word-and-image interplays that could not be used like poems in the BAM, such as Haki Madhubuti's "Awareness" (1966), as a way of making words gain the hypnotic power of posterized consciousness (a black consciousness that created a new literacy). But in "Awareness," the repetition of the capitalized words "THINK BLACK" is only one version of the BAM sign-making around "Think Black."[44]

Another version, much closer to Pope.L's "private with public aspirations" sign-making, is found in the archives of Tom Dent. In this lost-in-the-archive "Think Black" doodle, the words "think black" are not tied to collective consciousness but to personal salvation. In this unidentified notebook, in Tom

Dent's papers (but not Dent's handwriting), there are a series of drawings.[45] The drawing with the words "think black" includes a quickly doodled, vague sketch of what appears to be a map of a crossroads and the slanted words: "To think black is to say, I'm the only one to save myself." This personal-salvation approach to "thinking black" gives us a glimpse into the BAM's awareness that collective consciousness could be the bridge to a particular type of self-enclosure that would not be individuality for individuality's sake.

This notion of a self-enclosure that thrives on the open air that it shares with others is one way of understanding the vision of black aesthetics that Pope.L delivers in "Some Notes on the Ocean . . ." and the *Skin Set Drawings* introduced by this essay. Just as the oceanic air seems to be shared without ever really feeling like somebody else's air, the eccentric, quirky claims made in "Some Notes on the Ocean . . ." are offered as ideas that can be shared only when they remain too slippery to entirely *own*. Pope.L's claims are the type of ideas that have the most power when they are whispered and not screamed. This whisper is what we hear when Baraka's "bass" softens in *In Our Terribleness,* as he confesses, "I can't say more than that except all the visions and thoughts you've had actually exist."[46]

This whisper is the peculiar interiority created when black people who have been mobilized by black consciousness-raising realize that the black safe spaces of the movement produce the black *unsafe* spaces where interiority is too delicate, vulnerable, and maddening to ever really be shared. In one of Carolyn Rodgers's 1968 letters to Hoyt Fuller, she apologizes for her emotional outburst, and her language reveals much about the honest discussions of the unshared inner spaces that BAM comrades had after they discovered the power of the collective black public interiority. Rodgers writes: "I think that often, my depressing overwhelming sensitivity to people, moods, and situations makes me re-act and say things, frequently, which seem unthinking, crude, and nonsensical, in my blind helter-skelter attempts to counteract what I feel, but can neither understand or aid."[47] Rodgers's correspondence gives a glimpse into the vulnerability and fragility of the black public interiority embraced during the BAM. The power of shared, collective, public black inner space should not be romanticized as only power; it was also what Rodgers refers to as "blind helter-skelter attempts" to find kindred spirits in an inner space that could not be fully shared. Twenty-first-century black aesthetics continue to engage the sheer complexity of this black public interiority.

7

Who's Afraid of the Black Fantastic?
The Substance of Surface

If we think of the fantastic as a genre that destabilizes, at least momentarily, our understandings of the distinctions between the reasonable and unreasonable [. . .], I would suggest its effects are not all that dissimilar from those of blackness, with its compulsive externalities and unintended consequences.

—Richard Iton, *In Search of the Black Fantastic*

Black post-blackness is a holding on and letting go of blackness that requires a move beyond the assumption that playing with blackness is a betrayal of commitment to struggle against oppression. Playing with blackness takes a particular form in black popular culture. As Richard Iton has shown in *In Search of the Black Fantastic* (2008), black popular culture, when it becomes the "black fantastic," contains a form of black political life that is not legible in dominant ways of understanding the political.[1] The Black Arts Movement had a complex relationship with black popular culture. The movement critiqued black popular culture, but, as BAM writers critiqued the seeming desire for whiteness in 1960s and 1970s black popular culture, they unconsciously unveiled the complexity of popular culture—popular culture's ability to make the superficial (the surface) matter.

The 2015 Rachel Dolezal controversy put the issue of the substance of black style in the national spotlight. The popular-culture spectacle of Dolezal (the comedians' parodies of her and the sensational news coverage) produced newspaper, magazine, television, and internet caricatures of her "Afro" hair and other images that ridiculed black style in a manner that approached the Blaxploitation 1970s movie images. When this NAACP leader was "outed" as being a white woman passing for black, the media spectacle led quickly to a questioning of her hair. Dolezal told interviewers that her hair was a weave.

The curly hair weaves and braided hair weaves were, more than the tanned skin, the reason why her passing for black was so successful.

The issue of surface versus depth emerged, for me, when a black undergraduate student asserted, "It's fine for her to feel black, but as long as she herself knows, *deep down*, that she is passing, she can't know what it is to be black" (emphasis added). Dolezal herself, in a *Vanity Fair* interview, explained that she considers herself "black" and not "African American." The BAM mobilized "black" as a word that meant the full self-determination of African Americans. The BAM response to Rachel Dolezal would be a critique of the whiteness of her very desire to appropriate blackness. The BAM would critique her inability to understand that white people cannot become the very force that the movement defined, in the words of A. B. Spellman, as being "the sensuality of a collective consciousness that declared itself" as not white.[2]

The BAM response to Dolezal would critique her inability to grasp that she can put on the "black hair" and the darkened skin, but she cannot simply decide when in her life she is white and benefitting from white privilege and when she is black. The BAM would insist that black people do indeed have the right to limit how white people use the very word "black" that the BAM mobilized as the tag of African American and African diasporic self-determination. The *whiteness* of her seizure of the right to call herself "black" would incite the BAM's rage against the violence of white power.

The most vivid image in popular culture's response to the Dolezal "passing for black" controversy may be the one that appeared in the *New York Daily News*, of a shirt (that covers her body and face) being unzipped to reveal the "black person" inside the "white" exterior.[3] This image captures the issues of surface versus depth that put this twenty-first-century passing for black in full conversation with the BAM's investment in the substance of style. In the eyes of those who view her passing as problematic, Dolezal was simply showing the "surface of style" as she wore black hairstyles and darkened her skin. The critics of her passing for black could not imagine the black interior that is visualized in the unzipped-jacket image. Many of the plentiful outraged internet responses (to the scandal of her being "outed" by her parents as white) simply saw her "black" surface as lacking depth; she demonstrated the superficiality and meaninglessness of surface as opposed to the sincerity of an actual lived experience of blackness that does not require any bodily performance and passing.

The notion of her "surface as pure surface" that lacks substance takes on a new dimension when looked at through the lens of the BAM. The legacy of the BAM is the radical use of surface to produce the substance of feeling black and empowered. Dolezal may have upset some people who *feel* black, because it is hard for them to believe that she feels black in a manner similar to how they feel black. But through the lens of the BAM investment in the substance of style, the Dolezal scandal also shows the reasons why BAM leaders and artists often worried about popular culture's use of surface. If black style and surface can be appropriated by white people, the movement knew this style and surface could easily become something so different from the Black Power "substance of surface" the movement was hailing.

When the BAM really leaned into its black post-blackness, black radical superficiality abounded. This radical use of surface was the feeling produced with the inclusion of the mirror-page transparency at the beginning of *In Our Terribleness* (1970). The reader's literal movement through and past the opening mirror page allowed surface to be experienced as it is in film, as a flatness that creates a moving-picture effect. Baraka, in the beginning of *In Our Terribleness*, uses the words "long image story in motion." Experiencing surface as radical superficiality, as a substance that does not become a type of depth that cancels out the shiny surface of the mirror page, makes readers/viewers of this word-and-image text experience blackness itself as the emotional truth of surface, as "it is what it is," not the factual truth of "black is. . . ."[4] This emotional truth of radical superficiality that proclaims "it is what it is" differs greatly from Dolezal's investment in using the superficial (her altered hair and skin) to pass for black.

The radical superficiality of the BAM was a *passing* and *moving* with the surfaces and styles to create the black "long image story in motion." In Barbara Mahone's BAM poem "With Your Permission," the poet imagines a lover enjoying the sheer intensity of the surface of skin: "smooth surfaces are easy / . . . I would rather deal with / what moves you / explore the fire and texture / of your soul / with your permission / I would chart a course / across your skin / and travel all day / all night / up and down that rocky road."[5] This BAM poem's depiction of a lover's exploration of the skin of the beloved conveys the BAM's larger love affair with blackness and working of surface for its most fantastic possibilities.

Anne Cheng, in her theory of the modernist overcoming of the binary of surface and depth, fully approaches the postmodern surface-and-depth experimentation with blackness that shapes the BAM. She writes: "Of course it can be said that all these moves to the surface are not really moves to the surface and in the end reconfirm the surface-depth binary (by, for instance, reproducing the surface as essence). Yet I want to suggest that, for a brief period in the early twentieth century, before cultural values collapsed back once again into a (shallow) surface and (authentic) interior divide, there was this tensile and delicate moment when these flirtations with the surface led to profound engagements with and re-imagings of the relationship between interiority and exteriority, between essence and covering."[6] The cultural nationalism of the BAM was also "this tensile and delicate moment" when people, consciously and unconsciously, experimented with ways of letting surface remain surface so that black style is not reduced to shallowness and is also not frozen when it is given a fixed "deep" meaning.

The BAM's Complex Relation to Popular Culture

The BAM does not simply precede the 1970s rise of the Blaxploitation popular-culture industry.[7] In its later (early 1970s) stages, the BAM wrestled to protect the substance of its surface from what the movement viewed as the commercial, white, oppressive use of surface and style in Blaxploitation. The BAM's relation to popular culture was sometimes a strong reaction against what the movement saw as black entertainers' "shuffling and jiving" for the oppressors. One poem that embodies this version of the BAM anti–popular culture stance is Haki Madhubuti's "On Seeing Diana Go Madddddddddd" (1970). After the epigraph—"on the very special occasion of the death of her two dogs—Tiffany & Li'l Bit—when she cried her eyelashes off"—the opening words in the poem are:

> a dog lover,
> a lover of dogs   in a land where poodles
> eat/live cleaner than their masters
> & their masters use the colored people
> to walk that   which they love, while they
> wander in & out of our lives running the world.
>
> (stop! in the name of love, before you break my heart)
>
> u moved with childlike vision
> deeper into lassieland to become
> the new wonderwoman of the dirty-world
> we remember the 3/the three young baaaaad Detroiters
> of younger years when i & other blacks moved with u
> & all our thoughts dwelled on the limits of forget & forgive.
>
> (stop! in the name of love, before you break my heart)[8]

Diana Ross, through the lens of this poem, has gone mad in the process of being seduced by a white-dominated popular-culture industry. Madhubuti dramatizes what he views as Ross's loss of soul (what was called "Soul Power" during the BAM) by using her own song "Stop! In the Name of Love" (recorded in 1965 by the Supremes for the Motown label), as he shifts the song's individual romance narrative to the collective love affair with blackness (during the BAM) and the "black hearts" broken by Ross's move from the "baaaaad Detroiter" to mainstream celebrity.

But the BAM relation to popular culture also included the movement's embrace of what Richard Iton names the "black fantastic." As this movement of black self-determination raged against the insidious white aesthetic of dominant popular culture, it also found ways to bridge the gap between black popular culture and black cultural nationalism.[9] In *The Autobiography of LeRoi Jones* (1997), Amiri Baraka argues that black bohemianism is at the core of black cultural nationalism.[10] The pleasure of performing black eccentricity, during the era of the BAM, was sometimes situated on the edge or outside of black cultural nationalism.[11] Whereas the nationalism was sometimes framed as a seriousness that was not performance or *play*, some of the performances of "black is different" (in the 1960s and 1970s black popular-culture zone) reframed the meaning of the political and produced what Iton uncovers as the power of the alternative politics of the black fantastic—the power of productive *play*.

Iton's theory of black popular culture's ability to create a powerful groove of the black fantastic illuminates what is at stake in the deeper examination of the role of artifice and the "unnatural" in performances of "black is beautiful." We often think that black bodies will be fully liberated when they are no longer politicized—when, as some argue, hairstyles are simply hairstyles and there is no sense that dreadlocks are, as a woman in the documentary *Nappy* (1998) asserts, a Ph.D. in black consciousness.[12] But Iton's theory of the black fantastic pushes past the sense that the state of nonpoliticized bodies is the goal, as if we are only struggling with erasing the ideology that has been written on black bodies. Iton pushes us to the illegible work of resistance and struggle performed as black subjects reanimate the *overwritten* black body and denaturalize the notion that political resistance cannot be tied to pleasure and play.

The poems of Julia Fields offer a full entrance into the playful black popular-culture bodily aesthetics of the BAM era, which sometimes differed greatly from the natural-black-beauty discourse that the movement privileged. Fields's poem "I Loves a Wig" was published in a 1975 issue of *Black*

World, the most central BAM magazine, but it takes readers to a zone of black popular culture that, on the surface, does not link the cultural and political in the typical manner of the BAM. The speaker inveighs against the assumption that particular body adornments (worn by black women) must be read as racial self-hatred: "Precious Lord, what am I to do with smart people / That want me to get rid of my wig? I rake and scrape / To get me a wig and they come here telling me to / 'Go natural.'"[13] Joe Goncalves's BAM manifesto "Natural Black Beauty" (1969) crystallizes the "black is beautiful" policing of the body that frustrates the speaker in Fields's poem. Goncalves explains the movement's "natural beauty" sensibility in the following manner: "As for our natural beauty: Our lips complement our noses, our noses 'go with' our eyes and they all bless our skin, which is black. If your face does not complement itself, you are in a degree of trouble. . . . The real geometry of our faces, the natural geometry in terms of art is found, among other places, in African sculpture. Our natural architecture, our natural rhythm."[14] This BAM manifesto shows that the movement imagined natural black beauty as not only an alternative self-image (a black gaze) but also as an alternative aesthetic that could decolonize the mind and the body. The worry over disorder, in this manifesto, is the worry over the distortions of black beauty created by antiblack racism. This rage against the violence of the antiblack distortions fuels Madhubuti's poem "On Seeing Diana Go Madddddddddd." Madhubuti cannot see any liberating aspects of Ross's performance of the black fantastic.

Reconsidering *Mahogany* as the Black Fantastic

Diana Ross's performance in the film *Mahogany* (1975) helps us understand the freedom tied to the black female fantastic, that which is often unimaginable in ways of thinking about the political.[15] The seduction and pleasure created by the commercial popular-culture industry (that *Mahogany* embodies in its depiction of Diana Ross as a fashion designer and model) allows us to see that BAM resistance to white aesthetics and white cultural and economic power also included the pleasure of what Baraka described, in *In Our Terribleness*, as "putting on new clothes."[16] The tension between the political and the aesthetic is dramatized throughout *Mahogany* as Billy Dee Williams plays the earnest "Power to the People" character, Brian, who is running for political office and in love with the "I want to be a star" character, Tracy (Ross), who loves looking beautiful and wearing and creating beautiful clothing (and who is bored with race and black-community issues).

When Iton insists that the words "black fantastic" are redundant (a "pleonasm"), he offers a lucid way of breaking the boundaries between political mobilizations of blackness and cultural and performative mobilizations of blackness.[17] At the end of *Mahogany*, when Tracy gives up the world of glamor and returns from Rome to the United States, viewers may think that she is giving up the fantastic as she chooses a black family and community over the white world that her time in Rome represents in the eyes of Brian. But what if we do not assume that this iconic scene must be read as the post-fantastic? Could it be that Tracy returns to Brian with a renewed appreciation of the black fantastic? Does she return to the black Chicago community, not beaten down by the white gaze that has exoticized her, but with a renewed sense of black glamor? In the final scene of the film, is the crowd of people in the community rally witnessing Tracy's seduction by the charismatic black male leader, or are they witnessing Ross's seduction *of* the male leader?

The most apt reading of this scene is a two-way seduction in which the political speech delivered by Brian is productively interrupted by Tracy's litany of questions, as she insists that his campaign promises make room for the more abstract (and concrete) need for love and happiness. The most powerful part of black popular culture (in the midst of oppressive commercialism) is the zone where black people find a space to express love, happiness, and fantasy. When the crowd (in the final scene of *Mahogany*) witnesses a political campaign speech transform into a sharing of vows by two reunited lovers, the passion of campaign politics is rendered less important than the passion of black people finding room, in the midst of the historical and current racial trauma, to love and be loved. *Mahogany* shows, in this final scene, how fantastical this love (in the midst of war) can be.

Since the BAM was a collective love affair with blackness, BAM critiques of black entertainers' participation in white-dominated popular culture become an ideal lens through which to think about the complexity of self-love and the performances of self-love that are not recognized as liberating when our understanding of politics and resistance does not include the black fantastic. Madhubuti's poem "On Seeing Diana Go Madddddddddd" and *Mahogany* are not, simply, entirely different registers (black cultural nationalism versus popular culture entertainment). Madhubuti calls for Diana Ross's recovery from the "madness" of "selling out." The plot of *Mahogany* also pivots on her move from "selling out" to "coming back home," but "home" in the movie is not the "nation" hailed by the BAM, and Billy Dee Williams is not Malcolm X, Stokely Carmichael, or the other revolutionaries that set the BAM in motion. In spite of these differences, *Mahogany* nonetheless captures a "black is beautiful" sensibility that is not entirely different from the 1960s and 1970s BAM version. Madhubuti mourns Ross's "going mad," but in the film, Ross's performance creates a most heightened "black is beautiful" aura when she almost loses her mind as she struggles to escape the power of the white photographer who treats her like an exotic animal. When the photographer fully succumbs to madness, Tracy finally realizes she must return to the United States and escape the stardom that reduces her to such a disempowered object of the white gaze.

Tracy learns the lesson that the speaker in Madhubuti's poem wants to teach Diana Ross, but the poem shapes this lesson around black solidarity and black aesthetics, whereas the film shapes this lesson around the value of privileging love over success and money. Aesthetics are the core issue in the film, but the film is not, like the BAM, invested in the *substance* of style. Throughout the film, flashes of something that the BAM would call the Black Aesthetic emerge as a surprise. The most compelling flashes of Ross's black beauty are the ones that present her as "black is beautiful because it is fantastic." The most black-fantastic image of Ross in the film may be the one with circular braids that are wrapped with thread—an image that evokes the Afrofuturism of the clothing worn by Sun Ra's Arkestra. As opposed to the *unnatural*, in this image, which actually captures the fabulousness of the *natural* black beauty that the BAM celebrated, Madhubuti, in "On Seeing Diana Go Madddddddddd," rages against the wigs that Ross wears. This futuristic hairstyle would not be read, within the BAM gaze, as comparable to a wig (a sign of Ross's racial self-hatred). The hairstyle is so fantastically unnatural and otherworldly that, in the BAM gaze, it depicts the power of natural black beauty.

Other BAM poems by Madhubuti show that he was drawn to the black fantastic, even as he, like many other leading architects of the movement, insisted on natural black beauty. In the poem "Gwendolyn Brooks," Madhubuti revels in the full range of blackness as he celebrates "spaceman black" and "unsubstance black."[18] When BAM writers lean into black people's ability to love being themselves, the movement's approach to the political gains the popular-culture twist of the black fantastic. The black cultural nationalism surely does not disappear, but it deepens as the self-determination of black nationalism meets the self-determination of black pleasure. As Baraka, in *Black Music*, recognizes the ways that Sun Ra became the muse of the BAM, he also decides that Sun Ra's black otherworldliness cannot be separated from James Brown's soulful popularity. Baraka decides that we need "James-Ra and Sun-Brown." Baraka writes, "The Rhythm and

Blues mind blowing evolution of James-Ra and Sun-Brown. That growth to include all the resources, all the rhythms, all the yells and cries, all that information about the world, the Black ommmmmmmmm-mmmmmm, opening and entering."[19] Baraka captures the type of madness that is so different from the madness critiqued by Madhubuti in "On Seeing Diana." This beautiful madness ("all the yells and cries") is what made the cultural nationalism of the 1960s and 1970s into so much more than the bourgeois nationalism that, as Baraka explains, it was always on the verge of becoming. Madhubuti's words "Don't Cry, Scream" remind us that as he was raging against the madness of black participation in white commercialism, he was calling for a madness that would be black aesthetics unbound.

This unboundedness is what we see in *Mahogany* as Ross continues to dance and whirl as if she is performing Langston Hughes's poem "Dream Variations"—"To fling my arms wide / in some place of the sun, / To whirl and to dance."[20] But the final words in this iconic Harlem Renaissance poem are "Till the white day is done," and, through the lens of the BAM, Diana Ross remains trapped in whiteness once she chooses stardom over community. When we recognize how the black fantastic travels between the BAM and 1970s black popular culture, it is hard to believe that some of those "trapped in whiteness" are not subverting their containment, but the two-way flow of black fantastic energy, between black popular culture and black cultural nationalism, also shows that, as the BAM artists were purposefully enclosing themselves in blackness, they were often, simultaneously, subverting the containment. The movement's grassroots focus made their critiques of white popular media's brainwashing of the black masses coexist with a deep desire to make black cultural nationalism make sense on the streets, not only in the Black Arts collectives, journals, dramatic performances, visual art, and books.

Mahogany's focus on clothing as art connects directly to the clothing art of Jae Jarrell (one of the BAM visual artists in the AfriCOBRA collective). When Jarrell made the revolutionary suit that included bullets, she created art that was as fantastic as Sun Ra's clothing and the image of Diana Ross in *Mahogany*. When Baraka insists, "You can put on new clothes," in *In Our Terribleness*, we may only hear the political urgency of the BAM call for "Negroes" to become "black" and forget about Baraka's call for the actual sensation of putting on new clothes (the pulling off of the old, the unbuttoning and zipping on, the looking in the mirror to see how the new clothing looks).[21] When we connect Baraka's words "You can put on new clothes" to another moment in *In Our Terribleness*, when he writes, "Sun Ra is to teach

Freud, not the reverse," we gain a deeper understanding of Eleanor Traylor's frustration with what she views as the reduction of Black Arts theorists to ideologues.[22] Traylor argues, "Who was more theoretical than the Black Arts Movement, but we've been treated as ideologues."[23] Baraka develops a theory of the black mind as the black body, as he crushes the old tired binaries of (white) mind and time over (black) body and space.[24] The black fantastic, in this word-and-image text, is the nitty-gritty texture of new ideas about self that seem like new clothing that makes a body move with new energy and the urgency of "Nation Time," when the black body is the most local alternative nation state.

It is hard to watch *Mahogany* and feel the tremble of Baraka's call for Nation Time, but, in both *Mahogany* and *In Our Terribleness*, it is easy to feel the exhilaration of putting on new clothes that make one move through the world with a new sense of style and self-determination. In black popular culture, when this self-determination does not take the form of natural black beauty, it is sometimes misread as black self-hatred. Some BAM writers and leaders participated in this misreading of the body politics of black popular culture, but the BAM also included a profound engagement with the black self-determination in popular culture that sometimes looked very different from the "black is beautiful" images produced by the movement.

It may seem odd that Julia Fields's poem "Art," with the lines "Whenever I goes to black art shows, I sees / The ugliest black women in the whole world," would be published in the most central BAM magazine, *Black World*.[25] Both this poem and Fields's poem "I Loves a Wig" were published in a 1975 issue of *Black World*, the same year that *Mahogany* was released. In these poems, Fields imagines the point of view of a woman who is "black folk" and fully skeptical about the natural-black-beauty ethos of the art of the BAM and the everyday encounters between black "smart people" and the folk. Fields begins "I Loves a Wig" with the question, "Precious Lord, what am I to do with smart people, / That want me to get rid of my wig." The most intriguing part of this poem is the reclamation of intelligence as that which enables someone to know that the visual is the zone of play, not truth. Fields writes, "Wigs is for intelligent, sophisticated people—not Fools / That think that things is what they is or what they seems."[26] Fields's emphasis on the *common* black person's reaction to the "sophisticated" person's investment in natural black beauty dramatizes the everyday complexity of black popular aesthetics. The speaker enjoys wearing a wig because it is labor-free and because "all wigs have good hair." This notion of good hair is, of course, the madness that the BAM rages against, but the speaker is also critiquing the very notion of good hair, as she implies that just as "all wigs have good hair," all people have "good" hair. In this poem, the black fantastic emerges when the trauma of black self-hatred is denaturalized in such a fantastical manner. During the BAM, it would be easy to think that a black woman insisting on her self-love while wearing a wig is delusional, but Fields makes readers step into this world of seeming delusion and begin to understand the "love" and pleasure that the speaker feels when she puts on that which Madhubuti describes as "other people's hair."[27]

Fields's poem "Art" appears immediately before "I Loves a Wig." In "Art," Fields depicts the gendered dimension of some investments in natural black beauty and the gendered dimension of some erasures of the black fantastic. After the opening line—"I am glad that no revolutionary artist has ever made any / Painting of me"—the speaker proceeds to state, "The person who can make the ugliest picture of a black / Woman is a black man."[28] Fields imagines a black woman who looks at BAM paintings and sculpture and sees "blunt, basic, and ugly." She craves more adorned images; she wants to see more glamor. The idealization of the unadorned black woman during the BAM often represented an attempt by black men to purge themselves of the dominant-culture images of white feminine beauty; black women were imagined as the pure, "basic" beauty that did not need flowing hair or any intentionally seductive flair. But this stripping of black women to the "natural black beauty" ideal, as Fields shows in her poem "Art," shut down the play and performance that can shape the pleasure of performances of femininity. Some BAM women writers such as Julia Fields refused to accept this canceling-out of the play of black femininity.

Black male fear of the black feminine fantastic is one clear way to read Madhubuti's critique of Diana Ross in "On Seeing Diana Go Madddddddddd," Baraka's depiction of the nonrevolutionary "sister" in *Madheart* (with the blond wig), and many other images of black women in male-authored BAM texts.[29] But the more complex readings take us to signs of the black male writers' own boredom with images of black men and women simply loving each other by agreeing "to be black together" and their desire to locate the fantastic in black women (not "the natural"). We see this latent desire in Madhubuti's "On Seeing Diana Go Maddddddddd," as the speaker laments Ross becoming a "moving star" in what he views as her post-black period. As Madhubuti breaks the word "moving" apart ("mov ing"), slow motion is implied; the sense of a star that is not really moving makes the poem itself slow down each time he repeats this breaking apart of the word. In each of these slower sequences, he creates a desire to see Ross really move, a desire to not only critique what he sees as her post-blackness but also a desire to see her become a genuine "moving star."

This desire, in the male-authored BAM literature, to see a "black post-black" female fantastic looms at the end of Baraka's short story "Answers in Progress" (1967). In this story, Baraka moves to a literal post-blackness—the arrival of blue people from another planet in the middle of a black urban rebellion (also known as a "black riot"). At the very end of this story, after the narrator and other black people living in the area of the black urban rebellion realize how "almost black" the blue people are—how their style almost seems black and how they are most interested in the "out" part of the BAM (the free jazz, in particular)—one of the narrator's friends, Ball, wonders what the "blue chicks looked like."[30] The narrator expresses his seeming lack of desire to know the blue women, but the final sentences of the story imply that he realizes that he has blueness waiting for him at home. The story ends with the suggestion that black is blue.

The Undressing of the Political

An answer to Ball's question (what do "blue chicks look like?") literally appears in Erykah Badu and Robert Glasper's song and video "Afro Blue" (2012). Badu's blue lips in the video conjure up Afrofuturism and also the iconic Louis Armstrong question, "What did I do to be so black and blue?" Badu and Glasper's use of the words "Afro Blue" is a mood-shifting alternative to some of the current uses of the word "Afropessimism" that mistake what James Baldwin calls the "deep water" of the blues for the shallow water of skepticism about pan-Africanism and the need for black unity. As Badu and Glasper's video imagines a black futuristic world, the "blue" (a neo-blues sensibility) is figured as a fantastic force that will see black people through the future challenges.

We need to remember Toni Morrison's depiction, in her novel *Paradise* (1997), of how a woman with natural hair is treated by other black women whose respectability and investment in racial uplift makes them shun anyone who wears her hair natural. Morrison describes Anna's feelings as the only person in the town who wears her hair natural: "She was certain the disapproval was mostly because of her unstraightened hair. My God, the conversations she had been forced to have when she came back from Detroit. Strange, silly, invasive probings. She felt as though they were discussing her pubic hair, her underarm hair. That if she had walked completely naked down the street they would have commented only on the hair on her head."[31]

This crisis of black people being so oppressed by the gaze that makes them feel that their natural hair is shameful and must be "processed" before appearing in public is the very type of self-hatred that the BAM was fighting. Morrison's brilliant connection of black hair and black nudity—the idea that the gaze of internalized white aesthetics makes natural black hair comparable to pubic hair and underarm hair—opens up the deepest dimensions of the natural-black-beauty politics of the BAM. To destroy the "good hair/ bad hair" residue of the colonized mind that happened during slavery and was passed on throughout generations, the BAM mobilized the "natural" as a value system that made many young black women in the 1960s realize, for the first time, that they could *show* their unprocessed hair and defy the gaze that made their very bodies a source of shame.

Nikki Giovanni's poem "Seduction" (1967) stages another type of black women's seizure of the power of "uncovering" the black body. This poem also leads us to a deeper understanding of Iton's theory of the black fantastic; both Giovanni and Iton recognize that the black fantastic makes us rethink ingrained assumptions about the boundaries between play and politics. In the poem, there is stripping of a "long African gown" by a woman, as she listens to a man talk about the black revolution. After he continues to talk and pretend not to notice her removal of her clothing and his clothing (his dashiki), she removes his shorts, which makes him finally notice his "state of undress." As the woman speaker imagines the unfolding of this seduction scene, she wonders if he would ignore the "heat" of the moment and rush back to the seriousness of his movement *talk*:

> one day
> you gonna walk in this house
> and i'm gonna have on a long African
> gown
> you'll sit down and say "The Black . . ."
> and i'm gonna take one arm out
> then you—not noticing me at all—will say "What about
> this brother . . ."
> and i'm going to be slipping it over my head
> and you'll rap on about "The revolution . . ."
> while i rest your hand against my stomach
> you'll go on—as you always do—saying
> "I just can't dig . . ."
> while i'm moving your hand up and down

and i'll be taking your dashiki off
then you'll say "What we really need . . ."
and I'll be licking your arm
and "The way I see it we ought to . . ."
and unbuckling your pants
"And what about the situation . . ."
and taking your shorts off
then you'll notice
your state of undress
and knowing you you'll just say
"Nikki,
isn't this counterrevolutionary . . . ?"[32]

Giovanni "undresses" the category "revolutionary" and opens up new dimensions of this black cultural revolution—dimensions that show people wanting blackness to be a collective *release*, not the collective robotic nature embodied in the man addressed in the poem.

Other BAM poems, such as Baraka's "An Agony. As Now" (1964), also "undress" the collective nature of blackness to show an awareness that any elements in the movement that "policed" people's relation to the freedom of their own body was a problem.[33] A. B. Spellman captures this problem when he writes, "I do regret the culture cops."[34] The sheer desire for full freedom is at the core of "An Agony. As Now." The poem is typically read as expressing the pain of a black person trapped inside a white, overwhelmingly oppressive force, but the poem also pivots on the horror of "flesh" being contained "inside his books, his fingers." "Flesh," in this poem, is trapped inside what Baraka refers to as the "enclosure," and this "enclosure" is whiteness, of course, but it is also anything that presses in such a painful manner against the openness and excessiveness of *flesh*. When black-nationalist rhetoric becomes anti-erotic, as figured in Giovanni's "Seduction," it becomes another type of enclosure of flesh. "Flesh," as theorized by Hortense Spillers, is what the Middle Passage makes of black bodies. Fred Moten captures the core of Spillers's insight when he refers to "[t]his flesh that we might call a body."[35] This language makes me think about the black love of blackness that creates tender ways of treating each other's flesh. This tenderness would work against any enclosure, any containment of the flesh created by the unspeakable containment of the Middle Passage and its legacies. This tenderness is lost when some twenty-first-century black artists fail to recognize that the critique of the enclosures of black flesh is an *undressing* of black-nationalist ways of seeing black bodies, not a repudiation of the BAM itself, since the movement's liberation of flesh from antiblack violence is what produces the next step of this full freedom of the black undressed subject.

The electricity of the black natural/unnatural mix is canceled out in some BAM male-authored representations of black women. In many BAM texts, it is hard to find a female counterpart to Larry Neal's celebration of "Bobby Blue Bland with a dashiki and a process." But when we recognize that Madhubuti's description of black aesthetics unbound, in his poem "Gwendolyn Brooks," really can be read as one of the most lucid expressions of the role of the black fantastic in the BAM, we appreciate the natural/unnatural mix in the explosive, playful stanza that epitomizes the dramatic, complex performance of black post-blackness in this movement. We can grasp the black female fantastic of Brooks and many other black women when we lose ourselves in Madhubuti's uncontainable stanza that begins with the words "black doubleblack purpleblack blueblack beenblack was" and ends with "black unsubstanceblack."[36] Like Madhubuti, Amiri Baraka, in some of his BAM texts, wants to know the black female fantastic in spite of his own lapse, in *Madheart* and other BAM texts, into the assumption that black women's play with artifice and the "unnatural" must be a sign of racial self-hatred. Of all of Baraka's representations of black women, his tribute to Billie Holiday, "The Dark Lady of the Sonnets," is the most complex. In this tribute, Baraka presents his own version of the black female version of "Bobby Blue with a dashiki and a process." Baraka moves to a deep desire to feel (and a recognition that he cannot know) black-female-fantastic outer space. His love of Sun Ra, throughout *Black Music*, transmutes, in this verbal-abstract portrait of Holiday, into the love of her otherworldliness. When Baraka moves from "More than she has ever felt is what we mean by fantasy" to "Sometimes you are afraid to listen to this lady," we hear an honest response to the power of the black female fantastic and realize the power of the energy that Badu is channeling when she reenergizes the "Afro Blue" (a mix of neo-soul and neo-blues) in both the black cultural nationalism of the 1960s and the music and visual style of Lady Day, who died the year before the decade that mobilized "black" in such a fantastic manner.[37]

At the very end of *The Black Fantastic*, Iton analyzes Badu's video performance of the song "Bag Lady." This video begins with Badu literally opening up the sides of our viewing screen to make room for her and the other performers, who are all dressed in different mono-color flowing clothing that evokes Ntozake Shange's use of different colors as a way to identify the black women characters in *For Colored Girls Who Have Considered Suicide / When the Rainbow Is Enuf* (1975). Iton's focus on the movement of Badu's hands as she "push[es] back the frame past the standard margins" reminds us that to comprehend the black fantastic, we need to step out of certain frames that do not allow black pleasure and black political resistance to coexist and sustain each other. Badu performs the mix of pleasure and political resistance in a photograph of a side view of her seemingly unclothed body (her hand covering the visible part of her breast). In this photograph, buttons that would normally be pinned to clothing are on her bare skin, in a vertical arrangement from her shoulder to almost the midpoint of her arm. Two of the buttons have a picture of Badu and the words "Free Badu" surrounding the circle of her Afro. The most visible button (the one easiest to read) contains the words "I LOVE BEING BLACK" (with the heart shape instead of the word "love"). This button has a green background; the red, black, and green colors signal that this love of being black is, for Badu, a steady reenergizing of the colors, the vibrancy, of pan-Africanism and black cultural nationalism.

In this period that Iton calls the "post-post," Badu entangles the ongoing black freedom struggle and the heightened interest among young black people in the twenty-first century to claim their right to be individuals (not only a part of a black collective). The buttons with the words "Free Badu," of course, echo the "Free Angela Davis" campaigns, but they also echo the black fantastic energy, in Baraka's *In Our Terribleness*, that makes the most individual type of freedom-searching inseparable from the larger black freedom struggle. When Badu's embrace of individuality and critique of "groupthink" (in her "Window Seat" performance) is connected to her many songs and performances that reinvigorate 1960s black cultural-nationalist style, we see that the recovery of that which Baraka identified as the black bohemianism of cultural nationalism is the most riotous aspect of remembering black cultural nationalism and fighting against the current tendency to flatten it. Bohemianism and cultural nationalism constituted each other as investments in being black became inseparable from investments in performances of the black fantastic.

When Erykah Badu's first album put her in the public spotlight, she always wore her hair wrapped in an upward style that inspired imitations by young black women in Manhattan and Brooklyn, in particular. Badu put the 1960s and 1970s natural black hairstyles back in motion in urban black style. The covering of the hair with African prints had, during the BAM, a "black is beautiful" pull that was as strong as the movement's embrace of the Afro hairstyle and the "natural" (the shorter version of the Afro). After Badu gained success with her first album, the covering of her hair became a sensational issue discussed in magazine interviews. When she was asked what was under the covering, she explained in one interview that she had locks and that the locks were fake (i.e. that they were hair extensions). Through the years, as the trajectory of her hair play has continued, Badu first began to perform with the locks uncovered and then moved to a new public image when her hair was cut very short. Since the short-haired look, she has continued to perform and be photographed with many different hairstyles, but the cap that looks like a cap worn under a wig, in her public performance art at the site of John F. Kennedy's assassination in Dallas, is the moment when her play with the role of covering and uncovering in black aesthetics (putting on and taking off) gains the most power.

In 2010, as Badu unveiled her body at the site of JFK's assassination, the Queen of Neo-Soul performed a reclamation of the most "natural" type of blackness—the nude body with no covering or artifice whatsoever. As she walks down the street in the video for "Window Seat," she slowly removes her clothing and then simulates her own assassination before the performance ends with an image of Badu with a purposefully exaggerated African braid hairstyle and a wry smile.[38] She critiques the ongoing assassination of black people who claim their freedom in the most militant and public manner. She performs freedom as she takes off her clothes and pretends that she need not care about any external gaze. Baraka's words "You can put on new clothes" echo and take on new shapes in the twenty-first century neo-soul reenergizing of the BAM performance of the free black body as free black mental space. In contrast to Baraka's "You can put on new clothes," the neo-soul icon of cultural-nationalist style nonverbally proclaims, in this 2010 performance art, "You can take off your clothes." The 1960s putting on of "blackness" was always partially a taking off of an ideology of blackness in order to find what Madhubuti, in the poem "Gwendolyn Brooks," calls an "unsubstance" (a state of becoming, comparable to the word "Evolving" on Badu's back, after she unveils). The putting on and taking off is the ethos of black post-blackness that shapes Badu as much as it shapes the BAM women writers, such as Nikki Giovanni, who are not afraid of the black female fantastic.

The difference between Badu's performance of her assassination and the assassinations that the BAM staged (black people assassinated by white power) is the fact that, in "Window Seat," the question "Who assassinated her?" lingers. Badu as a neo-soul icon stages the public stripping of her clothes as a form of liberation that leads to her assassination, and there is no way of knowing who or what kills her. The words in the most famous BAM poem, "Black Art"—"we want 'poems that kill.' Assassin poems, Poems that shoot guns"—show how the BAM made art itself into a form of assassination.[39]

Badu's twenty-first-century performance is not an "assassination" performance; it is a stripping of the texture of what is recognized as assassination. As Badu makes people think about the ongoing assassination of black women, she does not identify who or what is killing them. The violence against black women's bodies is figured as a violence that can't be known or understood.

Badu's stripping in "Window Seat" begs to be compared to Baraka's use of the word "stripping" in "Black Art." Baraka writes, "Put it on him, poem. Strip him naked to the world!" The "negro leader" that needs to be "stripped naked" is catering to global white supremacy. Baraka asks the "poem" to make this "negro leader" feel so disempowered that he feels naked.[40] In "Window Seat," Badu is vulnerable once she strips; her act of stripping seems to be a transgression that means she must be assassinated. Badu seems to say, "I strip myself naked to the world." The "negro leader" in "Black Art" is missing the blackness that the BAM hailed as the movement called for the conversion of "Negroes" into "black people." The poem's stripping of the leader represents a stripping of his "Negro" power, his lack of blackness. Badu's stripping is a stripping of something that she doesn't name—it seems to reject everything that male and white gazes have projected onto her body. The style of her walk is black urban style. The style of the stripping is a letting go of any gazes (including black gazes) that fix her. One example of the gazes that try to fix her is an online blog about Badu's 2012 performance in Wayne Coyne's controversial video of "The First Time Ever I Saw Your Face." Tiffani Jones, the blogger, writes, "Erykah is a virtuosa at provocation. Got these people slipping and sliding, dipping and diving. Getting all deep, going all shallow. People are a hot mess."[41] In one of Badu's performances of the song "Tyrone," we see this "slipping and sliding" when she slightly pulls her long traditional West African dress and begins, for a moment, to lift the long dress. As she gestures to the unveiling that happens, years later, in "Window Seat," she performs a desire to be a potential stripper even as she wears the African clothing. She holds on to the clothing of the "respectable" African queen even as she simulates the moment of letting go of this clothing. Kalamu ya Salaam, in his interpretation of Badu's *sound* control, approaches this notion of holding on by letting go. In his tribute to Badu, Salaam writes:

> What it is, is Erykah is controlling the shit by letting it go, by giving basic tracks away, she is garnering truckloads of remixes, boxcars of attention, got producers worldwide working on her music and considering the result 'their/ our' music. This raises the notion of 'collective' to a truly cosmic level. So the greater control is achieved by letting go.[42]

In her song "Other Side of the Game," Badu sings, "Peace after revolution / I know there's confusion / We gotta do this thing together / Through whatever [. . .] Peace after revolution / You gotta do what you gotta do."[43] The sheer freedom, the "whatever," lingers when Badu holds onto the groove of "revolution" decades after the BAM and almost makes the words "peace after revolution" the *signature* added at the end of the song. Who is afraid of the black fantastic? Who is afraid of black post-blackness? These are the questions hovering around "Window Seat" and other black popular-cultural productions that take us to the complex performance of black post-blackness.

The Radical Sonic-Visual Surface

One of Badu's album covers captures the full spirit of the BAM's black radical use of surface. The cover art for *Worldwide Underground* (2003) features a profile image of Badu with a large Afro in front of a background of words (such as "our story," "neo-soul," and "are you afraid of dollars?") that begs

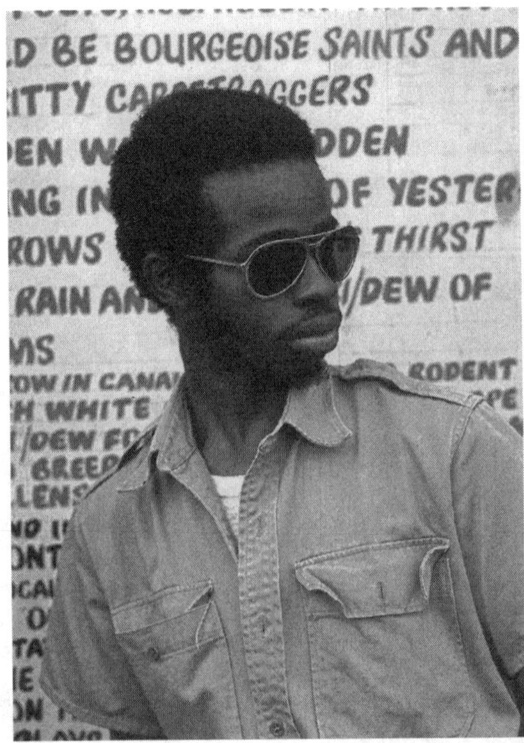

Figure 30. Joel Brandon ("master whistler"), 1968. Photo: Bob Crawford, Chicago, 1968.

to be compared to a BAM photograph by the Chicago photographer Bob Crawford of the "master whistler" musician, Joel Brandon, standing in front of a BAM poem painted on the wall of a building (fig. 30).[44] These images dramatize the tension between the surface of words and the surface of the body. Crawford's photograph shows how BAM photographers were, like the writers of the movement, attempting to reclaim the black body and resituate it in a black gaze. When we compare the *Worldwide Underground* cover and the classic BAM photograph, it is clear that Badu's neo-soul shares the BAM's interest in the alternative, Black Power rewriting of (and "on") the black body and also the movement's interest in the substance of surface. In both images, the bodies and words, the foreground and the background, become layered surfaces that do not need to collapse into each other. The words are not written on the body; the written surface and the body surface are in a state of productive tension. And the interplay between the embodied foreground and written background conjures up the possibility that sound has a certain surface, an edge that we could learn to hear in a radical way that destroys the surface/depth binary. Black sound could be the substance of surface that cannot be contained or commodified. Badu's album cover makes us want to hear the music, since we cannot really read the words; Crawford's photograph makes us want to hear the full performance of words such as "bourgeoise saints" and "carpetbaggers" in the BAM painted poem. The images gesture to a sonic dimension that is not *deeper* than the surfaces celebrated in the images; the sonic is rendered through the surfaces as a sonic visuality is produced.

The BAM mobilization of the substance of style was most closely tied to the black masses and the popular when the artists made art that seemed so "hands on" and a part of everyday life that any "black" person tired of being a "Negro" could grab on to this surface. The painted cardboard album covers and hand-drawn grooves on cardboard records of Mike Stevens ("Mingering Mike") are a profound example of the radical use of surface in some waves of 1960 and 1970s black popular culture that flowed smoothly with the mission of the BAM. In "The Changing Same," Baraka merges soul music and jazz as he calls for "James-Ra and Sun-Brown."[45] Mingering Mike imagined himself as a soul singer with celebrity status. His record covers (figs. 31 and 32) and simulations of records with actual grooves were discovered in 2003.[46] This folk art is a stunning example of someone realizing that the surface really can be the substance (that the black fantastic really might be the imagining of what we cannot hear *yet*). In "The Mystery of Mingering Mike: The Soul Legend Who Never Existed" (2015), Jon Ronson explains:

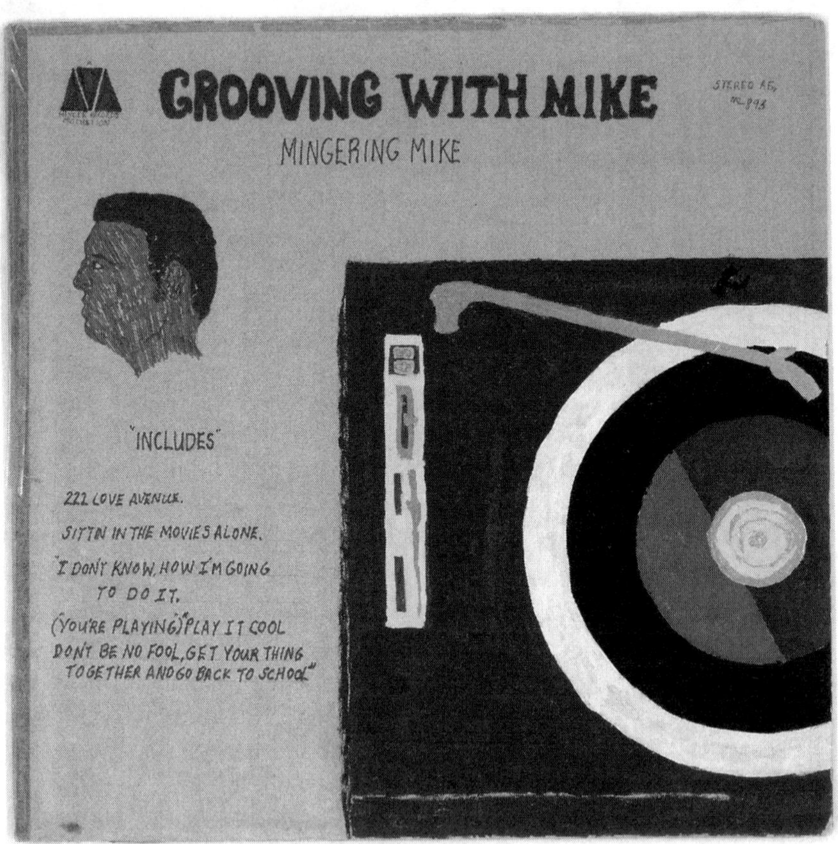

Figure 31. *Grooving with Mike*, Mingering Mike, 1970. Mixed media paperboard, 12½ × 12½ in. (31.8 × 31.8 cm.). Gift of Mike Wilkins and Sheila Duignan and museum purchase through the Luisita L. and Franz H. Denghausen Endowment. Smithsonian American Art Museum, Washington, D.C. Photo Smithsonian American Art Museum, Washington, D.C. / Art Resource, N.Y.

At first Mike concentrated on the cover artwork, but his cousins told him they were too flimsy without a record inside, so he added cardboard discs, drawing the groove lines with a pencil and a compass. He'd always double-check that the number of bands tallied with the number of song titles on the cover. Vinyl discs tended to hold "38 to 43 minutes of music," Mike says, so he'd estimate how long his imaginary songs would last, and made sure they stayed within that limit.

"I just wanted to be as real as possible," he says.

Sometimes he'd sing his imaginary songs into a cassette recorder, which made them no longer imaginary.[47]

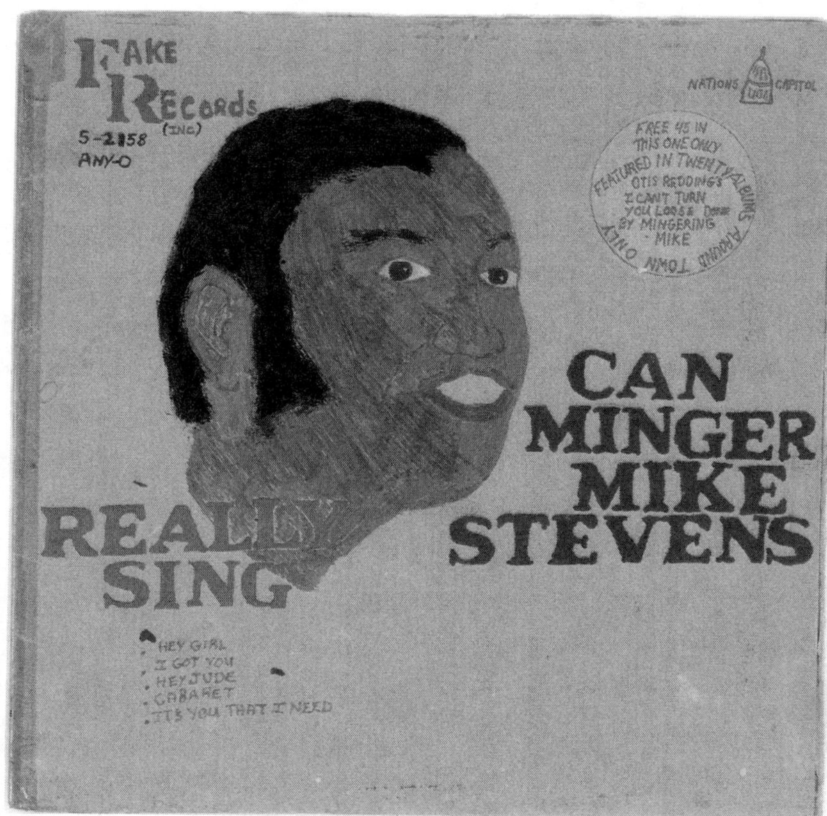

Figure 32. *Can Minger Mike Stevens Really Sing*, 1969. Mixed media on paperboard, 12 × 12 in. (30.5 × 30.5 cm.). Gift of Mike Wilkins and Sheila Duignan and museum purchase through the Luisita L. and Franz H. Denghausen Endowment. Smithsonian American Art Museum, Washington, D.C. Photo Smithsonian American Art Museum, Washington, D.C. / Art Resource, N.Y.

Mingering Mike was a teenager during the Black Arts and Black Power movements. When he uses the pan-African, black-nationalist colors of red, black, and green in his record covers, such as *Grooving with Mike*, he leans into the style of the BAM to imagine the unimaginable (to imagine that he, like Erykah Badu, could create his own "worldwide underground"). The "groove lines" drawn on the records exemplify the power of surface remaining surface. Mingering Mike's spirit of black post-blackness is evident in his holding on to the possibility of "real" black sound even as he moved fully to the realm of fantasy and imagination.

Glenn Ligon's Play with Commercial Surface

Mingering Mike's fake albums would be hard to find in the fake store that Glenn Ligon imagines. In a 2006 installation art, *Untitled*, Ligon created a neon light display that evokes a storefront window with the words, "I sell the shadow to sustain the substance." The large round lettering evokes urban, contemporary glitter, but the cords trailing down the wall and across the floor signal the clumsy artifice that sustains this glitter and commercialization. This installation is a profound engagement with Sojourner Truth's famous words, "I sell the shadow to support the substance."

In the 1860s, Truth sold her *carte de visite* daguerrotype portraits to raise funds to continue her travel and public speaking. She included the words "I sell the shadow to support the substance" as a caption to the portraits. Since this early form of photography was referred to in every-day talk as a "shadow," Truth found poetry in the everyday when she used these words.[48] The historian Nell Irvin Painter has uncovered Truth's self-conscious arrangement, in these photographs, of the clothing, eyeglasses, yarn, flowers, and bodily pose.[49] The eyeglasses are the punctum, Roland Barthes's term for the "prick" that makes a photograph work.[50] As we look at the spectacles, we see a framing of her eyes that begs to be connected to the words that frame the daguerreotype. Whereas W. E. B. Du Bois, more than four decades after these images were created, made the veil the prime metaphor for the black gaze, Sojourner Truth's portraits dare us to try to find the actual eyes lost behind that veil. Truth knows that daguerreotypes trick people into believing that they are seeing the real person, not an image. The use of daguerreotypes as visual evidence, in nineteenth-century antiblack racist discourse, made this trick very pernicious. When Truth sold these self-fashioned images as she spread her antislavery and feminist theology of liberation, she used the accepted realism of daguerreotypes to present visual evidence of the intellect, grace, and delicate strength of African American women.

Ligon's twenty-first-century image removes the black body from the space of representation. Truth's original dramatizes a nineteenth-century African American woman's counter-image (against the dominant degrading images of black womanhood). The word "shadow," in Truth's original, evokes the negativity tied, in the white gaze, to blackness and also the Du Boisian veil of double consciousness ("that peculiar sensation of always looking at oneself through the eyes of another") that makes one's own self-image a shadow in the bright, dominant glare of "another." The shadow behind the veil of double conscious-

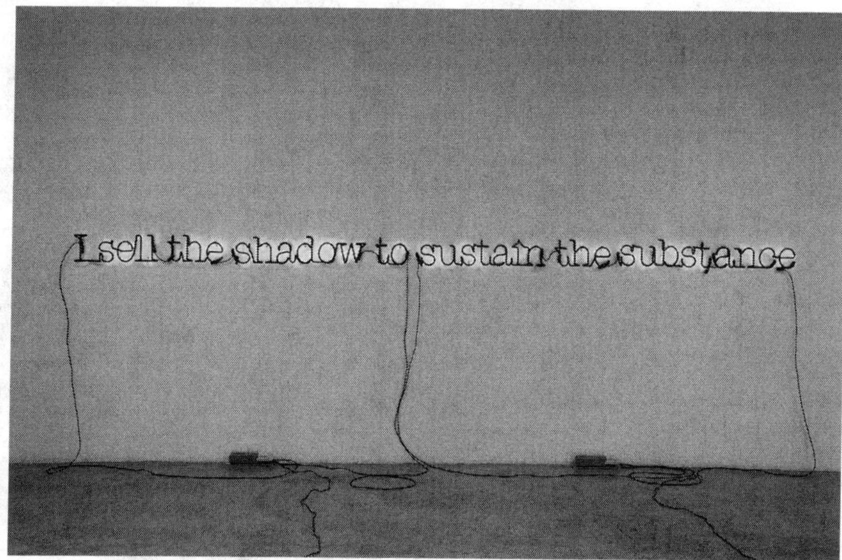

Figure 33. Glenn Ligon, *Untitled (I Sell the Shadow to Sustain the Substance)*, 2006. Neon and black paint, 8.5 × 185 in. (21.5 × 469.9 cm.). © Glenn Ligon, Courtesy of the artist, Luhring Augustine, New York, Regen Projects, Los Angeles, and Thomas Dane Gallery, London.

ness was reclaimed, during the BAM, as "black light." The words "black light" circulate widely in poetry, manifestos, essays, and titles of visual art during the BAM. In "The Tide Inside, It Rages!" one of the essays in the anthology *Black Fire*, the novelist Lindsay Barrett theorizes about black light: "Today, what the artistic sensibility of the black man spreads before the world as evidence of his social and historic dilemma, is really the articulation of a protest against the white denial of the possibility or existence of black light, and the superimposition, on his knowledge of this black light, of the hostile white light of Western history."[51] Barrett recognizes that the very "possibility" and "existence" of black light is hard to imagine due to the glare of white light.

Decades after the BAM, Ligon dramatizes the aesthetic struggle for black light in his artistic reshaping of Truth's *carte de visite* portraits (fig. 33). As Ligon makes the words "I sell the shadow to sustain the substance" appear to be a storefront sign, the exposed "nakedness" of the cords and plugs dramatize the fact that there is no interior to this surface. The neon lights allow the dark letters to glow. Ligon illuminates the letters in a manner that gives them a bright neon shadow and makes the light appear to enter the dark letters (as opposed to the etymology of the word "photography"—entering light and drawing with light).[52] Sojourner Truth's decision to "own" and "sell" the shadow (that the aesthetics of bright whiteness has projected on blackened subjects) inspired Ligon to create a twenty-first-century sign on a gallery wall, a sign that is lacking any interior depth.

The radicalness of this surface only emerges if viewers reflect on the image, walk around the cords, and think about the power and style of that woman who, in 1848, at the famous Seneca women's convention, may not have unveiled her breasts nor delivered the famous words "Ain't I a woman?" As Painter argues, it is much more likely that Frances Dana Gage invented the unveiling and the indignant question as she sensationalized what really happened when Truth spoke at the 1851 women's rights convention in Akron, Ohio. The question that has become a mantra in black feminism and the exposure of the breast may have been added as the white feminist abolitionist spectators and journalists continued to need to project *substance* onto their surface understanding of black womanhood.

Ligon's black post-blackness, in his revision of Truth's *carte de visite* portraits, is a profound play with the removal of the black body to force us to consider how the play of pure surface can spark the radical black imagination. In A. B. Spellman's BAM manifesto "Big Bushy Afros" (1998), this radical use of surface is depicted when Spellman explains, "It is hard to teach today the power of Black is Beautiful. The sensuality of a collective consciousness that declared itself on sight."[53] Spellman's words "*on* sight" and the very title of the manifesto, the words "big bushy Afros," capture the BAM's use of radical superficiality. "In sight" and "insight" are tied to a depth that makes it impossible for surfaces and edges to matter. Spellman's words "declared itself on sight" convey the sense that the "sensuality of the collective consciousness" speaks for itself (that the styles and surfaces have force precisely because they do not need mediation). Spellman may really be confessing that "it is hard to teach today the power" of the "bling bling," the shine, the nitty-gritty glamor of "black is beautiful." When surfaces like "big bushy afros" are treated, post-movement, like they were not surfaces with texture and edges, we cannot see the radical edges of black aesthetics. These radical edges (whether the BAM's edge in the black popular culture coterminous with the movement or the edges that bring surface and depth together so that they are not a binary) "declare themselves on sight" in the edge embedded in the words "black post-blackness."

Epilogue
Feeling Black Post-Black

In *The Fierce Urgency of Now: Improvisation, Rights, and the Ethics of Cocre-ation* (2013), the "cocreators" (George Lipsitz, Ajay Heble, and Daniel Fisch-lin) argue that "black nationalism" was "itself a kind of ingenious improvi-sation."[1] When cultural nationalism is improvised, it is always on the verge of becoming something that is closer to an aesthetic than a programmatic ideology. The "post" in black post-blackness is, partially, post-ideological blackness. This worry about ideological blackness is embedded in the de-bates that unfolded during the BAM. In a 1974 issue of *Black World*, a debate titled "The Black Aesthetic" was staged, with the "opponent" Martin Kilson and the "defender" Addison Gayle. Kilson makes the word "ideology" signal the greatest limits of the BAM. He writes, "The new Black Arts is nothing more than an ideology; it is an effort to subordinate the deeply profound and penetrating creative processes of Black people to an ideological move-ment."[2] But Addison Gayle's response shows how the BAM uncovered the role of aesthetics in any attempt to defeat programmatic ideology: "Their opposition to the New Black Arts, never stated, is due to the fact that it calls for re-evaluation of white values, a questioning and challenging of the ethics and morals of this country, a belief that man's humanity to man is possible once the symbols, images, and metaphors bequeathed by white men to Black men are redefined and re-structured."[3] Gayle's focus on new image-making is a fascinating way to rethink the common assumption that the BAM revolved around an ideological understanding of blackness. Gayle, in this passage, im-plies that new "symbols, images, and metaphors" could produce a new sense of what it means to be human. He offers an aesthetic approach to moving beyond ideological blackness. The aesthetic warfare of the movement has been misread as pure ideological warfare; we have lost a clear sense of the work that aesthetics were doing during this cultural movement. Ideology was not the end and aesthetics the means. As the movement constantly asserted the inseparability of aesthetics and ideology, it also constantly performed ideology's inability to contain aesthetics.

Baraka writes in *In Our Terribleness* (1970), "Ideology and style are the same thing," but he also asserts, in the new, twenty-first-century (2007) edition of *Black Fire* (1968), that "blackness is not an ideology."[4] What is blackness if not an ideology? The black post-blackness zones of the BAM make blackness into a perpetual complex love interest that makes one perpetually fall in and out of love as the relationship gains new dimensions. How does a collective love affair with blackness become a collective aesthetic experience? When the overt pronounced love affair becomes subdued to the point that it almost seems to end, what are the collective aesthetics that linger? Is the mood of black post-blackness the aesthetic residue of the overt love affair?

The aesthetic residue (the exhaustion with the ideological and also the aesthetic experience that there really is something else beside the ideological we can call *black*) is produced not after the movement that mobilized this collective love affair, but during the movement itself. This questioning of post-ideological blackness takes a different (but related) form in the cultural productions of twenty-first-century black aesthetics. For example, in the exhibition catalog for the 2012 Studio Museum exhibit *Fore*, the assistant curators (Lauren Haynes, Naima J. Keith, and Thomas J. Lax) wonder, "So what happens to black after post-black?" as they consider the relation between the 2012 exhibit and the 2001 "post-black" *Freestyle* Studio Museum exhibit.[5] One answer to this question may be: after an understanding of post-black as post-ideological blackness, we move to the new understanding of "black" as an emptied but full space of imagining the unimaginable. Fred Moten's question lingers, "What will blackness be?"[6]

The difference between this sheer wonder about the unimaginable and the call for the end of blackness is profound. Debra J. Dickerson's *The End of Blackness: Returning the Souls of Black Folk to Their Righful Owners* (2004) is one of the post-black texts that cancels out the wonder as it assumes that blackness cannot be a beginning or a break out of the binary of beginning versus ending. Dickerson dedicates *The End of Blackness* to Baraka and others who "loved us more than they hated anyone else."[7] Her call for African Americans to let go of the past in order to seize their right to create a better future is framed as an "end of blackness," but the book's dedication can easily be read as a call for the black post-blackness embedded in the BAM and some twenty-first-century black art. The full dedication reads:

> To James Baldwin, Amiri Baraka, W. E. B. Du Bois, Ralph Ellison, E. Franklin Frazier, Dr. Martin Luther King Jr., Albert Murray, Thomas Sowell, Malcolm X, and especially Frederick Douglass and Carter G. Woodson. Finally, worthy leaders and thinkers. Now I know how to be black and human. Now I know how to *think* because now, having sought out the un-Black History month, Chicken McNuggetized, contextless quote, I know how thoroughly I've been bamboozled as to my true intellectual and moral heritage and I know who did the bamboozling. Now I know that it's *black people* they strove to challenge and perfect, not the rest of the world. They loved us more than they hated anyone else. That's a gift beyond measure for an orphan race.[8]

Dickerson implies that her call, in the book proper after this opening dedication, for an end to black fixation on the oppression in the past is partially a recognition that the post–"black and human" work entails recognizing that racial oppression is not what it used to be and that African Americans have the "infinite possibilities" hailed at the end of Ellison's *Invisible Man* (1952). *The End of Blackness* is a very difficult book to place; it can easily be read as black conservatism, but it also has surprising swerves from the cookie-cutter black conservatism (such as the dedication to Amiri Baraka). The call for the "end of blackness," is most puzzling when she confesses, in the dedication and other parts of the book, that she understands the power of the black love affair with blackness. She understands that this complex love has been an inwardness of black self-reflection, and yet the entire book is a call for a looking inward by black people that would allow them to stop holding each other hostage in a "let's hold onto the past" collective paralysis: "In order to make progress possible, blacks have to give up on the past. Tomorrow is their only option."[9] Her association of blackness with the end has a longer tradition that Adam Lively, in *Masks: Blackness, Race, and the Imagination*, argues is the tradition of the American racial imagination's lapse into a fear of blackness that is produced by a sense of an apocalypse or a sense of a beginning of something new. He writes, "Blackness has spoken, to the Western imagination, of the beginning and end of things."[10]

The BAM and twenty-first-century spirit of black post-blackness denaturalizes this investment in blackness as a beginning or an end. Black post-blackness is a "weird expression of form" that produces what Ellison, in *Invisible Man*, describes as a "different sense of time."[11] Victor Estrada uses the words "a weird expression of form" to describe his art that is included in *Phantom Sightings*:

Art after the Chicano Movement (2008).[12] The "phantom sightings" of these "weird expressions of form" appear during (not only after) the cultural movements that seem, on the surface, to be so closely tied to the *normativity* that strategic essentialism and identity politics can lapse into. The BAM was most radical when it veered toward the "weird expressions of form."

The performance of weirdness, during a decolonizing, consciousness-raising movement, raises complicated questions about the relation of individual performance to collective performance. Many of the artists in the BAM were performing in both a powerfully collective manner and, also, in a profoundly individual manner. In the introduction to *Black Spirits* (1972), Nikki Giovanni captures the naturalness of this individual ethos in the midst of a collective movement when she first proclaims that the "newest people on earth are Afro-Americans" and then ends this introduction to one of the most pivotal Black Arts poetry volumes with a focus on why the self-love of the "newest people" should not be confused, too quickly, with group love. Giovanni writes, "And that's when we read a poem by a poet who loves, not us because he doesn't know us, but himself because he knows himself. For all that he is. Or might never be."[13] The words "he doesn't know us" are a remarkable framing of a BAM poetry anthology as art that speaks to "us" without claiming to "know us." Giovanni seems to grant that the audience for the poetry feels that a love of "us" is embedded in the poems, but she reminds the audience that what appears to be a "love of us" is really a self-love that opens up into a collective feeling.

BAM artists were participating in a collective love affair with blackness—the *collective* performance of *self*-love. The cultural nationalism of this movement was the style counterpart to the seemingly antistyle, pure mission zone of revolutionary nationalism. But cultural nationalism was also the zone where emotions and desire could be expressed in contrast to the focus on "what needs to be done" in revolutionary nationalism. The art created during the Black Power movement is an archive of the emotional release that paralleled the political urgency. Of course, the art was political (that is the most obvious layer of the BAM). The art was also a very complicated expression *and* sublimation of desire that was much more complicated than the overt political mission. The art of Black Power was often the art of emotional release. In the foreword to the new edition of *Black Fire*, Baraka offers "emotional spontaneity" as his explanation of the complexity of the movement: "In that emotional spontaneity there was not an advanced enough unity to maintain the eclectic entity that 'Black' had brought together."[14] The emphasis on the uncontainable affect, in this retrospection, matters. As Baraka looks back, he still remembers the "emotional spontaneity" that "black" was during the BAM. Baraka ultimately understood the deepest registers of the BAM as this feeling of "emotional spontaneity." The BAM's spirit of black post-blackness was a novel, spontaneous idea struggling in a discourse that was not yet prepared for it.

Imagining Black Post-Blackness as Home

A comparison of Nikki Giovanni's *My House* (1972) and Mat Johnson's *Loving Day* (2015) shows how the spirit of black post-blackness travels through the BAM to the twenty-first century as a "structure of feeling."[15] In both of these texts, the architecture of houses is used as a way of thinking about blackness as a structure of feeling, not a fixed ideology. As a structure of feeling, blackness can produce what Fred Moten, in the poem "There Is Blackness," describes as the state of being "homelessly in love."[16] This phrase captures the metaphor of architecture in *My House* and *Loving Day*, as Giovanni and Johnson depict a black post-blackness that is a "living within" surprisingly sustained by a desire, sometimes, to run away.

As twenty-first-century African American literature builds, sometimes unconsciously, on the BAM, there is a repetition of tender, "black interior" confessions about the need to break away and breathe more deeply, such as Giovanni's admission, in the poem "Categories," that "if this seems / like a tentative poem it's probably / because I just realized that / I'm bored with categories."[17] Johnson's character Warren, in *Loving Day*, confesses, "Every time I want to escape someone starts hugging me."[18] As Johnson foregrounds the complexity of the black love affair, the unwelcome "hug" is a repeated image: "He [Sirleaf Day] hugs me like he knows I'm trying to get away" (5). Warren, the biracial character who can pass for white, returns, at the beginning of the novel, to the black neighborhood of his childhood, and is embraced by Sirleaf Day, who literally wears black nationalism ("It's like Africa finally united, but just in his wardrobe" [5]). Giovanni's Black Power feminist confessions in *My House* are not so different from Johnson's twenty-first-century vision of hugs and embraces that hold together what is always falling apart. In *Loving Day*, the power of holding on to blackness *and* mixture is the power of love as a way of holding together that which could easily fall apart and become the "Mulattopia" that views feeling black as "mold-y," as "the racial mold set by slavery" (26, 27).

When Johnson's critique of "Mulattopia" begins to merge with Giovanni's critique of "blackness as an ideology," Johnson and Giovanni meet in the space of black post-blackness (the structure of feeling that helps us understand why both texts revolve around images of "the house"). Johnson begins this quintessentially twenty-first-century African American novel, full of references to Facebook and cell phones, with language that would sound like, "In the beginning there was black interior space and it was large," if the house being described in this opening line was not Warren's inheritance from his white father: "In the ghetto there is mansion, and it is my father's house" (3). The inherited house, throughout the novel, is a symbol of black urban space (in Philadelphia) and also a symbol of the interracial excess that black as biology or blackness as an ideology can never contain.

The mansion Warren inherits is falling apart and does not have a roof. It is a huge house full of ghosts that make Warren muse, in one scene, about Eddie Murphy's joke about horror films with white people who continue to live in the haunted houses that black people would just leave. Warren tells Sun, his lover and one of the leaders of the Mélange Center (committed to the "inclusion of all perspectives of the black and white, mixed-race experience" [69]): "Well, you know that joke? That black people would just leave at the first creepy sound? I've been thinking about that. Escaping? That's actually normative behavior. Staying, when you know there's a ghost, that's what makes no damned sense. So when you think about it, that's really the pretense of all ghost stories: white people are so confident of their omnipotence that they've lost their goddamn minds" (151). Just as Sun replies, "Sunflower bullshit" (the conditioning of "yellow," biracial people to think "brown"), Johnson, throughout the novel, complicates the idea that black people do not linger even when they want to escape. Black post-blackness is signaled by Warren's frustration with the haunted house, the mansion that remains in the "ghetto" after "white flight." Warren's love for his biracial teenage daughter Tal, whom he only meets when she is a teenager, makes him linger in the literal structure, the house that he has inherited, and, also, the structure of feeling black post-black. Tal becomes a consummate "post-black" artist when she transforms a Frederick Douglass action figure into a sculpture that includes the transformation of Douglass's Afro into blond hair, a literal stripping of his body to reveal a huge phallus, and the painting of half of his body pink to signal his biracialness. Warren, who wants so badly to make up for all the years of Tal's life that he missed, wants to let her experiment with her identity as a mixed person, and yet he remains offended by the sculpture. Tal makes him want to hold on to and pass on a black consciousness that helps her understand how history affects the present and how "whiteness—that's not really something you can be half of [. . .] [t]hat's more of an all or nothing privilege, perspective thing" (216). His love for Tal also makes him want to let go of any need to pass on anything that might make it harder for her to feel that the past does not have to be the future.

Johnson shows that the problem with the Mulattopia of Sun and others who teach Tal at the Mélange Center is their investment in mixed-race identity being an ideology, as opposed to a structure of feeling, a way of feeling *mixed*. In *Marxism and Literature*, Raymond Williams describes "structures of feeling" in the following manner: "It is a structured formation which, because it is at the very edge of semantic availability, has many characteristics of a pre-formation, until specific articulations—new semantic figures—are discovered in material practice: often, as it happens, in relatively isolated ways, which are only later seen to compose a significant (often in fact minority) generation; this often, in turn, the generation that substantially connects to its successor."[19] Just as these "pre-formations" begin to gain shape, they hail and merge with other pre-formations. Black post-blackness is a structure of feeling, a productive tension between the residual and the emergent. When the legacies of the black post-blackness of the BAM merge with the twenty-first-century feelings of mixedness depicted in *Loving Day*, feeling black merges with feeling mixed. "Black" and "mixed" both emerge as pre-formations. Sun Ra's reference to "chromatic-black" is a stunning move to the mixture that is black. A handbook for painters describes "chromatic black" in the following manner: "A *mixed* paint color that looks black but doesn't contain any black pigment in it. None of the pigments in a chromatic black mix have a PBk (Pigment Black) Color Index. Instead, a chromatic black is created by mixing dark versions of other colors, typically a red and green or blue and red. [C]hromatic black is a more complex, interesting color, with a subtlety that *straight* black lacks."[20] Black post-blackness is chromatic black, not "straight" black. What will mixture be? What will blackness be?

The issue of pre-formation is also at the core of Nikki Giovanni's use of the symbol of the house. In *My House*, with the two sections "The Rooms Inside" and "The Rooms Outside," Giovanni sets up a poetics of space that is overdetermined by the feeling that the "revolution [is] screeeeeeeeeeeching / to a halt" (66). She makes us wonder what is beginning in this prolonged space of screeching. We reconsider the BAM itself as the "screeeeeeeeeeeeching," as if poets like Giovanni were always aware that, as Ralph Ellison writes, the "end is in the beginning and lies far ahead" and that black thunder is black emptiness inhabited.[21] After the lines "we were seeing the revolution screeeeeeeeeeeeching / to a halt," Giovanni writes, "trying to find a clever way / to be empty" (66). As Buddhism teaches, emptiness is not nothingness.

In the poem "Straight Talk," appearing earlier in this same volume, Giovanni describes the fullness of "empty" pages: "i'm giving up / on language / my next book will be blank / pages of various textures and hues" (31). Emptiness is a state of pre-formation that is not aspiring to become cluttered. It allows people to breathe. Immediately after the poem "We," which ends with the note of emptiness, Giovanni concludes the collection with the title poem, "My House." This poem is a full celebration of the living that happens in the "empty spaces." As the speaker confesses, "it's my house / and I plan to live in it" (67). This is a love poem and, as the speaker states, "a silly poem" (68). The playfulness emerges as the speaker narrates, to the love interest, all of the simple but whimsical things that can happen in "my house." Black post-blackness emerges when Giovanni imagines the difference between "speaking English" and "trying to speak through it" and hails readers who will see the BAM as both "speaking blackness" and "trying to speak through it" (68). The black post-blackness is crystallized, in the poem "Straight Talk" (in the "The Rooms Inside" section), when Giovanni writes, "i'm black not only / because it's beautiful but because it's me" (32). The "me" that contains blackness is the "me" that carries blackness forward even as the BAM lets go of the "black is beautiful" frame as the only way to see blackness. When BAM writers such as Giovanni move to blackness as what simply *is*, the is-ness is the long poem that the BAM became as Giovanni and others wrote past the "main frame" of the movement.

Lingering While Moving On

This "long poem" of the movement is what Nathaniel Mackey describes so lucidly as a "lingering while moving on by way of recursiveness and feeling-with."[22] The phrase "lingering while moving on" encapsulates the torque of black post-blackness. Torque is the twist of an object; the twist of black post-blackness is what we see in Claudine Rankine's long poem *Citizen* (2014). Rankine, toward the midpoint of this poem, writes:

> You could build a world out of need or you could hold
> everything black and see. You give back the lack.
>
> You hold everything black. You give yourself back until
> nothing's left but the dissolving blues of metaphor.[23]

The twist of black post-blackness (the lingering while moving on) is crystallized in the words "you could hold / everything black and see. You give back the lack." Rankine connects the play with the "lack" in "b(lack)" and the idea of "holding back" or restraining oneself. Instead of "holding back," she calls for "holding black." She suggests that once the ideology of blackness "dissolves," we really can grip blackness ("You hold everything black"). Rankine's twist of black post-blackness is the grip and the "give back" (words that signal James Brown's words "need some get back" in the iconic Black Power song "The Payback," and also a refusal to hold on to any understanding of blackness that converts black people into lack).

When Rankine writes, "And so it goes until the vista includes only displacement of feeling back into the body, which gave birth to the feelings that don't sit comfortably inside the communal," it is clear that she is thinking about blackness as a feeling (152). The structure of ideology makes feelings "communal." The structures of feeling are too liminal and "pre-formed" to be completely communal. Black post-blackness is that gap between the individual and the communal; it is the gap that Baraka decides to "dig in" (according to Rankine's own analysis of Baraka in her review of his 2014 posthumous collection *SOS*, edited by Paul Vangelisti). Rankine analyzes Baraka's poem "Note to AB," which begs to be read as one of Baraka's edge-of-the-twenty-first-century meditations on his years in the BAM. In this poetic tribute to A. B. Spellman, Baraka writes, "I felt I knew / who I was but had to / Struggle, to catch up / w/my self. / Now I do see me / sometimes, a few worlds / ahead, & I speed up, then, / put my head down, / Stretch my stride out / & dig / There me go, I scat & / sing, there me go."[24] These lines stage the space between the self he thought he knew (the communal self where he and Spellman first connected while comrades in the BAM) and the self that is in motion (the individual who could never be contained by a movement). The limit of any communal spirit that replaces the openness of feeling with the fixity of ideology is staged in the BAM itself. In the BAM poem "friends i am like you tied," A. B. Spellman connects poets' literal move to the "far end of the page" to the freedom of "moving on down the line." A few lines after the self-reflection, "a.b. break something action i've / acted who mans the far end of the i?" Spellman performs the move to the "far end": "moving on down the line you now we."[25] Baraka's words "there me go," in "Note to AB," take on another dimension when we read this poem as a response to "friends i am like you tied." Spellman's image of the "far end of the i" and Baraka's words "there me go" convey the sense that both BAM literature and the artists' retrospective reflections on the movement demand a stretching out of self that is very similar to Walt Whitman's words "I am large, I contain multitudes."

Terrance Hayes uses Whitman's very words as one of the epigraphs in his twenty-first-century poetry volume *Wind in a Box* (2006), which revisits the poetics of the BAM with persona poems such as "The Blue Baraka." As Hayes tries, in "The Blue Baraka," to imagine what holding on to Baraka's BAM sensibility feels like in our twenty-first-century post-BAM point of view, he uses the phrase "floundering interiors."[26] With these words, Hayes meets Baraka in the liminal space of the preformed (the interiority that has not settled into an ideology). This language is, surely, the language of the structure of feeling, not the language of ideology. Baraka's BAM poetry is situated in these "floundering interiors," but Hayes's post-BAM persona poem names this "floundering" the "Blue Baraka," as opposed to the BAM naming of it as "black." Louis Armstrong's "What did I do to be so black and blue?" is the space of "blue and black" where Hayes enters into the "floundering" (the black post-blackness) of the BAM.

Hayes moves from this persona poem focusing on Baraka to a wide range of other persona poems, including one titled "The Blue Seuss," which imagines the voice of Dr. Seuss (one of the most hypnotizing, sonic-driven writers of children's books) as he thinks about "blacks." The shift from Baraka to Dr. Seuss foregrounds the productive play with blackness as one legacy of the BAM. Hayes also draws upon the sound of Dr. Seuss as a means of remembering how playful the hypnotic power of BAM poetry was. Hayes plays with the repetition, in so many BAM poems, of the word "black." In "The Blue Seuss," "blacks on" is repeated as Hayes uses the word "box" to signal the literal structure of feeling that blackness is. The first lines of the poem are:

> Blacks in one box
> Blacks in two box
> Blacks on
> [. . .]
> Blacks in boxes stacked on shores[27]

In an interview, Hayes explained his interest in the "box" as both a way of thinking about the historical oppression of African Americans (the Middle Passage, in particular) and a way of thinking about the open and closed forms of poetry. He asks, "What do boxes do for poems, and what do they do for our people?"[28] The tension between Hayes's words "blacks in a box" and "blacks *on*" signals the difference between the open feeling that black post-blackness becomes, during the BAM and in twenty-first-century responses to the BAM, versus any impulse to reduce and flatten the BAM into a *black box* of thwarted art. Hayes imagines that the "box" opens up; resumption is redemption. The containment happens as the subversion happens. The structure (the box) of *feeling* and *living* and *loving* blackness is always opening up to a "blacks on" sentiment that can be aptly described as black post-blackness. Every attempt to move beyond blackness should remind us that blackness has always been *beyond*.

Notes

Introduction

1. Paul C. Taylor, *Black Is Beautiful: A Philosophy of Black Aesthetics* (Malden, Mass.: Wiley Blackwell, 2016), 12.

2. "What Is Rhythm?" (Advertisement for *Black Power!*), *Soulbook* 2.2 (1967): 152.

3. Martha Buskirk, *The Contingent Object of Contemporary Art* (Cambridge: Massachusetts Institute of Technology Press, 2003), 11.

4. The time of the present is often crushed by the past and the future. For the twenty-first-century post-black impulses, this presentness often takes the shape of, "But things have changed, antiblack racism is not what it used to be." In the BAM mobilizations of "black" as a decolonizing, unifying concept, this presentness often took the shape of, "Let's free ourselves now, we can't afford to wait." Cultural movements like the BAM allow people to collectively imagine a stretched-out present that makes the radical seizure of the "here and now" as important as telling the truth about injustices in the past and creating a better future.

5. Amiri Baraka, "The Changing Same (R&B and New Black Music)," in *Black Music* (1968; reprint, New York: Da Capo Press, 1998), 180–211.

6. In *In Our Terribleness*, Baraka writes, "And what is the changing same for us, the reality beneath illusion that binds us, as the body is bound by its motion its intent." Imamu Amiri Baraka (LeRoi Jones) and Fundi (Billy Abernathy), *In Our Terribleness (Some Elements of Meaning in Black Style)* (Indianapolis: Bobbs-Merrill, 1970), n.p.

7. Kalamu Ya Salaam, "BlkArtSouth—New Orleans," *Black World*, April 1972, 41.

8. Amiri Baraka, Introduction to Larry Neal, *Black Boogaloo: Notes on Black Liberation* (San Francisco: Journal of Black Poetry Press, 1969), i; Amiri Baraka, "It's Nation Time," in *The LeRoi Jones/Amiri Baraka Reader*, ed. William J. Harris (New York: Thunder's Mouth Press, 1991), 242.

9. Nathaniel Mackey, *Splay Anthem* (New York: New Directions Publishing, 2006), xiv.

10. Nathanial Mackey, "An Interview with Kamau Brathwaite," in *The Art of Kamau Brathwaite*, ed. Stewart Brown (Bridgend, Mid Glamorgan, Wales: Seren, 1995), 14.

11. James Smethurst, *The Black Arts Movement: Literary Nationalism in the 1960s and 1970s* (Chapel Hill: University of North Carolina Press, 2005); Amy Abugo Ongiri, *Spectacular Blackness: The Cultural Politics of the Black Power Movement and the Search for a Black Aesthetic* (Charlottesville: University of Virginia Press, 2009); Daniel Widener, *Black Arts West: Culture and Struggle in Postwar Los Angeles* (Durham, N.C.: Duke University Press, 2010); Howard Rambsy, *The Black Arts Enterprise and the Production of African American Poetry* (Ann Arbor: University of Michigan Press, 2013); and Carter Mathes, *Imagine the Sound: Experimental African American Literature after Civil Rights* (Minneapolis: University of Minnesota Press, 2015).

12. Amiri Baraka, *Tales of the Out & the Gone* (New York: Akashic Books, 2007), 9.

13. Darby English, *How to See a Work of Art in Total Darkness* (Cambridge: Massachusetts Institute of Technology Press, 2010).

14. Edward Spriggs, Nikki Giovanni, Jaci Earley, Elaine Jones, Sam Anderson, Joe Goncalves, Ahmed Alhamisi, Carolyn Rodgers, Julia Fields, Akinshiju, A. B. Spellman, Ted Joans, and K. W. Kgositsile, "Black Dialogue," in *Black Dialogue* 4.1 (Spring 1969): 2.

15. Tom Dent, *Blue Lights and River Songs* (Detroit: Lotus Press, 1982), 50–51.

16. Carolyn Rodgers, "Uh Nat'chal Thang—The WHOLE TRUTH—US," *Black World* 20.11 (September 1971): 10.

17. Charles Johnson, *Half-Past Nation Time* (Westlake Village, Calif.: Aware Press, 1972), n.p.

18. Edward Spriggs, "Toward a True 'Black Art,'" in exhibit catalog for Afri-COBRA III (University Art Gallery, University of Massachusetts at Amherst, September 1973).

19. Derek Conrad Murray, *Queering Post-Black Art: Artists Transforming African-American Identity after Civil Rights* (London: I. B. Taurus, 2016), 24–25.

20. Larry Neal, "Some Reflections on the Black Aesthetic," in *African American Literary Theory*, ed. Winston Napier (New York: New York University Press, 2000), 89–91.

21. The ephemerality of the chalk resonates with Raymond Saunders's discussion of his use of chalk in his black abstraction: "A lot of things that are delicate and beautiful, a lot of things that I observe, are just as fleeting as chalk on a chalkboard." Hank Chase, "Raymond Saunders: Come Full Circle," *Black Renaissance* 7.3 (Fall 2007): 51.

22. Danzy Senna, "Admission," in *You Are Free* (New York: Riverhead Books, 2011), 20. Cassie thinks, "*Don't you dare take this from me, I'm almost there, I've almost made it to the other side, don't fuck this up for me.* But instead she said, 'Not everything has to be a political statement, Duncan'" (20).

23. Carolyn Rodgers, "What Color Is Lonely?" in *The Black Poets*, ed. Dudley Randall (New York: Bantam Books, 1970), 265–66.

24. Thelma Golden, "Post . . . ," in *Freestyle* (New York: The Studio Museum in Harlem, 2001), 14.

25. When we read Golden's post-black marker as post–Black Power and post–Black Arts, her emphasis on an interior space with no need for explanation represents a shift from the different type of Black Arts interior where explanations of the function of aesthetics abound.

26. Mark H. C. Bessire, ed., *William Pope.L: The Friendliest Black Artist in America* (Cambridge: Massachusetts Institute of Technology Press, 2002), 62.

27. Larry Neal, "Don't Say Goodbye to the Porkpie Hat," in *Hoodoo Hollerin' Bebop Ghosts* (Washington, D.C.: Howard University Press, 1974), 21.

28. A. B. Spellman, "Big Bushy Afros," *International Review of African American Art* 15.1 (1998): 53.

29. Fred Moten uses the phrase "frame cuts frame" in: Fred Moten, *In the Break: The Aesthetics of the Black Radical Tradition* (Minneapolis: University of Minnesota Press, 2003), 109. Harryette Mullen, *Sleeping with the Dictionary* (Berkeley: University of California Press, 2002), 19.

30. Baraka, Introduction, i.

31. Carolyn Rodgers, "All the Clocks," in *Black Spirits: A Festival of New Black Poets in America*, ed. Woodie King (New York: Vintage, 1972), 184.

32. Kevin Quashie, *The Sovereignty of Quiet: Beyond Resistance in Black Culture* (New Brunswick, N.J.: Rutgers University Press, 2012).

33. Tricia Rose, *Black Noise: Rap Music and Black Culture in Contemporary America* (Middletown, Conn.: Wesleyan University Press, 1994).

34. Yvonne Tasker and Diane Negra, eds., *Interrogating Post-Feminism: Gender and the Politics of Popular Culture* (Durham, N.C.: Duke University Press, 2007), 1.

35. Moten, *In the Break*, 22. Touré, *Who's Afraid of Post-Blackness? What It Means to Be Black Now* (New York: Free Press, 2011).

36. Claire Colebrook, "Queer Aesthetics," in *Queer Times, Queer Becomings*, ed. Mikko Tuhkanen (Albany: State University of New York Press, 2011), 31.

37. Amiri Baraka, "Heathen Technology at the End of the Twentieth Century," in *Tales of the Out and the Gone* (New York: Akashic Books, 2007), 158.

38. Ibid.

39. Ibid.

40. Ibid.

41. English, *How to See*, 222.

42. Kenneth W. Warren, *What Was African American Literature?* (Cambridge, Mass.: Harvard University Press, 2012); Charles Johnson, "The End of the Black American Narrative" in *Best African American Essays 2010*, ed. Gerald Early and Randall Kennedy (New York: Random House, 2010).

43. Warren, *What Was*, 43.

44. Ibid., 3.

Chapter 1. The Aesthetics of Anticipation

1. Dudley Randall, *Roses and Revolution: The Selected Writings of Dudley Randall*, ed. Melba Joyce Boyd (Detroit: Wayne State University Press, 2009), 37.

2. As Randall highlights the difference between "ugly too" and "always beautiful," he shows that Hughes was anticipating some strands of post-black discourse. "We know we are beautiful. And ugly too" is similar to the more nuanced post-black discourse that, unlike the more facile strands, works hard to not be post-race or anti-black.

3. Randall, *Roses and Revolution*, 38.

4. Kalamu Ya Salaam, interview with the author, July 11, 2013, Tulane University.

5. Alain Locke, "The New Negro," in *The New Negro*, ed. Alain Locke (1925; reprint, New York: Touchstone, 1992), 13.

6. Locke writes, "But fundamentally for the present the Negro is radical on race matters, conservative on others, in other words, a 'forced radical,' a social protestant rather than a genuine radical" (ibid., 11).

7. Countee Cullen, "Colors," in *The Copper Sun* (New York: Harpers and Bros., 1927), 11–12.

8. Ibid., 11.

9. Ibid., 12.

10. Jennifer Wilks, *Race, Gender, and Comparative Black Modernism: Suzanne Lacascade, Marita Bonner, Suzanne Cesaire, Dorothy West* (Baton Rouge: Louisiana State University Press, 2008), 84.

11. George Hutchinson, *The Harlem Renaissance in Black and White* (Cambridge, Mass.: Harvard University Press, 1995); Houston A. Baker Jr., *Modernism and the Harlem Renaissance* (Chicago: University of Chicago Press, 1987); Wahneema Lubiano, "Black Nationalism and Black Common Sense," in *The House that Race Built: Black Americans, U.S. Terrain*, ed. Wahneema Lubiano (New York: Pantheon Books, 1997), 233.

12. Marita Bonner, *The Purple Flower*, in *Black Female Playwrights: An Anthology of Plays before 1950*, ed. Kathy Perkins (Bloomington: Indiana University Press, 1989), 192.

13. Ibid., 191.

14. Ibid., 199.

15. Jean Toomer, *Cane* (New York: Norton, 2011), 114.

16. Tom Dent to Calvin Hernton, March 30, 1969, box 2, folder 3, Amistad Research Center, Tulane University, New Orleans.

17. Toomer, *Cane*, 81, 105.

18. Baraka writes, "And only Jean Toomer, Richard Wright, Ralph Ellison, and James Baldwin have managed to bring off examples of writing, in this genre, that could succeed in passing themselves off as, 'serious' writing." Amiri Baraka, "The Myth of a 'Negro Literature,'" in *Within the Circle: An Anthology of African American Literary Criticism from the Harlem Renaissance to the Present*, ed. Angelyn Mitchell (Durham, N.C.: Duke University Press, 1994), 166.

19. Walker writes, "*Cane* was for Toomer a double 'swan song.' He meant it to memorialize a culture he thought was dying, whose folk-spirit he considered beautiful, but he was also saying good-bye to the 'Negro' he felt dying in himself. *Cane* then is a parting gift, and no less precious because of that. I think Jean Toomer would want us to keep its beauty, but let him go." Alice Walker, *In Search of Our Mothers' Gardens* (Orlando: Harcourt, 1983), 65.

20. Toomer, *Cane*, 25.

21. Ibid.

22. In Shange's iconic black feminist choreopoem, the healing of the women characters is depicted as "I found God in myself and I loved her fiercely." Ntozake Shange, *For Colored Girls Who Have Considered Suicide / When the Rainbow Is Enuf* (New York: MacMillan, 1976), 63.

23. Imamu Amiri Baraka (LeRoi Jones) and Fundi (Billy Abernathy), *In Our Terribleness (Some Elements and Meaning in Black Style)* (Indianapolis: Bobbs-Merrill, 1970). Baraka writes, "Try to see your own face, when you close your eyes" (n.p.).

24. Toomer, *Cane*, 67.

25. Ibid., 66.

26. Ibid., 57.

27. Langston Hughes, *Ask Your Mama: 12 Moods for Jazz* (1961; reprint, New York: Art Farm West, 2009), 8.

28. Scott Saul, *Freedom Is, Freedon Ain't: Jazz and the Making of the Sixties* (Cambridge, Mass.: Harvard University Press, 2005), 131.

29. Ibid.

30. Hughes, *Ask Your Mama*, 55.

31. Zora Neale Hurston, *Mules and Men* (1935; reprint, New York: Perennial Library, 1990), 18.

32. James T. Stewart, "The Development of the Black Revolutionary Artist," in *Black Fire: An Anthology of Afro-American Writing*, ed. Amiri Baraka and Larry Neal (1968; reprint, Baltimore: Black Classic Press, 2007), 4.

33. Under Asch's leadership, Folkways became one of the first record companies to produce "world music" records. The recordings of Leadbelly are a prime example of the company's interest in black folk sounds.

34. Hughes, *Ask Your Mama*, 51–52.

35. Carlene Hatcher Polite, *The Flagellants* (New York: Farrar, 1967).

36. Hughes, *Ask Your Mama*, 77.

37. Langston Hughes, foreword to *Fire!! A Quarterly Devoted to the Younger Negro Artists* 1.1 (1926): 1.

38. Ibid.

39. Ed Bullins, "A Short Statement on Street Theatre," *TDR: The Drama Review* 12.4 (Summer 1968): 93.

40. Kalamu Ya Salaam, interview with the author. Salaam explained that Sun Ra delivered this speculation during many of his performances.

41. In "The Changing Same," Baraka describes this "black world" in the following manner: "But dig, not only is it a place where Black People live, it is a place, in the spiritual precincts of its emotional telling, where Black People move in almost absolute openness and strength." Amiri Baraka, "The Changing Same (R&B and New Black Music)," in *Black Music* (1968; reprint, New York: Da Capo Press, 1998), 186–87.

42. Countee Cullen, "Heritage," in *The New Negro*, ed. Alain Locke (1925; reprint, New York: Touchstone, 1992), 252–53.

43. Fred Moten, *In the Break: The Aesthetics of the Black Radical Tradition* (Minneapolis: University of Minnesota Press, 2003).

44. Baraka, "Changing Same," 187.

45. Robert Farris Thompson has mobilized the term "flash of the spirit" as a way of understanding diasporic African aesthetics.

46. Amus Mor, "Poem to the Hip Generation," in *Black Spirits: A Festival of New Poets in America*, ed. Woodie King, (New York: Vintage Books, 1972). 134.

47. Ibid.

48. Ibid., 135.

49. Gwendolyn Brooks, *Report from Part One* (Detroit: Broadside Press, 1972), 167.

50. Gwendolyn Brooks, "We Real Cool" in *Blacks*, Gwendolyn Brooks (Chicago: Third World Press, 1987), 407. Brooks, "In the Mecca," in *Blacks*, 423.

51. Brooks, "In the Mecca," 423–24.

52. Gwendolyn Brooks, Introduction to *My Name is Afrika*, by Keorapetse Kgositsile (New York: Doubleday, 1971), 15.

53. Keorapetse Kgositsile, "Exile," in *If I Could Sing: Selected Poems* (Roggebaai, South Africa: Kwela, 2002), 49.

54. Gwendolyn Brooks, "Kitchenette Building," in *Blacks* (New York: Third World Press, 1987), 20.

55. Raymond Williams, *Marxism and Literature* (Oxford: Oxford University Press, 1977).

56. Claudia Rankine, *Citizen: An American Lyric* (Minneapolis: Graywolf Press, 2014), 139–46. (subsequent references appear parenthetically in the text).

57. Toomer, *Cane*, 3.

58. Baraka and Fundi, *In Our Terribleness*, n.p.

59. Baraka and Fundi, *In Our Terribleness*, n.p.

60. Claudia Rankine, *Don't Let Me Be Lonely: An American Lyric* (Minneapolis: Graywolf Press, 2004), 23.

61. Lauren Berlant, "Claudia Rankine," *Bomb* 129 (Fall 2014), accessed August 5, 2016, http://bombmagazine.org/article/10096/claudia-rankine.

62. Chester Pierce, "Psychiatric Problems of the Black Minority," in *American Handbook of Psychiatry*, ed. Silvano Arieti. (New York: Basic Books, 1974), 515.

63. Nathanial Mackey, "An Interview with Kamau Brathwaite," in *The Art of Kamau Brathwaite*, ed. Stewart Brown (Bridgend, Mid Glamorgan, Wales: Seren, 1995), 14.

64. Larry Neal, "And Shine Swam On," in *Black Fire: An Anthology of Afro-American Writing*, ed. Amiri Baraka and Larry Neal (1968; reprint, Baltimore: Black Classic Press, 2007), 652.

65. Brooks, "Kitchenette Building," 20.

Chapter 2. The Politics of Abstraction

1. Amiri Baraka, "Black Art," in *The LeRoi Jones/Amiri Baraka Reader*, ed. William Harris (New York: Thunder's Mouth Press, 1991), 219.

2. Raymond Saunders, *Black Is a Color* (San Francisco: Arts Magazine, June 1967), n.p. Subsequently reprinted in 1989 as a brochure (*Raymond Saunders: Some Choices*—a group exhibition curated by Saunders for Long Beach Museum of Art, 24 June–23 July 1989).

3. Ibid.

4. I received this tweet in February 2015 from Deepna Oshun.

5. Q-Tip, "Vivrant Thing," *Amplified* (Arista Records, 1999).

6. Amiri Baraka, "The Man Who Sold Pictures of God," in *The Fiction of LeRoi Jones/Amiri Baraka* (Chicago: Lawrence Hill Books, 2000), 9.

7. Ibid., 11.

8. Ibid.

9. Kalpana Seshadri-Crooks, *Desiring Whiteness: A Lacanian Analysis of Race* (New York: Routledge, 2000).

10. Wesley Brown, "I Was Here but I Disappeared," in *Breaking Ice: An Anthology of Contemporary African-American Fiction*, ed. Terry McMillan (New York: Penguin Books, 1990), 98.

11. Charles Johnson, "A Capsule History of Blacks in Comics," in *I Call Myself an Artist: Writings by and about Charles Johnson*, ed. Charles Johnson and Rudolph Byrd (Bloomington: Indiana University Press, 1999), 209.

12. Darby English, *How to See a Work of Art in Total Darkness* (Cambridge: Massachusetts Institute of Technology Press, 2010), 12.

13. Ibid., 1..

14. Larry Neal, "Perspectives/Commentaries on AfriCobra," in *AfriCobra: Universal Aesthetic* (Washington, D.C.: Howard University Press, 1979), n.p.

15. Jeff Donaldson, "Ten in Search of a Nation," *Black World* 19.12 (October 1970): 86.

16. Originally published in the exhibition catalogue *AFRI-COBRA III* Exhibition catalog (Amherst: University of Massachusetts Art Gallery, 1973), n.p.

17. Donaldson, "Ten in Search," 85.

18. Ed Bullins, "A Short Statement on Street Theatre" (1968), in *Ed Bullins: Twelve Plays and Selected Writings*, ed. Mike Sell (Ann Arbor: University of Michigan Press, 2006), 288.

19. Nelson Stevens, interview with the author, October 20, 2011, Amherst, Mass.

20. Gerald Williams, interview with the author, March 7, 2012. The quotation from Spellman can be found in A. B. Spellman, "Big Bushy Afros," *International Review of African American Art* 15.1 (1998): 53.

21. Amiri Baraka, "It's Nation Time," in *The LeRoi Jones/Amiri Baraka Reader*, ed. William J. Harris (New York: Thunder's Mouth Press, 1991), 240–42.

22. Terezita Romo, *Malaquais Montoya* (Los Angeles: Chicano Studies Research Center, 2011).

23. Imamu Amiri Baraka (LeRoi Jones) and Fundi (Billy Abernathy), *In Our Terribleness: Some Elements and Meaning in Black Style* (Indianapolis: Bobbs-Merrill Co., 1970), n.p.

24. Edward Spriggs, "AFRICOBRA: An Intermediarily Pro/position," in *AFRICOBRA II* (New York: The Studio Museum in Harlem, 1971), 2.

25. Gerald Williams, interview with the author, March 2012.

26. Donaldson, "Ten in Search", 85.

27. Barbara Jones-Hogu, "The History, Philosophy and Aesthetics of AFRI-CO-BRA," in *AFRI-COBRA III* Exhibition catalog (Amherst: University of Massachusetts Art Gallery, 1973), n.p.

28. Donaldson, "Ten in Search," 85.

29. Nubai Kai, "Africobra Universal Aesthetics," in *AFRICOBRA: the First Twenty Years* (Atlanta: Nexus Contemporary Art Center, 1990), 8.

30. Gwendolyn Brooks, "Kitchenette Building," in *Blacks* (Chicago: Third World Press, 1987), 20.

31. Donaldson, "Ten in Search," 85.

32. Larry Neal, "The Narrative of the Black Magicians," in *Black Fire: An Anthology of Afro-American Writing*, ed. Amiri Baraka and Larry Neal (1968; reprint, Baltimore: Black Classic Press, 2007), 314.

33. On the lower frequencies, Adrienne Rich's iconic feminist essay "Notes toward a Politics of Location" (1984) is misread as solely a theory of the political uselessness and dangers of abstraction. When we reread the essay as a move to embodiment as the fight against that which Rich refers to as "lofty and privileged abstraction," *and* as a move to the inseparability of location and dislocation, we see that the recognition of a different type of *grounded abstraction* is embedded in the politics of location.

34. Ed Roberson, Foreword to *Seismosis*, text by John Keene, drawings by Christopher Stackhouse (Chicago: 1913 Press, 2006), n.p.

35. Eric Shouse, "Feeling, Emotion, Affect," *M/C Journal* 8.6 (2005), accessed February 7, 2015, http://journal.media-culture.org.au/0512/03-shouse.php.

36. Barbara Simmons, "Soul," in *Black Fire: An Anthology of Afro-American Writing*, ed. Amiri Baraka and Larry Neal (1968; reprint, Baltimore: Black Classic Press, 2007), 305, 307.

37. Baraka and Fundi, *In Our Terribleness*, n.p.

38. Richard Iton, *In Search of the Black Fantastic: Politics and Popular Culture in the Post-Civil Rights Era* (Oxford: Oxford University Press, 2008), 290.

39. Fred Moten, "The Case of Blackness," *Criticism* 50.2 (Spring 2008): 203.

40. Ibid., 204.

41. Spellman, "Big Bushy Afros," 53.

42. Sala Udin, "A Conversation with Amiri Baraka: Civil Rights, Black Arts, and Politics," *Sampsonia Way*, September 16, 2011, accessed August 8, 2016, http://www.sampsoniaway.org/bi-monthly/2011/09/16/a-conversation-with-amiri-baraka-civ-il-rights-black-arts-and-politics/.

43. Glenn Ligon, "Sound and Vision," in *Sun Ra + Ayé Aton: Space, Interiors and Exteriors 1972*, ed. John Corbett (New York: PictureBox, 2013).

44. Ranciere refers to the "the meta-political idea of global political subjectivity, the idea of the potentiality inherent in the innovative sensible modes of experience that anticipate a community to come." Jacques Ranciere, *The Politics of Aesthetics* (London: Continuum, 2004), 30.

45. Fred Moten, *In the Break: The Aesthetics of the Black Radical Tradition* (Minneapolis: University of Minnesota Press, 2003), 22.

46. Nelson Stevens, interview with the author, August 2011.

47. Glenn Ligon, *Yourself in the World: Selected Writings and Interviews*, ed. Scott Rothkopf (New Haven, Conn.: Yale University Press, 2011), 3.

48. Ibid.

49. Baraka and Fundi, *In Our Terribleness*, n.p.

50. Edouard Glissant, *Poetics of Relation*, trans. Betsy Wing (1990; reprint, Ann Arbor: University of Michigan Press, 1997), 111–20.

51. Percival Everett, *Erasure* (New York: Hyperion, 2001), 3 (subsequent references appear parenthetically in the text).

52. Samuel A. Hay, "Structural Elements in Ed Bullins' Plays," *Black World* 23.6 (April 1974): 21.

53. Fred Moten, *Hughson's Tavern* (Providence: Rhode Island, 2008), 40.

54. Baraka, "Black Art," 219.

55. Colson Whitehead, *The Intuitionist* (New York: Anchor Books, 1999), 5 (subsequent references appear parenthetically in the text).

56. Stephen Henderson, "Saturation: Progress Report on a Theory of Black Poetry" in *Understanding the New Black Poetry: Black Speech and Black Music as Poetic References* (New York: William Morrow, 1973), 64.

57. Touré, *Who's Afraid of Post-Blackness? What It Means to Be Black Now* (New York: Free Press, 2011). Kerry James Marshall, *Who's Afraid of Red, Black and Green Secession* (Berlin: Revolver Publishing, 2012), 53.

58. Ibid.

59. Marcus Garvey, *Philosophy and Opinions of Marcus Garvey or Africa for the Africans*, ed. Amy Jacque Garvey (London: Frank Cass, 1989), 124–25.

60. Rael Jero Salley, "The New Danger of the Pure Idea," in Kerry James Marshall, *Who's Afraid of Red, Black and Green Secession* (Berlin: Revolver Publishing, 2012), 26.

61. Wahneema Lubiano, "Black Nationalism and Black Common Sense: Policing Ourselves and Others," in *The House that Race Built*, ed. Wahneema Lubiano (New York: Vintage Books, 1998), 233.

62. Ben Jones, interview with the author, April 24, 2016, Jersey City, N.J.

63. Barbara Chase-Riboud, "The *Malcolm* Steles and the Silenced X," in *Barbara Chase-Riboud: The Malcolm X Steles*, ed. Carlos Basualdo (New Haven, Conn.: Yale University Press, 2014), 84.

64. Amiri Baraka, foreword to *Black Fire: An Anthology of Afro-American Writing*, ed. Amiri Baraka and Larry Neal (1968; reprint, Baltimore: Black Classic Press, 2007) xviii.

65. Chase-Riboud, "*Malcolm* Steles," 83–84.

66. Spellman, "Big Bushy Afros," 53.

67. Michelle Alexander, *The New Jim Crow: Mass Incarceration in the Age of Colorblindness* (New York: New Press, 2012), x.

68. Adia Harvey Wingfield, "Color-Blindness is Counterproductive," *The Atlantic*, September 13, 2015, http://www.theatlantic.com/politics/archive/2015/09/color-blindness-is-counterproductive/405037/

69. David C. Driskell, ed., *Kevin Cole Straight from the Soul: 25 Years in the Making* (New York: Blue Lotus, 2012), 26.

70. Brenda M. Greene, "The Black Artist as Activist and Transformative Agent," in *The Black Artist as Activist*, exhibition catalogue (Brooklyn: Corridor Gallery, 2010), n.p.

71. Phillip Brian Harper, *Abstractionist Aesthetics: Artistic Form and Social Critique in African American Culture* (New York: New York University Press, 2015).

Chapter 3. The Counter-Literacy of Black Mixed Media

1. Stephen Henderson, "Saturation: Progress Report on a Theory of Black Poetry," *Black World* 24.8 (June 1975): 4–17.

2. Angela Jackson, *Where I Must Go* (Evanston, Ill.: Northwestern University Press, 2009), 3.

3. Ibid., 4.

4. Zora Neale Hurston, "Characteristics of Negro Expression" (1934), in *Double-Take: A Revisionist Harlem Renaissance Anthology*, ed. Venetria K. Patton and Maureen Honey (New Brunswick, N.J.: Rutgers University Press, 2001), 61–62.

5. See Katherine Capshaw, *Civil Rights Childhood: Picturing Liberation in African American Photobooks* (Minneapolis: University of Minnesota Press, 2014).

6. Imamu Amiri Baraka (LeRoi Jones) and Fundi (Billy Abernathy), *In Our Terribleness (Some Elements and Meaning in Black Style)* (Indianapolis: Bobbs-Merrill, 1970), n.p.

7. Jacques Derrida, "Signature, Event, Context," in *Margins of Philosophy*, trans. Alan Bass (Chicago: University of Chicago Press, 1982).

8. Fred Moten, *In the Break: The Aesthetics of the Black Radical Tradition* (Minneapolis: University of Minnesota Press, 2003), 22.

9. Ben Sidran, *Black Talk* (New York: Holt Rinehart Winston, 1971), xvi.

10. Dennis Hevesi, "Milton Meltzer, Prolific Author, Dies at 94," *New York Times*, September 25, 2009.

11. June Jordan, *Who Look at Me* (New York: Thomas Y. Crowell Co., 1969), 1 (subsequent references appear parenthetically in the text).

12. Baraka and Fundi, *In Our Terribleness*, n.p.

13. Ibid., n.p.

14. Diana Taylor's insistence that the archive cannot contain the live resonates here. See Diana Taylor, *The Archive and the Repertoire: Performing Cultural Memory in the Americas* (Durham, N.C.: Duke University Press, 2003), 173.

15. Amiri Baraka, "Black Art," in *The LeRoi Jones/Amiri Baraka Reader*, ed. William Harris (New York: Thunder's Mouth Press, 1991), 219.

16. Haki Madhubuti, *GroundWork: New and Selected Poems of Don L. Lee/Haki Madhubuti* (Chicago: Third World Press, 1996), 21.

17. I am drawing upon Michael Warner's theory in *Publics and Counterpublics* (Brooklyn: Zone Books, 2005).

18. Baraka and Fundi, *In Our Terribleness*, n.p.

19. Fundi Abernathy to Amiri Baraka, May 5, 1969, Amiri Baraka Papers, box 12, Moorland Spingarn Research Center, Howard University.

20. Middleton A. Harris, with the assistance of Morris Levitt, Roger Furman, and Ernest Smith. *The Black Book* (New York: Random House, 1974), cover quotation.

21. Toni Morrison, preface to *The Black Book*, by Middleton A. Harris (New York: Random House, 1974), n.p.

22. Mitchell explains the concept "imagetext" in the following manner: "The term 'imagetext' designates composite, synthetic works (or concepts) that combine image and text. 'Image-text,' with a hyphen, designates *relations* of the visual and verbal. The necessity of a concept such as the 'imagetext' was first made clear to me by Robert Nelson in our team-taught seminar on 'Image and Text.'" W. J. T. Mitchell, *Picture Theory: Essays on Verbal and Visual Representation* (Chicago: University of Chicago Press, 1994), 89.

23. In the catalog for the 1973 AFRI-COBRA III exhibit at University of Massachusetts at Amherst, the "aesthetic principle" of mimesis at midpoint is described in the following manner: "B. *MIMESIS AT MID-POINT*, design which marks the spot where the real and the unreal, the objective and the non-objective, the plus and the minus meet. A point exactly between absolute abstractions and absolute naturalism." (*AFRI-COBRA III* Exhibition catalog (Amherst: University of Massachusetts Art Gallery, 1973), n.p.)

24. This mural was created in 1973 at United Community Construction Workers Labor Temple in the Roxbury neighborhood of Boston.

25. In the 1973 AfriCOBRA catalog, the principle of lettering is described in the following manner: "The subject matter must be completely understood by the viewer, therefore lettering would be used to extend and clarify the visual statement. The lettering was to be incorporated into the composition as a part of the visual statement and not as a headline."

26. Tricia Rose, *Black Noise* (Middletown, Conn.: Wesleyan University Press, 1994).

27. Larry Neal, *Black Boogaloo: Notes on Black Liberation* (San Francisco: Journal of Black Poetry Press, 1969), 40.

28. Ibid., 43.

29. Larry Neal, "Some Reflections on the Black Aesthetic," in *The Black Aesthetic*, ed. Addison Gayle Jr. (Garden City, N.Y.: Doubleday and Co., 1971), 13.

30. Baraka and Fundi, *In Our Terribleness*, n.p.

31. Ibid., n.p.

32. Jackson, *Where I Must Go*, 3.

33. Ibid., 4.

34. Charles Johnson, "The End of the Black American Narrative" in *Best African American Essays 2010*, ed. Gerald Early and Randall Kennedy (New York: Random House, 2010), 111–22.

35. *Seismosis*, text by John Keene, drawing by Christopher Stackhouse (Chicago: 1913 Press, 2006), 36. (subsequent references appear parenthetically in the text).

36. *Seismosis*, 19.

37. Ed Roberson, Foreword to *Seismosis*, text by John Keene, drawing by Christopher Stackhouse (Chicago: 1913 Press, 2006), n.p.

38. Don L. Lee, *Think Black* (Detroit: Broadside Press, 1967), 24.

39. National Ocean Service, "What Is Geodesy?" accessed August 9, 2016, http:// oceanservice.noaa.gov/facts/geodesy.html.

40. Kimberly Ruffin, *Black on Earth: African American Ecoliterary Traditions* (Athens: University of Georgia Press, 2010); Camille T. Dungy, ed., *Black Nature: Four Centuries of African American Nature Poetry* (Athens: University of Georgia Press, 2009).

Chapter 4. The Local and the Global: BLKARTSOUTH and *Callaloo*

1. Amiri Baraka, "A Post-Racial Anthology?" *Poetry* 202 (2013): 168; *Angles of Ascent: A Norton Anthology of Contemporary African American Poetry*, ed. Charles Henry Rowell (New York: Norton, 2013).

2. Author's interview with Kalamu ya Salaam, July 12, 2013.

3. Ibid.

4. *The Penguin Anthology of Twentieth-Century American Poetry*, ed. Rita Dove (New York: Penguin, 2013).

5. Rita Dove, "Upon Meeting Don L. Lee, in a Dream," in *Selected Poems* (New York: Vintage, 1993), 12.

6. Jerry Ward, interview with the author, July 20, 2013.

7. Ibid.

8. Baraka, "A Post-Racial Anthology?" 168.

9. Jerry Ward, interview with the author, July 20, 2013.

10. Ibid.

11. Jerry W. Ward Jr., "Introduction: A River Talking Time and Revolution," in *Blue Lights and River Songs*, by Tom Dent (Detroit: Lotus Press, 1982), n.p.

12. Thomas C. Dent, Richard Schechner, and Gilbert Moses, preface to *The Free Southern Theater by the Free Southern Theater*, ed. Thomas C. Dent, Richard Schechner, and Gilbert Moses (Indianapolis: The Bobbs-Merrill Co., 1969), xi.

13. Ibid.

14. Kalamu ya Salaam, *The Magic of Juju: An Appreciation of the Black Arts Movement* (Chicago: Third World Press, 2016), 2.

15. Tom Dent to Calvin Hernton, March 30, 1969, box 24/4, Thomas Dent Correspondence, 1969 Jan.–June, Amistad Research Center, Tulane University.

16. Tom Dent, "For the Southern Univ. in New Orleans Students Arrested Attempting to Raise the BLK Flag of Liberation," *Nkombo* 2.2 (1969): 46.

17. Kalamu ya Salaam, "Food for Thought," *Nkombo* 2.3 (1969): 4.

18. Zora Neale Hurston, introduction to *Mules and Men* (1935; reprint, New York; Harper Perennial, 2008), 2.

19. Ed Bullins, "Black Theatre: The 70s Evolutionary Changes" (New York: Black Theatre, 1971), Box 88, Folder 9, Amistad Research Center, Tulane University.

20. Ibid., 1.

21. Nayo Ola (Barbara Malcolm), "today, tomorrow, sister," *Nkombo* 2.3 (1969): 18.

22. Ibid., 20.

23. *Uncommonplace: An Anthology of Contemporary Louisiana Poets*, ed. Ann Brewster Dobi (Baton Rouge: Louisiana State University Press, 1998).

24. Fred Moten, "There Is Blackness," in *Hughson's Tavern* (Providence, R.I.: Leon Works, 2008), 40.

25. Quo Vadis Gex-Breaux, "Jazz Rain," in *Uncommonplace: An Anthology of Contemporary Louisiana Poets*, ed. Ann Brewster Dobi (Baton Rouge: Louisiana State University Press, 1998), 90.

26. Kalamu ya Salaam, Introduction to *Dark Waters*, by Quo Vadis Gex (New Orleans: BLKARTSOUTH, 1969), 2.

27. Gex-Breaux, "Jazz Rain," 90.

28. Ibid., 90–91.

29. Fred Moten, "Jurisgenerative Grammar (For Alto)," in *The Oxford Handbook of Critical Improvisation Studies*, vol. 1, ed. George Lewis and Benjamin Piekut (Oxford: Oxford University Press, 2016), 133; James Baldwin, "Sonny's Blues," in *Going to Meet the Man* (New York: Vintage, 1965), 138.

30. Moten, "Jurisgenerative Grammar," 133.

31. Ibid.

32. Amiri Baraka (LeRoi Jones), "Black Dada Nihilismus," in *The Dead Lecturer* (New York: Grove Press, 1964), 61.

33. Quo Vadis Gex-Breaux, "The Long and Short of It," in *Uncommonplace: An Anthology of Contemporary Louisiana Poets*, ed. Ann Brewster Dobi (Baton Rouge: Louisiana State University Press, 1998), 92.

34. I'm echoing Tom Dent's language in his 1969 letter to Calvin Hernton, cited earlier, when he describes the need for a "southern orientation" to the "Black Arts concept" (box 24/4, Thomas Dent Correspondence, 1969 Jan–June, Amistad Research Center, Tulane University).

35. Dara Ebun Ola, untitled poem, *Nkombo* 2.3 (1969): 22; Amiri Baraka, *The Le-Roi Jones/Amiri Baraka Reader*, ed. William J. Harris (New York: Thunder's Mouth Press, 1991), 218.

36. Catherine Michna, "We Are Black Mind Jockeys: Tom Dent, the Free Southern Theater, and the Search for a Second-Line Literary Aesthetic in New Orleans," *Journal of Ethnic American Literature* 1 (2011): 1–31.

37. Vertamae Smart-Grosvenor, *Vibration Cooking: Or the Travel Notes of a Geechee Girl* (New York: Doubleday, 1970), xiii.

38. Mona Lisa Savoy, "A Few Words on My Words," in *Red Beans and Ricely Yours* (Kirksville, Mo.: Truman State University Press, 2005), 19.

39. Quo Vadis Gex-Breaux, interview with the author, October 24, 2013.

40. Ibid.

41. Tom Dent, "From the Kitchen," *Nkombo* 2.2 (1969): n.p.

42. Kalamu ya Salaam writes, "*we are black mind jockeys I look for us everywhere.*" Kalamu ya Salaam, "Food for Thought," *Nkombo* 2.2 (1969): n.p.

43. Amiri Baraka, "Black Art," in *The LeRoi Jones/Amiri Baraka Reader*, ed. William Harris (New York: Thunder's Mouth Press, 1991), 219.

44. Nikki Giovanni, *Black Feeling Black Talk/ Black Judgement* (New York: Morrow Quill, 1979 [1968]). I'm referring to Giovanni's use of "feeling," in the layered title of this poetry volume, as a means of celebrating the excessiveness of blackness.

45. Thomas C. Dent, *The Free Southern Theater by the Free Southern Theater*, ed. Thomas C. Dent and Richard Schechner (Indianapolis: Bobbs-Merrill Co., 1969), 233. In "The Free Southern Theatre, 1963–1979," Genevieve Fabre explains the blackening of the FST in the following manner: "In 1965 nationalist-separatist ideologies permeated the FST membership, as they did most militant organizations. A number of issues were debated concerning the advisability of having white members, or performing before whites, and of going to white-dominated towns. New slogans were launched— 'The Fire Next Time in Mississippi' or 'Good Bye Godot.' The FST thus bade farewell to the white god—white liberal, patron, playwright—from whom no salvation could be expected, and expressed its dissatisfaction with the help of 'benevolent' whites. It was decided that the FST should become a 'black' theatre for blacks, performed and managed by blacks. The theatre moved its base to an all-black neighborhood in the Desire district of New Orleans, where it would be easier to solicit black talent and involvement" (56).

46. Salaam, *Magic of Juju*, 2–3.

47. Author's interview with Quo Vadis Gex-Breaux, October 24, 2013.

48. Tom Dent to Dr. Thomas Brayboy, May 28, 1968, Box 2, folder 1, Amistad Research Center, Tulane University.

49. Ibid., 13.

50. Ibid., 3.

51. Jean Toomer, *Cane* (1923; reprint, New York: Norton, 1988), 3.

52. LeRoi Jones, *Blues People: The Negro Experience in White America and the Music that Developed from It* (New York: William Marrow, 1968), 95.

53. Tom Dent to Dr. Thomas Brayboy, 3.

54. Kalamu ya Salaam, "Leroi." *Nkombo* 1.1 (1969): 66.

55. Bill Withers, *The Best of Bill Withers: Lean on Me*, CD (Sony Legacy, 2000)

56. Neal writes, "The motive behind the Black aesthetic is the destruction of the white thing, the destruction of white ideas, and white ways of looking at the world." Larry Neal, "The Black Arts Movement," in *SOS—Calling All Black People: A Black Arts Movement Reader*, ed. John H. Bracey Jr., Sonia Sanchez, and James Smethurst (Amherst: University of Massachusetts Press, 2014), 56.

57. Alice Walker, "Everyday Use," in *The Norton Anthology of African American Literature*, ed. Henry Louis Gates and Nellie Y. McKay (New York: Norton, 2004), 2441.

58. Alice Walker to Tom Dent, undated, circa 1971–1973, Thomas Dent Papers, Amistad Research Center, Tulane University.

59. Alice Walker to Tom Dent, November 6, 1971, Box 2, folder 8, Thomas Dent Papers, Amistad Research Center, Tulane University.

60. Alice Walker, "The Labels Slip Sometimes," *Nkombo* 9 (June 1974). 56.

61. Alice Walker to Tom Dent, May 24, 1972, Box 3, folder 1, Thomas Dent Papers, Amistad Research Center, Tulane University.

62. Fred Moten, *In The Break: The Aesthetics of the Black Radical Tradition* (Minneapolis: University of Minnesota Press, 2003), 69. Moten writes, "We'll see how Amiri Baraka, for instance, in both approach and avoidance, enacts such a cut interpellation. But maybe all such resignifications or redeployments bear this active, if muted, infelicity, this unhappiness of nomination or incomplete christening" (69). The words "frame cuts frame" are used in the following manner: "At the place where Shakespeare, Baraka, and Eisenstein do not meet, not in between but outside and home, race cuts race and frame cuts frame" (109).

63. Quo Vadis Gex, "Song to Be Sung for Poets," *Nkombo* N9 (June 1974), 6.

64. Neal uses the word "weird" in many of his texts. He writes, for example, in the poem "Don't Say Goodbye to the Porkpie Hat": "Shape to shape, horn to horn / the Porkpie Hat resurrected himself / night to night, from note to note / skimming the horizons, flashing bluegreenyellow lights / and blowing black stars / and weird looneymoon changes, chords coiled about him / and he was flying." Larry Neal, *Hoodoo Hollerin' Bebop Ghosts* (Washington, D.C.: Howard University Press, 1974), 21.

65. Gex, "Song to Be Sung for Poets," 6.

66. Greg Thomas, professor of global black studies at Tufts University, offered this theory of the BAM move from poetry to poesis in a 2014 conversation with the author.

67. Ken Friedman, *The Fluxus Reader* (New York: Academy Editions, 1998), 4.

68. David Henderson, "Jass Funeral," *Nkombo* 9 (June 1974), 70.

69. Kalamu ya Salaam, interview with the author, July 12, 2013.

70. See Nato Thompson, ed., *Living as Form: Socially Engaged Art from 1991–2011* (New York: Creative Time Books, 2012).

71. Sam Cornish, "Marcus: A Student Who Writes Backwards and Sits Close to Me Even If I Am Reading Dr. Suess," *Umbra* 5, "Latin Soul" issue (1974): 91.

72. Victor Hernandez Cruz, "Walking Faces," *Umbra* 5, "Latin Soul" issue (1974): 95; Victor Hernandez Cruz, "African Things," in *Maraca: New and Selected Poems, 1965–2000* (Minneapolis: Coffee House Press, 2001), 65.

73. LeRoi Jones (Amiri Baraka), "The World You're Talking About," in *Felix of the Silent Forest*, by David Henderson (New York: Poets Press, 1967), n.p.

Chapter 5. The Satire of Black Post-Blackness

1. Ralph Ellison, "An Extravagance of Laughter," in *Going to the Territory* (New York: Vintage, 1995), 145.

2. Anca Parvulescu, *Laughter: Notes on a Passion* (Cambridge: Massachusetts Institute of Technology Press, 2010), 70.

3. Jelani Cobb, "The Path Cleared by Amiri Baraka," *New Yorker*, January 15, 2014, http://www.newyorker.com/news/news-desk/the-path-cleared-by-amiri-baraka. Cobb writes, "In *Home*, a collection of Baraka's essays from this period, published in 1966, he wrote: 'The black artist's role in America is to aid in the destruction of America as he knows it. His role is to report and reflect so precisely the nature of the society, and of himself in that society, that other men will be moved by the exactness of his rendering and, if they are black men, grow strong through this moving, having seen their own strength, and weakness; and if they are white men, tremble, curse, and go mad, because they will be drenched with the filth of their evil.' Reading these lines now, in an era defined by a black Presidency, the kill-whitey rhetoric has an almost comic undertone."

4. Ishmael Reed, *Mumbo Jumbo* (New York: Scribner, 1972), 25 (subsequent references appear parenthetically in the text).

5. Gates writes, "As many critics have gone to great lengths to demonstrate, *Mumbo Jumbo* is at thematic allegory of the Black Arts Movement of the 1960s rendered through causal connections with the Harlem Renaissance of the 1920s." Henry Louis Gates, *The Signifying Monkey: A Theory of African-American Literary Criticism* (Oxford: Oxford University Press, 1988), 232–33.

6. Amiri Baraka, "Return of the Native," in *The LeRoi Jones/Amiri Baraka Reader*, ed. William J. Harris (New York: Thunder's Mouth Press, 1991), 217.

7. Reed uses the words "Afro satire" in the following passage as he describes African art that depicts European colonists in caricatured ways—thus positing the roots of this satirical impulse far earlier than the Harlem Renaissance or the Black Arts

Movement: "But the figures on the desk, these grotesque and laughable ivory and bronze cartoons represent the genius of Afro satire" (97).

8. Ruthe Sheffey, "The Sardonic Vision: Wit and Irony in Militant Black Poetry," *Black World* 22.8 (June 1973): 15. Sheffey explains BAM satire in the following manner: "From the womb of disillusion over the condition of Blacks in American society, from a social indignation, often deepened into disgust, from a sense of moral outrage at cruelty and hypocrisy, the Black ironist declares beyond rancorous sensibility the warfare against racism. Sometimes the angle of vision is from Black social solidarity, sometimes from private introspection, but always from the conviction that we are at war, that there is an enemy, and that poems are weapons in which the strong antipathy of the oppressed for his oppressor finds its locus. As in all good satire, the appeal is to those deep-laid elements of human personality, anger, and contempt, the love of mockery or laughter, but moral and social correction are the primary objectives" (19).

9. Amiri Baraka, "It's Nation Time," in *The LeRoi Jones/Amiri Baraka Reader*, ed. William J. Harris (New York: Thunder's Mouth Press, 1991), 242.

10. Frantz Fanon, *The Wretched of the Earth* (1961; reprint, New York: Grove Press, 2004), 43.

11. Larry Neal, "New Space/The Growth of Black Consciousness in the Sixties," in *The Black Seventies*, ed. Floyd B. Barbour (Boston: Porter Sargent, 1970), 29.

12. Ed Bullins, *The Theme Is Blackness: "The Corner" and Other Plays* (New York: William Morrow and Co., 1973).

13. Amiri Baraka, "Sound for Sounding," in *Black Boogaloo: Notes on Black Liberation*, by Larry Neal (San Francisco: Journal of Black Poetry Press, 1969), i.

14. Amiri Baraka, Introduction to *Black Fire: An Anthology of Afro-American Writing*, ed. Amiri Baraka and Larry Neal (1968; reprint, Baltimore: Black Classic Press, 2007), xviii.

15. Amiri Baraka, "A Post-Racial Anthology?" *Poetry* 202 (2013): 168.

16. Paul Beatty, *Slumberland* (New York: Bloomsbury, 2008), 16 (subsequent references appear parenthetically in the text).

17. Baraka, "Sound for Sounding," i.

18. Carlene Hatcher Polite, *Sister X and the Victims of Foul Play* (New York: Farrar, Straus, and Giroux, 1975), 3–4 (subsequent references appear parenthetically in the text).

19. Edouard Glissant, *Poetics of Relation*, trans. Betsy Wing (Ann Arbor: University of Michigan Press, 1997 [1990]), 41.

20. Like Martin, Paul Beatty, in *Slumberland*, thinks about the difficulty of finding language for the aesthetics of "yesterday," but he focuses on the "day before yesterday," which seems to represent a layering of the "memory and mood" of yesterday versus the "memory and mood" of the day before yesterday. Beatty uses this meditation on the "day before yesterday" to shape his twenty-first-century play with blackness around the temporality of that which has just passed and that which passed immediately before. In this "blurring" of the layers of the very recent past, he locates a

temporal rhythm of a past that is too recent to be past—a temporal rhythm that, in the following passage, is depicted as an impatient "tapping" and waiting for words to understand this very recent past: "Most languages have a word for the day before yesterday. *Anteayer* in Spanish. *Vorgestern* in German. There is no word for it in English. It's a language that tries to keep the past simple and perfect, free of the subjunctive blurring of memory and mood. I take out a pen, tapping the end impatiently on a bar napkin as I try to think of a English word for 'the day before yesterday'" (13).

21. Sharon Stockard Martin, *Edifying Further Elaborations on the Mentality of a Chore*, Free Southern Theater Records, 1960–78, box 86, folder 40, p. 64, Amistad Research Center, Tulane University, New Orleans (subsequent references appear parenthetically in the text).

22. Willie Abraham, Introduction to *dem*, by William Melvin Kelley, 2nd ed. (New York: Collier Books, 1969 [1967]: xi.

23. Ibid., vii.

24. Willie Abraham, introduction to *dem*, by William Melvin Kelley, 2d ed. (1967; reprint, New York: Collier Books, 1969), 128 (subsequent references appear parenthetically in the text).

25. Souleymane Bachir Diagne, "Re-Reading Senghor Today," Paper delivered at Global Black Consciousness Conference, Dakar, Senegal, May 11, 2014.

26. Charles Johnson, "The End of the Black American Narrative," *American Scholar* 7.3 (Summer 2008): 42.

27. Charles Johnson, *Half-Past Nation Time* (Westlake Village, Calif.: Aware Press, 1972), n.p.

28. Charles Johnson, *Black Humor* (Chicago: Johnson Publishing Co., 1970), n.p.

29. Carolyn Rodgers, "Uh Nat'chal Thang—The WHOLE TRUTH—US," *Black World* 20.11 (September 1971): 10.

30. Ibid., 10.

31. Ibid., 10.

32. Maulana Ron Karenga, *The Quotable Karenga* (Los Angeles: US Organization, 1967), 3.

33. Souleymane Bachir Diagne, "Re-Reading Senghor Today," Paper delivered at Global Black Consciousness Conference, Dakar, Senegal, May 11, 2014.

34. Amiri Baraka, *Tales of the Out and the Gone* (New York: Akashic Books, 2007), 11 (subsequent references appear parenthetically in the text).

35. Baraka describes the out and gone in the following manner: "The out is out, even if in plain sight. Though it would not have to be. The 'Gone' could be seen or unseen or obscene. But even farther 'Out,' crazier, wilder, deeper, a 'heavier' metaphor, a deeper parable. We'd say that's 'way out'" (12).

36. Imamu Amiri Baraka (LeRoi Jones) and Fundi (Billy Abernathy), *In Our Terribleness* (Indianapolis: Bobbs-Merrill Co., 1970), n.p.

37. Percival Everett, *Percival Everett by Virgil Russell* (Minneapolis: Graywolf Press, 2013), 3 (subsequent references appear parenthetically in the text).

38. Amiri Baraka, "Adventures in Negrossity," in *Un Poco Low Coup* (Berkeley: Ishmael Reed Publishing Co., 2004), 19.

39. Mat Johnson, *Pym* (New York: Random House, 2011), 30.

40. Ibid., 28.

41. Amiri Baraka (LeRoi Jones), *Dutchman and The Slave* (New York: HarperCollins, 1964), 44, 45.

42. Ibid., 45.

Chapter 6. Black Inside/Out: Public Interiority and Black Aesthetics

1. For example, Ernest Allen (Ernie Mkalimoto) used the words "black collectivity" in the following manner: "[I]n short, black life-style—was created by political means, by the pale fist of white state power wielded against the black collectivity by the slave master." Ernie Mkalimoto (Ernest Allen), "The Cultural Arm of Revolutionary Nationalism," *Black World* 19.2 (December 1969): 14.

2. Quo Vadis Gex-Breaux, interview with the author, October 24, 2013.

3. Ibid.

4. Amiri Baraka, *Tales of the Out and the Gone* (New York: Akashic Books, 2007), 12.

5. Sun Ra, *Super Sonic Sounds*, LP (New York: ABC/Impulse AS-9271, 1974). This is a reissue of *Super Sonic Jazz* (Chicago: Saturn LP 204 clone 1956)

6. Samella Lewis and Ruth Waddy, eds., *Black Artists on Art*, Vol. 1 (Los Angeles: Contemporary Crafts, 1969), 4.

7. Nelson Stevens, interview with the author, October 20, 2011, Amherst, Mass.

8. Ibid.

9. A. B. Spellman, "Big Bushy Afros," *International Review of African American Art* 15.1 (1998): 53.

10. Call for papers, *Interstices: Journal of Architecture and Related Arts*, 2011 (circulated online).

11. Amiri Baraka, "Black Art," in *The LeRoi Jones/Amiri Baraka Reader*, ed. William Harris (New York: Thunder's Mouth Press, 1991), 219.

12. Kara E. Walker, *Kara Walker: My Complement, My Enemy, My Oppressor, My Love* (Minneapolis: Walker Art Center, 2007), 220.

13. Keith Morrison, Catalog, "The Thirty-Ninth Arts Festival Exhibition," Fisk University Art Gallery, 1968.

14. Kirsten Buick, "L'Effet de Réel: Showing (and Telling) Kara Walker" in *Kara Walker No/ Kara Walker Yes/ Kara Walker-?*, ed. Howardena Pindell (New York: Midmarch Arts Press, 2009), 22.

15. Benjamin Sutton, "Here It Is, the Kara Walker Selfie Generator," *Artnet News*, July 1, 2014, accessed August 20, 2016, https://news.artnet.com/in-brief/here-it-is-the-kara-walker-selfie-generator-52094.

16. Hoyt Fuller to Carolyn Rodgers, May 6, 1970, Hoyt W. Fuller Collection, Archives Research Center, Atlanta University Center, Robert W. Woodruff Library, box 33, folder 6 (hereafter Fuller Collection).

17. Kara Walker, *Narratives of a Negress* (New York: Rizzoli, 2007), 18

18. Ibid., 7.

19. Qtd. in Andrea Burns, *From Storefront to Monument: Tracing the Public History of the Black Museum Movement* (Amherst: University of Massachusetts Press, 2013), 20.

20. "We Are Here: Black Women Claim Their Space at Kara Walker's Controversial Sugar Sphinx Show," *Ebony*, accessed October 11, 2016, http://www.ebony.com/entertainment-culture/kara-walker-domino-003#axzz4LspW3qk6.

21. Jamilah King, "Kara Walker's Sphinx Evokes Call from Black Women: 'We Are Here,'" *Colorlines*, June 23, 2014, accessed August 20, 2016, http://www.colorlines.com/articles/kara-walkers-sugar-sphinx-evokes-call-black-women-we-are-here.

22. Jane H. Carpenter with Betye Saar, ed. *Betye Saar* (Petaluma, CA: Pomegranate Communications, 2003), 45.

23. Gwendolyn Brooks, *Report from Part One* (Detroit: Broadside Press, 1972), 167.

24. Toni Morrison, *A Mercy* (New York: Vintage Books, 2008), 3.

25. Amiri Baraka, "Black Art," in *The LeRoi Jones/Amiri Baraka Reader*, ed. William Harris (New York: Thunder's Mouth Press, 1991), 219.

26. Nina Simone, *Baltimore*, LP (Brussels: CTI, 1978)

27. Esther Terry, professor emeritus at the University of Massachusetts at Amherst, used these lucid words "we have our own eyes" in a 2008 conversation with the author.

28. Ernest Shaw, interview with the author, April 10, 2016.

29. Carolyn Rodgers, *2 Love Raps*, Folded broadside (Chicago: Third World Press, 1969), handwritten note, Fuller Collection, box 23, folder 16.

30. Hoyt Fuller to Carolyn Rodgers, October 2, 1970, Fuller Collection, box 23, folder 16.

31. Hoyt Fuller to Carolyn Rodgers, February 12, 1971, Fuller Collection, box 23, folder 16.

32. Amiri Baraka, "Black Art," in *The LeRoi Jones/Amiri Baraka Reader*, ed. William Harris (New York: Thunder's Mouth Press, 1991), 219.

33. Hoyt Fuller to Carolyn Rodgers, June 24, 1971, Fuller Collection, box 23, folder 16.

34. Fuller to Rodgers, June 24, 1971, Fuller Collection, box 23, folder 16.

35. Carolyn Rodgers to Hoyt Fuller, July 24, 1970. Fuller Collection, box 23, folder 16.

36. Fuller to Rodgers, June 24, 1971, Fuller Collection, box 23, folder 16.

37. Carolyn Rodgers, "For H. W. Fuller," Broadside no. 50, Broadside series (Detroit: Broadside Press, 1969), 1.

38. Carolyn Rodgers, "Black against the Mothafuckas," folded broadside in *2 Love Raps* (Chicago: Third World Press, 1969), n.p.

39. Carolyn Rodgers, "For H. W. Fuller," 1.

40. Hoyt Fuller, Introduction to *Paper Soul*, by Carolyn Rodgers (1968), Fuller Collection, box 23, folder 16.

41. *Night Catches Us*, dir. Tanya Hamilton, DVD (Magnolia Pictures, 2010).

42. William Pope.L, "Some Notes on the Ocean . . . ," in *Black People Are Cropped: Skin Set Drawings* (Zurich: JRP/Ringier, 2012), 11.

43. Albert Bostick to John O'Neal, August 2, 1978, Free Southern Theater Records, box 1/23, Amistad Research Center, Tulane University. This letter ends with the words "P.S. (Like my stationery???)," as this Oklahoma-based visual and performance artist revels in the art of this private correspondence.

44. Haki Madhubuti, *Think Black* (Detroit: Broadside Press, 1967), 24.

45. Unidentified notebook, Thomas Dent Papers, Box 40, folder 30, Amistad Research Center, Tulane University.

46. Imamu Amiri Baraka (LeRoi Jones) and Fundi (Billy Abernathy), *In Our Terribleness (Some Elements and Meaning in Black Style)* (Indianapolis: Bobbs-Merrill, 1970), n.p.

47. Carolyn Rodgers to Hoyt Fuller, April 14, 1968, Fuller Collection, box 23, folder 16.

Chapter 7. Who's Afraid of the Black Fantastic?
The Substance of Surface

1. Richard Iton, *In Search of the Black Fantastic: Politics and Popular Culture in the Post–Civil Rights Era* (Oxford: Oxford University Press, 2008).

2. A. B. Spellman, "Big Bushy Afros," *International Review of African American Art* 15.1 (1998): 53.

3. Linda Stasi, "Rachel Dolezal Not Only Thinks She's Born into the Wrong Race, She Has Everyone Believing It . . . Including the NAACP," *New York Daily News*, June 14, 2015, accessed August 21, 2016, http://www.nydailynews.com/entertainment/gossip/white-wrong-rachel-dolezal-article-1.2257666.

4. Imamu Amiri Baraka (LeRoi Jones) and Fundi (Billy Abernathy), *In Our Terribleness (Some Elements and Meaning in Black Style)* (Indianapolis: Bobbs-Merrill, 1970). Anne Cheng critiques the insidious binary of surface and depth. She argues that modernist art allowed many artists to imagine a type of surface that could not be understood within this binary of surface versus depth. See Anne Cheng, *The Second Skin: Josephine Baker and the Modern Surface* (New York: Oxford University Press, 2011).

5. Barbara Mahone, "With Your Permission," qtd. in Carolyn Rodgers, "Black Poetry—Where It's At," in *SOS—Calling All Black People: A Black Arts Movement Reader*, ed. John H. Bracey Jr., Sonia Sanchez, and James Smethurst (Amherst: University of Massachusetts Press, 2014), 193.

6. Cheng, *Second Skin*, 11.

7. Gil Scott-Heron's iconic critique of televised blackness and the Black Power movement's critique of Blaxploitation reveal the movement's great understanding

of the market forces eager to reduce Black Power to a televised brand. In the novel *The Nigger Factory* (1972), Scott-Heron situates the problem of "televised" cultural revolutions as the problem of a certain generation's inability to really know the struggle because they did not live it. But the key tension that we often fail to realize is the fact that Scott-Heron and others locate this post-knowing in the 1970s; they begin to think about the "post" generation as the movement is about to end. Just as Blaxploitation films do not really start after the movement, the worry about the black counterrevolutionary and the post-movement lack of understanding happens *during* the movement. Scott-Heron, in *The Nigger Factory*, depicts post-movement consciousness as a certain process of gathering and responding that does not shape one era into an ending and set up the other as a beginning. This is the challenge of black post-blackness. Gil Scott-Heron, *The Nigger Factory* (New York: Grove Press, 1972).

8. Haki Madhubuti, "On Seeing Diana Go Maddddddddd," in *Groundwork: New and Selected Poems, Don L. Lee/Haki R. Madhubuti* (Chicago: Third World Press, 1996), 84.

9. In the BAM, we see flashes of an interest in artifice and adornment that is not *only* tied to what the movement viewed as "natural" and "African." Baraka's great interest in Sun Ra is one of the flashes of the black fantastic that shape the BAM. Sun Ra's involvement in the BAM collectives (Spirit House) and his presence on the Spirit House jazz mobile that literally moved Spirit House to the streets is as important to remember as the popular-culture flow of Sun Ra when the movie *Space Is the Place* was released in 1974. Sun Ra's otherworldly dress had deep connections to the clothing of the BAM. When Larry Neal, in "Some Reflections on the Black Aesthetic," uses the image of "Bobby Blue Bland with a dashiki and a process" as one way to encapsulate his sense of the raw core of the aesthetics of the BAM, the mix (of the African, "natural" beauty that the dashiki embodied in the BAM ethos and the straightening, "processing," of black hair) crystallizes, for Neal, the hipness of black aesthetic bohemianism. The mix of the natural and the unnatural in the *electricity* of Bobby Blue Bland (not the pathological confusion and madness that Madhubuti assigns to Diana Ross) is comparable to the electricity that Sun Ra's black otherworldliness creates. Larry Neal, "Some Reflections on the Black Aesthetic," in *African American Literary Theory*, ed. Winston Napier (New York: New York University Press, 2000), 89–91.

10. Baraka writes, "My own wife, who met me in what appeared to be the dying days of my bohemianism, really had got to me when that bohemianism had changed its color. It is my contention that much of the cultural nationalism young people fervently believe is critically important to the struggle is just a form of black bohemianism." Amiri Baraka, *The Autobiography of LeRoi Jones* (Chicago: Lawrence Hill Books, 1997), 424–25.

11. In an editorial in a 1970 issue of *Black World*, the editor Hoyt Fuller directly engages the problem and usefulness of play and performance in the BAM. He writes, "For

some people, game-playing is a full-time preoccupation. [. . .] But the Black Revolution is not a game. Nor are the legitimate aims of the Black Revolution served by assorted poseurs and hustlers playing revolution. Across the country, a small but determined body of black men and women are dedicating their energies—and, in many cases, their lives—to the task of liberating black people from the psychological shackles which have rendered them powerless for centuries." Hoyt Fuller, "Mod, Modish, and Militant: Keeping on Top of the Scene, *Black World* 9.5 (March 1970): back cover.

12. *Nappy*, dir. Lydia Ann Douglas, DVD (New York: Women Make Movies, 1997).

13. Julia Fields, "I Loves a Wig," *Black World* 26.4 (February 1975): 47.

14. Joe Goncalves, "Natural Black Beauty," in *Black Arts*, ed. Ahmed Alhamisi and Harun Kofi Wangaga (Detroit: Black Arts Publications, 1969), 19–20.

15. *Mahogany*, dir. Berry Gordy, DVD (Paramount Pictures, 1975).

16. Baraka and Fundi, *In Our Terribleness*, n.p.

17. "In other words, my reference to a black fantastic is to some degree a pleonasm or, to borrow from Zora Neale Hurston's anthropologies of negro syntax, a double descriptive: separately and in tandem, blackness and the fantastic work to disrupt the bodily imperialisms of the colonial and corrupt the related, innocent representations of the modern." Iton, *In Search of the Black Fantastic*, 290).

18. Don L. Lee (Haki Madhubuti), "Gwendolyn Brooks," in *Directionscore: Selected and New Poems* (Detroit: Broadside Press, 1971), 88–90.

19. Amiri Baraka, *Black Music* (1968; reprint, New York: Da Capo Press, 1998), 211.

20. Langston Hughes, "Dream Variation," in *Voices from the Harlem Renaissance*, ed. Nathan Irvin Huggins (Oxford: Oxford University Press, 1995), 358.

21. Baraka amd Fundi, *In Our Terribleness*.

22. Theorizing about a specifically black aesthetic occurred more in this period than any earlier period. Baraka defines the word "aesthetic" as "freedom": "For black people, *freedom* is our aesthetic and our ideology. *Free Jazz, Freedom Suite, Tell Freedom, Oh, Freedom!* And on!" Amiri Baraka, *Tales of the Out and the Gone* (New York: Akashic Books, 2007), 133.

23. Eleanor Traylor, keynote address at the "Don't Say Goodbye to the Porkpie Hat: Larry Neal" conference, Brooklyn College, October 19, 2006.

24. Sharon Patricia Holland considers the performances of race that make white people occupy time and black people occupy space. See Sharon Patricia Holland, *The Erotic Life of Racism* (Durham, N.C.: Duke University Press, 2012).

25. Julia Fields, "Art," *Black World* 26.4 (February 1975): 46.

26. Fields, "I Loves a Wig," 47.

27. Madhubuti, "On Seeing Diana Go Maddddddddd," 84.

28. Fields, "Art," 46.

29. Amiri Baraka, *Madheart* (1969), in *Four Black Revolutionary Plays* (New York: Marion Boyars Publishers, 2000).

30. Amiri Baraka, "Answers in Progress" (1967), in *Tales of the Out and the Gone*, 132.

31. Toni Morrison, *Paradise* (New York: Penguin, 1997), 119.

32. Nikki Giovanni, "Seduction," in *Black Feeling, Black Talk/Black Judgement* (1968; reprint, New York: Morrow Quill, 1979), 38.

33. Amiri Baraka, "An Agony. As Now," in *The Dead Lecturer* (New York: Grove Press, 1964), 15.

34. Spellman, "Big Bushy Afros," 53.

35. Fred Moten used this phrase during the "Black Popular Culture" panel at the "Feeling the Black Fantastic" symposium at Northwestern University, May 17, 2014. Hortense Spillers, "Mama's Baby, Papa's Maybe: An American Grammar Book (Chicago: University of Chicago Press, 2003), 206.

36. Lee, "Gwendolyn Brooks," 88–90.

37. Amiri Baraka, "The Dark Lady of the Sonnets," in *Black Music* (1968; reprint, New York: Da Capo Press, 1998), 25.

38. Erykah Badu, "Window Seat: A Story by Erykah Badu," dir. Erykah Badu; co-dir. Coodie and Chike, prod. Kareem Johnson (Creative Control, 2010), accessed October 10, 2016, https://www.youtube.com/watch?v=9hVp47f5YZg

39. Amiri Baraka, "Black Art," in *The LeRoi Jones/Amiri Baraka Reader*, ed. William J. Harris (New York: Thunder's Mouth Press, 1991), 219.

40. Ibid., 219.

41. Tiffani Jones, "No Disrespect: Erykah Badu Falls Victim to the 'Male Gaze,'" *The Intersection of Madness and Reality*, June 8, 2012, accessed October 10, 2016, http://www.rippdemup.com/video-articles/no-disrespect-erykah-badu-falls-victim-to-the-male-gaze/.

42. Kalamu ya Salaam, "Breath of Life: a Conversation about Black Music," January 12, 2009, accessed October 11, 2016, www.kalamu.com/bol/2009/01/12/erykah-badu-"erykah-badu-live-remixes-mixtape"/.

43. Erykah Badu, "The Other Side of the Game," *Baduizm* (Kedar Entertainment/Universal Records, 1997).

44. The location of this word painting is unknown. Crawford identified the man as Joel Brandon, but he did not have more information about the location, the painter, or the writer of the poem that is painted on the wall.

45. Baraka, *Black Music*, 211.

46. Dori Hadar found the collection of albums in a Washington, D.C., flea market. Since being "discovered" in 2003, Mingering Mike's work has now been recognized as groundbreaking black "outsider art." The Smithsonian American Art Museum acquired a large collection of his work in 2015.

47. Jon Ronson, "The Mystery of Mingering Mike: The Soul Legend Who Never Existed," *The Guardian*, February 11, 2015, accessed August 25, 2016, http://gu.com/p/45yvm/sbl.

48. The daguerreotype was created by the use of glass within the camera obscura (the box with the hole of light) to create a shadow.

49. Nell Irvin Painter, *Sojourner Truth: A Life, a Symbol* (New York; Norton, 1997).

50. Roland Barthes, *Camera Lucida: Reflections on Photography*, trans. Richard Howard (New York: Hill and Wang, 1981).

51. Lindsay Barrett, "The Tide Inside, It Rages!" in *Black Fire: An Anthology of Afro-American Writing*, ed. LeRoi Jones and Larry Neal (New York: William Morrow and Co., 1968), 150.

52. During the Black Arts Movement, black-and-white photography was reclaimed as the process of embodying darkness as opposed to entering light. The racially inflected understanding of photography is crystallized in the following passage by the French psychoanalyst Jacques Lacan: "It is through the gaze that I enter light and it is from the gaze that I receive its effects. Hence it comes about that the gaze is the instrument through which light is embodied and through which—if you will allow me to use a word, as I often do, in a fragmented form—I am *photo-graphed*." Jacques Lacan, "What is a Picture?" in *The Four Fundamental Concepts of Psychoanalysis: The Seminar of Jacques Lacan*, vol. 11, ed. Jacques Alain Miller, trans. Alan Sheridan (1977; reprint, New York: Norton, 1981), 106.

53. Spellman, "Big Bushy Afros," 53.

Epilogue: Feeling Black Post-Black

1. George Lipsitz, Ajay Heble, and Daniel Fischlin, eds., *The Fierce Urgency of Now: Improvisation, Rights, and the Ethics of Cocreation* (Durham, N.C.: Duke University Press, 2013), 149.

2. Martin Kilson and Addison Gayle, "The Black Aesthetic," in *Black World* 24.2 (December 1974): 30.

3. Ibid., 42–43.

4. Imamu Amiri Baraka (LeRoi Jones) and Fundi (Billy Abernathy), *In Our Terribleness (Some Elements and Meaning in Black Style)* (Indianapolis: Bobbs-Merrill, 1970), n.p. In the 2007 edition of *Black Fire*, Baraka added a new introduction in which he approaches the issue of ideology and blackness in the following manner: "The Black Arts Repertory Theater School self- (and FBI) destructed because 'Black' is not an ideology and so the unity gained under that finally nationalist but reductionist label, though it was an attempt to locate & raise the National Consciousness, could not hold." Amiri Baraka, "Black Fire: A New Introduction," in *Black Fire: An Anthology of Afro-American Writing*, ed. Amiri Baraka and Larry Neal (1968; reprint, Baltimore, Md.: Black Classic Press, 2007), xviii.

5. Lauren Haynes, Naima J. Keith, and Thomas J. Lax, *Fore* (New York: The Studio Museum in Harlem, 2012), 22.

6. Fred Moten, *In the Break: The Aesthetics of the Black Radical Tradition* (Minneapolis: University of Minnesota Press, 2003), 22.

7. Debra J. Dickerson, *The End of Blackness: Returning the Souls of Black Folk to their Rightful Owners* (New York: Anchor Books, 2004), opening page (unnumbered).

8. Ibid.

9. Ibid., 26.

10. Adam Lively, *Masks: Blackness, Race, and the Imagination* (Oxford: Oxford University Press, 1998), 280.

11. Ralph Ellison, *Invisible Man* (New York: Vintage, 1952), 8.

12. Victor Estrada, qtd. in "Victor Estrada," by Rita Gonzalez, in *Phantom Sightings: Art after the Chicano Movement*, ed. Rita Gonzalez, Howard N. Fox, and Chon A. Noriega (Los Angeles: University of California Press, 2008), 144.

13. Nikki Giovanni, introduction to *Black Spirits: A Festival of New Black Poets in America*, ed. Woodie King (New York: Vintage, 1972), x.

14. Baraka, "Black Fire," xviii.

15. The idea of a "structure of feeling" (as opposed to other ways of understanding ideology and the Marxist dialectic) is introduced in Raymond Williams, *Marxism and Literature* (Oxford: Oxford University Press, 1977).

16. Fred Moten, "There Is Blackness," in *Hughson's Tavern* (Providence: Leon Works, 2008), 40.

17. Nikki Giovanni, *My House* (New York: Perennial, 1972), 30 (subsequent references appear parenthetically in the text).

18. Mat Johnson, *Loving Day* (New York: Spiegel and Grau, 2015), 52 (subsequent references appear parenthetically in the text).

19. Williams, *Marxism and Literature*, 134.

20. Marion Boddy-Evans, "Chromatic Black," August 31, 2016, accessed October 11, 2016, http://painting.about.com/od/colourtheory/ss/chromatic-black.htm.

21. Ellison, *Invisible Man*, 5.

22. Nathaniel Mackey, *Splay Anthem* (New York: New Directions Publishing, 2006), xi.

23. Claudia Rankine, *Citizen: An American Lyric* (Minneapolis: Graywolf Press, 2014), 70 (subsequent references appear parenthetically in the text).

24. Amiri Baraka, "Note to AB," *SOS: Poems 1961–2013*, ed. Paul Vangelisti (New York: Grove Press, 2014), 397.

25. A. B. Spellman, "friends i am like you tied," in *Black Fire: An Anthology of Afro-American Writing*, ed. LeRoi Jones and Larry Neal (New York: William Morrow and Co., 1968), 248–49.

26. Terrance Hayes, "The Blue Baraka," in *Wind in a Box* (New York: Penguin, 2006), 19.

27. Terrence Hayes, "The Blue Seuss," in *Wind in a Box* (New York: Penguin, 2006), 43 (italics added).

28. "The idea of the box is a kind of interesting image, both for me as a poet, and, you know, historically speaking," Hayes tells NPR's Melissa Block. "What do boxes do for poems, and what do they do for our people?" "MacArthur Fellow Terrance Hayes: Poems Are Music, Language Our Instrument," *All Things Considered*, NPR, September 17, 2014, accessed October 11, 2016, http://www.npr.org/2014/09/17/349272690/macarthur-fellow-terrance-hayes-poems-are-music-language-our-instrument.

Index

MARGO NATALIE CRAWFORD is an associate professor of English at Cornell University.

The University of Illinois Press
is a founding member of the
Association of American University Presses.

———————————————————————

University of Illinois Press
1325 South Oak Street
Champaign, IL 61820-6903
www.press.uillinois.edu